child development

child development

John R. Bergan

University of Arizona

Ronald W. Henderson

**University of California
at Santa Cruz**

Charles E. Merrill Publishing Company
A Bell & Howell Company
Columbus   Toronto   London   Sydney

Published by
Charles E. Merrill Publishing Company
A Bell & Howell Company
Columbus, Ohio 43216

This book was set in Helvetica.
The production editor was Linda Hillis Bayma.
The cover was designed and prepared by Ron Starbuck Design.

Photos: p. ii, Ron Starbuck Design; pp. 8, 34, 166, 211, 229, 284, 358, 359 by
Bernstein Photo; pp. 24, 26, 38, 139, 157, 197, 286 by Celia Drake; pp. 70, 246, 276 by
Larry Hammill; p. 66 by Editorial Photocolor Archives/Susan McKinney; pp. 93, 109
by EPA/Blair Seitz; p. 126 top by EPA/Arthur Sirdofsky; p. 126 bottom by EPA/James
Carroll; p. 75 by St. Ann's Hospital, Columbus, Ohio; pp. 97, 363 by Bill Stoll; p. 208
by Tim Chapman; pp. 309, 327 by Joan Bergstrom; pp. 6, 10, 25, 62, 129, 206, 220,
287 by Charles E. Merrill Publishing Co.; all other photos by Ronald W. Henderson.

Library of Congress Catalog Card Number: 78–62025

International Standard Book Number: 0–675–08371–0

Printed in the United States of America
2   3   4   5   6   7   8   9   10/ 85   84   83   82   81   80   79

Preface

This book is directed at undergraduate students in introductory child development courses. It is especially designed to provide a practical introduction to individuals who'll work with children as either a parent or child care worker in educational, social service, or health service professions.

Most child development textbooks introduce students to the field of development by describing developmental processes and characteristics. Some books describe elements of development which convey psychological principles and processes, but which generally lack specific guidelines for applying these principles to socializing children and youth. In contrast, books describing the characteristics of ages and stages often fail to communicate the continuity of psychological influences which are applicable across the span of development.

To benefit from both the topical and the age-stage orientations, and to avoid the limitations of each, we have treated developmental principles and processes in an integrated way by linking topical, theoretical chapters to applied ages and stages chapters. Developmental principles and socialization practices are illustrated through numerous extended examples integrated into the text. In addition, significant issues and problems in socialization are highlighted through the use of inserts set apart from the text. The inserts contain case studies, discussions of current issues in socialization, and practical suggestions for guiding development.

The first two chapters in the book provide an overview of principles of development and socialization as they relate to contemporary social conditions. The first of chapter discusses the nature of childhood in a society characterized by cultural diversity and change. The second chapter presents an introduction to the principles of development and socialization in the context of contemporary social conditions.

The next two chapters present information on the biological bases and physical processes of development. In chapter 3 the mechanisms and processes of biological transmission of individual characteristics are presented. The interactive influences of genetic and environmental factors on development are discussed. Chapter 4 deals with physical growth and motor-skill development and the biological and cultural factors that influence them.

Chapters 5, 6, and 7 deal with intellectual development. Chapter 5 discusses psychometric and sociological perspectives used in the measurement of intellectual functioning. Chapter 6 deals with the major theoretical perspectives on the process of intellectual development, while chapter 7 considers the task of guiding intellectual growth at different stages in the developmental process.

Chapters 8 and 9 discuss language development. In chapter 8 the major perspectives on how language is acquired are considered. Chapter 9 presents information on socialization practices to guide language growth.

Chapter 10, 11, 12, and 13 examine personality development. This section emphasizes the importance of developing personal and social competence. Chapter 10 deals with psychological processes involved in affective development. Chapter 11 discusses conditions that foster positive emotional growth at various stages of development. In chapter 12 the basic principles governing social development are presented, while chapter 13 provides information regarding the socialization influences that guide this aspect of development.

Chapter 14 provides a brief review at what has been learned about development, and a look forward to future directions in the field. The discussion focuses on socialization needs produced by the changing conditions of modern life.

The book contains a number of features designed to facilitate and to motivate student learning:

- combined topical and ages and stages organization

- interesting inserts on controversial issues

- case studies

- objectives at the beginning of chapters

- outlines of chapter content

- marginal notes signalling key concepts

- new terms introduced in another color

- definitions of terms in a glossary

- summary tables of difficult concepts

- photographs and drawings

We wish to express our appreciation to Rosemary Rosser for reading portions of the manuscript and to Yvette Lehman, George Morrison, Phyllis Seabolt, and Antoinette Lenahan for their thoughtful and constructive reviews of various drafts of the book. We would like to thank Francie Margolin for her careful and creative editing of the manuscript. We would also like to give special thanks to our wives, Kathy and Lea, for their careful editing and thoughtful suggestions during text preparation.

To our wives and children:

**Lea, Holly, Paige and Tom;
Kathy, David and John**

Childhood Today

Understanding how children develop is a challenging goal. This chapter is a first step in that direction. When you have finished the chapter, you should understand that the ways people think about children are affected by their societies. You should be familiar with some past and present American views on childhood and child-rearing practices. Especially important, you should know about some of the changes in American society and the American family today that are affecting our children. When you have read the chapter, you should be ready for a more in-depth look at how children grow up to be adults.

3

Everywhere you look, Americans are reading, writing, and talking about children and their welfare. Numerous community, state, and federal agencies publish pamphlets and books on topics ranging from prenatal care to the kinds of toys kids should play with to teenagers' mental health problems. Your Sunday newspaper magazine supplement gets in on the act by giving advice on the problems of "parenting." Women's magazines include regular columns on child rearing, and any bookstore worth its salt has a large section of pop treatments of child development. In exchange for a fee and a few hours, middle-class couples can join groups of like-minded mothers and fathers in workshops intended to teach them to be more effective parents. On every hand, we see evidence that America is a child-centered society. Or at least we are concerned about our children enough to employ many bureaucrats and to make fortunes for those business people who take advantage of this child-centered orientation.

child-centered society

Interest in children and their development is not new, even though it may be more pronounced now than in the past. One interesting thing about all the information that has been published to guide parents in raising their children is that the advice has changed substantially over a relatively short period of time. The same can be said of advice offered to teachers, who share with parents the responsibility of guiding the learning and development of youth. The "expert" advice is always changing for two important reasons: first, new information is being discovered all the time; and second, the society itself is changing. Thanks to child development researchers, the information we have about the ways children grow and mature is constantly growing. As new facts are discovered, the theories we use to explain them must be refined and revised. Occasionally a new point of view will become popular quite suddenly, and the information provided to parents and other caregivers changes dramatically. For instance, **genetic**[1] interpretations of development were replaced relatively rapidly with *environmentally oriented* points of view. (This particular shift is discussed in detail in chapter 2.)

developmental theory is dynamic!

But scientific information about development—no matter how current—can never stand alone. Scientific detail takes meaning from its social, political, and economic context. The ways facts are interpreted, and even the kinds of issues scientists choose to study, are strongly influenced by the political events and social philosophy of their times. Childhood cannot be separated from the society in which it exists.

science and social circumstances are interdependent

Children and Youth in Social History

Many people argue that Americans are not nearly as child-centered as we would like to believe. They point to such evidence as the fact that we have done less than many other developed countries to provide high quality care for children whose parents both work. They call attention to

child-centeredness as a myth

1. Words appearing in boldface in this text are defined in the glossary.

the alarmingly high rate of child abuse and neglect in this country. American children are abused sexually, battered physically, and they are emotionally and biologically neglected by their parents so often that public concern led to the passage of the Child Abuse Prevention and Treatment Act in 1974. This legislation is designed to provide protection and treatment for abused children. It also provides a means to find out how to prevent child abuse by establishing a National Center on Child Abuse and Neglect (Ferro, 1975).

Clearly, you can make a convincing case that as a society we have a long way to go before we'll have optimal conditions for our children. Nevertheless, we can take some comfort in the fact that many people are worried about this issue. Many agencies are actively trying to improve the quality of life for all our children. Today most people believe that children are as much a product of their experiences as of their biological inheritance. Thus by improving the circumstances of childhood, we can raise children who are intellectually, socially, and emotionally better equipped to be adults. As parents, they will be even better equipped than their own parents were to rear their children.

Of course, this is an oversimplification of current beliefs about childhood, but it helps us emphasize the point that the theories of child development held by the members of any society influence how they treat their children. These theories may be formal or informal; the people may or may not be consciously aware of how they view children. Concepts of childhood also affect the institutions outside the family that help raise the children. The theories of childhood we hold today are markedly different from the beliefs of our forefathers. *beliefs shape socialization institutions*

COLONIAL BELIEFS ABOUT CHILDHOOD

With the exception of the people whom Columbus mistakenly called Indians because he did not know where he was, there are no native Americans. Our population is comprised of people from all over the world; we are a "nation of nations" (Hicks, 1955). The immigrants came in separate waves, first from northern Europe, primarily from England. The English, the first to come in large numbers, set the pattern for American society (Hicks, 1955), including the treatment of children. Their Calvinist doctrine included some very definite ideas about children and how they should be treated. *religious influences*

It may be hard for you to think of a newborn infant as evil or wicked. Not so for the puritanical Calvinists who settled in New England. Their doctrine taught that children were born wicked, filled with evil inclinations. As if that were not enough, there was always the influence of the Devil to reckon with. To prove this, they pointed to the disobedience of their children (Martin, 1818, as cited in Kessen, 1965). *native depravity* *Satanic influences*

Children were regarded as imperfect versions of adults, and parents were urged to develop socially acceptable qualities in their children. Counted among the most important were obedience, honesty, industry, and piety (Cotton Mather, as cited in Rippa, 1969). Disobedience was not to be tolerated (Sunley, 1955). *valued characteristics*

In some cultures, children are given responsibility at an early age.

Each stage of life was thought to be more prone to certain types of sins than others. The special sins of childhood were stubbornness and falseness, while pride and sensuality were the troubles typical of adolescents. Punishment was used freely to correct the sins and follies of childhood and youth. In addition to punishment, admonition (advising and preaching) and example were common. Children were told stories of others who had met with a sorry fate at the end of a path of sin. The messages of these stories were clear:

> if young people ignored the instruction and authority of their elders and abandoned themselves to a life of pride and sensuality, they would face physical or spiritual death, or both. The wages of sin, even for youth, were certain. (Hiner, 1974, p. 9)

THE OTHER AMERICANS

Hispanic traditions

The British were by no means the only people busy exploring and spreading their influence in colonial America. While the British were occupied on the East Coast, the Spanish were just as busy in the Southwest. Their religious heritage was Catholic rather than Protestant, but their concept of the basic nature of children was quite similar to that of the British. The Catholic belief in original sin carried with it the assumption that the human being is predisposed to rebellion and disobedience. They believed that children must be corrected through the efforts of the family and other social and religious institutions.

The idea of original sin and the resulting belief that children must be "shaped up," often through physical punishment, was very foreign to most native Americans. The Navaho point of view is fairly representative of the attitude of most of the Indians in North America. The idea that children are "born bad" did not occur to them, nor did the idea that the human being can become perfect through knowledge and religious devotion. They assumed that everyone has a blend of good and evil at the moment of birth, and that "no amount of 'religious zeal' can do more that alter somewhat the relative proportions of 'bad' and 'good' in any given person" (Kluckhohn & Leighton, 1946).

native American beliefs

Perhaps as a result of these beliefs, Navahos and many other groups of native Americans have shown respect for the integrity of individuals, including children, that people of European backgrounds find difficult to comprehend. This tradition has been carried down to the present day among many of these native American groups.

respect for the individual

INDUSTRIALIZATION AND EXPANSION

A Population of Immigrants   Once the fledgling colonies had settled down, the "new land" became attractive to more immigrants: first hundreds of thousands of Scotch, Irish, and Germans and then a new wave from eastern and southern Europe (Hicks, 1955). They saw America as the land of opportunity for the oppressed and homeless. Developing industry offered jobs in the cities, and the open frontier offered room for expansion.

These newcomers arrived expecting to find personal freedom and economic well-being; they wanted nothing more than to become "Americans"—to fit in. The "melting pot" became the American ideal, held both by the original settlers and the immigrants. The best elements of the different cultures whose people became Americans were to be fused into a common pattern. Of all the social institutions, the schools were particularly important in helping people become part of the general **culture.** If the melting pot was the ideal, the public school was the chief tool for blending the ingredients into a stew.

expectations of immigrants

school as the instrument of assimilation

Cultural Values in Transition

The mood of the country has been changing significantly during the last few years. The 1960s and 1970s, in particular, brought mounting dissatisfaction with many traditional values, including assimilation. The discontent did not spring from any single event. First, American youths have become keenly aware of some of the effects of our traditional goals—effects like the damage to the environment and to the human spirit that has come from blind pursuit of economic goals.

technological goals and dehumanization

Second, as an outgrowth of the civil rights movement of the 1960s, minority groups have begun to insist on keeping their identities and valued portions of their own native cultures. They argue, and many educators and social activists agree, that there is richness in diversity.

legacy of the civil rights movement

During adolescence, friends become an important force in socialization.

The mass media have also played an important role in changing values. According to anthropologist Margaret Mead (1970), one result is that there are now many more similarities among certain types of people across cultures than across types within a single culture. Television has helped make children and young adults around the world more and more alike.

mass media
influences

THE RISE OF PLURALISM

The United States still includes many members of minority groups whose distinct ways of life and values are clearly different from the mainstream of American life. However intense the heat in the melting pot, some ethnic groups have so far proved "unmeltable." As ethnic pride increases (Cardenas & Fillmore, 1973), the concept of pluralism becomes more important in our understanding of child development.

tolerance and
equal power

Concepts of Pluralism The term cultural pluralism means different things to different people. At one level, it simply implies that culturally distinct groups should live next to each other, respect each other's traditions, and have equal access to power and resources. The interests of no one group would be served at the expense of the overall society (Havighurst & Dreyer, 1975). Others are more concerned with eliminating the injustices of the past; with equalizing access to schooling and other resources (McNeil & Laosa, 1975).

equality of
opportunity

learning style
and cultural
democracy

Others suggest that children from different ethnic backgrounds may have different "learning styles." The schools should recognize these differences, they argue, and adapt to them. Education should be "culturally democratic" (Ramirez & Casteneda, 1974).

beyond tolerance
and cultural
democracy

Still others argue that all children should be exposed to all of the cultures in the pluralistic society. Children should learn to function in the dominant culture as well as in their own ethnic subcultures. The schools, the family, and the mass media should all work toward this goal. Advocates of this view feel that it is not enough—indeed it is not appropriate—to simply teach African history to blacks, for example. It should be taught to all children. Any practice that leads to segregation of ethnic subcultures produces people who cannot talk to each other. It leads to ignorance and suspicion, and makes cooperation impossible (Pearl, 1972).

These competing points of view have implications for social policy, which in turn affects the developmental environment of our children. At present we do not know very much about how to identify the skills that are unique to a given subculture, or how to turn these skills to the advantage of the minority child. While we assume that there is a single set of principles of learning and development that operates in all cultures, most of the studies on which these principles are based have been done with Western European and middle-class American children. Therefore, we don't know how the environment of specific subcultures influences development. Finding this out, and finding ways to use cultural diversity to the advantage of future generations of Americans, lies ahead.

While we cannot predict the future precisely, we can make some guesses based on the past. We know that human beings have changed, have evolved to fit their environments. And we know that change is the most constant fact of modern life. To us it seems that diversity may well provide the survival value today that the ability to adapt provided in the evolutionary past. If, as a society, we produce highly specialized people who can function only as cogs in a technological society, we might lose the capacity to adapt to unforeseen changes. At least it is a point to ponder.

Where We Are Today

Putting cultural diversity aside for the moment, there are certain things that are happening in the United States today that are affecting all of our children. As we have become an urban, industrial culture, our traditional institutions—particularly the family—have changed.

THE CHANGING FAMILY

Before the Industrial Revolution, the family was an economic unit and the center for most of a child's activities. The child was a functional member of the economic unit, and virtually all important influences in the child's life drew him in toward the family. With industrialization all that changed. Forces now radiate out from the family. (See the story of Rosa.) The family is no longer a unit of economic production. Easy transportation has changed the relationship between parents and their children. The nature of work has changed. The family is no longer surrounded by a relatively *homogenous* community whose values directly support those of the parents. The children spend more and more time away from their families. They are bombarded by the messages of the mass media, which tends to distort reality because "it presents the unusual as the representative" (Pearl, 1972, p. 281).

Preschools in a pluralistic America should encourage children to value their own cultural backgrounds.

social change and
personal decisions

Rosa, a young Mexican-American girl from a relatively large city in the Southwest, came from a large and poor family. She planned to go to the state university in her hometown, earn a teaching credential, and get a job in her community. She was a very able student; before graduation she became a student assistant for a research project that used bilingual interviewers. Rosa became intrigued by research and, immediately after receiving her B.A. degree, went on to earn a master's degree at the same university. Her relationship with her family was still relatively undisturbed.

Then came a difficult decision point. She won a fellowship to work for a doctoral degree at one of the nation's most prestigious universities. She knew full well that if she took the fellowship and earned a Ph.D, the chances of finding suitable employment in her hometown would be very slim indeed. Rosa finally made the agonizing decision to accept the fellowship.

One of the most visible features of the family that has changed is its size. In an agrarian society there was work for children to do. They made a direct contribution to the welfare of the family. Today many families still place a high value on children, but largely because of the pleasure children can provide or because of some social or religious obligation. In an urban society, children are economic liabilities rather than assets. The trend is therefore toward smaller and smaller families, and an increasing number of couples are choosing not to have any children at all.

the shrinking
family

And number of children is not the only size change. The nuclear family, a pair of parents and their offspring, has become the standard of American life, replacing the extended family. An extended family includes two or more generations of relatives, such as parents and grandparents, plus children and a number of uncles, aunts, and cousins. It can even include people who are not biologically related—godparents, for example. Extended families serve several functions; the members provide moral support for each other; all the adults may help raise all the children.

Some ethnic groups still place a particularly high value on the extended family. Orientals and Mexican-Americans, for example, have traditionally had strong social, emotional, and economic ties to the extended family. But modern life threatens this form of family life.

It is not only the support of the extended family that is being lost. In the small communities of an earlier day, there were many people besides relatives who were interested in a child's welfare. From the child's point of view, that had both advantages and disadvantages. Someone would surely let his parents know if he was seen doing something he shouldn't. And neighbors never seemed hesitant to give advice. As one observer of the social context of childhood put it, "Sometimes you liked it and sometimes you didn't—but at least people cared" (Bronfenbrenner, 1970b, p. 96).

In our cities today and in the suburbs that surround them, people live near each other, but most keep a careful psychological distance between themselves and their neighbors. Often next-door neighbors barely know each other, and for children the circle of people who care about them may be very small.

As the family has been changing, so has marriage. Divorce has become commonplace. In 1974 it was estimated that one out of every six American children was being raised in a one-parent home. Of these homes, 95% were headed by the child's mother (Hetherington, 1976). A single-parent home *the single-parent family* gives a child a markedly different kind of experience than a two-parent home. Countless other children live in homes where divorce has been followed by remarriage. The scenario in which children are shuttled from one parent's family to the other's new family on weekends or for summer vacations is becoming more and more common. It is the subject of both serious sociological discourse and situation comedy.

Another factor contributing to changes in the ways children grow up is *working mothers* the increasing numbers of women in the work force. Whether women work because they have to, or because they find it challenging and self-fulfilling, alternative provisions for child care are required. We have good reason to believe that some child-care arrangements are better than others. Nevertheless, as a society, we have not devoted much systematic attention or resources to quality child care.

Many American children whose parents are divorced are raised by their mothers, with only brief visits with their fathers.

Mobility   More and more families are moving more and more frequently—
not just across town, but across the country. This mobility affects children; it may make them feel defensive (see the story of Tim). Children
whose roots have been repeatedly torn tend to avoid forming human ties.
The child's social responses seem to suffer more often than academic
performance (Moore, as cited in Toffler, 1970).

Tim is the son of a rising young business executive. When he had been
in a new school in a West Coast suburb for several weeks, his teacher
became concerned that he still had made no friends among the other sixth
graders in his class. He was a good-looking boy. He was well coordinated,
and was usually one of the first selected when sides were chosen up for
sports. He was a good student and was cordial in his responses to the
teacher and to other students, but he had developed no close relationships
with other children. He kept to himself much of the time, and never stayed
after school for any of the organized clubs or activities. There were times
when the teacher was sure that Tim wanted to strike up a friendship with
one of the other children; but after a guarded initial response, he always
seemed to back off.

When Tim's cumulative records arrived from the last school he had
attended, the teacher learned that he had attended five different schools
during the past 6 years. For Tim's father to rise in his corporation, the
family had moved frequently. By putting bits of information from the file
together with snatches of conversation with Tim about his previous

Mobility among American families disrupts children's friendships.

schools, the teacher concluded that Tim was afraid to become friends with other children. He had been disappointed so often in the past when his friendships had been disrupted that he had adopted the tactic of protecting himself by avoiding close ties.

THE ISOLATION OF CHILDHOOD

Many "old timers" think that children have never had it so good; and there's evidence to believe they are right. Children are no longer pressed into service from dawn to dark in the mines or factories. While some parents still use harsh punishment, most do not. Many children have more toys and gadgets than they know what to do with, and parents feel like taxi drivers as they take their children to piano lessons, soccer practice, the tennis league, the orthodontist, and on and on and on. The benefits modern American middle-class children have cannot be denied. But even so, affluent suburban life has its drawbacks.

Many suburban neighborhoods are scarcely more than places to retreat to eat, sleep, and watch television. Most of the rest of the family's activities take place outside the home. For parents, these places may include the office and clubs or volunteer organizations. For children, they are the school, the scout troop, the Little League.

Unlike the small towns we used to have, suburban neighborhoods lack diversity. The people who live in a given neighborhood often come from the   lack of diversity
same social background, have similar incomes, and similar occupations. We have a friend who lives in a suburb of Washington, D.C. who has pointed out that his neighborhood consists of families with a status of GS-13, plus or minus 1, plus nongovernmental professions of comparable rank. Before the boom of suburbia, communities included a wider range of people, of events for children to experience (Bronfenbrenner, 1970b).

Another serious drawback of suburban life is the separation of the children from the adults. Play experiences are highly organized and conducted in different places than where parents find recreation. Only a few organizations include whole families. And children never have the chance to experience the world of work. Few suburban children have any real concept of the kind of work their parents do outside the home, where in small communities, and on farms, children can work alongside their parents. At least they can have a chance to hang around a variety of work settings, to do occasional odd jobs. These are problems the schools and other social institutions have barely recognized, let alone dealt with.

A Look Ahead

During the last century the treatment of children and attitudes toward them have become more humane. Part of this shift is the result of new theories of development. We will look at these influences in later chapters. At the same time, however, changes set in motion by industrialization and urbanization pose problems for all of the groups that make up our society. How can our social institutions deal with the alienation that seems to stem in part from the lack of shared experiences of children and adults? What effect does the absence of a parent have on the development of children from single-parent homes? How are children whose mothers work outside the home affected by this change in the traditional maternal role? And how adequately do contemporary child-care arrangements for them meet their developmental needs? Does the experience of having ties of friendship severed time after time have any long-range influence on the social adjustment of children of highly mobile families?

These are just a few of the questions that we can ask about how our society affects our children. There are no final answers to any of them, but neither can we proceed in ignorance. For most of these questions, we have at least enough information available to suggest courses of action. In some cases the choices are in the hands of parents, and all that we can do is give them an estimate of the probable consequences of some alternative courses of action. In other cases, the information we have may suggest the need for broad action, for new social policies.

This book is arranged to give you basic information derived from theories and research on the development of children and youth. This information describes how we think children develop; how they learn things from walking to talking to being confident to being assertive. After the basic facts and principles are presented, the information will be applied to the development of children at different stages. This second kind of information describes the kinds of changes children go through. It also describes some things adults can do to help further the changes they want to see in children. But there are no simple answers; working with children is complex and demanding!

Suggested Readings

Bronfenbrenner, U. *Two worlds of childhood: U.S. and U.S.S.R.* New York: Russell Sage Foundation, 1970.

Bronfenbrenner, U. The changing American family. In E.M. Hetherington & R. O. Parke (Eds.), *Contemporary readings in child psychology.* New York: McGraw-Hill, 1977. Pp. 315-331.

Kessen, W. *The child.* New York: Wiley, 1965.

Kramer, R. You've come a long way, baby, in three centuries. *The New York Times Magazine,* March 15, 1970. Reprinted in S. White (Ed.), *Human development in today's world.* Boston: Little, Brown, 1976. Pp. 40-44.

Mead, M., & Wolfenstein, M. *Childhood in contemporary cultures.* Chicago: Phoenix Books, 1955.

Tiger, Lionel. Omnigamy: The new kinship system. *Psychology Today,* July 1978, pp. 14–17.

Scientific Perspectives

*This chapter presents a basic framework for our study of child develop-
ment. When you have finished reading it, you should understand the
definitions of development and socialization and how the ways we look at
these concepts are influenced by our culture. You should be familiar with
the two most popular perspectives on child development—the structural
view and the behavioral view. We will be using these two perspectives
throughout this book as we look at specific types of development:
physical-motor, intellectual, language, emotional, and social. As we look
at the stages children go through in each of these domains, we will be referring to these perspectives.*

*You should be familiar with the early biological structural view and its
cultural bases. You should also be familiar with interactive view and the
currently popular concept of developmental stages and its foundations.
You should know how structural analysis is used to guide development.
The concepts of maturation and readiness should be understood, as well
as structural ideas about socialization practices.*

*The two behavioral perspectives—operant and social-learning—and
their historical bases are topics you will need to be able to describe.
You should know what a behavior-contingency unit is and how the behaviorists view developmental stages. You should be able to analyze a
behavior to be changed in functional terms, and to describe common
behavioral socialization practices and terminology.*

In nonindustrial societies, custom dictates the way people look at children and child rearing. Ideas about how to raise children are passed on from generation to generation, and often do not change much for long periods of time (LeVine, 1969). Custom also affects *our* notions about children and child rearing. However, more and more, the social sciences, particularly psychology, are altering our views of children and how to guide their development.

The influence of psychology has grown tremendously in a short time. During the nineteenth century, there were only a handful of psychologists in the United States; the body of knowledge in the field was quite limited. Today 3,000,000 college students each year take psychology courses; 3,000 students a year receive psychology doctorates (McKeachie, 1976). Both increased knowledge and widespread dissemination of it have made psychology a major popular force. It affects the ways we think about ourselves, our roles, and our children.

development defined

The science of psychology influences the way we think about children first of all by affecting our ideas about development. **Development** is those changes in capability and functioning that occur as a function of time. Psychology provides information about the processes by which developmental change takes place and about the hereditary and environmental conditions that influence change. In addition, psychology affects cultural views about socialization. Socialization is concerned with the social conditions that affect the behavior of the individual, and "tie it to the cultural system in which an individual lives" (Hess, 1970, p. 457). Research on socialization gives us knowledge about child-rearing practices and about how socializing agents influence children's development.

socialization defined

This chapter looks at the major perspectives that have guided scientists in accumulating psychological knowledge of development and socialization practices. It presents the central tenets of these perspectives and examines their cultural foundations and their relationship to our pluralistic society. Table 2–1 outlines these perspectives.

Structural Perspectives

Much of today's knowledge about development and socialization comes from scholars such as Freud, Piaget, Rogers, and Lewin. While these men developed specific theories (some of which we'll look at in more detail later), they have a common approach. All take a structural view of the ways children develop. Structural theorists see behavior as being controlled by common characteristics working inside each person. In other words, each child has a set of structures that control the ways in which he or she grows. For example, if a child does very well in school, the teacher may say that the child is highly intelligent. Intelligence is a structure; it implies certain internal mental structures that control the way the child functions intellectually. High intelligence implies a set of structures that make it possible for the child to perform well in school.

structural view of behavior

Table 2–1   Perspectives on development and socialization

structural perspectives		behavioral perspectives	
biological	interactive	operant	social learning
Development occurs through the acquisition of genetically determined structures.	Development occurs through the acquisition of structures determined by the interaction of genetic and environmental factors.	Behavior is controlled by reinforcement	Behavior may be acquired through observation without reinforcement.
		Development results from the interaction of behavior with environment. Heredity influences development, but individual variations are controlled largely by environment. The outcome of development is the acquisition of behavior-contingency units.	
Age is an index for establishing developmental stages.	Structural change is the basis for developmental stages; children are asked questions aimed at revealing how they think.	Developmental stages are based on qualitative changes in interactions with the environment.	
Socialization practice is guided by the need to adapt child rearing to the maturational level of the child.	Socialization practices such as affection and punishment affect child behavior such as aggression and dependency across a wide variety of settings.	In socialization, behavior is analyzed to determine the environmental factors controlling it. Procedures such as modeling and reinforcement are used to affect specific behaviors.	

VIEWS ON DEVELOPMENT

Structural theorists think of development as a process of acquiring complex arrangements of internal traits. These traits allow a person to display a broad range of behaviors. Infants' internal structures permit only the most basic forms of behavior. But as children grow, they develop new structures that let them perform more complex acts. They acquire these more complex behavioral patterns in distinct stages. At any point, children can only do those things characteristic of the particular stage they have reached. Early structural viewpoints emphasized the role of genetic factors in determining progress from one stage to the next. Current views recognize the contribution of both heredity and environment.

Development: Genetic, Environmental, or Both?   During the early part of this century, the first structural theorists used a biological model. Led by G. Stanley Hall, they thought internal structures were genetically determined (Hunt, 1961). Development, according to their model, consisted of slowly acquiring the structures that had been determined at the time of conception.

English competition and the biological model

The cultural origins of early structural views emphasizing biological control of development can be traced to nineteenth century England (Riegel, 1972). During that period, England was a dominant sea power. People who could effectively meet the demands of competition could become financial and social successes. The biological model, closely linked to Darwin's notion of the survival of the fittest, stressed the competitive environmental selection of superior individuals.

descriptive research and the biological model

This early viewpoint held that internal structures determine behavior. Evidence for this belief came from descriptive research. This research has set the pattern for scientific investigations of development. Two types of descriptive investigations are used. In one, the **longitudinal method**, behavior is observed at successive time periods. For instance, intellectual development has been studied by observing the performance of one group of children several times, at each of several different ages (Bayley, 1949). In a second type of investigation, the **cross-sectional method**, information is collected on individuals who differ in age. For instance, intellectual development can be investigated by assessing several groups of children, each at a different age.

Most of the early structural studies were longitudinal. For example, Coghill (1929) conducted several influential studies showing that behavioral development in the salamander follows structural development. He found that structural development proceeds from the head downward and that behavioral development also follows that sequence. He also observed that the salamander's body develops before its limbs and that it gains control of body functions before gaining control of the movements of its extremities. Shirley (1931) conducted research on child development that supports Coghill's findings. She pointed out that infants achieve control over head movements before they master behavior such as walking.

Not all structural theorists hold that the development of internal structures is genetically predetermined. Some, including Sigmund Freud, believe that it is the result of an interaction between genetic and environmental influences. Freud (1938) described three internal structures: the **id** (which is the source of instinctual impulses), the **ego** (which governs rational thought), and the **superego** (which is responsible for determining values and guiding behavior to fit those values). He assumed that the id is controlled by heredity. However, he said that both the ego and the superego are the result of environment. The child's actions are affected by all the structures. For example, consider a familiar situation: 6-year-old Sean is tempted to take a cookie from the cookie jar when his mother is not looking. According to Freud, the hunger impulse to take the cookie comes from the id and is genetically determined. The little voice inside Sean's head saying "No, don't take that cookie; it would be wrong; it will spoil your dinner" comes from the superego, which was developed through Sean's interactions with his parents. The judgment that it might be possible to take the cookie without getting caught comes from the ego, developed from Sean's previously acquired knowledge of his parents' behavior.

Although some structural theorists, particularly those who are popular today, recognize the role of environment, most deny direct and unrestrained control of behavior by the environment. An example is Jean Piaget (1971), an eminent Swiss psychologist who has established a comprehensive theory of intellectual development. He sees the environment

SIGMUND FREUD (1856–1939)

Sigmund Freud was born in Czechoslovakia. However, he spent most of his life in Vienna. In 1881 he obtained a doctorate in medicine. His specialty was neurology, and for a number of years he conducted research on neuronatomy. In the course of his work, he discovered that many of the disorders he encountered were based in psychological rather than physical problems. This observation radically changed psychological and psychiatric practice in the 20th century. Before Freud introduced his views on mental illness, it was generally assumed that mental disorders were caused by brain pathology. Freud was responsible for making mental-health professionals aware that in many instances mental illness occurs largely as a result of experience. Freud's theory of development was derived from his clinical observations. These observations led him to conclude that the most crucial experiences of an individual's life were those during the early years of childhood. Freud was a hard worker. He wrote most of his many books and papers in the evenings after his daily work with patients had been completed. He was also a man of great personal courage. Despite repeated attacks by members of his profession, he held to his views and developed and elaborated his theories. No theorist has had a greater impact than Freud on psychological theory and practice in the 20th century.

JEAN PIAGET (1896–   )

Jean Piaget was born in Neuchâtel, Switzerland. He was introduced to scholarly pursuits early in life by his father, who was a professor of medieval literature. By the time Piaget was 15, he had already published papers in scientific journals in the field of biology. One of these led to an offer of a job in a museum which, of course, had to be rejected, since Piaget was still in secondary school. Young Piaget received his Ph.D. in biology from Neuchâtel University at the age of 21. After postgraduate study in Paris, he was appointed director of research at the Jean Jacques Rousseau Institute, which is affiliated with Geneva University. For many years it has been Piaget's habit to retreat to his Alpine farmhouse in the summer time. There he does much of his writing. The result has been some 30 books and hundreds of articles presenting what many theorists regard to be the most revolutionary and insightful contributions to our knowledge of child development to appear in the 20th century.

as a set of opportunities that let children construct internal structures. These structures—not the environment—control the ways children think. According to Piaget, the mind of the child is not a blank slate to be written upon by experience. Rather, the child *acts upon* the environment. By doing so he or she constructs internal structures.

European class system and contemporary structural theory

The roots of contemporary structural views such as those of Piaget can be found in the rise of the middle class in continental Europe. In the European class system, the competition that had characterized life in England was largely absent. The existence of distinct classes with distinct roles led people to be aware of group and age differences. This produced a social and educational philosophy that recognized the worth of individuals from different generations and cultural backgrounds. Piagetian theory is the contemporary legacy of this philosophy (Riegel, 1972). It does not emphasize individual differences; children are not compared to one another. Rather, thinking processes are described in reference to particular stages of development, and a child does not pass from stage to stage by competing with others. Just as people from different social classes had different responsibilities, so also children in different stages of development display different ways of thinking.

Developmental Stages   For the most part, development involves gradual, continuous change occurring as a function of time (Ausubel & Sullivan, 1970). For instance, the child grows taller slowly and continuously throughout childhood, although there are, of course, certain sharp spurts. But despite the fact that most development takes place gradually, certain characteristics show substantial jumps. Accordingly, some structural theorists describe developmental change in terms of qualitatively distinct stages.

Early structural theorists used age as an index for establishing developmental stages. An example is Arnold Gesell (1940), whose books on child development are still widely read. Gesell compiled a vast collection of motion picture films showing a wide range of behaviors of children at different ages. Each age was regarded as a separate stage in the child's development. Because Gesell considered behavior genetically predetermined, he treated age as though it caused behavior. For instance, the 2-year-old children he studied were somewhat unruly. Gesell not only documented their unruliness in great detail, but also assumed that they behaved that way *because* they were 2.

age as an index of stage

Theorists who use age as a basis for developmental stages often construct **developmental norms.** These **norms** are standards against which to judge individual children. To construct norms, the researchers select a large sample of individuals representing different ages. Next the developmental characteristic that is being studied is assessed in each child. Their scores are then used as standards. For example, a child's intellectual development is often assessed by specifying his or her position in a norm group composed of age mates. The score that the child receives on the assessment can be compared to the scores of the children in the norm group.

norms

Studies using developmental norms to assess children's development have invariably revealed marked individual variations. Children differ greatly from one another in the rate at which they develop. Not only that, but also there are often substantial variations within the individual child. The child who excels at reading will not necessarily excel in math. Thus age has proven to be a poor index of developmental stage.

individual differences

ARNOLD GESELL (1880–1961)

Arnold Gesell grew up in the little town of Alma, Wisconsin along the Mississippi river. He was the eldest of five children in a closely knit family. His mother and father both valued education highly, and Gesell was oriented early in life toward a career in teaching. He took undergraduate training at Stevens Point Normal School and graduated in 1889. After graduation, Gesell taught high school for 2 years and then attended the University of Wisconsin where he obtained a bachelor of philosophy degree. Upon completing his work at Wisconsin, he became a high school principal. However, he stayed in that position for only 1 year before deciding to pursue his Ph.D. in psychology at Clark University under G. Stanley Hall. Hall had a great influence on Gesell, but it was not until 2 years after he had received his doctorate that Gesell finally decided to spend his life studying the development of children. Despite all of his previous training, he felt unprepared for this task because he lacked knowledge of the physical bases and physiological processes underlying growth. Thus he decided to return once more to school. After 5 years of study beyond the doctorate in psychology, Gesell obtained a medical degree from the school of Medicine at Yale University. He remained at Yale until his retirement in 1948. In his laboratory he compiled the most complete descriptive record of children's development ever to be constructed.

During the sensorimotor period, babies learn basic skills.

structural change
as an index of
stage

Contemporary theorists such as Piaget and his followers generally hold that age should not be used as a basis for determining developmental stages. The development of structures does not necessarily correspond to a particular age level (e.g., Flavell, 1963).

Modern structural theorists use hypothesized structures as a basis for developmental stages. For example, Piaget discusses three broad periods of development. We'll look at them briefly here, and in detail in later chapters. The first period is called the **sensorimotor period** of development. At this stage the child tends to represent the environment through physical acts. Objects are understood in terms of the actions that the child associates with them. For instance, a spoon might be represented in the child's mind by the act of using it to ingest food. The second major period is the period of **concrete operations**. It includes a large substage called **preoperational thought.** During the preoperational subperiod, the child learns to represent experience with words and other symbols. In the advanced stages of concrete operations, the child uses symbols to represent logical relationships among objects. Piaget calls the last phase the period of **formal operations.** During this phase the individual is able not only to represent concrete events symbolically, but also to conceptualize abstract possibilities.

Structural theorists use their stages to explain the behavior of the developing child. For example, 7-year-old Sara used to believe stories about a jolly old man with flying reindeer, to the delight of her parents at Christmas. Now she is beginning to question those yarns, because she is reaching the concrete operations stage. According to Piagetian theory, children in the concrete operational period can use symbols to represent objects because they have the necessary intellectual structures. Parents or teachers who know that a child is functioning at that stage can know what to expect of the child. This information can be used to determine what the child is likely to be able to learn and what in all probability is beyond him.

Structure Analysis   In addition to knowing a child's developmental stage, it can be useful to know just which structures the child has developed. Many structural theorists analyze the characteristics of internal structures that control a child's behavior. Piaget (1963) uses a **clinical method** of investigation to determine internal intellectual structures. His clinical method involves interviewing children to get them to talk about or act out the ways in which they think. The procedures are based on techniques used in psychiatric clinics.

clinical method of analysis

An adult using the clinical method asks a child a series of questions on his or her views on something in the environment or on a problem situation. For example, a mother might learn something about her daughter's concept of life by asking the child about the things that she regards as being alive. Thus, the mother might say: "Is Teddy Bear alive? How about the mountain—is it alive?" From questions like these, Piaget has concluded that young children tend to attribute their own personal characteristics, like life, to environmental phenomena.

To decide what questions to ask, the investigator develops **hypotheses** about internal structures. These hypotheses are based in part on observations of the ways children act and in part on psychological theory. For ex-

Children in the period of concrete operations make great strides in their use of language.

ample, Piagetian theory suggests that preschool children generally do not yet have the intellectual structures needed to understand logical concepts such as quantitative relations among objects. A father using this approach might test the hypothesis by asking the child questions to determine how she conceptualizes quantity. For instance, he might place two sets of four jacks in parallel rows and then ask the child if one set has more than, the same as, or less than the other. If the child responds that they are both the same, the father might say: "This will be my set." Then he might elongate his set by increasing the distance between the jacks and again ask the child whether her set had more than, the same as, or less than his. Piaget has observed that young children usually cannot answer a question like this correctly.

To apply the clinical method effectively the investigator must not suggest answers to the child or criticize the child's responses. If the adult suggests answers, the child will probably say or do what the adult expects regardless of the child's own perspective. If the adult criticizes the child, the child may very well stop saying or doing anything at all. The following protocol from one of Piaget's (1963) experiments shows how to avoid suggestion and criticism in applying the clinical method:

> Where does night come from? -*The sky.* -How is the night made in the sky? *-Because there's a watch, and in the morning it points right up and in the evening it's let down.* -Why? *-It's down because night-time is coming?* -And what does that do? *-Because it's night.* -What does the night do when the hand points down? -(The night comes) *because there's the hand pointing down.* Have you known this long? . . .*-Because at home there's a sort of lamp, then a hand; when it falls that makes it night.* (Piaget, 1963, p. 202)

During the period of formal operations, children begin to develop the ability to reason.

By avoiding the temptation to tell the child how night comes and goes and by not criticizing the child for his unique conceptions, the adult was able to learn a great deal about how the child was thinking. The adult could use this information in guiding the child's further development.

VIEWS ON SOCIALIZATION

The early structural theorists who supported the biological model relied heavily on the ideas of maturation and readiness in formulating their views on socialization. Contemporary theorists emphasize the internal structures. Both groups stress the need to adapt socialization practices to the developmental level of the child. Let's look at each approach more closely.

Maturation, Readiness, and Socialization   Early theorists used the term **maturation** to explain changes in development occurring over time. Maturation referred to developmental change controlled by genetic factors (Gesell, 1940; Olson, 1959). They believed that maturation set limits on growth. Within those limits, learning could produce changes in behavior. Development resulted from the combined influence of maturation and learning.

> maturation

These theorists assumed that children who were asked to learn skills beyond their maturational level would inevitably be frustrated and would fail. Effective socialization required a match between the child's current developmental level and the kinds of activities provided to stimulate further learning. They used the term **readiness** to refer to this match. The idea of readiness was most frequently used in reference to reading instruction.

> readiness

The commonly accepted views of maturation and readiness have changed considerably since these terms were first used. It is now recognized that maturation is not independent of environment. From the moment of conception, the environment can influence genetic structures. And heredity may affect the kind of environment provided (Bell, 1968). For example, some infants seem to have a genetic predisposition to cry and squirm when being held by adults. Those children often get less attention from adults than more placid babies. The less adult attention, the greater the chance of a detrimental effect on the child's social and intellectual growth.

> changing views on maturation and readiness

Jerome Bruner (1960) led the first major attack on the concept of readiness. He argued "that any subject can be taught effectively in some intellectually honest form to any child at any stage of development" (1960, p. 33). His approach said that traditional procedures for organizing school subjects should be altered to match the developmental level of each child. For example, Bruner pointed out that advanced topics in mathematics can be presented to young children if they are taught in a way that is appropriate to the child's developmental level. He advocates a spiral approach to curriculum organization in which basic concepts are presented in increasingly complex form at several successive developmental levels.

JEROME BRUNER (1915–   )

Jerome Bruner is a native of New York City. He became interested in psychology while attending Duke University as a result of an unusual incident. Bruner was threatened with being expelled from school for failing to attend chapel. William McDougall, an outstanding psychologist on the faculty at Duke, stepped in in Bruner's behalf. Bruner subsequently worked in McDougall's laboratory and then went on to Harvard to get his Ph.D. in 1941. During World War II, he conducted research for the Foreign Broadcast Intelligence Service, the Department of Agriculture, and the office of Public Opinion Research at Princeton University. Following the war, he returned to Harvard, where he formulated his views on development and education. Bruner has conducted extensive research on the process of intellectual development and has written widely on the education of the young. In 1962 the American Psychological Association formally honored Bruner with a distinguished scientific contribution award, and in 1969 he served as president of the association. Currently he is a professor at Oxford University.

Other theorists have challenged the concept of readiness on the grounds that it does not recognize the impact of instruction on development (Ausubel & Sullivan, 1970). For example, a child may fail to learn not because he is not ready, but because he is not being taught effectively.

Socialization Practices   One question that many structural theorists are trying to answer is which socialization practices affect the development of the structural characteristics that control child behavior. These investigators want to identify *categories* of practices that could have long-term and widespread effects on a whole class of behaviors. For instance, there have been many investigations of the effects of punishment on aggression in children. These studies support the assumption that in both middleclass and lower-class children, parental punishment is associated with later aggressive behavior (Martin, 1975).

Many theorists have drawn up *systems* to describe the categories of socialization practice that can affect children's development (Martin, 1975). However, none of them provides a complete account. One system, developed by Schaefer (1959) to analyze maternal behavior, is representative. Schaefer has drawn a two-dimensional framework (see figure 2–1). One dimension ranges from autonomy to control. At the autonomy end of the scale we find behaviors like freedom, detachment, and indifference. At the control end we find classes such as possessiveness and authoritarianism. The second dimension ranges from love to hostility. Practices at the love extreme include acceptance and indulgence. Practices at the hostility end include rejection and antagonism. Ideally, any behavior of the mother could be located on the grid and evaluated to see how it would probably affect the child.

Schaefer's classification of socialization practices

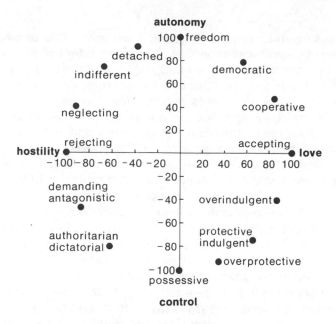

Figure 2–1 A hypothetical circumplex of maternal behavior concepts.

From "A Circumplex Model for Maternal Behavior" by E. S. Schaefer, *Journal of Abnormal and Social Psychology*, 1959, *59*, 226–235. Copyright 1959 by the American Psychological Association. Reprinted by permission.

General categories of socialization practices like these are related to a variety of child behaviors, including such diverse characteristics as aggression, dependency, and moral standards. For instance, several investigations have shown that parental warmth or affection is related to the development of internalized moral standards (Hoffman, 1970). Children who have been raised in a warm home are more likely to resist temptation, confess their misdeeds, and express remorse when they do misbehave than children who have not been reared in a warm home atmosphere. Punitiveness has also been related to the internalization of standards of conduct. Parents who control their children by punishing them are likely to have children who do not internalize standards of personal conduct to the same extent that children from a less harsh environment do.

A third variable that has been related to the internalization of moral standards is **cognitive structuring.** When an adult describes to a child how he expects the child to act and why, he is using cognitive structuring. For example, a parent might say "You shouldn't play with that toy. It belongs to Mary, and if you broke it she would not be able to play with it. That would make her sad." As you might expect, cognitive structuring is more effective with older children than with younger ones (Martin, 1975).

Until recently, structural theorists have assumed that influence in the socialization process was essentially a one-way street. They assumed that adults influenced the child's development of the internal structural charac-

socialization and internalized moral standards

teristics that in turn controlled the child's behavior. The behavior of the adult socializing agent was thought to be independent of the behavior of the child. The possibility that the child might affect the adult was largely overlooked. But recently a number of theorists (e.g., Bell, 1968) have challenged this view. Bell and others suggest that the behavior of the child may affect the socializing practices adults use. For example, it is possible that punitiveness in parents is not the only significant social cause of aggressiveness in children. Aggressive children may evoke the punishment from parents. From this perspective, socialization involves complex interactions: socializing agents affect the behavior of children, and children in turn influence the practices of socializing agents.

The research investigating the influences of child behavior on the practices of socializing agents is still quite meager. However, some studies have shown that children *do* affect the behavior of the adults responsible for guiding their development. For example, Yarrow, Waxler, and Scott (1971) found that nursery school teachers were likely to return to a child sooner if the child smiled at the adult or gave the adult other social rewards. Sherman and Cormier (1974) showed that child behavior influencing the behavior of a socializing agent can be modified. They used tangible rewards to reduce the highly disruptive classroom behavior of two elementary school children. When the children's inappropriate behavior decreased, the teacher's positive practices increased. Marcus (1975) showed that child behavior may influence the behavior of parents as well as teachers. He showed parents videotapes of children solving a problem. Some children acted dependent; others were more independent. The parents were then asked to indicate what they would do or say in response to the child. The children who acted dependent elicited greater encouragement of their dependence and more directiveness than the children who acted independent.

child influences
on socialization

Although we do have evidence that children may influence the socializing behavior of adults, the extent of their influence is still being debated. Hoffman (1975) argues that parents exert significantly greater control over the behavior of children than children exert over the behavior of parents. For example, he cites research evidence presented by Barker (1963) that children try to change parent behavior in only a small percentage of their interactions. By contrast, parents try to discipline their children in a very large percentage of their interactions. Hoffman also points out that, even if children significantly influence the behavior of their parents, it does not negate the effects of the parents' behavior on the children. For example, an aggressive child may cause her parents to punish her. The punishment may in turn call forth further aggressiveness on the part of the child.

Behavioral Perspectives

Behavioral psychology is a second major source of knowledge about development and socialization. It began as a reaction to the structural ap-

JOHN B. WATSON (1878–1958)

John Broadus Watson received his Ph.D. from the University of Chicago in 1903. He remained at Chicago for 5 years after receiving his degree and then became a professor at Johns Hopkins University. His professorship at Johns Hopkins lasted for only 12 years. During this relatively brief time span, Watson developed his ideas on behaviorism and communicated them to the scientific community. In 1920 Watson's career in psychology ended abruptly when he was forced to resign from Johns Hopkins because he had divorced his wife. After his expulsion from academic life, Watson pursued a successful career in advertising and gradually withdrew entirely from the field of psychology.

proaches that dominated the field in Europe and the United States during the early years of psychology. John Watson, the founder of behaviorism, wrote an article entitled "Psychology as the Behaviorist Views It" in 1913. There he advocated a science of psychology like the natural sciences. This new science would focus on the study of observable behavior and would try to describe, predict, and control observable actions.

Behaviorism has its origins in the rise of science and technology. Its philosophical foundations were laid by British empiricists in the seventeenth century. They believed that all knowledge is derived from sensory experience. This belief is the basis for the behavioral emphasis on environmental influences and for the stance that psychology should be based on the study of observable action.

Behavioral psychology formally began in the United States in the early part of this century. American philosophy during that period was practical; it reflected rising industrial production. This pragmatism was more compatible with the behavioral concern for doing and acting than with structural views emphasizing internal processes (Buss, 1975). Behaviorism was also influenced by the philosophy of logical positivism. This position advocated value-free, disinterested scientific study.

American pragmatism and behaviorism

positivism and behaviorism

There is also a close association between behaviorism and the American democratic ideal that people can shape their own destinies by actively manipulating the environment (Wispé & Thompson, 1976). Structural views that stress the role of heredity imply that behavior is unchangeable. This belief is antagonistic to the characteristic American ideal that people can control their environment and rise above poverty and adversity.

Today there are two approaches to behaviorism: the operant perspective, as represented by B. F. Skinner (1953, 1974) and his colleagues, and the social-learning or cognitive view, advanced by theorists such as Albert Bandura (1969, 1971, 1977) and Walter Mischel (1968, 1973). The operant view holds that behavior change occurs when an individual emits a response that operates on the environment to produce reinforcing consequences that increase the likelihood that the response will occur again. For example, a child who reaches into the cookie jar and gets a cookie is likely to try again on other occasions. The social-learning view holds that behavior change may be the result of observation of the behavior of others. No direct reinforcement is required to learn something new. Thus, if our cookie-snatching little girl were to be watched by her brother as she munched her prize, the brother too might subsequently be able to find his way to the cookie jar.

Both positions place heavy emphasis on the role of environment in determining behavior. However, the operant view holds that environment may influence behavior directly, where the social-learning position assumes that environmental influences are affected by internal mental processes (Bandura, 1977). For instance, they might say that, if a person is rewarded for doing something, he might anticipate receiving further rewards for doing it again. This anticipation might lead him to repeat the previously rewarded response.

VIEWS ON DEVELOPMENT

Bijou and Baer (1961) describe development from the behavioral viewpoint as "progressive changes in the way an organism's behavior interacts with the environment" (p. 1). Their description implies both genetic and environmental influences on development. For example, heredity may affect how receptive an individual is to environmental influences. During the course of development, the child continually changes physically. These changes are based in part on genetic makeup, and may determine the kinds of environmental **stimuli** that affect behavior. Newborn infants, for example, cannot respond to verbal requests because they are not physiologically ready to.

Although behaviorists recognize the influence of heredity on development, they generally hold that the individual variations in behavior that we associate with a particular level of development are largely a function of environment. The environment affects development in two ways. First, the experiences each child has as he or she grows up give a learning history. This bank of experiences influences the way in which he may respond in any given situation. For instance, as they develop, children learn to respond to a broad range of verbal **cues** such as "Open your book to page 24" or "Watch what I do." The experiences the child has with these cues will influence what the child will do when he hears the phrase again. Second, the environment in the immediate situation where behavior is taking place also affects children's responses. For example, if a child is praised for eating appropriately at dinner time, the likelihood that she will behave appropriately at other meals is increased.

Development as the Acquisition of Behavior-Contingency Units The outcome of development may be thought of as a series of **behavior-contingency units.** A behavior-contingency unit is made up of a behavior and the conditions that control the likelihood of its occurrence (Mischel, 1973). For instance, Carol, a 14-year-old, was highly sensitive to the opinions of her peers. She was often subjected to behind-the-back sniping by her classmates. Their sniping served as a cue that led Carol to make

behavior-
contingency
unit defined

abusive verbal assaults on her classmates. When she did that, she was rewarded; her classmates temporarily stopped sniping at her. In this example, the complete set of events, including the cue, the verbal abuse and its rewarding consequences, would be a behavior-contingency unit.

Behaviorists hold that behavior-contingency units are restricted to a specific and limited set of situations. For instance, although Carol responded with verbal abuse to the sniping of her classmates, she would not necessarily respond the same way to sniping remarks by her parents or teachers. The behavioral position is in sharp contrast to the structural perspectives in this regard. Structural theories assume the child develops stable characteristics as he grows up. These characteristics influence the child's behavior in a wide variety of situations (Mischel, 1968). For instance, when a child is labeled "aggressive," it is usually assumed that his aggressiveness is a general trait that will characterize his behavior in many circumstances. But although intellectual capabilities are to some extent generalizable this way, social behaviors are not (Mischel, 1968; Bandura, 1969). For instance, children who are aggressive in one situation may not be aggressive at all in another situation.

Behaviorists focus their child development studies on how individual children acquire behavior-contingency units. They use *single subject research designs* in their work (Kratochwill, 1978). These designs show how the environment affects what one person or a small number of people do. One example is the *reversal design.* Allen, Hart, Buell, Harris, and Wolf (1964) used this design to prove that teacher attention could be used to affect a preschool child's interactions with adults and other children. The child's teacher was concerned because she felt that Cheryl wasn't spending enough time with the other children. For several days the researchers measured how much time Cheryl spent with adults and how much time she played with children. Their measures showed that Cheryl spent most of her time with adults. Next the researchers asked the teacher to praise Cheryl when she played with other children. When praise was used, Cheryl spent much more time playing with other children and much less time with adults. The researchers wanted to make sure that they were advising the teacher to use a method that really worked. To make sure that praise was really what caused Cheryl's increase in play, they *reversed* the contingency. The teacher praised Cheryl when she did not play with other children and withheld her praise when she did. Under the new set up, Cheryl promptly began to spend most of her time with adults. Once they had learned that praise was indeed affecting Cheryl's actions, the contingency was reversed again, and Cheryl once more spent most of her time with her classmates.

Developmental Stages Behaviorists place very little emphasis on the concept of developmental stages in their work. Nonetheless, Bijou and Baer (1961) suggest a set of stages that they believe to be useful. These stages represent qualitative changes in the kinds of interactions that occur between children and their environments as they grow up.

Relying heavily on the work of Kantor (1959), Bijou and Baer designate three broad stages of development: the **universal stage**, the **basic stage**,

[margin note:] situational specificity of behavior-contingency units

Children in the basic stage learn by interacting with the objects—including toys —around them.

the universal stage

and the **societal stage**. The universal stage begins at birth and continues until the child has functional verbal behavior. At the beginning of this period, the child's behavior is controlled mainly by biological processes, as in breathing and sucking (Bijou & Baer, 1965). At birth certain stimuli bring out certain reflexive reactions, such as blinking, sucking, and head turning. As children develop, an increasing number of environmental stimuli affect their behavior. They gradually learn to operate on their environments and to produce increasing numbers of consequent stimuli. These **consequences** in turn influence the children's behavior. For instance, during the first year of life, most children learn to reach for and grasp objects such as rattles and other crib toys. The pleasant consequence of controlling a rattle by grasping it increases the chance that the child will repeat the behaviors leading to that consequence; that is, he will reach for the toy again.

the basic stage

The basic stage begins with the onset of language at about the age of 2 and extends to about the age of 5 (Bijou, 1975). The behavior of the child in the basic stage depends on the learning history established during the first 2 years and on the environmental circumstances of the basic stage. The child now has a repertoire of responses that make it possible to develop a highly complex set of cognitive, social, and emotional response patterns. Parents provide the major social stimuli influencing development during the basic stage. However, the child's increasing interactions with objects in the environment also exert a powerful influence on behavior.

the societal stage

The societal period of development begins when the child starts to have extensive contacts with people outside of the home; it continues throughout adulthood. The child entering this period is a complex individual with a multitude of cognitive and social behavioral patterns. At this point the environmental influences on behavior are greatly expanded over what they were in the basic stage. The family continues to play an important role in influencing behavior. However, peers, teachers, and other adults are more and more influential.

VIEWS ON SOCIALIZATION

To help socialize a child from a behavioral viewpoint, we must first of all analyze the environmental conditions that may be leading to the behavior. Socialization practices are selected and implemented on the basis of this kind of analysis. This analysis not only makes it possible for adults to guide a child's development, but also it helps children acquire the necessary competencies to direct their own growth. A child who is aware of the conditions controlling his or her own behavior is in a good position to control that behavior.

Behavior Analysis in the Socialization Process   A behavior is analyzed to find the stimulus conditions that lead to it. This analysis is generally referred to as a **functional analysis** (Skinner, 1953). The first steps are to precisely describe the behavior you're investigating and the environment under which it usually occurs.

functional analysis

As any parent or teacher knows, there are vast numbers of things a young child does that adults would like to change. A preschool child, for instance, may spill the water colors, poke another child with a paint brush, and smear paint on his hair, all within the span of a few seconds. Behaviorists usually pick a limited set of responses to change. For instance, consider the difficulties faced by Brian's parents. He cried incessantly every night when he was put to bed. His wailing extended into the wee hours of the morning, making it impossible for the parents to get enough sleep at night. These blurry eyed parents would have no difficulty deciding what behavior to focus on in a functional analysis.

specifying behaviors

Although the strategy of selecting a limited number of behaviors as targets for change is useful in many situations, it does have its shortcomings. It makes it easy to overlook the relationship between immediate problems and long-range developmental goals. Behaviorists have been criticized for using powerful tools to achieve trivial and sometimes questionable socialization goals. Some educational theorists, for example, have questioned the value of behavior change programs designed to make children sit in their seats and work silently throughout the the school day (Winett & Winkler, 1972).

The problem of selecting significant behaviors can be dealt with by systematically relating specific behaviors targeted for change to long-range developmental goals. A set of procedures for determining such a relationship has been established (Bergan, 1977). In brief, it involves setting up long-range general socialization goals. Then subordinate goals are specified that are related to the general, long-range goals. Finally, specific behavioral goals are established for each subordinate goal.

Adult socializing agents tend to describe the behavior of other people in rather global terms (Mischel, 1973). A teacher may describe a child as "shy" or "aggressive." A parent may indicate that his son is "ambitious" or "unmotivated." Global descriptions like this do not indicate anything very precise about the child's behavior.

To conduct a functional analysis of behavior, global descriptions must be put aside in favor of concrete specifications of what the child actually does. This can be accomplished by asking questions about the child's behavior (Bergan, 1977; Bergan & Tombari, 1975). For example, a teacher might say to herself, "What kinds of things does Alice do to show her immaturity?" This question will generally lead to the specification of a number of examples of immature behavior. For instance, the teacher might answer, "When Alice asked Bobby to share the blocks and he refused, she cried. That was immature."

specifying
conditions

After a behavior of concern has been specified, it is necessary to find the conditions under which the behavior usually occurs. This is done in order to identify the things in the environment that might be influencing behavior. For instance, consider the case of JoEllen, a seventh grade girl who had a habit of lighting fires in a science laboratory. The fires were generally lit when the teacher had her back turned to the class, and the ensuing blazes were usually accompanied by cheers and laughter from JoEllen's classmates. Both of these facts were important in explaining her behavior. When both the teacher and the classmates changed their behavior, JoEllen stopped building fires.

Specifying conditions involves both those things that happen right before the behavior of concern and those things that occur immediately afterwards. Incidents that occur immediately before the behavior may be cues signalling the occurrence of the behavior. For instance, JoEllen's teacher's act of turning her back on the class probably functioned as a cue signalling the onset of the fire building. Events occurring immediately after behavior may increase the likelihood that the behavior will be repeated. For instance, her classmates' cheering and laughter were probably rewarding to JoEllen. It would be likely that she would continue to build fires to get this attention from her peers.

Socialization Practices   There are several quite specific practices that behaviorists use to socialize others. The first group includes responses, emitted by socializing agents after behavior, that are or may be related in a **contingent** way to child behavior. For instance, a mother might want to control her child's coming to dinner by saying "I'm so glad you came to dinner on time." To do so, she will only say that when the child behaves appropriately. The mother's statement is verbal praise *contingent* on arriving at dinner on time.

Socialization practices also include responses made immediately before a behavior, called **antecedent** behaviors. For instance, the mother may signal to the child that it is time to come to dinner by calling to him. Table 2–2 summarizes the major types of antecedent and consequent socializing behaviors identified by behaviorists.

reinforcing
behavior

Reinforcment is among the most widely used behavioral socialization practices. A reinforcer is a consequence of behavior that increases the likelihood that the behavior will happen again (Skinner, 1974). Thus, if a teacher uses verbal praise to increase the probability that his students will

Table 2–2 Behavioral socialization techniques

technique	definition	example
Reinforcing	administering a positive reinforcer or withdrawing a negative reinforcer following a response	I really appreciated your picking up your room.
Extinguishing	withdrawing a positive reinforcer contingently related to a given behavior	A teacher ignores a child's yelling.
Punishing	adding an aversive stimulus or removing a positive stimulus to reduce behavior	Since you hit Ted you can't go outside for recess.
Cueing	signaling the occurrence of a response	Pass the butter.
Modeling	demonstrating a response to be acquired by a learner	You say thank you when someone gives you a present.

stay on-task, then praise is a reinforcer. Similarly, if a teacher's reprimands increase the probability that a child will be disruptive, then reprimands serve a reinforcing function. In other words, an adult can reinforce an undesirable behavior.

There are two types of reinforcement: **positive reinforcement** and **negative reinforcement**. Positive reinforcement involves adding a consequence that increases the probability of a response. For example, a parent may increase the probability that a child will make her bed in the morning by serving breakfast only after the bed has been made. Breakfast in this example is a positive reinforcer; it is a consequent event added after a desired behavior to increase the probability that the behavior will occur. Negative reinforcement involves removing a condition previously in effect to increase the probability of a response. For instance, a parent might increase the probability that a child would complete homework assignments by nagging the child incessantly until the child did the homework. In this illustration, doing homework is negatively reinforced by the removal of parental nagging.

positive and negative reinforcement

Some reinforcers are associated with basic body needs. These reinforcers are called **primary reinforcers**. Food and water are familiar examples. When a stimulus that is not a reinforcer is repeatedly paired with a primary reinforcer, it will gradually become a reinforcer. These reinforcers are called **secondary reinforcers**. For example, if you repeatedly reward a child with food and verbal praise, verbal praise may gradually become an effective reinforcer itself.

The fact that a stimulus that at one time is not reinforcing can become a reinforcer probably accounts for much of the variation in what is reinforcing for different people. To socialize a child, you must keep this variation in mind. Different consequences are reinforcers for different people. An adult must find out what things are reinforcing for a child whom he wishes to teach. He can do this by watching how the child acts in specific situations. He can also ask the child directly. For instance, a teacher may simply ask a pupil what he would like to do when he finishes his assignment.

Reinforcement may be given either every time a desired behavior occurs or only some of the time. For instance, a teacher may praise a child every time he turns in an assignment (called a **continuous schedule** of reinforcement) or only some of times (called an **intermittent schedule**). Intermittent schedules are particularly useful because they tend to increase the rate of responding and are easy to administer. For instance, a mother may increase the chance that her son will sit up straight at the dinner table by praising him for that behavior. At first she might praise him every time that he sits up straight. Then she might praise him less frequently. If she followed this plan, the chances that he would sit up straight would very likely increase, and he would probably continue to sit up straight over a period of time.

A second socializing technique advocated by behaviorists is **extinction**. Extinction is used to decrease an undesirable behavior. To extinguish a behavior, you stop reinforcing it and pair it with a stimulus that is not reinforcing (called a **neutral stimulus** [Bijou & Baer, 1961]). For instance, consider Greg. While reading one night, he noticed his 2-year-old son pulling vigorously on one of the drapes in the room. Greg said immediately, "Don't do that, John." The child was apparently delighted to see that his father had finally taken his nose out of the book and that he was at last going to get some attention. A big smile came over John's face, and he began pulling at the drape again. A second reprimand produced more vigorous tugs at the drape. At this point Greg caught on to the game and ignored the child's behavior, with the result that it soon stopped.

Extinction is a difficult tool to use because it must be applied absolutely consistently. If not, the child is in effect receiving intermittent reinforcement. For example, suppose a student is disruptive in order to get the teacher's attention. The teacher may say something like, "I try to ignore James when he's cutting up because I know he's doing it to get my attention, but sometimes his behavior gets so bad that I just have to do something about it." Her comments suggest that James is receiving intermittent

schedules of reinforcement

extinguishing behavior

Simple affection can be a powerful reinforcer for a child.

B. F. SKINNER (1904–   )

Burrhus Frederic Skinner was born into a professional family in Sus-quehanna, Pennsylvania. He majored in English at Hamilton College and was elected to Phi Beta Kappa at that institution. His initial ambition was to become a writer. However, after a two-year effort to establish himself in that field, his interests turned to the study of psychology. He received his Ph.D. from Harvard University in 1931, taught for a few years in Minnesota and Indiana and then returned to Harvard where he has remained throughout his long and productive career. In his years at Harvard, he developed his views on behaviorism and on the applica-tion of behavioral technology toward the solution of significant social problems. A skillful writer, Skinner has been able to communicate his ideas effectively not only to the scientific and professional community in the field of psychology, but also to the general public. He stands today as the most articulate contemporary spokesman for the behavioral position.

reinforcement. Sometimes he gets attention for his disruptions, and some-times he doesn't. It's likely that his disruptions will increase rather than decrease.

Extinction is particularly difficult to use when a child's behavior has negative consequences for the other people around him. For instance, a teacher may be reluctant to ignore a child's aggressive behavior if he is afraid that the child may hurt the other children. Pinkston, Reese, LeBlanc, and Baer (1973) found a potential solution to this problem. They observed that a preschool teacher was reinforcing a child's aggression with atten-tion. To make it practical for the teacher to use extinction, they devised the following plan. Every time the child choked, hit, or verbally assaulted another child, the teacher would rescue the "victim" rather than scolding the assailant.

Punishment is one of the more commonly used techniques for reducing the incidence of undesirable behavior. But despite the frequency with which it is used, it has both practical and ethical limitations. Punishment is defined technically as a consequence that decreases the probability that a response will occur (Azrin & Holz, 1966). It may consist of adding an unpleasant consequence (called an **aversive** consequence) following a behavior or of withdrawing a positive reinforcer. Reprimands and spank-ing are familiar aversive consequences. Withdrawal of affection and special privileges are examples of withdrawal of positive reinforcers.

punishing behavior

Punishment must be used with caution. It is easy to overuse or abuse it, to punish without being sensitive to the rights of the child. Because of its potential problems, it is best used as a last resort under strict guidelines.

Of course, there are degrees of aversiveness and hence of acceptabil-ity. Harsh techniques should rarely if ever be used. When positive proce-dures cannot be used for one reason or another, mild punishment can sometimes be effective and quick. It can be a humane and useful tool in

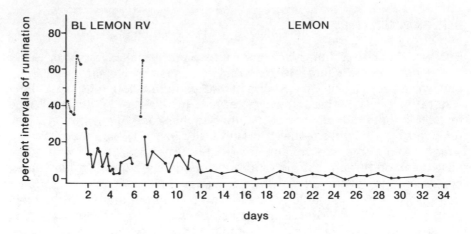

Figure 2–2 Percentage of 10-second intervals of rumination during the 20-minute postfeeding periods during baseline (BL), lemon-juice therapy periods (LEMON), and brief cessation of therapy (RV).

From "Lemon-Juice Therapy: The Control of Life-Threatening Rumination in a Six-Month-Old Infant," by T. Sajwaj, J. Libet, and S. Agras, *Journal of Applied Behavior Analysis*, 1974, *7*, 560. Reprinted by permission.

situations in which it is necessary to change a child's behavior immediately. Sajwaj, Libet, and Agras (1974) report an instance where lemon juice was used as a mild punishment to help save a child's life. These men were faced with the problem of a 6-month-old with chronic rumination. Rumination is the bringing up of food without nausea. The food is then spit out or reswallowed. It appears to be voluntary, in that children have been seen straining vigorously to bring the food back up. Serious problems, including malnutrition, dehydration, and lowered resistance to disease, can result from rumination. And some children die from it. It has been treated with procedures ranging from the extremes of surgery and electric shock to almost constant adult attention. Attention is effective, but it generally takes a relatively long time to work. The child Sajwaj and his colleagues were trying to help was already seriously ill. They were looking for something that would work more rapidly than attention and be less severe than surgery or electric shock. They hit upon the idea of squirting a small amount of lemon juice in the child's mouth immediately after food was brought up. As shown in figure 2–2, this mildly punishing procedure was highly effective. The child's rate of rumination quickly decreased and she got better.

limitations of punishment

Although punishment can be effective when used cautiously and sparingly, its usefulness is limited. It sometimes decreases behaviors other than the one targeted for change (Bandura, 1969). And in some cases the suppressed behaviors may be ones that are highly desirable. For example, if a teacher reprimands a child who has poor communication skills for talking out of turn in class, he may also reduce the rest of the child's speech.

A second limitation of punishment is that it may lead the child to avoid the situation completely (Bandura, 1969). For instance, a child punished too much in school may try to avoid being there whenever possible.

A third difficulty is that punishment may increase the occurrence of undesirable responses other than the one being punished. For example, consider the case in which a child's flying paper airplanes is being positively reinforced by attention from the other students. If the teacher punishes the child, he may simply find another way to get attention. One way to get around this problem is to punish the new responses as well (Clark, Rowbury, Baer, & Baer, 1973).

A fourth limitation is that punishment, like extinction, must be applied completely consistently to be effective. Finally, punishment may increase a child's aggressive behavior. There is substantial evidence that children who observe aggression in adults will imitate what they have observed (Martin, 1975). For example, a child who is often punished by her parents will probably learn to control the behavior of other people by being aggressive.

Behaviorists frequently use **cueing** in teaching. A cue is a signal for a response to occur. For instance, a parent may say "Pick up your room" to signal to his son what response he wants to see. According to behaviorists, cues influence behavior because they are associated with reinforcement (Skinner, 1974). In this example, if the father hugs the child after he has picked up the room, he will strengthen the power of the cue. cueing

Cueing can produce rapid changes in behavior. For example, Glynn and Thomas (1974) found that verbal cues combined with reinforcement abruptly increased the amount of time students spent on task. When they began their study, they had the students record and reinforce their own time spent on task in the classroom. While this was somewhat effective in increasing on-task behavior, many of the children seemed confused about precisely what they should be doing at any given time. The teacher then built signs to show the kinds of activity called for. These signs were used effectively to cue the students to stay on task.

Modeling is another widely used practice. It involves demonstrating a behavior that the observer is supposed to learn or perform. The term also refers to the behavior of the observer. For example, we may say "Robert modeled George's behavior," meaning that Robert imitated George. modeling

Modeling is particularly effective when the goal is to introduce something new or strengthen a response that occurs very infrequently. Haskett and Lenfestey (1974) observed that the children in a preschool classroom spent very little time in activities relating to reading. When the adults in the classroom modeled reading for the children, there was an immediate and substantial increase in the children's reading.

Modeling also may be useful in showing children what *not* to do (Bandura, 1969). The child's physical environment can be highly punishing— think of the many bumps, scrapes, and bruises that most children suffer in the course of growing up. By noticing the misfortunes of others, some children learn to avoid the risks of certain unwise actions.

Another use of modeling is to eliminate inhibition. Bandura and Menlove (1968) used modeling to help children overcome a fear of dogs. The children in this study watched a film in which children interacted with a dog without being afraid. Some children who, before the experiment, had been quite afraid of dogs, had their fear disappear completely as a result of watching the film.

Psychology in a Pluralistic Society

We tend to think of psychology as a dispassionate discipline, a science. However, psychology has developed and taken shape within a cultural context, and it has been and continues to be influenced by cultural forces. In this final section of the chapter, we shall briefly look at how our perspectives on development and socialization are related to our society.

The social forces that shape the structural and behavioral viewpoints today are different in many ways from the forces that initially supported these perspectives. Science and technology are now much more potent than they used to be. Culture changes much more rapidly than it once did. And there is a growing awareness of the significance of cultural diversity. For a scientific view on anything to be useful and accepted, it must relate to its social context. In those instances where there is disparity between scientific theory and current cultural needs, we can expect pressure from the culture to lead to changes in the theory. Theories are merely attempts to explain the things we observe; as such, they can be modified when they no longer seem useful.

STRUCTURAL PERSPECTIVES TODAY

contemporary culture and the genetic stance

Nowhere is the cultural pressure for change in a scientific theory more apparent than in today's criticisms of the early genetic structural perspective. The focus of these criticisms has been on the use of the structural model to assess and describe children's intellectual functioning. As we will see in detail in chapter 5, the assumption of genetically based individual variations in intellectual development was accepted uncritically until the early 1960s. Since that time there has been mounting dissatisfaction with the once-predominant genetic view. Moreover, this dissatisfaction has been buttressed by scientific evidence refuting the early genetic stance.

The genetic position once served a need in American society, and perhaps this is why it flourished. The American culture in the first half of this century was oriented toward consuming not only natural resources, but also human resources. Tests of "predetermined" intellectual functioning were used to identify bright children who could be channeled into advanced education and ultimately assigned to positions of leadership.

In contrast the pluralistic society of contemporary America is becoming more and more oriented to conservation. There is a growing commitment to develop the full intellectual potential of all children, rather than to focus on identifying those of special ability.

Obviously we still need to find able people. Thus the technology of intellectual assessment that was based on the Darwinian view of the survival of the fittest is still widely used. Nonetheless, the scientific theory underlying the assessment of intellectual ability is not in harmony with our current needs. We can expect to see increased pressure for changes in scientific theory and accompanying technology in the next few years.

Contemporary structural theories such as Piaget's have fared much better than has the early structural perspective. Because the Piagetian point of view does not emphasize comparisons among individuals and groups, it has not been used to assign inferior positions to certain people. Piaget's theories can accommodate cultural diversity—a strong point in a society that stresses the value of pluralism and the contributions of individuals from varied backgrounds.

contemporary culture and modern structural views

Although contemporary structural views are compatible with some current cultural movements, they do have certain shortcomings (Riegel, 1972). They do not emphasize the capability of individuals to alter their own destiny by manipulating the environment. Piaget recognizes the influence of environment on development. However, changes in the environment are not perceived as sources of significant or fundamental developmental change.

BEHAVIORAL PERSPECTIVES TODAY

The environmental emphasis of the behavioral position relates well to the current view that individuals can change their lives. Moreover, the stress on environmental determinants of behavior avoids the difficulties of the early structural position. The behavioral view does not emphasize comparisons among individuals and groups and does not place certain people in inferior social positions.

environmental viewpoint in contemporary society

Behaviorists have been sensitive to the charge that their position puts powerless people in a particularly vulnerable position, because the controlling environment is made up of people in power. Recently there have been significant changes in the behavioral position related to the issue of power. For example, in recent years behaviorists have placed increasing emphasis on the capability of human beings to manipulate the environment to control their *own* behavior (Bandura, 1974; Mahoney & Thoresen, 1974; Thoresen & Mahoney, 1974). Many behaviorists no longer give the environment the primary position in controlling behavior that it once had (e.g., Bandura, 1974). Rather, they see the individual as an active agent who continually interacts with his surroundings. The environment may affect individual behavior, but people may also influence the environment, and thereby control their own actions.

self-direction

Suggested Readings

Bandura, A. Behavior theory and the models of man. *American Psychologist*, 1974, *29*, 859–869.

Bijou, S. W. Development in the preschool years: A functional analysis. *American Psychologist*, 1975, *30*, 829–837.

Buss, A. R. The emerging field of the sociology of psychological knowledge. *American Psychologist*, 1975, *30*, 988–1002.

Elkind, D., & Duckworth, E. The educational implications of Piaget's work. In C. E. Silberman (Ed.), *The open classroom reader*. New York: Vintage, 1973.

Riegel, K. F. Influence of economic and political ideologies on the development of developmental psychology. *Psychological Bulletin*, 1972, *78*, 129–141.

Skinner, B. F. The steep and thorny way to a science of behavior. *American Psychologist*, 1975, *30*, 42–49.

Before Birth:
The Influence of Biology
and Prenatal Development

By the time children are born, they have already been developing for 9 months. This chapter looks at the basic biological processes of conception, prenatal development, and birth. When you have finished reading it, you should be familiar with these processes, and with the basic facts of genetics. You should know what genes, chromosomes, and DNA are, and their parts in prenatal development. You should understand how parents pass traits on to their children. You should be familiar with some harmful genes and chromosomal conditions and how they can affect children. You should know something about birth—full-term or premature, single or multiple. Finally, you should be aware of some environmental conditions that can affect prenatal development.

If you are studying in the library right now, look around you at the other people in the room. Or if you are at home, glance through your high school yearbook at the pictures of old friends. Notice how much people differ in physical appearance, even when you disregard differences like clothing and hair style. One of the most striking things about people is the extent to which every one of us differs from every other—the tremendous variability of human beings. And, of course, these differences include far more than obvious differences in physical appearance. If you call to mind some of the people you know well, the first qualities you think of probably include things like their typical behaviors, their mannerisms or their personalities, rather than their physical appearance.

Biological Transmission of Traits

How these differences in the ways people look and behave come about is one of the most fascinating questions asked by developmental biologists and psychologists. The other side of the question is equally challenging: What biological and physiological processes are common to everyone?

INTERACTION OF BIOLOGY AND ENVIRONMENT

We already know a lot about the factors that contribute to the differences between people. As we saw in chapter 2, in the past some scientists emphasized the influence of biology on development, while others thought that the environment plays the starring role in creating these differences. But it is now very clear that biology and environment *interact* to produce all the little variations that make people different from one another—even some traits that seem on the surface to be exclusively biological.

development of
biological
structures

One impressive demonstration of the interaction between biology and environment comes from studies of the eyes of young chimpanzees. The **retina** is a layer of light-sensitive cells at the back of the eyeball. Light entering the eye strikes the retina, which transmits the image to the brain. When infant chimpanzees are reared in total darkness, the retina does not develop properly. This finding suggests that the *potential* for normal development of the retina is transmitted biologically, but that it can only be realized if the chimpanzee is exposed to light (Riesen, Chow, Semmes, & Nissen, 1951). Obviously, we cannot try this experiment with human infants, but we have no reason to suppose that human babies need different conditions for normal development of the retina than chimpanzee babies do.

physical stature

There are many naturally occurring examples of the interaction between environment and biology. For instance, the chances are excellent that you are taller than your great-grandparents were. Of course there are many exceptions, but over the past five or six generations the average height of adults from the developed nations has been increasing. These increases are due in part to improved health and nutrition, and in part to a redistribution of the genes for "tallness" that is the result of intermarriage among ethnic groups (Dunn & Dobzhansky, 1952). Increases in height among the Japanese and the Chinese over the past few generations are especially marked (Hulse, 1971). These changes seem to stem from rapid improvements in the average standard of living, since these groups have a relatively low rate of intermarriage. Apparently they had the potential for greater stature all along, but the less than optimal health and nutrition of the people held them back. But before we can understand just how biology and environment interact, we need to take a closer look at how biology affects us, and how parents pass biological characteristics on to their children.

HEREDITARY TRANSMISSION

Conception occurs when a male's **sperm** penetrates a female's **ovum**, or egg. At this moment, which is also called **fertilization**, a new life begins.

People must have come to realize thousands of years ago that there is a relationship between sexual activity and reproduction. The most obvious clue is the fact that children usually look more like their parents and their brothers and sisters than like other people. But even though people have long suspected that something that happened during sexual intercourse gave the child some characteristics of the parents, they were largely unaware of the details of the process. Only recently have we known the precise way that one generation passes characteristics on to another.

Some scientists who thought about this question thought that an animal could pass along a trait acquired during its lifetime to its offspring. This idea was promoted by Lemark, a French scientist interested in evolution. Lemark's idea has been generally discarded, and Darwin's concept of natural selection has been accepted in its place.

> belief in transmission of acquired characteristics

When the microscope was invented, scientists could see the tiny sperm for the first time. The early instruments could not provide a clear view of the sperm, and many thought that they saw a tiny person there. The little being was named *homunculus*, and the theory that developed said that a tiny version of a complete human being was passed from male to female during intercourse (Scheinfeld, 1965). A competing school of thought held that the ovum contained a tiny embryo that would begin to develop when a male sperm activated it. Of course, both views were wrong, and we shall now look at the process by which parents make equal contributions to each child. Since (except for identical twins) the children of a given pair of parents differ considerably from one another, we will also look at some of the factors that contribute to differences between people.

Hereditary Material All organisms, both plant and animal, are made up of cells—tiny structures that have all the characteristics of living things, including the ability to reproduce themselves. In fact, in a suitable environment, such as a laboratory culture, single cells can live and produce more of their own kind for years—perhaps indefinitely. Apparently only when cells become part of a complex, multicellular organism do maturing, aging, and dying become a problem (Hardin, 1953).

> cells

Cells differ from one organism to another; and even within a single organism the cells of different organs and tissues vary in size, shape, and function. In humans, the cells on the inside of the cheek are relatively large, and you can easily scrape a few loose with the blunt end of a toothpick to look at under a microscope.

There are two main parts of a cell. The central part is called the *nucleus.* The material surrounding the nucleus is the *cytoplasm.* The entire cell is bounded by a *cell membrane.* Collectively, all the living material of the cell (the nucleus, the cytoplasm, and the membrane) is called *protoplasm.*

body cells and
sex cells

Humans and other higher organisms have two basic kinds of cells: **somatic,** or body cells, and the germ cells, which are involved in reproduction. These germ cells are also called **gametes** or *sex cells.* Male gametes are called spermatoza, or simply sperm. The female gamete, or egg, is the ovum.

chromosomes

Within the nucleus of both somatic and sex cells there are threadlike bodies called **chromosomes.** When a cell is stained with certain dyes, the chromosomes take on a deep color. In Greek, *chromo* means color, and *soma* refers to body—hence the name *chromosome.* Each body cell in a human being contains 46 chromosomes arranged in 23 pairs. Each sex cell contains only 23 chromosomes, or one member of each pair in the body cells. As we shall soon see, there is a very good reason for this difference.

genes

The chromosomes are the physical carriers of hereditary material (McClearn, 1970). The **genes,** which are small particles of hereditary material, lie in a line along the threadlike chromosomes. Each chromosome carries thousands of genes, and each gene has a fixed position on a given chromosome. These small chemical particles are arranged like beads along the chromosomes. The chromosomes keep the hereditary material organized. The genes contain the "instructions" that govern biological development.

DNA

Scientists have known for some time that an important compound called **deoxyribonucleic acid (DNA)** is present in the chromosomes of all cells. They assumed that this nucleic acid was involved in the transmission of hereditary traits. However, the structure and exact functions of DNA were unknown until an American biologist, James D. Watson, and an English bio-

FORBIDDEN KNOWLEDGE

For most scientists, it is unthinkable that there should not be free and open research on any topic they choose. But some concerned scientists are beginning to question the assumption that the unrestricted gathering of scientific information is always good. Robert Sinsheimer, a well-known biologist who is the Chancellor of the University of California at Santa Cruz, suggests that some knowledge may be, if not "forbidden," at least "inopportune" and contrary to general human welfare at a given point in history. For example, since the break-through discovery of the nature of DNA, genetic engineers can now create new organisms and

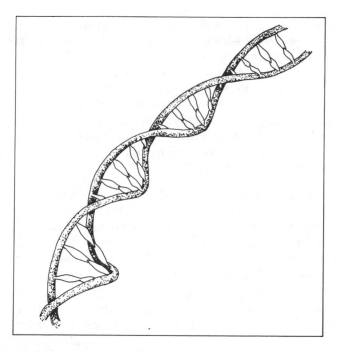

Figure 3–1   Artist's conception of the double helix.

physicist, Francis Crick, stimulated by X-ray pictures taken by an English biophysicist, Maurice Wilkins, found the key to the genetic code. They were able to show how the DNA molecule works.

The DNA molecule consists of two long strands linked together by four different kinds of compounds (see figure 3–1). Compounds that are compatible with one another line up in pairs, and the pairs are linked together by weak chemical bonds. The two strands coil around each other like a spiral staircase or a twisted rope ladder. Watson and Crick named this peculiar structure the *double helix.*

double helix

DNA is considered the basic substance of all living matter. Each DNA molecule may represent many genes (Ziegel & Van Blarcom, 1972). This remarkable molecule has two unique properties. First, it can copy itself. Cells can divide again and again, producing identical copies of them-

override the wisdom of billions of years of biological evolution. The scientists involved in this work may be well trained in science and technology, but do they have the individual and collective wisdom to engineer the future evolution of all organisms, including humans? Other critics (for example, Howard & Rifkin, 1977) argue that the leading scientists in the field of genetic engineering face a conflict of interest because they stand to make money from corporate use of the new genetic technology.

Sinsheimer feels we should even look carefully at the possible risks of such apparently beneficial inquiry as research on aging. We have not yet developed, and show few signs of being able to develop, social solutions to problems of overpopulation on a finite planet.

duplication

selves each time. During cell division, the DNA molecule "unzips" itself along the weak chemical bonds. Then each half duplicates itself from materials in the surrounding cell.

RNA

DNA's second unique characteristic is that it carries the basic instructions for the characteristics of the developing organism (Howe & Hunt, 1975). When it "unzips," the DNA molecule creates a second type of nucleic acid, **ribonucleic acid (RNA)**. RNA acts as a messenger to carry the instructions coded in the DNA to the cytoplasm of the cell. DNA cannot move out of the nucleus into the cytoplasm, but the RNA messenger can (Ziegel & Van Blarcom, 1972).

zygote

chromatids

Mitosis—The Duplication of Body Cells   The male sperm cell and the female egg each have 23 chromosomes. When the sperm penetrates the ovum at the time of fertilization, a new cell with 46 chromosomes is formed. This new cell, the fertilized ovum, is called a **zygote**. The zygote begins to grow immediately through cell division. This process is called **mitosis**. Through the process that we already described, each of the 46 chromosomes duplicates itself by splitting along its length, forming two new chromosomes called **chromatids**. The members of the chromatid pairs are then pulled to opposite sides of the original cell. As the chromatids are pulled apart, a new cell wall develops, dividing the original cell and forming two new cells (Fraser, 1966). This process is diagrammed in figure 3–2. Each of the new cells has 46 chromosomes, and each is identical to the original cell from which they were formed. The process then begins all over again as each new cell divides, then divides again, and again, and on and on.

If the sex cells contained as many chromosomes as the body cells, the union of sperm and egg would result in a zygote with 92 rather than 46

Figure 3–2   Mitosis: The process of duplication of body cells
a. A body cell with chromosomes (actual human body cells have 46 chromosomes in 23 pairs).
b. Each chromosome duplicates itself, and the halves (chromatids) begin to separate.
c. Chromatid pairs are pulled to opposite sides of the cell by tiny fibers.
d. The cell begins to separate, with half of the chromosomes on each side.
e. Cell division is now complete. Each of the two cells will now go through the same process, resulting in four cells. They, in turn, will form new cells.

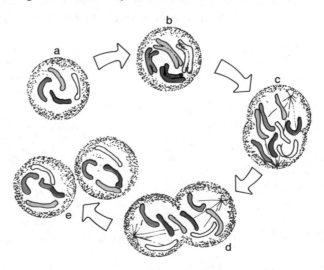

chromosomes. If that were possible, the resulting child would have gametes with 92 chromosomes. The number of chromosomes in each generation would double. Clearly, this is not what happens, so there must be a way for the number of chromosomes in the cells to remain constant. The process of meiosis **(reduction division)** provides this mechanism.

reduction division

Meiosis—Reduction Division in the Germ Cells   Soon after the zygote begins to divide into new cells, differentiation begins. Under instructions from the genetic code carried in the DNA, cells begin to specialize. Eventually this specialization produces different tissues like muscle and skin. (We will describe this process in more detail later in this chapter.) Among the cells that develop specialized functions are the sex cells. In **meiosis,** sex cells divide and redivide.

At this point remember that the cell contains 46 chromosomes, 23 from the mother and 23 from the father. Each chromosome from one parent is comparable to a chromosome from the other parent. Therefore, when the two sex cells unite at fertilization, the resulting zygote has 23 *pairs* of chromosomes. These are called **homologous** *pairs*, and each member of a pair is called a **homologue.**

homologous chromosomes

Two cell divisions take place during meiosis (see figure 3–3). In the early stages of the first division, meiosis is very similar to mitosis. Each chromosome duplicates itself, but the two chromatids remain connected at a point called the **centromere.** Each duplicated chromosome now begins to move toward its homologue. The homologues line up closely, side by side, to form homologous pairs. Since the chromosomes have doubled,

Figure 3–3   Meiosis: The process of reduction division.

a. Sex cells originate from a cell with 46 (23 pairs) of chromosomes (only two single chromosomes are shown here).
b. Each chromosome duplicates itself.
c. The duplicate halves of the chromosomes (chromatids) split. Members of the chromatid pairs are pulled to opposite sides of the cell by tiny fibers.
d. The cell begins to divide, resulting in two cells with the same number of chromosomes as the original cell.
e. Each of these cells divides.
f. There are now four cells, each with half as many chromosomes (23) as the original cell.

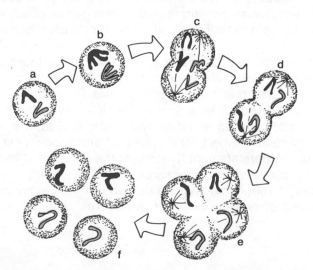

each pair now consists of four chromatids. The members of the homologus pairs then begin to move away from one another, toward opposite poles of the cells. A new cell membrane forms between the two sets of chromosomes. The result is two new cells, each with 23 chromosomes.

Until now the chromatids of the duplicated chromosomes were connected at the centromere. They then separate; one member of each chromatid pair moves to one side of the cell and its homologue moves to the opposite side. Again a new membrane is formed, so now there are four cells, each with 23 chromosomes, when before this all began there was only a single cell.

FACTORS CONTRIBUTING TO HUMAN VARIABILITY

Mendel's discoveries

Some of the most basic rules of genetic inheritance were discovered during the mid-nineteenth century by Gregor Mendel, an Augustinian monk. He spent his time carefully breeding pea plants, counting and classifying, and recording the results. He published his findings in 1866, but no one paid much attention to them until after his death. His works were rediscovered at the beginning of this century (McClearn, 1970; Hulse, 1963).

Mendel noticed that some peas have smooth seeds while the seeds of other plants are wrinkled. Some plants have green seeds and some have yellow. The flowers of some plants appear in one position, while other plants have flowers in a different position. He crossbred these plants in various ways and kept careful records of the offspring produced and the proportions in which the characteristics he was watching appeared. It just so happened that the characteristics he studied were controlled by genes situated on different chromosomes. This fact is important because during meiosis, some chromosomes end up in one sex cell while others end up in different sex cells. In this sorting out process, each chromosome is entirely independent of any other chromosome. That is, as each pair of homologous chromosome breaks up, the individual chromatids go to new

principle of independent assortment

cells independently. Any given chromatid may end up in any one of the four new sex cells. This process is called the *principle of independent assortment* of chromosomes. In effect it means that if the gene calling for wrinkled pea seeds is on one chromosome and the gene calling for green seeds is on another chromosome, these two genes could end up in the same sex cell or in different sex cells. This factor contributes to variety in offspring.

individual uniqueness

In human beings, with 23 pairs of chromosomes, there are 8,388,608 possible combinations of chromosomes that could result from this random assortment. Not only that, but the chance that any particular sperm of the 8,388,608 that are possible will combine with any specific one of the 8,388,608 possible eggs is less than one in about *64 trillion*. And these are only the possible outcomes of the mating of one specific set of parents. It seems a gross understatement to say that the chances of two people ever being exactly alike are very, very small.

Even these astronomical possibilities do not truly exhaust the possible recombinations of genetic material. Additional recombinations may oc-

cur during cell division by a process called *crossing over.* Early in the crossing over
process of meiosis, when homologous chromosomes from the maternal
and paternal sex cells are lined up side by side, the homologues may exchange genetic material. Thus, when the homologues part company and
move to different sex cells, they may contain some genetic material from
the mother and some from the father. This process is depicted in figure
3–4.

Mendel concluded from his breeding of pea plants that individual characteristics must be controlled by some kind of hereditary material. He
called it a *gene.* The simple characteristics he observed were controlled
by single pairs of genes, one of which is contributed by each parent. He
concluded that the gene for a given condition may have more than one
form. Let's look at pea seed color as an example. A pea seed can be
either green or yellow and, obviously, not both. A gene that controls alternative expressions of a given characteristic is called an **allele.** Alleles   alleles
are located on homologous chromosomes. If both alleles carry the same
message, say green, then the plant with these alleles is called **homozygous**
for seed color. On the other hand, if the plant has one allele for greenness
and the other for yellowness, it is **heterozygous** for seed color.

Mendel discovered that some genes may be dominant and others re-   dominant and
cessive. Again, let's use pea plants instead of people, because heredity   recessive genes
in peas is simpler. In pea plants yellow is dominant over green. Thus, if a
plant receives one allele for yellowness from each parent, it will produce

Figure 3–4 Crossing over. Chromosomes may exchange genetic material during
mitosis.
a. Chromosomes In this diagram are depicted as strands of genes. Here, two pairs of
   chromosomes line up alongside each other during mitosis.
b. Adjacent members of two chromosome pairs cross over each other.
c. Sections of each of the crossed chromosomes become attached to the member of
   the adjacent chromosome pair.

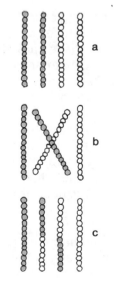

yellow seeds itself. For convenience, let's call this allele for yellow seeds *Y,* and the allele for greenness *y.* The new plant will also produce yellow seeds if it receives one *Y* allele from one parent and one *y* allele from the other, because the dominant gene for yellow *(Y)* masks the recessive allele *(y).* The offspring will produce green seeds only if it receives a double dose of the *y* gene. Thus a plant with green seeds must be homozygous for *y.* If the plant is yellow, we cannot tell by looking at it whether it is homozygous *(YY)* or heterozygous *(Yy).* If two heterozygous plants were mated, each parent would contribute the dominant allele *(Y)* about half of the time and the recessive allele for the other half of the time. The likelihood that both germ cells would be recessive is one in four.

For most human characteristics, inheritance is much more complicated than the simple dominant-recessive pattern. Many characteristics are controlled by more than a single set of alleles, and some can blend contrasting features rather than having one dominant over the other. Some genes can modify the expression of other genes. Nevertheless, some human characteristics are dominant-recessive. If your earlobe is attached at its lower tip, you are homozygous for the attached earlobe trait, because it is controlled by a recessive gene. If you have detached earlobes, you may be homozygous for the dominant gene or heterozygous. If you take a random sample of the people in your class, about ¼ of them should have attached earlobes, while the others are detached.

Thus some genes are directly reflected in observable characteristics, while others are not. Those characteristics that we can observe constitute

phenotype and genotype

the individual's **phenotype.** For a given characteristic, the phenotype may or may not correspond to the genotype. **Genotype** is an individual's actual genetic makeup, whether or not it is directly observable. For example, if your earlobes are attached, that is both your phenotype and your genotype. However, if your phenotypic characteristic for earlobes is detached, no one can tell by looking at you whether or not your genotype is *YY* or *Yy.*

Except in the case of biological accidents, such as genetic mutations, the environment has no influence over people's genotypes. On the other hand, many phenotypic characteristics are affected by the interaction between heredity and environment. An infant might inherit genes for superior intellectual capability; but if he were not given the chance to develop it, he would probably perform at a very low level and there might be no clue to his true potential.

Not all human traits that are dominant-recessive are as trivial as attachment of earlobes. Certain relatively infrequent but serious hereditary diseases are controlled this way. And to complicate the issue, the inheritance of certain characteristics, including some that are quite harmful, is linked to the another important aspect of human variability. That aspect is sex.

Sex Determination   Twenty-two of the pairs of chromosomes in a human

autosomes and sex chromosomes

body cell are called **autosomes.** Each of the two members of an autosome pair looks just like its mate, but the twenty-third pair is different. One member of this pair is longer than the other. These are the sex chromosomes. The longer member of the pair is called the X chromosome, and the smaller one is called the Y chromosome. Genetically, the difference between male and female sex cells is that females have two X chromosomes, while males have one X and one Y chromosome. Each time meiosis takes place in a male sex cell, one of the new cells receives an X chromosome and the other receives a Y chromosome. As a result, it is actually the male's contribution that determines the sex of a child. The Biblical husbands who blamed their wives for failing to bear sons were dead wrong about which partner was responsible for the sex of a child. The zygote will always receive an X chromosome from the mother's egg. About half of the male sperm contain X chromosomes and the other half Y chromosomes, so if the first male sperm to reach the ovum contains a Y chromosome, the zygote will carry the XY genotype. Phenotypically the child will be a boy.

sex-linked inheritance

Some inherited characteristics are sex-linked. The principle of independent assortment applies only to the chromosomes and not to the genes themselves. The X and Y chromosomes carry a number of genes in addition to those that determine sex, so the characteristics controlled by those genes will be associated with the child's sex. Since genes from the same chromosome are likely to be inherited as a unit, they are said to be *linked*. The closer together genes are on the chromosome that carries them, the less likely they are to be separated by crossing over. Traits controlled by genes carried on the X and Y chromosomes are *sex-linked*, since these characteristics are usually inherited along with the individual's sex. So far, at least 150 specific sex-linked characteristics have been identified in humans (McKusick, 1971).

color blindness

Red-green color blindness is one sex-linked trait. The gene for normal red-green color vision is dominant, while the gene for red-green color blindness is recessive. If a female has the recessive gene for color blindness on both of her X chromosomes, she will be red-green color blind. The chances of this happening are quite small. On the other hand, there is no gene for red-green color vision on the Y chromosome at all, so if a male receives the recessive gene for color blindness from his mother, he will be color blind. There is no chance for him to have a dominant gene to counteract the effects of the recessive gene he received from his mother.

hemophilia

Hemophilia, or bleeders' disease, is an inherited disorder in which blood does not coagulate properly. Like red-green color blindness, hemophilia is a sex-linked characteristic contolled by a gene on the X chromosome. It is quite rare. Nevertheless, it is rather famous because it has afflicted some very famous people. Queen Victoria of England passed the recessive gene for hemophilia on to several members of European royal families. The affliction appeared in only a few princesses, because to have hemophilia a female must receive the recessive gene on each of her two X chromosomes. Royal males were not nearly so lucky as the females. No fewer than ten European princes, dukes, and viscounts had the disease within the first three generations following Queen Victoria. Hemophilia played a role in the political intrigue that preceded the Russian

Revolution. The infamous monk, Rasputin, manipulated the Czar and Czarina of Russia by holding out hope for a magical cure of their son, whose hemophilia is traceable to Queen Victoria (Scheinfeld, 1965).

genetic mutations

Mutations By now you might be wondering why we haven't mentioned hemophilia in the royal line before Queen Victoria. It appears that the gene causing hemophilia occurred as a result of a **mutation** during Queen Victoria's own prenatal development, or perhaps in one of her parents. Mutations are accidents that occur while DNA is reproducing itself. They provide the primary source of new variations in a species. Mutations may occur spontaneously, or they may be caused by things like radiation, chemicals, or high temperatures. Mutations may occur either in the body cells or in the sex cells. A mutation in a body cell will appear in only those cells that are direct descendants of the cell in which the mutation occurred. That is, they are not passed on to later generations. But when a mutation occurs in a sex cell, it may be transmitted to successive generations (Ziegel & Van Blarcom, 1972).

Most mutations have harmful effects. Usually they disappear or remain rare because the people who carry them have less chance of growing to adulthood and passing the harmful gene on to their own children than people who do not have the mutant gene. But some harmful genes do not disappear from the population. In the case of hemophilia, new mutations resulting in the gene that causes the disease occur at the rate of about one gene in 50,000 (Dunn, 1959).

characteristics providing natural selection

Natural Selection New forms of genes can only get into a population through mutations or through interbreeding between distinct populations. While most mutations are harmful, over the long course of human evolution some mutations have given their bearers a better chance to survive and reproduce themselves than their neighbors. Traits that improve their carriers' chances of surviving and producing offspring have an *adaptive advantage.* In later chapters we shall see that some psychologists explain certain developmental characteristics of children on the basis of their probable adaptive advantage during human evolution.

Genetically Determined Defects

aberrant genes and chromosomes

Luckily, most of the characteristics we get from our parents and pass on to our own children have been well tested for their adaptive value over thousands of years. But unfortunate children may also inherit characteristics that put them at a developmental disadvantage, or that may even be deadly. Some of these disabilities result from abnormal genes, called **aberrant** genes. Other defects are the result of abnormalities in the chromosomes. In this section we will describe a few examples of each.

DEFECTS CAUSED BY HARMFUL GENES

Phenylketonuria (PKU) is one of several hereditary conditions that can result in mental retardation. It is inherited through a simple recessive gene that is carried by about one in every 20 people. This gene leads to a metabolic breakdown that causes irreversible damage to the central nervous system. Unfortunately, phenylalanine, the chemical that causes the damage, is found in milk, which is the most basic food in an infant's diet.

PKU can be identified by a urine test taken within the first 24 to 40 hours after an infant's birth. Once the condition is identified, its effects can be controlled by diet. Because phenylalanine is essential to growth, it cannot be eliminated entirely. The diet of an infant with PKU must include a small amount of phenylalanine plus an artificial replacement for natural dietary proteins. During the first few weeks of life, careful measurements of height, weight, and general development, as well as blood tests, are taken every week to make sure that the diet is just right (Getchell & Howard, 1975). After this time, monitoring can be less frequent; but as the child grows, the diet must be continuously checked and adjusted to meet his or her changing needs. To compound the problem, the diet is quite unpalatable. It is often very difficult to make sure that growing children follow the diet as strictly as they should.

The birth of a child with PKU generally means financial hardship and emotional stress to the family. These tensions can affect the parent-child relationships and other interpersonal relationships within the family. The parents' attention is understandably focused on the demands of the child's physical well-being. It is especially important that parents give the child the chance to develop socially and emotionally as well.

PKU develops only if a child is homozygous for the harmful gene. People with a single recessive gene for PKU will have no symptoms and thus will not be aware that they are carriers. If two carriers mate, the chances are one in four that their child will receive a double dose of the harmful gene and develop the disorder. Luckily, today it is possible to detect the presence of a single recessive gene through chemical tests. This information would be of great value in genetic counseling (Reed, 1963; Scheinfeld, 1965; Stern, 1960). If there is a history of PKU on either side, a couple planning to have children would be well advised to take the tests.

Amaurotic family idiocy is another genetic disorder that leads to mental retardation. **Tay-Sachs disease** is one of the most common forms of this disorder. It is caused by a recessive gene that occurs with relatively higher frequency among Jewish families than in other populations (Reed, 1975). Tay-Sachs disease develops only when a child is homozygous for the harmful gene. Like PKU, Tay-Sachs disease results from a metabolic disorder. This disorder causes fatty deposits to build up in the nerve cells of the brain and spinal cord. The condition results in mental deterioration, blindness, paralysis, and finally death by age 4 or 5. There is no known cure.

phenylketonuria

early detection of PKU

impact on family

Tay-Sachs disease

microcephaly

Microcephaly may also be genetically determined, although it can also result from environmental factors such as maternal infections or X-ray exposure during pregnancy (Sisson, Clatworthy, & Zadroga, 1975). In microcephaly the sutures of the skull close before they should. Both the skull and the brain stop growing at an early age, often causing severe mental retardation.

hydrocephaly

Hydrocephaly is a neurological disorder that is genetically determined, although the exact hereditary causes have not been clearly identified. The condition becomes evident at birth or soon after. There is an abnormal increase of cerebrospinal fluid in the skull. The skull becomes enlarged, and mental deficiency develops if it goes untreated. Hydrocephaly can be treated, often successfully, by draining the excess fluid from the skull.

epilepsy

The causes of **epilepsy** are not completely known, but it is usually hereditary. Epilepsy involves recurring convulsive disorders or seizures. The seizures may be relatively mild, involving temporary loss of conciousness, rolling of the eyes, and perhaps a slight quivering of the body. Slight

petit mal

seizures like this are known as *petit mal.* Petit mal epilepsy usually disappears by adolescence. Teachers and others who work with children often mistake mild episodes of petit mal as day dreaming or inattention.

grand mal

Grand mal seizures involve generalized convulsions and disturbances in brain function. The child may fall to the ground, the eyes may roll upward or to one side, the trunk muscles may be rigid while the limbs are either rigid or contract irregularly. The child may bite his tongue as jaw muscles contract. Sleep follows a seizure (Sisson, Clatworthy, & Zadroga, 1975).

Epilepsy does not seem to be inherited as a specific disorder. Instead, many people seem to inherit a susceptibility or predisposition to it. People with this susceptibility may or may not develop the syndrome, depending upon the experiences they have. The specific environmental events that may trigger epilepsy are not yet known, but once the disorder is diagnosed it can often be controlled by medication.

sickle cell anemia

Sickle cell anemia is a particularly interesting and serious disorder. When a child is homozygous for the recessive sickle cell gene, there is a defect in the way red blood cells form. Early signs of the disorder include retarded growth, frequent infections, irritability, paleness, jaundice, and a general failure to thrive (Green & Cooper, 1975). Unfortunately, these symptoms are also associated with a number of other childhood disorders. However, if these symptoms are noticed in a black child, the possibility of sickle cell anemia should be investigated right away. While the gene occurs very rarely in most populations, it is found in almost 40% of certain groups of African descent.

sickle cell trait

People who are heterozygous for the sickle cell gene have *sickle cell trait.* There are usually no ill effects from sickle cell trait, unless the person with it is deprived of oxygen. Generally, people with sickle cell trait can expect to live a normal life span but people with sickle cell disease usually cannot expect to live beyond early adulthood.

One intriguing question about this disorder is how such a deadly gene can remain so frequent in a population. Under normal circumstances, we would expect natural selection to have reduced the frequency of the gene. The answer lies in a peculiar kind of environmental-genetic interaction. Malaria is prevalent in the region of Africa where the groups carrying the mutant sickle cell gene came from. Individuals who have a single sickle cell gene have some resistance to malaria. Therefore, people who are *heterozygous* for sickle cell are more likely to live to maturity and pass the gene on to their own children than their neighbors in that malaria-infested environment who do not have the gene (Allison, 1955; Dunn, 1959).

adaptive advantage of sickle cell

In the United States, the sickle cell gene does not offer the adaptive advantage it did in its original environment. Therefore, while sickle cell anemia presents a serious health problem for American blacks (Schein-feld, 1965; Boyd, 1950; Dunn, 1959), we might expect to see its relative incidence decrease over the next centuries.

GENETIC COUNSELING

Scientists have identified about 2,000 genetically transmitted diseases. Many of these can be spotted by a qualified genetic counselor, who will analyze the family trees of a couple and compute the odds of their having a child with a genetic defect. Before long, even more detailed and precise information may be routinely made available through screening immediately after birth. We already have the technology to analyze a chromosome sample soon after the birth of a baby. Dr. Robert Ledley of the National Biomedical Research Foundation has developed a technique for analyzing these samples with computers programmed to identify genetic defects.

Many people consider genetic counseling a blessing. Ledley feels that a couple who has reason to fear that they may be carriers of a dread genetic disease will probably refrain from having a child if the chances are too great that the child will be afflicted. On the other hand, a couple may be relieved to learn that their chances of having an afflicted child are small. They might decide to have a child, where without the information provided by genetic counseling they might refrain.

Other people are not so sure that it is a blessing to have this information. They argue that our knowledge of genetics is more refined than our knowledge of how to use genetic information. They feel the genetic counselor is playing God, and that her own values may be imposed on the people who are counseled. It is also argued that unwanted genetic information may cause unnecessary fears for relatives who themselves may or may not be at risk for the same defect. (See Restak, 1975, in Suggested Readings, for this point of view.)

Genetic counselors naturally disagree with this view. They argue that the counselor should provide the genetic information and explore a variety of options with the patient. The counselor's own opinion should not be expressed. The prospective parents are the ultimate decision makers, but without all the relevant information, they have no basis for an informed, rational choice. (See the reading by Shaw, 1974.)

DEFECTS CAUSED BY ABNORMAL CHROMOSOMES

Certain developmental disorders are caused by abnormal conditions in the chromosomes. In fact, it has been estimated that somewhere between 22 and 46 % of spontaneously aborted fetuses (miscarriages) are probably caused by chromosome abnormalities. Some sort of major chromosome abnormality is involved in about one out of every 200 live births (Reed, 1975).

spontaneous aborting

One common disability caused by an abnormal chromosomal arrangement is **Down's syndrome**. Children with Down's syndrome have a fold of skin over their eyes that makes them look somewhat Oriental. This characteristic led to the name *mongolism,* which was once widely used to refer to Down's syndrome. The term *mongolism* is rarely used today, because it is considered insensitive.

Down's syndrome

Other features of Down's syndrome include a flat, sunken nose bridge, small malformed ears, a large and misshapen forehead, a fissured tongue, and fingers and hands that may be webbed or otherwise misshapen. Children with Down's syndrome are frequently dwarfed and may have a number of serious health problems. These problems include heart defects and susceptibility to infections. Until recently, children with this disorder could not expect to live to reach their teens; but with improved medical treatment and modern antibiotics to fight their frequent infections, it is not unusual for them to live well into middle age. Down's syndrome is also associated with mental retardation. Fortunately, the plight of these children

Lucia has physical features characteristic of Down's syndrome.

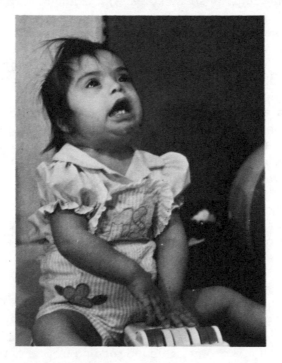

has been improved by educational innovations. New educational techniques make it possible for them to learn both academic and social skills that only a short time ago were considered far beyond their capabilities.

Children with Down's syndrome have a total of 47 rather than 46 chromosomes. They usually have an extra number of one particular pair of chromosomes—the number 21 pair. This extra chromosome develops when the number 21 chromosome fails to separate from its mate during meiosis. If this happens in a young woman, there is very little risk that it will happen again and affect another child born to the same parents. However, the chance that it will happen again is about one in 40 if the mother is 45 years old or over (Reed, 1975). In general, older mothers are more likely to have Down's syndrome children than younger mothers. This suggests that as a woman ages, her reproductive system operates less efficiently.

causes

failure of chromosome 21 to separate

Down's syndrome may also occur when the extra number 21 chromosome becomes attached to another chromosome. This accident is called a *translocation,* and either parent may be the carrier of the extra chromosome. If one parent is the carrier, the chance of producing a Down's syndrome child is about 15%, a risk that many parents would not take if they were aware that one of them is a carrier (Reed, 1975).

translocation of chromosome 21

Since accidents during meiosis happen so much more often among older women, middle-age pregnancy causes anxiety and concern. Fortunately, it is now possible to tell whether an unborn child will have Down's syndrome. Parents who discover that their unborn child will have Down's syndrome can consider having a therapeutic abortion. The test, called **amniocentesis**, involves extracting a small amount of **amniotic fluid** from the mother and analyzing the chromosomes in it. This test makes it possible to detect Down's syndrome during the first trimester (three months) of pregnancy. Amniocentesis can also be used to detect Tay-Sachs and other deadly disorders.

early identification

An abnormality in the number of sex chromosomes a child receives may result in deviations in sexual development. For example, people with **Klinefelter's syndrome** usually have an extra X chromosome. Phenotypically they are males, but their testes do not develop completely and they cannot produce sperm. They have related deficiencies in the production of certain male hormones that are essential to the development of male secondary sexual characteristics.

Klinefelter's syndrome

Males with Klinefelter's syndrome may also have a somewhat feminine body build, with rounded hips and enlarged breasts. Often they show signs of mental retardation and antisocial behavior. The disorder does not appear until adolescence; when it is detected, the boy can take male hormones to promote male secondary sexual characteristics and a more masculine appearance.

Turner's syndrome is seen in females with only one X chromosome. Phenotypically, they are female, because they have no Y chromosome to influence the development of male sexual characteristics. On the other hand, since they have only a single X chromosome, they do not develop

Turner's syndrome

complete female secondary sex characteristics unless they take hormones. Their internal female sex organs do not develop fully, and they can never conceive children.

AMNIOCENTESIS

Amniocentesis is a relatively simple procedure that makes it possible to identify hereditary defects and other genetic characteristics of unborn children still in the mother's womb. It lets doctors determine the sex of the unborn child, plus find out about around 50 genetic disorders, including Down's syndrome and Tay-Sachs disease. A small amount of the fluid surrounding the fetus is withdrawn with a syringe through a thin needle inserted through the mother's abdomen. This fluid contains fetal cells that can be put into a culture and analyzed.

While the medical procedure is simple, the ethical issues associated with amniocentesis are more complex. When parents request that it be done, their request implies that they are willing to consider abortion if a disorder is found. Even for parents for whom abortion for such reasons is not a problem, there may be some reason to hesitate. The procedure can only be performed when the pregnancy is fairly far advanced. Once the fluid is obtained, it takes an additional few weeks for the cells to grow so that the required tests can be done. By that time there are increased risks of complications in abortions.

Some doctors respond to concerns about amniocentesis by saying that it is actually a life-giving procedure. Most of the parents who request amniocentesis have either had a previous child with a genetic defect, or are older parents who know that children born to older mothers have an increased chance of having a defect such as Down's syndrome. Without the benefit of prenatal genetic screening, these parents, worried about the possibility of having a child with a serious disorder, are often reluctant to take the risk of having a baby.

Some people who believe in abortion to prevent the suffering associated with genetic defects are concerned that amniocentesis may be used for trivial and unethical reasons. Some people have already used it to make sure they have a baby of a particular sex, and boy babies are more often desired than girl babies. Margaret Mead, however, sees this as a possible benefit. She feels that girls born under these circumstances will at least be wanted. They will not be rejected by their parents for not being boys. Next, the critics fear, parents may decide whether or not to have a abortion on the basis of the child's hair or eye color.

Another concern among those who oppose prenatal screening is that it will lead to a lack of concern and compassion for individuals who aren't "normal." And, over time, our notions about what is normal may become more and more narrow. While all these concerns have some basis, advocates of amniocentesis feel the current benefits far outweigh the possible future disadvantages.

Multiple Pregnancy

Two or more children may develop during a single pregnancy. Multiple pregnancies may occur in two different ways. In one case the male sperm fertilizes a single ovum, but early in the development of the zygote it splits into two separate cell masses, each of which develops into a separate embryo. Twins that result from a single fertilization develop from identical genetic material, and they are technically known as **monozygotic** (MZ) twins. They are more commonly called *identical twins* because they are of the same sex, have the same blood type, will share the same hereditary disorders, and have a strong physical resemblance to each other. The term *identical twin* is somewhat misleading, however, because MZ twins do differ from each other in some ways. They may differ in birth weight because one embryo may be more crowded in the uterus or one may receive more nutrition from the **placenta** than the other twin. Some identical siblings are mirror images of each other, apparently because of the way the chromosomes split when the original zygote divided. When this happens, one twin may be left-handed and the other right-handed, their hair whorl and direction of hair growth will be opposite, and features such as birthmarks or other right- and left-sided physical features will be reversed (Howe & Hunt, 1975).

Occasionally the developing cell mass will split into three or more separate cell masses. When this happens, three or more embryos develop simultaneously, resulting in the birth of triplets, quadruplets, and sometimes even larger numbers of siblings.

Twin pregnancies may also result from the fertilization of two ova by two separate sperm. Twins from these pregnancies are commonly called *fraternal twins.* The more technical term is **dizygotic twins** (DZ), because they result from the development of two separate zygotes that originate from two separate fertilized eggs. Since the genetic material one dizygotic twin inherits is completely independent of the genetic material received by the other twin, they resemble one another no more than any other siblings born to the same parents. They may be of the same sex or different sexes.

Twins occur once in every 90 pregnancies, while triplets are born only about once for every 9,000 pregnancies. There is apparently some hereditary influence on the chance of multiple births, since twins are more common in some families than in others. There are also racial differences in the probability of multiple births. Black families have a higher proportion of twin pregnancies than white families, and the rate is lowest among orientals (Ziegel & Van Blarcom, 1972).

Since the introduction of birth control pills, multiple births have become more common. Birth control pills contain the hormone estrogen, which prevents ovulation while they are being taken regularly. However, when the woman stops taking them, several eggs that have been held back may

identical twins

fraternal twins

probability of multiple births

birth control and fertility

Identical twins are identical in genetic material as well as in appearance. Fraternal twins are no more similar to each other than any other pair of siblings.

be released at the same time. Thus there is the possibility that two or more of them will become fertilized (Howe & Hunt, 1975). Some drugs that are given to women having trouble becoming pregnant are also associated with increased multiple births.

age   Age is another factor that influences the likelihood of multiple births. Older women are more likely than younger women to release more than one ovum at a single ovulation (Greenhill, 1971).

From the moment of conception, it takes only about 280 days until an infant, capable of thriving in the relatively harsh environment outside the mother's uterus (womb), has developed. During that time an amazing sequence takes place. The period of prenatal development is composed of three different stages of development. These periods are the **germinal** stage, the **embryonic** stage, and the **fetal** stage.

STAGES AND STRUCTURES

The Germinal Stage The ovum is fertilized as it travels down the Fallopian tube toward the uterus. The zygote then begins the process of mitosis while it is still in the Fallopian tube, moving toward the uterus. Within 3 or 4 days the rapidly dividing zygote reaches the uterus, where it floats freely for another 2 or 3 days. On about the seventh day after conception, the zygote becomes implanted in the wall of the uterus, which has been prepared for it. Here it establishes the relationship of dependence on the mother that will last throughout the entire course of prenatal development.

> implantation

By the time the zygote reaches the uterus, it has changed from a single cell into a fluid-filled structure called a **blastocyst** The spherical blastocyst consists of an inner cell mass and an outer layer of cells. Some of the cells cluster along one side of the blastocyst and differentiate into three layers of cells from which the baby will develop. An outer layer of cells eventually develops into the outer layer of skin, hair, nails, the nervous system, and certain other tissues. A second layer of cells becomes the baby's inner layer of skin, bone, and muscle tissues, and the circulatory, urinary, and reproductive systems. The inner layer of cells develops into various glands and the organs of the respiratory system. The cells develop thread-like structures that attach to the wall of the uterus and implant the developing cell mass there. Once fully implanted, the developing organism is called the *embryo*.

> structural differentiation

The Embryonic Stage Some cells of the blastocyst develop into the **placenta,** the **umbilical cord,** and the **amniotic sac.** The amniotic sac is filled with fluid that protects the developing child. The umbilical cord forms to connect the embryo to a thick mass of tissue that develops within the uterus. This tissue, the placenta, serves several amazing functions (figure 3–5). It lets nourishment and oxygen pass from the mother's bloodstream to the infant through the umbilical cord. It also allows waste from the child's bloodstream to pass to the mother's bloodstream to be eliminated, but it prevents the blood cells themselves from passing between the circulatory systems of mother and child. The bloodstreams of mother and child are separate.

The early growth of the embryo is very rapid. Facial features begin to take form by about 9 weeks; and arms, legs, feet, and hands all make their appearance. By this time the embryo is no more than about an inch long. During this period the major organs and body systems also become differentiated and begin to develop. The child is especially vulnerable to developmental damage from maternal infections and other environmental causes.

The Fetal Stage   By the beginning of the third month after conception, the growing child enters the third and final stage of prenatal development.

functional differentiation

The word *fetus* is now used to refer to it. During the embryonic period, the organs and body systems are established. During the fetal period, these organs and systems continue to develop and begin to function. This distinction between the two periods is not sharp, because different body structures develop at different times and at different rates. In fact, some structures continue to develop after birth and on into infancy (Ziegel & Van Blarcom, 1972).

By about 28 weeks after conception, the infant is well enough developed to survive outside the mother's body if temperature and other conditions are strictly regulated. That does not mean that the infant's development is complete. The body systems continue to develop and refine until about 40 weeks or even later. Full-term birth normally takes place about 40 weeks, or 280 days, after conception.

ENVIRONMENTAL INFLUENCES ON PRENATAL DEVELOPMENT

We have already seen some of the hereditary factors that can influence the development of a child. But no matter what the inheritance, the prenatal development will not be optimal unless the environment is right.

deviation from normality

Environment causes about 20% of the cases of abnormal fetal development. Genetic factors account for another 20%, and the remaining 60% of developmental defects apparently result from complex environmental-

Figure 3–5   The relationship between a mature fetus and the placenta.

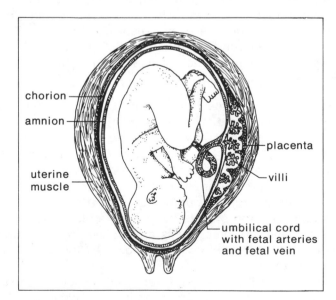

- chorion
- amnion
- placenta
- uterine muscle
- villi
- umbilical cord with fetal arteries and fetal vein

VIRGIN BIRTH?

Many plants and some animals produce offspring without sexual mating. New offspring develop from an unfertilized cell. This process is called *parthenogenesis*, which comes from a Greek word meaning *virgin*. Apparently, in very rare instances, a shock or accident of some sort may cause a cell in the uterus of a human female to divide and develop, resulting in the birth of a child. The child in this case would be an identical (but younger) twin of the mother. (See page 118 of the Howard and Rifkin reading, 1977, for a medically documented case of human parthenogenesis.)

Recent breakthroughs in genetic engineering have made artificial parthenogenesis possible. Scientists can produce individual organisms from the genetic information contained in a single cell. A single cell is sliced from an organism and stimulated, or "tricked into thinking" it has been fertilized. This process is called *cloning*. Since all of the genetic material in a clone comes from a single parent, the offspring will be identical to that parent.

So far there has been no reliably documented case of the cloning of a human being, but most experts agree that it should be technically possible within the next 15 years.

Why would anyone want to clone a human being? Some of the ideas proposed by enthusiastic biologists sound like the wildest science fiction. Some think it may be possible to bring back genetic copies of great historical figures. Others have seriously suggested that for every person we could keep a clone in storage to use for spare parts. A heart or kidney transplant from your own clone would not be rejected, because the donor would be genetically identical to the recipient. It is interesting to speculate what the clone would think of all this, since he or she would be as human as the "parent" (Howard & Rifkin, 1977).

Many parents have suffered the agony of losing a child. Through cloning, it would be possible to reproduce a loved one who died. And duplicates of our geniuses and other exceptional people could be produced in any quantity we want to make further contributions to human knowledge and welfare. Other scientists think we could use cloning to conduct social experiments. The nurture-nature controversy could be put to rest once and for all by assigning duplicate individuals to grow up in different environments.

Not all biologists go along with these "visionary" suggestions. A number of outstanding biologists believe that, while such applications of cloning are technically possible, they are ethically and morally unacceptable. Human cloning could lead to social and legal problems we are not equipped to deal with. And finally, the value of each individual may be diminished by the existence of multiple copies. Would it be as interesting to enter a room full of duplicates of Raquel Welch or Robert Redford as to be enticed by the presence of one such person?

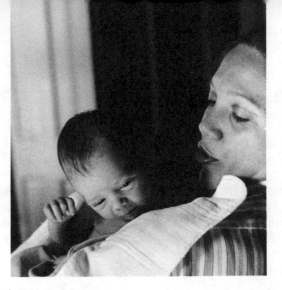

This is a healthy, full-term infant.

genetic interactions (Scipien, 1975). Nutrition, drugs, radiation, illness, and even the expectant mother's emotions may influence the development of the unborn child.

Maternal Nutrition Pregnancy makes heavy demands on a woman's body. To develop new tissues in her own and in the baby's body, she needs extra energy. She also needs added energy to move; her metabolism speeds up. Since the fetus depends upon the mother for its nutrition, the mother's diet must include vitamins, minerals, and proteins.

To a certain extent, the fetus is protected: it gets more than its share of the nutrients. This means that if the mother's diet is not sufficient, her own health is likely to suffer. Even so, the fetus develops so rapidly that it is more likely than the mother to suffer from malnutrition (Montagu, 1962; Pasamanick & Knobloch, 1966). If the mother does not take in enough nutrients, there is an increased chance that she will have a spontaneous abortion or that the baby will develop disorders like rickets and anemia.

Many infants who suffer from prenatal malnutrition are born to economically disadvantaged families. These low-income groups include members of certain ethnic and racial minorities who do not have the resources to obtain an adequate diet.

Drugs and Radiation Many mothers are not aware of the effects on their unborn children of taking drugs. All kinds of drugs can be hazardous for the developing fetus—including simple over-the-counter drugs, medication prescribed by doctors, and of course narcotics. Fortunately, the placenta prevents many potentially harmful substances in the mother's blood from reaching the fetus, but the system is not perfect.

thalidomide

A tragic illustration of this point is the drug *thalidomide*. This sedative was not generally available in the United States, but during 1961 and 1962 thousands of pregnant German women were given the drug during early pregnancy. Many of their children were born with severely deformed extremities, or even absence of limbs.

In many other cases the relationship between therapeutic medication taken by pregnant women and birth defects in their children is less clear. Children born to epileptic mothers who take medication to control their convulsions have a higher than normal rate of cleft lip or cleft palate or both. Certain heart defects also seem to be associated with these drugs. However, many women have taken these drugs during pregnancy with no apparent ill effect (Scipien, 1975).

Sedatives and pain killers taken during the last weeks of pregnancy and during labor may cause problems. Excessive sedation of a mother during the final weeks of pregnancy may cause permanent brain damage in an infant (Montagu, 1950). Recently it has been discovered that medication given during labor may slow down the newborn's motor abilities and ability to pay attention. These effects may last as long as 1 month after birth (Conway & Brackbill, 1970).

effects of sedation

Today it is more and more common for children to be born addicted to narcotics such as heroine or morphine. These infants are often premature and low in birth weight. After they are born, they go through withdrawal just as an adult would; they vomit, tremble, and cry shrilly. These children are poorly equipped to cope with the violent and painful shock of withdrawal, and they may not live for more than a few days.

addiction in the neonate

The use of hallucinogenic drugs such as LSD during pregnancy may also result in birth defects. The evidence on this question is mixed, but there is information available that suggests that there is at least a good possibility that the drug may cause malformations. There is some evidence that LSD may cause certain chromotids to break, with resulting malformations of the infant's lower extremities. Other studies suggest a connection between infant heart disorders and LSD use in the early stages of pregnancy. There is also some evidence that amphetamines ("speed") may produce abnormal development of the heart in infants whose mothers use the drug. The evidence on the harmful effects of these drugs is not yet conclusive, but it is strong enough to call for extreme caution by pregnant women.

Cigarettes are so widespread that it is easy to forget that tobacco, too, is a drug. Smoking by an expectant mother does affect the developing fetus (Ziegel &Van Blarcom, 1972). Mothers who smoke have a higher proportion of stillbirths than mothers who do not. Smoking retards the growth of the fetus, and babies whose mothers smoke have a better chance of being low in birth weight and dying in infancy than babies of nonsmoking mothers. There is also evidence that suggests that heavy use of marijuana can harm a mother's unborn baby.

Another common drug that is easy to overlook is alcohol. Excessive alcohol intake during pregnancy is associated with severe birth defects, including physical defects and mental retardation.

We have already seen that drugs taken for medical reasons may harm an unborn infant. This is also true of another form of therapy—radiation treatment. Disorders such as cancer are often treated with massive doses

radiation danger

of X-rays. X-rays are also used to detect certain organic disorders or orthopedic problems. Expectant mothers should be exposed to X-rays only when it is absolutely necessary because there is a known relationship between exposure to radiation and birth defects. Mothers who have been exposed to large doses of radiation have a higher than normal chance of having a baby with physical or mental disabilities (Montagu, 1962).

The potential danger of X-rays is not limited to the period of pregnancy. Radiation is a major cause of mutations in the sex cells of mature adults. Therefore, even low levels of radiation are potentially dangerous. Certain appliances that keep us entertained or make life a little easier may be harmful. A radiation leak in a broken color television set or a microwave oven is a potential hazard. We know the effects of large doses of radiation, but the effects of smaller amounts are less clear.

Viruses   If a pregnant woman contracts a disease, the effects on her un- born child depend on several factors, including the kind of infection and the stage of prenatal development. There are many infectious diseases, such as syphilis, chicken pox, mumps, and tuberculosis, that may be transmitted through the placenta to the fetus. German measles, or rubella, is one disease that may have particularly serious consequences for an unborn child. If a mother gets German measles during the first 3 months of pregnancy, the child may be mentally retarded, and may have eye, ear, and heart defects (Greenberg, Pelliteri, & Barton, 1957; Montagu, 1962). The chances are about one in 10 that a child whose mother contracts German measles during the first trimester will have one or more of these disorders. There is also a possibility that a woman who is exposed to German measles will carry the virus for a year or more. This possibility has not been proved; but just to be on the safe side, some doctors advise women to avoid becoming pregnant for at least 18 months after they are exposed to German measles (Scipien, 1975).

effects of measles

extended effects of measles virus

Toxemia   Toxemia is a possible complication of pregnancy. There are several types of toxemia; but they all result in high blood pressure and swelling in the face, ankles, and hands. Signs of toxemia include dizzi- ness, blurred vision, and headaches. In severe cases it may lead to con- vulsions, coma, and even death (Ziegel & Van Blarcom, 1972). The exact causes of toxemia are not known, but it occurs most frequently among low-income groups. It seems likely that general poor health, poor nutrition, and lack of professional prenatal care contribute to it.

toxemia and social class

Toxemia is an important cause of maternal and fetal deaths. It ac- counts for about 1/5 of the cases of death of the mother, and a large number of stillbirths and deaths of infants during the first days after birth (Ziegel & Van Blarcom, 1972).

The Mother's Emotions   Emotional stress during pregnancy may lead to complications, but the emotional state of an expectant mother is so inter- woven with other possible influences on prenatal development that it is difficult to find clear-cut relationships. For example, anxiety may have an indirect influence on prenatal development. If stress changes the mother's eating habits, the amount of nutrients the fetus gets could be affected (Montagu, 1962). Anxiety may also affect the mother's activity level. Again,

indirect influences

this could change the availability of certain compounds and carbon dioxide in the fetus' blood system. (Montagu, 1962; Pasamanick & Knobloch, 1966).

Rh Incompatibility   At some time or another you have probably had your blood type determined. You know that when you give blood or receive it in a transfusion, it is important to know your blood type because some types are not compatible with others. The blood produces substances known as **antigens** that are labeled *A* and *B*. People with blood type AB produce both kinds of antigens, and blood type O produces no antigens at all. If a different antigen enters the bloodstream, the body defends itself by producing **antibodies** that attack the intruding particle.

Blood types A, B, O, and AB cause no hazard for the developing fetus, but there are other substances in the blood that do. About 80% of the people have a substance called Rh factor in their blood. This factor is the result of a dominant gene, and people who have it are called *Rh positive.* People who are homozygous for the recessive gene are *Rh negative.*

If an Rh negative mother and an Rh positive father have a child, the child may either be Rh positive or negative, depending on whether the father's gene is dominant or recessive. If the child receives the dominant gene, he or she will be Rh positive. Often no ill effects occur if one child born to an Rh negative mother is Rh positive. But if any of the child's blood gets into the placenta and enters her bloodstream during labor or delivery, a problem may develop. The mother may become "immune" to her future Rh positive children. What happens is that, as the Rh positive substance from the child's blood enters the mother's system, the mother's blood builds up antibodies to fight the foreign substances. If a later pregnancy produces another Rh positive fetus, the antibodies (which remain in the mother's blood) will attack the baby's blood, causing *erythroblastosis fetalis,* or Rh disease. The antibodies cause the child's blood to clump, resulting in severe anemia and jaundice. With each pregnancy with an Rh positive child, additional antibodies accumulate in the mother's bloodstream. Eventually the attack on the red blood cells of the fetus may be fatal.

Rh disease

Until relatively recently, medical intervention involved replacing all of the newborn infant's Rh positive blood with Rh negative blood. Fortunately this is no longer necessary. Since the situation leading to Rh disease is well known, it can be anticipated in those cases in which the mother is Rh negative and the father Rh positive. There are now immunizations available that can be given to an Rh negative mother within 72 hours after a miscarriage or birth of an Rh positive child. The medication prevents the formation of Rh antibodies in the mother's bloodstream.

Birth Trauma

Even if a fetus is healthy and has no genetic defects, if it has not suffered from the effects of malnutrition, drugs, radiation, or other environmental agents, there is danger in the very process of being born. The mother's body provides a safe, warm, dark environment for the child. This fluid world protects the fetus from jars, bumps, and jolts; it muffles even the loudest sounds from the outside. Then in the space of a few minutes, the child leaves this shelter and enters a cold place full of lights and new sights and sounds. Even our greatest explorers never again experience such a rapid and dramatic change in environment. Some parents are now choosing to have their babies in especially warm, dimly lit rooms, to lessen the shock.

At the time of delivery the new child, who will be called a neonate for the first few weeks of life, may be physically injured. If labor is long and
oxygen deprivation
difficult, the child may not receive enough oxygen, which may permanently damage some nerve cells in the brain. This damage may hamper the development of the child's motor or intellectual abilities. As we have already seen, pain-killing drugs given to the mother in labor may also cause problems for the child.

CHANGING CHILDBIRTH PRACTICES

Not so long ago the birth of a child was generally attended by skilled midwives who had no formal medical training. Physicians were called upon only when there were serious complications. During the past century it became more and more common for doctors to preside over the birth process; but even within the memory of many people still alive, it was common for babies to be born at home. But while home delivery may have been convenient, morality was high and childbirth was generally painful.

With the development and spread of specialized medical facilities for obstetrical care, hospital birth became the norm. This was regarded as a major advance in health care. A hospital delivery carried the mysterious feeling of "science." Antiseptic conditions reduced mortality. The pain of childbirth could be reduced through the use of anesthesia, which was regarded as a major medical breakthrough. In the hospital, babies could be cared for by trained professionals in a sterile nursery with carefully controlled temperature and humidity. And the special equipment and personnel at the hospital made it possible to respond to emergencies and complications that would be difficult or impossible to deal with at home.

Today the advantages of the obstetrical practices that we have come to think of as standard are being increasingly questioned. The use of anesthetics, which was once regarded as such an advance, is being questioned for several reasons. Early in this century, Grantly Dick-Read, then a relatively obscure physician in England, expressed his concern with modern obstetrical practices. He taught his patients that childbirth is a natural process and that it need not be painful. He believed that most pain results from fear. In 1933 he published a book titled *Natural Childbirth* in which he presented his views. He told prospective mothers about the physiology of reproduction, and about prenatal health and physical fitness. Mothers, aided by their husbands,

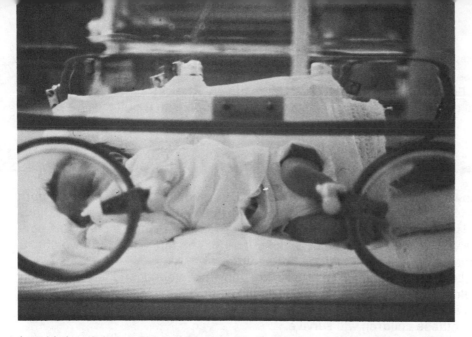

Low birth weight infants must be provided with a protective environment.

learned relatively simple breathing and relaxation techniques to ease the birth process. His ideas were later presented in a more comprehensive book called *Childbirth Without Fear.*

Besides teaching that childbirth could be a positive experience, Dick-Read said that fathers should be involved in the delivery of the child. He argued that the practice of isolating a father from the birth of his child leads to alienation, trouble, and sadness. By giving the father a supporting role and including him in the entire process, from the prenatal period through postpartum, fathers could share in the joy of birth. Dick-Read taught that the newborn baby should be wrapped in warm towels immediately and given to the mother instead of being sent to a nursery. He believed that skin-to-skin contact between mother and child, and soon after between father and child, would have a beneficial emotional effect on all three. If a mother must bottle feed, he suggested that it be done with the baby snuggled, skin to skin, to the mother's breast. And babies should not be sent to a nursery and isolated from their mothers. Even in the hospital, the baby should stay by the mother's side in a crib. This practice is called *rooming-in.*

These ideas won rather slow acceptance, but are very popular among young parents today. Many young parents attend Lamaze classes, named after the French physician who developed procedures for "prepared childbirth." Prepared childbirth encourages childbirth without the use of drugs. Many hospitals now allow fathers in the delivery room, and the practice of rooming-in is also quite widely available.

It is not yet known whether practices like involving the father, having skin-to-skin contact, or rooming-in have any long-term psychological benefit for parents and child, but it does seem likely that painless childbirth without drugs may benefit some infants. *All* forms of anesthetics administered during delivery have some effect on the baby. They pass through the placenta, often causing the baby to be unresponsive; and

Fortunately, most deliveries are relatively free of trauma; and as stressful as the process may be, most neonates cope with it quite well.

Premature Birth

Newborn babies who weigh less than 5½ pounds at birth or who are born less than 37 weeks after conception are considered "premature." Since it is impossible to know just how long it has been since a child was conceived, we use birth weight as the criterion. The term "low birth weight" is gradually replacing the term "premature."

Low birth weight babies are not fully developed and are extremely vulnerable. The lower the birth weight, the less likely the child is to survive. However, medical advances have dramatically improved the chances that these children will survive.

Premature babies generally lag behind full-term infants in the development of motor skills during their early years. Those born at extremely

some physiological processes may be slowed down for a week or more (Brazelton, 1970; Conway & Brackbill, 1970). Some authorities believe that the routine use of drugs during labor may account for the fact that the United States has a higher infant mortality rate than most other developed nations.

The early physical effects of an obstetrical anesthetic on the child generally wear off within a week or so. However, some people believe this may have a long-range impact on the relationship between the mother and her child, because mothers who try to nurse their babies may have less positive feelings toward an unresponsive infant than to one who acts alert.

Some new obstetrical practices may be traced to the psychoanalytic belief that birth is such a severe trauma for the infant that it may have lifelong negative effects on the child's behavior and personality. Whether you accept the psychoanalytic view or not, the hustle and bustle, harsh lights, and lowered temperatures of modern hospital delivery rooms must certainly exaggerate the difference between the warm protective environment of the uterus and the new environment. In a book called *Birth Without Violence,* a physician named Leboyer (1975) has suggested practices to reduce the birth trauma. At the time of delivery, lights are dimmed and the people in the delivery room talk in hushed voices. The old practice of slapping babies to get them to breathe is not used. Instead, the baby is placed on the mother's belly with the umbilical cord still attached. When normal breathing begins, the cord is cut. After a few minutes the infant is bathed in lukewarm water, intended to feel like the environment of the uterus the child has just left.

As with other new procedures, it is not yet known whether the gentle practices Leboyer advocates will have more favorable effects on development than conventional techniques.

low weights may continue to have difficulty with attention, intellectual performance, reading ability, and certain other behaviors (Ausubel & Sullivan, 1970).

Many premature infants cannot survive in the regular environment during their early weeks. They must have a controlled temperature and carefully prepared diet. As a result, they cannot live at home at first; they must be hospitalized. This has become a source of increasing concern, not just because it is emotionally hard on the parents, but also because the separation may interfere with the development of affection between the mother and the child. The bonds of affection and their significance are discussed in chapter 12. Because of this concern, some medical authorities now teach parents to feed and hold their hospitalized baby whenever possible. Teaching parents to care for their premature infants also makes it possible for the children to go home earlier, with good results reported (St. Petery, 1975).

Low birth weight, like most other hazards to developmental well-being, is much more common among poor families than in middle-class groups. Once again, this situation probably results from the nutritional advantages and professional prenatal care that are not widely available to economically disadvantaged people.

Postscript

The complex biological process of reproduction and prenatal development makes our most complex technology seem simple by comparison. In the brief descriptions provided here, we have only been able to hint at the elaborate complexity of the biological foundations of development. When we consider how delicate and finely tuned these processes are, it is not surprising that there are accidents and developmental defects. What is much more amazing is that developmental disabilities are as infrequent as they are. Even so, a great many of the developmental defects we discussed could be eliminated.

Genetic counseling is one means of reducing the frequency of hereditary defects. If a prospective parent comes from a family with a history of hereditary disorders, a counselor can tell them their chances of having a child with a genetic abnormality. Just as important, a genetic counselor may help to relieve the anxiety and distress of parents who have a child with a hereditary defect. Once parents have had a child with a genetic problem, they may be afraid to have more children. But often the chances of a reoccurrence are extremely small, and a genetic counselor can share this information with the couple trying to decide whether to take a chance and have another child. If they have decided to go ahead and take the chance, amniocentesis during pregnancy can often tell them if the fetus will be affected.

genetic counseling

One of the tragedies of society is that such a large proportion of the children who are born with disabilities, or who die at birth, or whose mothers die in childbirth, come from families with low incomes. And a disproportionate number of Americans living below the poverty level come from ethnic and racial minorities. The financial cost to our society to educate and sometimes institutionalize citizens disabled by birth defects is staggering; and there is no possible way to measure the heartbreak and anguish of the families into which these children are born. Many of these tragedies could be prevented through proper nutrition and prenatal care; but in a society that claims to be the most affluent and enlightened in the world, these benefits are very unevenly distributed. The rate of infant and maternal mortality in the United States is among the highest of the industrialized nations. Even the prenatal development of our children is completely intertwined with our economics and politics.

Suggested Readings

Birch, H. G. Health and the education of socially disadvantaged children. *Developmental Medicine and Child Neurology,* 1968, *10,* 580–599.

Bowes, W. A. Jr., Brickbill, Y., Conway, E., & Steinschneider, A. The effects of obstetrical medication on fetus and infant. *Monographs of the Society for Research in Child Development,* 1970, *35* (Y), (Whole No. 137).

Greenfield, J. Advances in genetics that can change your life. *Today's Health,* December, 1973. Reprinted in S. White (Ed.), *Human development in today's world.* Boston: Little, Brown, 1976. Pp. 27–30.

Hardy, J. B. Rubella and its aftermath. *Children,* 1969, *16,* 91–96.

Howard, T., & Rifkin, J. *Who shall play God?* New York: Dell, 1977.

Lynch, P.K., Women: The next endangered species? *Mademoiselle,* May 1977, *83,* 32–91.

Restak, R. The danger of knowing too much. *Psychology Today,* September 1975, *9,* 21–23.

Shaw, M.W. Genetic counseling. *Science,* May 17, 1974, *184,* 751.

How Children Grow

Physical growth itself is an important factor in how a child develops. When you have finished with this chapter, you should know what growth is, what patterns it follows, and how it is regulated. You should also understand how environmental factors such as nutrition and stimulation affect growth and what you can do to affect it.

Closely related to physical growth is the ability to control and use your body—motor skills. This chapter discusses ontogenetic and phylogenetic motor skills, the sequence of skill development, the relationship of skill development to intellectual development, and how culture can affect skill learning. Finally, you should have a basic understanding of how to foster skill development in children.

To improve the quality of human life around the world, we must find ways to promote both physical growth and motor skill development. At present we are less than effective in these tasks. Our difficulty is most obvious in the developing nations, where undernutrition threatens the lives of millions each year. However, it also can be seen in industrialized societies like ours. In certain parts of the United States, a lack of physical activity, coupled with poor diet, poses a serious threat to many people's health and life.

In this chapter, we shall discuss physical development and how culture affects it. In the first part of the chapter, we will focus on physical growth, while in the second half we will deal with the development of motor skills.

Physical Growth

Physical growth is, of course, largely controlled by heredity. However, environment, particularly activity and nutrition, also have a marked influence on growth. While economic conditions influence growth, our socialization practices also play an important role.

Physical growth is the enlargement of body structures occurring during the course of development. To some extent, different body structures grow at different rates. However, a number of body structures grow in similar ways. And there is some relationship between physical growth and other forms of development.

INDICES OF GROWTH

There are several ways we measure growth. The ones used most often include skeletal growth, growth in height, growth in weight, brain growth, and growth of reproductive organs.

skeletal growth

Skeletal growth is an excellent measure of physical growth because everyone eventually reaches the same degree of bone development. A newborn has much more cartilage than an adult. Skeletal growth represents the replacement of the child's cartilage with bone. It can be assessed by radiographs such as those shown in figure 4-1. As this figure shows, there is a marked increase in the number of wrist bones between the ages of 3 and 13 years.

height

Changes in height are perhaps the most familiar measure of growth. This cannot serve as a common index for all people, however, because adults vary greatly in height despite the fact that they are similar in bone growth.

Growth in height is highly predictable. By the time children are 9 years old, it is possible 90% of the time to predict their adult stature within ± 1½ inches (Tanner, 1970). The predictions are based in part on the children's height and age. However, skeletal maturity is also used. For example, a high level of his or her bone development may show that a child is closer to adult height than age alone would indicate.

There is some relationship between height and intellectual development (Tanner, 1970). Tall children tend to score higher on intelligence tests

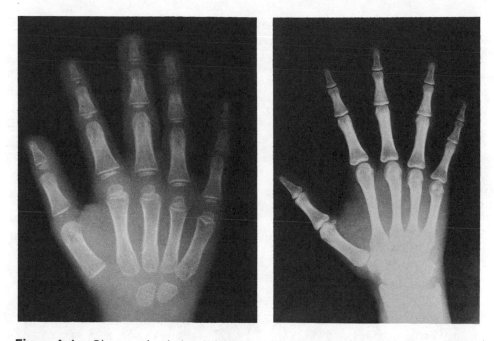

Figure 4–1   Changes in skeletal development reflecting typical growth in a boy ages 3 to 13 years.

than small children throughout the childhood and adolescent years. When the differences in height are large, the differences in intellectual performance may also be substantial. For instance, Tanner (1970) reports a difference of nine IQ points between children at the 75th percentile and children at the 25th percentile in height. We are not yet certain of the reason for this relationship. However, cultural factors that affect both height and intellectual functioning may be at least partially responsible.

Weight is another common index of growth. As might be expected, weight is related to height. Weight is, of course, much more sensitive to food intake than height is. Moreover, weight can be lost as well as gained, where height only increases during the growth period. Weight is particularly useful in trying to find the relationship between nutrition and growth.

weight

Table 4-1 gives weight and height data for boys and girls from birth to 18 years old. The table can be used as a standard against which to evaluate a child's development. If a child's weight and height shifts widely or falls at the extreme of the group, or outside it, he or she can be watched for possible abnormalities (Lowrey, 1973).

Neurological development, or more specifically brain growth, is a fourth common index of physical development. There are two types of brain growth. The first involves the formation of new cells, while the second involves the differentiation of existing cells. We think that virtually all of the cells in the adult brain are there by the time a child is 1 year old. Brain growth from then on occurs through cell differentiation (Winick, 1976). As children develop, various parts of their nerve cells grow. In addition, the sheaths that allow the brain impulses to be transmitted form around the nerve fibers. We can assess brain growth simply by measuring the weight

brain growth

Table 4–1 Weight and height percentile table

girls				age	boys			
weight (lbs.)		height (in.)			weight (lbs.)		height (in.)	
50%	range	50%	range		50%	range	50%	range
7.4	6.2– 8.6	19.8	18.8–20.4	Birth	7.5	6.3– 9.1	19.9	18.9–21.0
9.7	8.0– 11.0	21.0	20.2–22.0	1 mo.	10.0	8.5– 11.5	21.2	20.2–22.2
11.0	9.5– 12.5	22.2	21.5–23.2	2 mo.	11.5	10.0– 13.2	22.5	21.5–23.5
12.4	10.7– 14.0	23.4	22.4–24.3	3 mo.	12.6	11.1– 14.5	23.8	22.8–24.7
13.7	12.0– 15.5	24.2	23.2–25.2	4 mo.	14.0	12.5– 16.2	24.7	23.7–25.7
14.7	13.0– 17.0	25.0	24.0–26.0	5 mo.	15.0	13.7– 17.7	25.5	24.5–26.5
16.0	14.1– 18.6	25.7	24.6–26.7	6 mo.	16.7	14.8– 19.2	26.1	25.2–27.3
19.2	16.6– 22.4	27.6	26.4–28.7	9 mo.	20.0	17.8– 22.9	28.0	27.0–29.2
21.5	18.4– 24.8	29.2	27.8–30.3	12 mo.	22.2	19.6– 25.4	29.6	28.5–30.7
24.5	21.2– 28.3	31.8	30.2–33.3	18 mo.	25.2	22.3– 29.0	32.2	31.0–33.5
27.1	23.5– 31.7	34.1	32.3–35.8	2 yr.	27.7	24.7– 31.9	34.4	33.1–35.0
31.8	27.6– 37.4	37.7	35.6–39.8	3 yr.	32.2	28.7– 36.8	37.9	36.3–39.6
36.2	31.2– 43.5	40.6	38.4–43.1	4 yr.	36.4	32.1– 41.4	40.7	39.1–42.7
40.5	34.8– 49.2	42.9	40.5–45.4	5 yr.	40.5	35.5– 46.7	42.8	40.8–45.2
46.5	39.6– 54.2	45.6	43.5–48.1	6 yr.	48.3	40.9– 56.4	46.3	43.8–48.6
52.2	44.5– 61.2	48.1	46.0–50.7	7 yr.	54.1	45.8– 64.4	48.9	46.0–51.4
58.1	48.6– 69.9	50.4	48.1–53.0	8 yr.	60.1	51.2– 73.0	51.2	48.5–54.0
63.8	52.6– 79.1	52.3	50.0–55.3	9 yr.	66.0	56.3– 81.0	53.3	50.5–56.1
70.3	57.1– 89.7	54.6	51.8–57.5	10 yr.	71.9	61.1– 89.9	55.2	52.3–58.1
78.8	62.6–100.4	57.0	53.9–60.4	11 yr.	77.6	66.3– 99.3	56.8	54.0–59.8
87.6	69.5–111.5	59.8	56.1–63.2	12 yr.	84.4	72.0–109.6	58.9	56.1–62.2
99.1	79.9–124.5	61.8	58.7–64.9	13 yr.	93.0	77.1–123.2	61.0	57.7–65.1
108.4	91.0–133.3	62.8	60.2–65.7	14 yr.	107.6	87.2–136.9	64.0	59.9–67.9
113.5	97.4–138.1	63.4	61.1–66.2	15 yr.	120.1	99.4–147.8	66.1	62.1–69.6
117.0	100.9–141.1	63.9	61.5–66.5	16 yr.	129.7	111.0–157.3	67.8	64.1–70.7
119.1	102.8–143.3	64.0	61.5–66.7	17 yr.	136.2	117.5–164.6	68.4	65.2–71.5
119.9	103.5–144.5	64.0	61.5–66.7	18 yr.	139.0	120.0–169.0	68.7	65.5–71.8

of the brain. However, there are other, more sophisticated procedures to use also. For instance, the density of the neurons, which decreases as the cells differentiate, can be used.

Different parts of the brain develop at different speeds. For example, the nerve cells controlling the arm and upper trunk develop earlier than the nerve cells controlling leg movement. As we might expect, body control follows the same pattern as structural development (Tanner, 1970). Infants can control their arms and upper trunks before they can effectively guide their legs.

reproductive growth

A fifth widely used index is growth of the reproductive system. Reproductive growth is measured in terms of the size of the reproductive organs. The testes, prostate gland, and seminal vesicles are measured in males. Uterine and vaginal growth are the most frequently used indices in females. In addition, measures of secondary sexual traits (such as the acquisition of pubic hair) are sometimes used.

Dramatic changes in reproductive growth, some of which are shown in figure 4–2, occur at puberty. The term *puberty* referred initially to the period marked by the development of pubic hair. However, it is now assessed in terms of the growth of reproductive organs. For males, puberty begins with the enlargement of the testes, which is followed closely by the development of pubic hair. Penis growth and sharply accelerated increases in height follow about a year later. Approximately 2 years after the first pubic hair appears, axillary hair (under the arms) and facial hair can be expected to appear. Puberty begins in the female with marked growth changes in the uterus, vagina, and breasts. **Menarche,** the first menstrual period, may occur several years after the initial signs of puberty. Moreover, it can take as long as 18 months after the first menstrual period before pregnancy is possible.

There are vast differences between people in the rate of reproductive development and in other related growth processes (Keliher, 1938; Tanner, 1972). Figure 4–3 shows the extent of these variations. Because

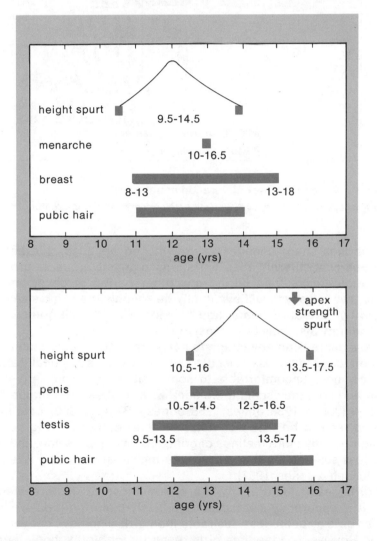

Figure 4–2   Sequence of events at adolescence in boys and girls. The average boy and girl are represented. The range of ages within which each event may begin and end is shown.

Adapted from "Variations in the Pattern of Pubertal Changes in Boys," by W. A. Marshall and J. M. Tanner, *Archives of Diseases of Childhood,* 1970, *45* 13. Reprinted by permission.

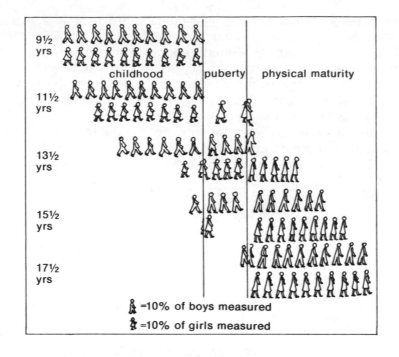

Figure 4–3   Variability in sex maturation in boys and girls.

Adapted from *Life and Growth,* by A. V. Keliher, New York: Appleton- Century, 1938, p. 185. Reprinted by permission.

puberty brings sharp changes in growth and because different people reach puberty at different ages, variations in growth are more pronounced during adolescence than during any other period of development. For example, two boys who will eventually be roughly the same size can vary in height by several inches at age 13. Moreover, the differences in their sexual maturity also may be extensive.

For boys there is an advantage to early maturation. Late-maturing boys have been found to be less poised, to be rated as less physically attractive, and to be more uncomfortable in social situations than early-maturing boys. In addition, they seem to be somewhat restless and unpopular with their peers (Jones, 1938; Jones, 1958; Jones & Bayley, 1950). Late-maturing boys also tend to be less well-adjusted than early-maturing boys. They show significantly more feelings of guilt, anxiety, depression, and inferiority and less self-esteem than boys maturing at an early age (Weatherley, 1964; Mussen & Jones, 1957).

For girls, early maturation is a mixed blessing. In late elementary school, it is apparently a disadvantage. Early-maturing girls are rated by the other girls as being less desirable than girls who have not yet reached puberty. However, by the time girls reach junior high school, there is no social disadvantage to early maturation (Faust, 1960). In fact, some research indicates that early maturation in girls is positively related to intellectual functioning. Girls who have had their first menstrual period score significantly higher on intelligence tests than girls of the same age who have not yet begun to menstruate (Tanner, 1970). The findings are not, however, entirely consistent. Waber (1977) did not find any advantage in early maturation. Indeed, she found that, for both sexes, performance on nonverbal intellectual tasks was higher in late-maturing individuals than in early-maturing people.

PATTERNS OF GROWTH

The indices of physical growth we have just looked at all involve highly predictable patterns of developmental change. Several growth indices share a common pattern, called the *general growth curve*. The general growth curve, shown in figure 4–4, was first documented by Count Philbert de Montbeillard over 200 years ago (Tanner, 1970). He took periodic measurements of his son's height from the time of birth until the child reached the age of 18. He found height increased rapidly during infancy and early childhood. Between the ages of 6 and 12 years, the rate of growth leveled off. However, during adolescence there was a sharp acceleration, generally referred to as the *adolescent growth spurt.* Many studies have documented these early observations of changes in height. And it has been found that a number of other indices, including skeletal growth and growth in weight, tend to follow the general growth curve.

general growth curve

The adolescent growth spurt is found only in human beings. We do not know what specific functions it serves. However, the slow pace of childhood growth does create a relatively long time during which children must depend on their parents to meet their physical needs. Tanner (1970) points out that this gives the child a long time to be socialized. Since our survival depends upon teaching elaborate cultural patterns to the young, the prolonged childhood dependency may help us survive as a species.

Although several indices of growth do follow the general growth curve, there are some that vary from it. One of these is brain growth. The brain develops rapidly during childhood. When children reach the age of 10, they will generally have reached 95% of their adult brain development, as measured by brain weight. The remaining 5% occurs slowly during later

indices that do not follow the general growth curve

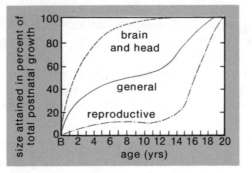

Figure 4–4   Growth curves.

From R. E. Scammon, "The Measurement of the Body in Childhood" by R. E. Scammon, in J. A. Harris, C. M. Jackson, D. G. Paterson, & R. E. Scammon. *The Measurement of Man.* Minneapolis: University of Minnesota Press, 1930, p. 193. © Copyright 1930 by the University of Minnesota. Reprinted by permission.

childhood and adolescence. A second index that does not follow the general growth curve is reproductive development. During childhood, the reproductive system grows very slowly. Then at adolescence, the acceleration in development is more pronounced for reproductive growth than it is for general growth.

THE REGULATION OF GROWTH PROCESSES

endocrine system

For the most part, growth is regulated by the endocrine glands (Tanner, 1970). The **endocrine** system is a group of ductless glands including the adrenal gland, the thyroid gland, the testes in males, the ovaries in females, the pancreas, and the pituitary gland. All of these glands secrete **hormones** that affect growth. For instance, in adolescent males secretions of testosterone from the testes produce male traits such as extensive facial hair. And in females, estrogen from the ovaries affects the development of female characteristics.

We sometimes call the pituitary gland the *master gland*. It controls both growth and the hormones released from the other endocrine glands. For example, the pituitary gland secretes hormones that make the testes or the ovaries grow.

Besides influencing the other endocrine glands, the pituitary gland directly influences the growth process. From approximately the 10th week after conception throughout childhood, the pituitary gland secretes a hormone that determines growth to a major extent. However, we do not yet know the role that this growth hormone plays in the adolescent growth spurt. Indeed the cause of that phenomenon is still something of a mystery.

environmental effects on the path of growth

The internal mechanisms that regulate growth are basically independent of environmental influences. A poor environment may disturb growth's original path. However, if the poor environment is not too extreme, the growth pattern can return to the original path if a supportive environment is again provided. Figure 4–5 shows how a child's growth pattern remains stable despite changes in environment. This figure shows the growth in height of a child who went through two periods during which he lost his appetite and ate considerably less than normal for him. During those periods, the child's gains in height slowed down. When he once again ate his normal amount of food, he began to grow at his original rate (Prader, Tanner, & von Harnack, 1963).

This tendency for growth to keep to a given pattern despite variations in environment is limited by the degree of change. For instance, in extreme cases of malnutrition, a child's growth may be permanently retarded (Tanner, 1970).

GROWTH AND CULTURE

As might be expected, we have known for some time that physical growth is largely controlled by heredity factors. For example, identical twin sisters reach menarche at very nearly the same time, but there may be marked differences for other pairs of sisters (Tanner, 1970). Similarly, there is a much higher correspondence between the skeletal growth of identical twins than for other **siblings** (Reynolds, 1943). Likewise, identical twins

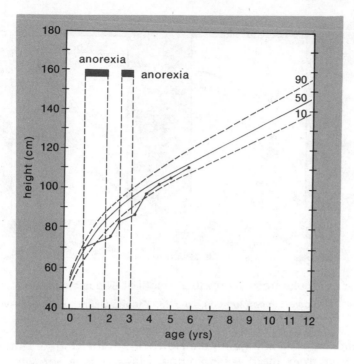

Figure 4–5   Two periods of catch-up growth following episodes of anorexia in a young child. The other lines indicate percentile ranks for height at successive age levels in the population.

From "Catch-up Growth Following Illness or Starvation". An Example of Developmental Canalization in Man, by A. Prader, J. M. Tanner, and G. A. von Harnack, *Journal of Pediatrics*, 1963, *62,* 648. Reprinted by permission.

are much more similar in height than siblings or parents and their offspring (Harris, Jackson, Paterson, & Scammon, 1930). But despite the strong influence of genetic factors on growth processes, culture is also prominent in determining growth.

Cultural Variations   Several studies have found distinct variations in growth in different cultures. And there are some differences in growth even when the cultures share a common physical environment. For instance, Hiernaux (1963, 1964) found substantial differences between the Tutsi tribe and the Hutu tribe, both of which live in Rwanda. The Tutsi tend to be tall and thin, while the Hutu for the most part are short and stocky. It is, of course, possible that these two groups differ because they have developed from different gene pools. However, there are different environmental conditions in the two cultures that could also account at least partially for the differences in weight and height. Specifically, the Tutsi are the ruling class in Rwanda and therefore are better nourished than the Hutu.

growth variations between cultures

There are also differences in growth occurring across generations. For the past 100 years, there has been an upward trend in growth. This change is generally referred to as the *secular trend*. In many parts of the world,

variations in growth across generations

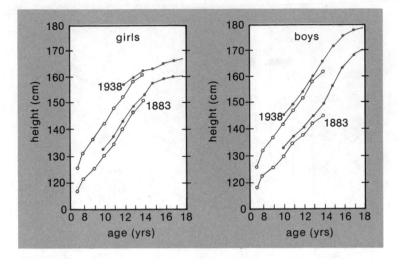

Figure 4–6   Secular trend in growth of height of Swedish children.

From *Growth at Adolescence* (2nd ed.), by J. M. Tanner. Oxford: Basil Blackwell, 1962, p. 144. Reprinted by permission.

the secular trend is still going on. However, in the United States, at least for children from middle- and upper-class homes, growth may have reached a maximum (Tanner, 1970).

The secular trend is illustrated in figure 4–6, which shows changes in the heights of Swedish children across generations. As the figure shows, the secular trend can be seen shortly after birth and continues through childhood and adolescence. In the early school years, there is only a small difference in height for children from different generations. This difference becomes rather substantial between the ages of 10 and 14 years. Although these differences in height for older children are relatively large, the differences in adult height are less pronounced. This is because in most societies today, children stop growing several years earlier than they used to. Where today 18- or 19-year olds will probably be as tall as they ever will, in the past people did not usually stop growing until the age of 25.

The secular trend can be seen in sexual development as well as in growth in height. Figure 4–7 shows variations in age at menarche for girls from several different countries. As the figure indicates, menarche occurs much earlier today than it did during the nineteenth century.

social class variations in growth   There are social-class differences as well as other forms of cultural differences in growth. Children from the upper levels of a society tend to be taller at all ages than children from lower levels. For instance, in England there is currently a 1-inch difference between the heights of 3-year-olds whose fathers have managerial jobs and 3-year-olds whose fathers are unskilled laborers. Class-related differences reach a peak of 3 inches during the adolescent years. To some extent, these differences are probably perpetuated by customs that help tall people move socially upward (Tanner, 1970). For instance, Tanner finds that tall women, regardless of their social station, marry men with occupations with higher social status than the occupations of the husbands of short women.

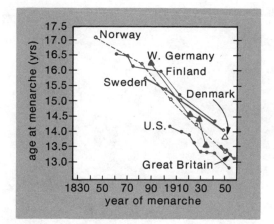

Figure 4–7   Secular trend in age at menarche.

From *Growth at Adolescence* (2nd ed.), by J. M. Tanner, Oxford: Basil Blackwell, 1962, p. 153. Reprinted by permission.

There are also class-related differences in sexual development. For instance, European girls from the lowest socioeconomic levels go through menarche 2 to 4 months later than European girls from the highest socioeconomic levels. These differences are probably produced by differences in socialization, including differences in sleep, nutrition, and exercise.

Class-related differences in weight are the most obvious case of growth being affected by socialization. In the lowest levels of society, particularly in the developing nations, many children are severely underweight. The principal cause of this problem is poor nutrition (Eckholm & Record, 1976). But in countries where most people *can* get enough to eat, people from the lower socioeconomic levels tend to weigh significantly more than people from the higher classes (Eckholm & Record, 1976). This is a reversal of a long-established trend. During much of human history, the vast majority of people could not get enough food to keep healthy. Weight was a symbol of well-being, and the rich tended to far outweigh the poor. Today weight remains a symbol of economic plenty. However, in modern technological cultures such as ours, we now know the health hazards of being overweight. This information is widely known among the upper socioeconomic levels. In addition, those elements in our diet that tend to produce weight gain are in many cases less expensive than foods that are low in calories. Thus, there is less tendency than there once was for people in the highest classes to be overweight.

Activity and Environmental Stimulation   To grow properly, children must be able to move around; they must live in stimulating surroundings. Without activity and stimulation, not only the child's physical growth but also the rest of his or her development may be slowed down.

We first found out about what happens to children who do not get enough physical activity and stimulation through studies of infants raised in institutions like foundling homes. An early study by Rene Spitz (1945) provided dramatic evidence of the damage that may occur when a child

institutional deprivation

Visual stimulation plays an important role in a child's development.

does not have stimulation and movement. Spitz studied two groups of children. One group was raised in a nursery; the other, in a foundling home. The nursery was used for the children of delinquent girls who were serving prison terms nearby. These children had toys to play with and their mothers and the employees of the nursery played with them. The conditions in the foundling home were markedly different. Although the children there had adequate physical care, they had very little chance to move around and got very little stimulation from the environment. Spitz reported that the children from the foundling home lagged well behind the children in the nursery in both physical growth and motor-skill development. He interpreted his findings as indicating the importance of mothering for adequate development. However, research since then (e.g., Dennis & Najarian, 1957; Provence & Lipton, 1962) suggests that lack of stimulation and of movement are more likely explanations for the differences.

stimulation and growth

The specific influence of stimulation on growth has been studied. Landauer and Whiting (1963), for example, observed that adults in cultures where children go through a lot of physical stress are taller than adults in cultures with low stress. They considered stress to be practices like making cosmetic changes in body features or subjecting children to extreme temperatures. But other factors could have produced the differences they found. For instance, a generally demanding environment could result in the natural selection of tall, strong people (Thompson & Grusec, 1970).

Rice (1977) recently did an experiment in which premature infants were given extra stimulation. Their bodies were systematically stroked for 15 minutes 4 times a day for a month. This was done by the infants' mothers beginning on the day that they were taken home from the hospital. At age 4 months, the infants who had been stroked were significantly heavier than those who had not been stroked. There were no differences in their heights.

Undernutrition   Undernutrition is undoubtedly the most serious obstacle to adequate growth throughout the world. Warren (1973) estimates that at least one billion people living today are or have been malnourished. The problem is most serious in developing nations with low income levels. For example, in Uganda the lives of between 1% and 2% of the children are threatened because of undernutrition, and between 5,000 and 7,000 children from 1 to 5 years old die of malnutrition annually. Moreover, growth is retarded in 30 percent of the population (Winick, 1976).

magnitude of undernutrition

While undernutrition is most serious in developing nations with low income levels, it also exists in rich countries. There is malnutrition in the United States. It is most prevalant among ethnic minorities from low socio-economic levels in the culture. It is most common among blacks, less so among Mexican Americans, and least among whites. A study of Navajo Indians in Arizona illustrates the problem of malnutrition in this country (Winick, 1976). Laboratory studies showed anemia in 17% and low iron levels in 23% of the people tested. Half of the Navajo children under 4 years of age were in the lowest 10% of the United States population in weight. Moreover, 68% of the children under 3 years old had head circumferences in the lowest 10% in the population.

undernutrition in the U.S.

Many studies have shown that undernutrition affects virtually all kinds of growth. For example, Tanner (1970) summarized data on the heights of children living in Stuttgart, Germany, from 1911 to 1953. These data, shown in figure 4—8, show a substantial decrease in the average height of

effects of under-nutrition on growth

This child is malnourished.

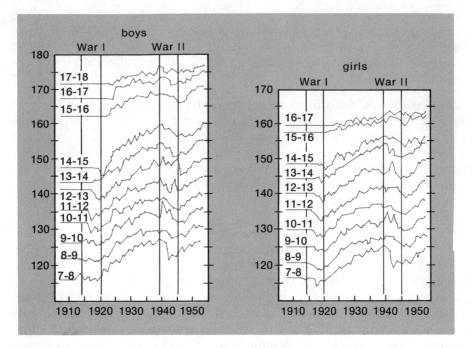

Figure 4–8   Effect of malnutrition on growth in height of Stuttgart schoolchildren.
From *Growth at Adolescence* (2nd ed.), by J. M. Tanner, Oxford: Basil Blackwell, 1962, p. 122. Reprinted by permission.

children toward the ends of World War I and World War II when the city's food supplies were inadequate. And the data show that malnourished children living in Ecuador were several centimeters shorter than adequately fed children in Ecuador and in the United States (Winick, 1976). In addition, the height difference between malnourished and adequately nourished children increases with age. The malnourished child may end up being 4 to 6 inches below average in height.

Retardation in skeletal development is also associated with malnutrition. Reisenger, Rogers, and Johnson (1972) looked at the skeletal growth of over 300 Navajo children who were not receiving enough nourishment. Compared to white children, the skeletal development of the Navajos was delayed about 14% for boys and 30% for girls. This represents a delay of about 1 year for boys and close to 2 years for girls.

One of the most important and at the same time controversial associations between nutrition and growth is the relationship between undernutrition and brain growth. Several studies show that there is an association between malnutrition and brain growth. For example, several investigations reveal that malnutrition, especially before birth and during the first 2 or 3 years of life, is related to delays in the rate of increase of head circumference. As documented in figure 4–9, this has been reported in malnourished children in every developing nation in the world. It was the first alarming sign that lack of proper nourishment might cause permanent brain damage (Winick, 1976). This is cause for concern because, while with adequate nutrition there is essentially no relationship between head size and intelligence, with malnutrition the association between intelligence and head circumference is substantial.

Autopsies done on children who died of malnutrition are a second source of information on the relationship between brain growth and nutrition. Winick, Rosso, and Waterlow (1970) reported on the autopsies of 16 Chilean and Jamaican children who died from malnutrition before the age of 2. All 16 children had fewer brain cells than normal for their age. Other studies have had similar results. For instance, Brown (1966) summarized investigations of the brain weights of 1,000 Ugandan children and concluded that brain weight was below average for undernourished children.

Several studies have shown a direct relationship between intelligence test performance and undernutrition. Stoch and Smythe (1967) matched 20 black infants living in South Africa and suffering from extreme undernutrition with children of the same sex and age who had not been malnourished. Although both groups of children came from the lowest socioeconomic levels of their society, the malnourished group scored well below the others on an intelligence test. In addition, the head circumference of the malnourished children was substantially smaller than for the well-fed children.

In spite of these studies and others like them, some people still question whether malnutrition causes inadequate brain growth and therefore intellectual delays. They base their challenge on the methods used in the field investigations (Warren, 1973). It is difficult to separate the effects of nutrition from the other factors that might retard growth. For example, malnourished infants are often not very active (Warren, 1973). Since there is a relationship between activity and mental development, it is possible that activity rather than nutrition accounts for some of the findings on nutrition and brain development.

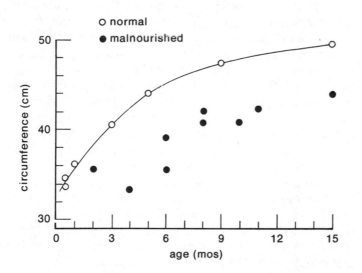

Figure 4–9 Head circumference in normal and malnourished children.

From "Head Circumference and Cellular Growth of the Brain in Normal and Marasmic Children, by M. Winick and P. Rosso, *Journal of Pediatrics*, 1969, *74*, 774–778. Reprinted by permission.

Actually, whether or not undernutrition directly affects mental development is to some extent a pointless question (Eckholm & Record, 1976). Undernutrition almost always occurs along with poverty, disease, and other conditions that, taken as a whole, delay not only brain growth, but other forms of development as well. Clearly, a major world-wide priority ought to be to stamp out undernutrition and the other social conditions associated with it.

causes of
undernutrition

Undernutrition can have many causes, such as poor eating habits or cultural bias against particular healthy foods. However, severe undernutrition is largely caused by economic circumstances. In many cases, low-income families simply do not have the money to buy the food that they need. For example, Winick (1976) reports low-income Navajo families consisting of five people spent about $4.54 per person per week in 1969. In households with nine people, the money spent on food per person averaged $2.99. As these figures imply, these Navajo families probably did not have enough money to buy the food necessary to sustain growth.

Although economic factors do influence nutrition, they are not solely responsible for the malnutrition we see around the world. The World Health Organization estimates that proper education could solve many nutritional problems. For example, recently severe undernutrition has be-

BOTTLE VS. BREAST FEEDING IN UNDERDEVELOPED NATIONS

The issue of bottle versus breast feeding in underdeveloped nations is currently a source of heated controversy. Some specialists feel that bottle feeding should be actively discouraged among the poor in underdeveloped countries. They argue that because poor women may not be equipped to prepare bottle formulas properly and to give sanitary bottle feedings, they should be encouraged to breast feed their children. Advocates of this view feel that manufacturers of baby formulas have a responsibility to protect the public by not encouraging the sale of formula in places in which it is likely to be used improperly. They are also concerned about relationships between manufacturers of formula and physicians. They believe that advertising that might encourage physicians to recommend bottle feeding to the poor should be eliminated.

Those favoring bottle feeding argue that a return to the breast is a threat to women's rights. They hold that breast feeding may excessively confine a woman and in some cases interfere with her right to earn a living. They argue that one aspect of becoming a modern mother is to learn to bottle feed. Furthermore, they suggest that the solution to the problem of improper bottle feeding is education.

At present there is no resolution to this controversy. The tragedy is that while the controversy continues, thousands of children in underdeveloped nations die of malnutrition each year.

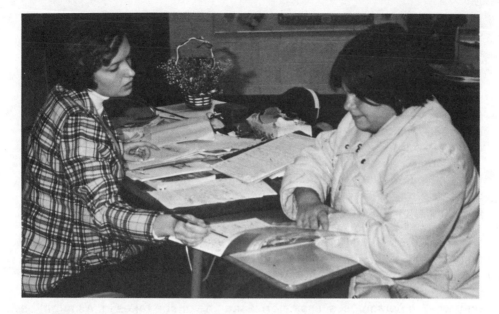

Obesity often begins during childhood.

come largely a disease of infancy (Winick, 1976). To a significant degree, this undernutrition can be traced to the practice of bottle feeding. Mothers who, a few decades ago, would have breast fed their children have now started bottle feeding them. However, although they use bottle feeding extensively, they are often not aware that they need to sterilize the bottles. When they are fed from unsterilized bottles, infants develop diseases, particularly diarrhea. Diarrhea robs the infant of needed nourishment. And, in an effort to reduce the diarrhea, the mothers often stop using milk and feed the babies mixtures of flour and water. These may help to control diarrhea, but unfortunately they also often lead to severe undernutrition (Winick, 1976).

Overnutrition   In technological societies such as the United States, overnutrition has become a significant problem in physical development. With the obvious exception of its influence on weight, overnutrition does not affect growth directly. However, the **obesity** related to overnutrition is associated with several serious threats to health and life, particularly during the adult years. Since obese children make up a large percentage of the grossly obese adults (Aragona, Cassady, & Drabman, 1975; Heald & Hollander, 1965), the potential dangers of heart enlargement, high blood pressure, **angina pectoris,** brain hemorrhage, congestive heart failure, diabetes, and **cirrhosis** of the liver due to obesity (Mahoney & Mahoney, 1976) must be considered even when dealing with children.

An obese person is usually defined as one who weighs more than 20% more than the mean weight for his or her height, age, and frame (Lowrey,   obesity defined extent of obesity in U.S.

1973). It has been estimated that 10% to 20% of all children in the United States are overweight (Eckholm & Record, 1976). Approximately 50% of the obese children seen in one clinic had at least one obese parent (Lowrey, 1958). The evidence is quite strong that this relationship results from environment rather than from heredity (Lowrey, 1958). Currently 35% to 50% of the middle-aged people in the United States are overweight (Eckholm & Record, 1976). Moreover, 20% of Americans are so overweight that their health is threatened (Eckholm & Record, 1976). This is a very real problem.

causes of obesity

The main cause of obesity is an imbalance between calorie consumption and calorie use. People who eat high calorie foods and who do not use these calories every day will become overweight. We live in one of several nations that has the "affluent diet" (Eckholm & Record, 1976). The meats, dairy products, cakes, and pies that you see on many American tables every day make up the diet of affluence. While this food may seem tasty, it is high in calories and thus poses a direct threat to an appropriate weight level.

Although high calorie intake is a direct cause of obesity, it is a problem only when a person uses less calories than he or she takes in. As might be expected, many obese youngsters, particularly adolescent girls, lead very inactive lives (Mayer, 1957). Reduced activity levels may have a substantial influence on weight level. Indeed, even a small reduction in activity may result in obesity. For example, a decrease in daily exercise equivalent to a 10-minute walk can produce a weight gain of 40 pounds over 10 years (Eckholm & Record, 1976).[1]

dealing with obesity

We have evidence that the best strategy for dealing with obesity is to prevent it before it occurs. It is not easy to reverse (Leon, 1976). And it is particularly difficult to treat effectively when people are extremely overweight (Penick, Filion, Fox, & Stunkard, 1971). Eckholm and Record (1976) suggest that one way to prevent obesity as well as other nutrition problems would be to establish a national nutrition strategy. They argue for the creation of a government agency to establish national nutrition policies. This agency would promote education to make the public aware of what we know about nutrition and health. It would work to create local environments to foster adequate activity and appropriate nutrition practices.

weight control programs

Obesity can, of course, be treated. Behavioral methods seem to be more effective than other procedures used to lose weight and maintain it (Leon, 1976). Effective behavioral weight control programs have generally involved a combination of techniques. One strategy that is often used is to have the individual trying to lose weight monitor his or her own weight and eating habits. In addition to monitoring weight and eating habits, the client in a behavioral weight control program is often asked to identify the specific conditions under which he or she usually eats. At first, a client will be asked to keep detailed records of when he eats and what conditions are present at those times. These records are used as a basis for controlling eating. For example, if an obese adolescent girl were to find

1. In addition to affecting weight, low activity levels play a significant part in a number of adult health problems. For example, several researchers have linked heart disease to inadequate exercise (e.g., Cooper, 1968).

that she tended to snack while watching television, she might be instructed to not eat then. She could teach herself to eat only at meal time and only in the dining room. The strategy of identifying conditions and establishing ways to control eating only under specific circumstances has been effective in helping people lose weight and maintain the loss (Stuart, 1971).

Another often used procedure in behavioral weight control programs is self-reward. For example, people might give themselves money for eating slowly or eating only in the kitchen or dining room at meals. Self-reward is

A CASE STUDY IN WEIGHT CONTROL

Alice was the mother of two adolescent girls, Carol and Mary. All three weighed close to 200 pounds. Alice was quite worried about her own weight and about the weight of her daughters. She believed that weight control was simply a matter of exercising will power. She had tried to lose weight many times and had convinced her girls that they should lose weight too. However, the results of their efforts were always the same. A few pounds would come off grudgingly. Then they would quickly return. Over the years Alice had steadily gained weight, and her girls appeared to be following the same pattern.

What might Alice and her children do to control their weight? There is, of course, no easy answer to this question. However, research does provide some guidelines that people like Alice, Carol, and Mary could follow (Leon, 1976). First, they should realize that weight control is a complex problem that usually is not solved simply through exercising will power. Second, they should recognize that, in light of their previous difficulties in controlling their weight, they would be well advised to seek help from a qualified professional. Third, they should learn to control the events in their environment that influence their eating. To do this, they might begin by keeping records of when and where they eat. They also might note what happens right before and after they eat. For instance, Alice and her daughters might find that they tend to eat while watching television. Once they have noted that turning on the television is a signal for having a soft drink or perhaps some crackers and cheese, they will be in a better position to control their tendency to eat in front of the television.

Fourth, Alice and her daughters might try to control their thoughts about eating. Some thoughts may be called "fat" thoughts and other thoughts "thin" thoughts. For instance, if Alice were to say to herself "I just love lemon cream pie," and then "One little piece wouldn't really hurt," she would be thinking a very blubbery thought. On the other hand, if she were to say "Carrots taste just as good as pie and they have a lot fewer calories," she would be thinking a thin thought. It goes without saying that to achieve weight control, Alice and her daughters ought to try to think thin thoughts.

Finally, Alice and her daughters should realize that it is more difficult to keep weight off than to lose it. *Permanent* weight control requires permanent changes in living and eating patterns.

most effective when it depends on eating appropriately rather than on loss of weight (Mahoney, 1974). Behavioral research on obesity suggests that permanent weight control requires that the person change his or her eating patterns. When good eating patterns are rewarded, it is easier to maintain an appropriate weight level.

We have discussed teaching an obese person to control his or her eating and exercise habits for a weight loss program. Another approach is to teach the parents of obese children techniques to alter their children's eating and exercise habits. In one study this procedure was effective in helping children lose weight but not maintain the lower weight (Aragona, Cassady, & Drabman, 1975). Thirty-one weeks after the program was stopped, the children in it were no longer lighter than their obese peers who had not been helped by their parents to lose weight. A future approach might be to combine parent assistance and self-assistance in an effort to both lose weight and maintain the lower weight.

Motor-Skill Development

Motor skills are made up of series of musle movements that meet an established performance standard. For example, if Jessie can put one foot in front of the other and move forward with at least some confidence that she will not find herself sitting on the floor all of a sudden, most people would say that she had developed the motor skill of walking. The socialization practices of a culture affect the development of motor skills. And the culture may also influence the extent that a skill is used in a society.

Virtually everyone who has no physical problem learns some motor skills, like walking. Other skills, like touch typing are highly specialized and may be developed by only a few people. The time and rate at which a skill develops varies according to the type of skill. The skills that everyone has develop in a fixed sequence early in life. Specialized skills do not necessarily come in a fixed order. As we might expect, there may be wide variations in the age at which they are mastered.

ONTOGENETIC AND PHYLOGENETIC SKILLS

ontogenetic skills   Those skills that some, but not all, people have are called **ontogenetic** skills. Hitting a baseball and throwing a football are familiar examples. Some people can hit a ball with great skill; others cannot.

Ontogenetic skills let people perform highly specialized functions. Sometimes these functions are related mainly to leisure activities. However, in other instances, ontogenetic skills may contribute directly to job activities. Many careers require the development of highly complex and specialized ontogenetic skills. Skilled trades such as masonry and typing and professions such as dentistry and surgery are examples.

The development of ontogenetic skills is strongly influenced by learning and motivation. A person masters a skill when he has appropriate instruction and the chance to practice and when he wants to learn (Ausubel & Sullivan, 1970). Maturation also plays a role. For instance, infants do not have the physical capability to throw a football.

Skills that everyone who does not have physical damage develops are called **phylogenetic** skills. Walking and the ability to grasp objects (**prehension**) are phylogenetic skills.

phylogenetic skills

Phylogenetic skills have very general functions that often help the species survive. For example, as Jerome Bruner (1970) has pointed out, if we could not grasp objects, we would not be able to use tools. Anthropologists have long known that the ability to use tools is critical to culture. As anthropologist Leslie White (1959) pointed out some years ago, culture develops as people learn to save their energy and still accomplish important tasks, other factors remaining constant (p. 55). Tools help us control our energy use.

Early developmentalists believed that phylogenetic skills were controlled almost entirely by genetics. Gesell and Thompson (1929) found that giving young children special practice in skills like stair climbing had little effect on their skill development. But several investigations since that time have shown that their extreme genetic stance was not justified. For instance, Johnston, Kelley, Harris, and Wolf (1966) have increased preschool children's climbing skills by rewarding them with adult attention.

SEQUENCE IN SKILL DEVELOPMENT

Early research showed that the development of basic phylogenetic skills follows a fixed sequence. Three trends have been identified. One is the tendency for development to proceed from the head downward. Infants can control head movements long before they can control their legs. A second trend is for control to move from the central regions of the body to the extremities. For example, arm control is achieved before finger con-

types of sequential trends in skill development

Hitting a baseball is an ontogenetic skill.

Table 4–2   The Development of Locomotion and Prehension Skills

age	development toward locomotion	development toward prehension
Newborn	Reflexive head and body movements.	Reflexive arm movements. Looking not coordinated with eye movements.
1-4 months	Reflexive head and body re-actions disappear.	Spontaneous hand-to-mouth movements. Objects placed in the hand are grasped.
4–7 months	Voluntary control of head and arms.	Successful reach for and grasp of objects in the palm of the hand.
7–10 months	Trunk control, unsupported sitting.	Grasp with opposable thumb and forefinger.
10–12 months	Control of the legs.	Eye-hand coordination permits tasks such as placing pegs in a peg board.
2nd year	Walking and running.	

This table is compiled from information summarized by Appleton, Clifton, and Goldberg (1975). There are substantial variations in the ages at which the various skills develop. The age ranges given reflect several experimental studies conducted in different locations.

trol. A third trend involves the change from highly generalized activity involving large muscles to more specialized movements involving small muscles.

The general sequences found in early studies have stood the test of time. However, more recent research has shown that the ages at which particular skills emerge may vary widely. We will discuss this further later in the chapter.

locomotion and prehension

The major phylogenetic skills that develop in a fixed sequence are **locomotion** and prehension. Table 4–2 shows the sequences of behaviors associated with these skills. As shown in the table, locomotion skills move from the head downward. At first, infants have very little control over the motor movements that will ultimately let them walk. During the first month of life, their reactions consist of reflexes. Between the first and the fourth month, infants develop some control over their head movements. Between the fourth and the seventh month, children learn to control their heads and arms voluntarily. They usually learn to sit alone between the seventh and the tenth month. They learn to control their legs, to creep, walk, and finally run, between the tenth month and the second year of life.

Prehension skills develop from the center out. Children can control their arms before they can control their fingers. Prehension begins with reflexive arm movements at birth. Between the first and fourth months, infants can usually grasp objects placed in their hands and bring them to their mouths. Infants will also reach for an object that touches their hands if they see the object and their hands at the same time. By the time infants are 15 weeks old, their reaching behavior is regulated by the distance from the infant of the object to be grasped (Field, 1976). Between

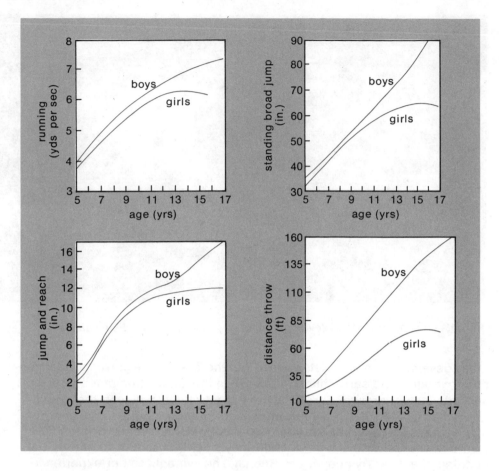

Figure 4–10   Age and sex differences in selected motor skills.
"Motor Development" by A. Espenschade and H. Eckert, in W. R. Johnson and E. R. Buskirk (Eds.), *Science and Medicine of Exercise and Sport* (2nd ed.), New York: Harper & Row, 1974. Reprinted by permission.

the fourth and seventh months, infants can reach for and successfully grasp objects in the palm. They refine their use of their fingers in grasping during the remainder of the first year.

Both locomotion and prehension skills begin with generalized activity involving large muscles and proceed to specialized activities involving small muscles. For example, prehension skill development begins with control of arm movements. As development progresses, children learn to control their hands and finally their fingers.

Phylogenetic skill development continues well beyond the first years of life. Figure 4–10 shows developmental trends through adolescence for four phylogenetic skills. Note that there is a constant increase in motor skill ability for both boys and girls until adolescence. At this time the rate of development declines for girls but not for boys. These differences between sexes may in part be due to cultural influences and personal interests, experiences, and attitudes (Espenschade & Eckert, 1974). We will discuss cultural factors influencing skill development later in the chapter.

Parents can encourage the development of phylogenetic skills like walking.

motor skills and
infant intelligence

Many developmental theorists believe that there is a close correspondence during infancy and early childhood between the acquisition of motor skills and intellectual growth. For instance, Piaget (1952) believes that intelligence has its roots in the actions infants perform during the first 2 years of life. He says that children learn to represent outside events through their own behaviors. For instance, a child may open her mouth to signify the opening of a door. By opening her mouth, she symbolizes her experience.

MOTOR SKILLS AND INTELLECTUAL DEVELOPMENT

Because of this relationship between intelligence and motor skills, some theorists have put measures of motor-skill development into tests of infant intelligence. Arnold Gesell (1925) developed an early scale to assess infant abilities that is heavily weighted with items on motor-skill development. The Baylay Scales of Infant Development (Bayley, 1969), one of the most widely used measures of intellectual functioning in infants, is also heavily loaded with motor skills items.

Tests of infant intelligence that are heavily weighted with motor-skill items reflect the kinds of intellectual capabilities Piaget says are critical to the development of early intelligence. For instance, Gottfried and Brody (1975) looked at the relationship between the performance of infants on the Bayley scales and their performance on tasks specifically designed to assess capabilities that Piaget says develop during the first 2 years of life. They found that the Bayley scales and the Piagetian tasks assess the same underlying abilities.

Although motor skills play a key role in infant intellectual functioning, early motor-skill development does not seem to indicate intellectual functioning after language develops. The relationship between measures of infant intelligence and tests of intellectual functioning given after the child learns language is generally quite low (Kessen, Haith, & Salapatek, 1970). But despite the fact that most studies have failed to reveal a significant relationship between infant intelligence and later intellectual performance, some research does indicate that infant intellectual functioning somewhat predicts later intellectual development. Wilson (1974) found that scores on the Bayley scales for children 1½ years old predicted their performance on an intelligence test at age 6 about 20% better than predictions not based on infant scores. *motor skills and intelligence after the onset of language*

MOTOR-SKILL DEVELOPMENT AND CULTURE

Motor skills develop in a cultural context; and, as we might expect, there are marked variations in how skills are acquired associated with differences in cultural experience. We should be particularly concerned about socialization practices that affect skill development because we know that physical activity is an important factor in overall health (Eckholm & Record, 1976).

Cultural Variations   Several studies have found significant cross-cultural differences in the rate of development of motor skills. For example, Geber (1958) found marked differences in early motor-skill development between black children from Uganda and European children. During the early years of life, Ugandan children far surpass their European counterparts in motor skills. In fact, on the first day after birth Ugandan children can usually keep their heads from falling backwards when they are put in a sitting position. At the age of 6 months, they can typically control their heads regardless of body position. By the time they are 4 months old, they can generally sit without support. When they are 8 months old, they can stand alone; and by the time they are 10 months, they can usually walk. These accomplishments place the Ugandan child an average of 2 to 3 months ahead of European age mates. However, later on, these early discrepancies disappear. *cross-cultural differences in skill development*

Geber traces the early skills of Ugandan infants in part to socialization practices in Ugandan families. Young Ugandan children receive a great deal of environmental stimulation. A Ugandan mother is with her child constantly during the early years of life. She carries the infant on her back as she does household chores. She sleeps with the infant and feeds the child on demand. Geber suggests that all this maternal stimulation may make the children active and promote motor-skill development.

During the past few decades, the rate at which children learn motor skills has differed across generations as well as across cultural subgroups. For instance, Bayley (1965) found that children assessed on her infant scales in the late 1950s were substantially ahead of children tested in the 1930s. Robertson (1973) compared the motor skills of children who were 7 in 1972 with those of children who were 7 in 1952. He found that the performance of the 1972 group on skills such as throwing and punting a ball surpassed the performance of the 1952 group. *cross-generational differences in skill development*

The differences in motor-skill mastery can be largely traced to changes in socialization practices. For example, Appleton, Clifton, and Goldberg (1975) argue that these differences are at least in part caused by changes in medical care, nutrition, and child rearing that have taken place during the last few decades.

We have only recently focused on another type of differential skill development related to culture—sexual differences in skill mastery. We're all familiar with sexual differences in motor skills. However, we have only recently begun to consider the idea that these differences might in part be culturally based. We have assumed that the males' superior athletic performance is a result of genetically determined differences between the sexes (Keller, 1976). But while genetic factors affecting size and strength undoubtedly contribute to sexual differences in motor skills, cultural factors may also be important. For example, girls are not rewarded to the same extent as boys for developing physical prowess.

During the last few years, it has been argued that women have not been given the same chances as men to develop their physical capabilities (Keller, 1976). For instance, girls have been excluded from competitive school sports. Because of this obvious inequality in educational experiences, the federal government developed regulations to prohibit sex discrimination in physical education by any educational institution receiving federal funds. Beginning in June of 1974, the Department of Health, Education and Welfare issued guidelines requiring that all elementary and secondary school physical education classes, except those involving a limited number of sports such as wrestling, be coeducational.

It is too early to see the effect of these new regulations on female physical development. Some studies have shown that girls in coeducational physical education classes are superior in skill development to girls in all-female classes (Nixon & Locke, 1973). In addition, many theorists

Today there are more and more opportunities for girls to develop motor skills.

now believe that, largely because of past discrimination, most women have not come close to reaching their full potential for skill mastery (Keller, 1976). Given the traditional lack of opportunity and encourage-

TOILET TRAINING

Toilet training is a difficult task for many parents. They are often unsure as to when to begin training and how to carry it out. Moreover, they may be afraid that improper training will have a bad effect on their child's future development. Sometimes parents begin training before a child is maturationally ready to be trained. Their own training failures often lead to frustration and anger. They scold the child for accidents or try to shame the child into appropriate toilet behavior. Early, punitive training tends to produce unfortunate results. The child may kick, bite, and scream when placed on the toilet and, most important, may simply refuse to eliminate. The overall consequence is often chronic bedwetting that may last for years (MacFarlane, Allen, & Honzik, 1954).

Fortunately, research exists which can help parents to be effective in toilet training. Research findings suggest two keys to effective training. One is to make sure that training is not started too early. Children as young as 16 to 18 months of age can learn toilet skills. However, the number of "accidents" encountered at this age is likely to be high even after training (Madsen, Hoffman, Thomas, Koropsak, & Madsen, 1969). By the time children are about 2, they can generally be trained easily and the incidence of accidents following training is likely to be low.

The second key to effective training is to reward the appropriate behavior when it occurs. Hugs, kisses, and tangible rewards such as sweets can help children to learn toilet skills painlessly and in a short period of time.

Foxx and Azrin (1973) have developed a highly effective toilet training program based on rewards that shows just how easy toilet training can be. In their research they demonstrated that basic toilet training skills could be taught in less than one day. Parents participating in the research brought their children to a clinic for a day of training. Each child was assigned to a trainer. After making friends with a child, the trainer offered the child as much soda pop as he or she wanted. The purpose of this, of course, was to produce a full bladder. The children were given a doll capable of emitting water in a fashion similar to urination. The trainer taught the child to raise and lower the doll's pants and to allow it to "urinate" in a potty chair. Following urination, the child was asked to give the doll candy and to praise it, saying, "The doll behaved like a big kid."

The child was then asked to sit on the potty chair. When urination occurred, the trainer hugged and kissed the child and gave the child some potato chips. The child's pants were checked every few minutes following successful urination. Reward accompanied dry pants, but not wet ones. Using these procedures it took an average of about four hours to send children on their way to a lifetime of dry pants.

ment for developing motor skills, it seems likely that the recent changes in physical education may have a marked positive effect on girls' physical development.

Socialization Practices   In this final section, we will take a look at some specific socialization practices that may affect motor-skill acquisition at different levels of development. It would be far beyond the scope of this book to cover these socialization techniques in detail. Nevertheless, we can give you some basic knowledge on how socializing agents can promote skill development.

movement and
skill development

During infancy, the chance to move around is particularly significant in determining motor-skill development. For example, Dennis and Najarian (1957) studied children raised in a foundling home in Beirut, Lebanon. They found motor retardation was caused largely because the children were restricted in their chances to move about and thereby to practice physical skills. Recently, Slovin-Ela and Kohen-Raz (1978) studied children in Jerusalem. They found that retarded skill development appears in institutionalized infants as young as 4 months old. They observed the reaching skills of institutionalized infants and middle-class babies being raised in their own homes. The institutionalized babies were in most cases about 3 months behind the middle-class babies in learning to reach for and grasp objects. Dennis and Sayegh (1965) also looked at how enriched chances for movement affect motor-skill development of infants raised in institutions.

They gave the infants practice in activities like sitting and manipulating objects. These infants made significantly greater gains on an infant intelligence scale heavily weighted with motor-skill items than other infants who had not had the enrichment.

Zelazo, Zelazo, and Kolb (1972) also found that opportunities to practice affect skill development. During the first week of life, infants who are held in a standing position will generally make primitive walking movements. By the end of the second month, most infants can no longer do this. However, if they have practice in walking, their primitive walking movements do not disappear. In the Zelazo study, mothers were asked to provide walking practice for their children for 12 minutes a day from the time the infants were 2 weeks old until they were 8 weeks old. The average age that these infants began to actually walk was 10 months, which is about 2 months ahead of the time when walking generally begins.

space and
equipment for
early skill
development

When children can get around on their own, during the second year of life, they need extensive space and equipment to develop their motor skills. Most homes and neighborhoods provide adequate chances for children to learn skills between ages 1 and 5 (Appleton, Clifton, & Goldberg, 1975). And we have standards to ensure that day-care centers have enough equipment and space. What is generally needed is enough room to do things like run and jump. In addition, children should have equipment to let them learn skills such as climbing and tricycle riding.

informal skill
instruction

During the years between 1 and 5, most motor-skill instruction is informal. The adult must look for opportunities to teach motor skills and seize them when they arise rather than planning to teach at a particular time and place. Behavioral techniques such as modeling and reinforcement can be particularly useful in this kind of informal instruction. Harris, Wolf, and Baer (1967) conducted a study that shows how behavioral principles can be used informally with preschool children. This preschool had a climbing frame that the children could use. One of the children rarely used this device, and consequently was not progressing as well as the teacher thought he should. To solve this problem, the teacher reinforced the child with attention. Whenever the child moved in the direction of the climbing frame, the teacher paid attention to him. When she was successful in encouraging him to approach the frame, she withheld her attention until he touched it. Next she attended only when he made some effort to climb on it. Finally, she attended to him only when he climbed on the frame. By this shaping procedure, the teacher was able to help the child develop climbing skills.

During the school years, children learn a variety of specialized skills like throwing and kicking a football, shooting and dribbling a basketball, and hitting a tennis ball. Many of these skills are learned through informal play. However, formal instruction is important in skill development during the school years.

A wide variety of techniques can be useful in formal motor-skill instruction. One of the most widely used is modeling, especially for introducing a new skill. For example, to teach a child how to hit a forehand stroke in tennis, a teacher might begin by demonstrating the stroke. Research indicates that there is some advantage to demonstrating not only the correct way to perform the skill being taught, but also the major errors that may occur (Nixon & Locke, 1973). Thus, a tennis teacher might model the forehand stroke with a firm wrist and then show students the disastrous results of snapping the wrist at impact with the ball. The demonstration of incorrect skill execution gives students clues to find the errors that they inevitably will make while learning the skill.

modeling in skill instruction

This Ugandan girl has well-developed motor skills.

component skills

When the skill being taught is very complex, it is often useful to break it into parts and then teach the parts separately (Nixon & Locke, 1973). A familiar example is the way children are taught handwriting. They are initially given easy-to-grasp large crayons and pencils. At this point in the process they are only expected to hold the instrument and make marks on paper. They are later taught other components one step at a time. They are taught to hold the standard thin pencil; they are taught the standard thumb, forefinger, and middle finger grasp of the writing instrument, and they are taught various fine finger movements necessary for printing letters.

A tennis serve is a second example of a skill that is best taught by breaking it down into components. To serve a tennis ball, it is necessary to do two things at one time. The ball must be tossed into the air to a place where it can be hit easily. At the same time, the racket must be moved into position to hit the ball to propel it into the opponent's court. Doing two things at once can be confusing. In this case, instructors often try to reduce the confusion by teaching the ball toss and the act of moving the racket into the hitting position separately.

overt and covert practice

Opportunities for practice are, of course, essential to motor-skill development. To master a complex skill requires countless hours of disciplined effort. But although extensive practice is required to master a new skill, the practice need not always take the form of actually performing the skill. A number of studies have shown that mental practice can be beneficial in learning skills (Richardson, 1967a, b). A person who spends time imagining how he or she will execute a particular skill is likely to improve the skill performance. For example, golfers often report that they think about how to swing while they are preparing to swing the golf club. Practice of this kind may improve execution of a skill.

feedback

Perhaps the most important function of socializing agents in guiding skill development is affording students with feedback (Nixon & Locke, 1973). Feedback can be of two types. Students may be told how well their performance meets the standard, or they may be given a description of the results of the action. In skills such as golf and springboard diving where the *form* of the action is critical, feedback on performance may be particularly helpful (Nixon & Locke, 1973). In skills, such as catching a baseball, that can be accomplished in many different ways, feedback on performance may be no better than feedback on results. Thus, a teacher might help a child learn to catch either by giving knowledge of results like "That one fell right off the tip of your glove," or by making comments about performance like "When you catch a ball below your waist, the fingers of your glove should point down."

motivation for skill development

Socialization aimed at helping children develop skills requires not only effective instructional techniques, but also encouraging the children to perform motor-skill activities (Ausubel & Sullivan, 1970). We have been reasonably successful in motivating boys to develop motor skills; but, at least in the past, we have spent little time on stimulating skill development in girls and in adults of both sexes. Because we are now aware of the role of exercise in overall health, we now need strategies to encourage girls and adults to increase their exercise. Institutions like the schools can play an important part in this. However, we also need to make adults more aware of the benefits of appropriate motor skill development and use.

Suggested Readings

Cooper, K. H. *Aerobics.* New York: M. Evans, 1968.

Dennis, W. Causes of retardation among institutional children: Iran. *Journal of Genetic Psychology,* 1960, *96,* 47–59.

Dennis, W., & Najarian, P. Infant development under environmental handicap. *Psychological Monographs,* 1957, 71, No. 7.

Dennis, W., & Sayegh, Y. The effect of supplementary experiences upon the behavioral development of infants in institutions. *Child Development,* 1965, *36,* 81–90.

Eckholm, E., & Record, F. *Worldwatch paper 9: The two faces of malnutrition.* Washington, D. C.: Worldwatch Institute, 1976.

Geber, M. The psychomotor development of African children in the first year and the influence of maternal behavior. *Journal of Social Psychology,* 1958, *47,* 185–195.

Leon, G. R. Current directions in the treatment of obesity. *Psychological Bulletin,* 1976, *83,* 557–578.

Mahoney, M. J., & Mahoney, K. *Permanent weight control.* New York: Norton, 1976.

Rice, R. D. Neurophysiological development in premature infants following stimulation. *Developmental Psychology,* 1977, *13,* 69–76.

Shirley, M. M. A motor sequence favors the maturation theory. *Psychological Bulletin,* 1931, *28,* 204–205.

Tanner, J. M. Physical growth. In P. H. Mussen (Ed.), *Carmichael's manual of child psychology* (Vol. 1) (3rd ed.). New York: Wiley, 1970.

Winick, M. *Malnutrition and brain development.* New York: Oxford University Press, 1976.

Zelazo, N. A., Zelazo, P. R., & Kolb, S. Walking in the newborn. *Science,* 1972, *176,* 314–315.

Intelligence:
What Is It?

We all know a meaning in our own minds for the word "intelligence." When you have finished this chapter, you should have an idea of what some other people think it is, as well. You should be familiar with two perspectives on the definition of intelligence: the psychometric perspective and the sociological perspective. You should know the meaning of the terms norm, norm-referenced assessment, mental age, and IQ. You should know what general intelligence is.

In addition, you should be able to describe the relationship between intelligence and race and social class and how roles and status labels affect intellectual behavior. You should understand how test norms and results are affected by society, and how intelligence tests can be culturally fair or biased. At that point, you will be ready to look at some theories on how intellect develops (chapter 6) and then at how you can affect intellectual development in children (chapter 7).

Most of us think of intelligence as a "thing"—something special that develops within each person. But, in fact, "intelligence" is only a concept we define in cultural terms. There can be different perspectives on the nature of intelligence and intellectual development, and the thoughts and actions of people who work with children are affected by how they view intelligence. Let's look at Elsa, a 13-year-old girl, whose case shows the far-reaching consequences that social notions about intelligence may have. We learned about Elsa's life by watching a school psychologist interview her. The interview took place in an empty classroom that had been well used during the school year. The walls were marred by heavy smudges of dirt, and the once glossy desks were extensively carved. Elsa's behavior during the early part of the interview blended with her drab surroundings. She sat motionless, her head bent forward and her eyes staring at the floor, as the psychologist went on about the teacher's concerns about Elsa's lack of progress in school.

After the psychologist's opening "speech," there was one of those seemingly endless silences that happen when one person expects the other to respond and no response comes. Then the psychologist asked a rather uncharacteristic question. "Why," he said, "Why don't you do better in school than you do?" Even as he spoke, he had the feeling that he should not have asked the question. After all, he was the expert, the skilled diagnostician. How could he expect Elsa to know what he did not know?

Then Elsa responded. "Because I'm too stupid. What's the use of trying to do something that you know you can't do?" "What makes you think that?" asked the psychologist. "I've known it for a long time now," the girl said. "When I was in the third grade, I took some tests pretty much like the ones you gave me. One night after supper my parents both came into my room. I could tell they were angry. They told me that they had just talked with the psychologist and that he said I was a dummy and that I would never be able to learn because my head was damaged." "That's not true," retorted the psychologist. "I have the test results right here in front of me. You have normal intelligence, and I have no information to suggest that there's anything the matter with your brain."

The child's lips began to quiver. Tears welled up in her eyes, and soon she began to sob. "My God," she said. "They told me I could never learn."

The Psychometric Perspective

Elsa's experiences relate to what we call the **psychometric perspective** on intellectual development. People who have this viewpoint describe intelligence in terms of test performance. Each year millions of children from every region in this nation take intelligence tests based on the psychometric perspective. In this section of this chapter, we will look at the characteristics of the psychometric viewpoint, its origins in nineteenth century England, and its use today.

CHARACTERISTICS

The two principal characteristics defining the psychometric perspective are the use of norm-referenced assessment and of correlational technology. Norm-referenced assessment is used to describe intellectual functioning as measured by test performance. Correlation analysis is the principal tool used to tell whether the test does what the designer wants it to.

Norm-Referenced Assessment Within the psychometric perspective, a person's intellectual capabilities are described in terms of his or her position in a group. For instance, when the psychologist told Elsa that she had normal intelligence, he was indicating that her performance on his tests was roughly the same as the average performance of a group of people of her age.

The strategy of measuring intellectual functioning in terms of group position is referred to as *norm-referenced assessment*. Francis Galton, an eminent nineteenth century British psychologist and cousin of the illustrious Charles Darwin, introduced the concept by measuring performance variation rather than performance averages.

norm-referenced assessment defined

Since the early part of this century, it has been common practice in the United States as well as other countries to use norm-referenced assessment to measure intelligence. To devise a norm-referenced test, the designer creates a list of items (questions). These items are given to groups of individuals called *norm groups*. To construct an intelligence test, most people use several norm groups representing different age levels. For example, the Wechsler Intelligence Scale for Children-Revised (WISC-R) (Wechsler, 1974), a widely used test, includes norm groups for children ranging from 6 to 16 years old. The performance of the children in each norm group is used as a standard to judge the scores of other children of the same age who take the test.

norm groups

In selecting norm groups, designers try to choose people who have the same characteristics as the people for whom the test is intended. For example, if the test is to be used with children from both urban and rural homes, then children from urban and rural communities will be included in the norm groups. Likewise, if the test is to be used with children of varying cultural backgrounds, then different ethnic groups will be included in the norms.

Group position may be described in a number of ways. An early procedure, which related well to developmental psychology, was to specify group position in terms of mental age. This technique, developed by Alfred Binet for use in his intelligence test, involved classifying the test items according to the age level at which they were likely to be passed. For example, a test item passed by the majority of 6-year-olds was assigned an age level of 6. An individual who passed the items assigned to the 6-year level along with the items for younger age levels was said to have a mental age of 6.

mental age

Each year, millions of American children are given intelligence tests.

Today the most widely used tool for describing group position in intelligence is an IQ score. The term IQ (**intelligence quotient**) originally indicated the mental age divided by the chronological age and multiplied by 100. However, IQ now simply designates an individual's standing in a norm group. An IQ of 100 indicates average performance. Values above and below 100 indicate the extent of variation from the average.

correlation
defined

Correlation Analysis   **Correlation** refers to the extent to which things vary in the same way. For example, suppose that a group of children take an intelligence test and an arithmetic achievement test. Assume that children who score above the average on the intelligence test also score above the average on the arithmetic achievement test, and that children who score below the average in intelligence are below average in achievement. We would say that these two tests are correlated because the people taking the tests varied in the same way on the two assessments.

Today there is a large technology for measuring correlation. It derives directly from the work of Galton. He reasoned that it ought to be possible to measure the extent to which things vary in the same way. He asked Karl Pearson, a well-known mathematician, to develop an index to assess the correlation between phenomena. The Pearson index of correlation, which we still use, ranges from -1 to $+1$. The $+1$ indicates a perfect positive relationship, while the -1 means a perfect negative relationship. Thus, for example, if the child with the highest score on the intelligence test got the highest score on the achievement test, and the child with the second

Pearson index of
correlation

highest intelligence score got the second highest arithmetic score, and so on down to the child with the lowest scores, the correlation between the two tests would be +1. On the other hand, in the unlikely event that high scores in intelligence were always associated with low scores in achievement and low achievement scores always indicated high intelligence scores, then the relationship between intelligence and achievement would be −1.

Psychometrists use correlations to evaluate intelligence tests. For example, before intelligence testing was widespread in this country, James McKeen Cattell had developed a number of tests that were widely regarded as measures of intelligence. However, when Clark Wissler (1901) proved that Cattell's tests did not correlate with success in school, professionals in the field questioned their **validity**. By contrast, Alfred Binet   test validity
wisely selected the items for his intelligence test on the basis of teacher judgments of school success. Professionals looked at the correlation of the Binet scale with academic performance as adequate evidence for the view that the Binet test was indeed a measure of intelligence.

The basic rationale for validity studies has not changed from its early days. To the extent that a test correlates with other measures in the ways we would expect, the test is regarded as valid.

The value of a test involves its reliability as well as its validity. The **reli-**   test reliability
ability of a test refers to the degree to which individual variations in performance on the test are consistent. We establish reliability, like validity, with correlation analysis. For example, we can look at the scores of people taking the same test on two different occasions. A high correlation would indicate a high degree of test reliability. Test reliability is important in establishing the credibility of intelligence tests. People would not be likely to believe that a test measured intelligence if an individual's scores changed extensively in short spans of time.

ALFRED BINET (1857–1911)

Binet, who was born in Nice, France, first studied law as a young man. From there, his interest turned to biology, and from there to psychology. He is considered the founder of French experimental psychology. With a colleague, he founded the first journal of psychology in France. He also helped start the laboratory school at the Sorbonne.

In 1904, the French minister for public education appointed Binet to study problems associated with identifying retarded children in order to educate them. This led to the creation of a metric intelligence scale, a new way to measure intelligence. In 1905 Binet developed a series of tests to measure intelligence. These tests were revised in 1908 to include a distinction between mental age and chronological age. This 1908 revision, which Theodore Simon contributed to, is the foundation of the standardized tests of intelligence we use today.

THE BEGINNINGS OF THE PSYCHOMETRIC PERSPECTIVE

The psychometric perspective had its origins in the layered society of nineteenth century England. This society was clearly divided into social classes; and, although some social mobility was possible, right-of-birth was a major factor in determining class. It is impossible to know the exact extent to which the psychometric view was shaped by social conditions of nineteenth century England. Nevertheless, in retrospect, it is clear that this position fit its circumstances well.

Intelligence and Social Position   Before the Industrial Revolution, social position in Western societies was invariably determined by family membership. As a consequence, the concept of intelligence was not very important. But the onset of industrialization brought increased demands and opportunities for people with ability. In this new age, family membership became less important and the role of ability in determining social status began to increase. There were ample opportunities for people with ability to move up the social ladder. Eventually a class-caste system developed; both ability and family membership helped determine status. Thus ability came to be linked with family background. Galton gave this notion a scientific basis in 1869 with the publication of *Hereditary Genius: An Inquiry into Its Laws and Consequences.* In this book Galton studied 300 families of high social station. From his observations, he concluded that intelligence was determined by heredity and that level of intelligence was related to social position.

England's class-caste system

link between ability and family background

It may seem surprising that Galton did not consider the possibility that environment could affect the way intellectual functioning relates to social class. However, the people of the English upper classes of the time were not familiar with the society of the lower classes. Many refused to recognize the sordid living conditions of the poor. And some people felt that to realistically discuss the way poor people lived was in bad taste.

Homogeneous Cultural Standards   Thus in nineteenth century England, behavior was judged according to a single set of cultural standards—those of the upper classes. There were, of course, cultural differences among subgroups in the population, but any variations from the norms established for the rich were regarded as inferior. As in other societies, language, dress, and actions all served as cues to social station.

As the concept of measuring intelligence developed, it too began to reflect a single set of cultural standards. A British psychologist, Charles Spearman (1904), advanced the view that intelligence is a unitary phenomenon. Initially he held that all intellectual activity was based on one fundamental function, which he called *general intelligence.* He later modified his position, asserting that intelligence includes both general and specific abilities (Spearman, 1927).

general intelligence

The notion of general intelligence was introduced into the United States through the widespread use of the Binet test (Terman, 1916). This was ironic because Binet himself believed that intelligence is composed of a

Table 5–1   Some examples of content from the 1960 Stanford-Binet
Intelligence Scale

subtest name	subtest activity
	Year 2
Three-Hole Form Board	The child must place three forms into the correct recessed areas on a form board.
Delayed Response	The child must locate an object after it has been hidden under a box and the box has been screened from view for 10 seconds.
Identifying Parts of the Body	The child is asked to point to various body parts (for example, the hair) on a paper doll.
Picture Vocabulary	The child is asked to name 18 common objects pictured on cards.
	Year 6
Vocabulary	The child is asked to define words ranging in difficulty from very easy to very difficult.
Differences	The child must be able to tell the differences between specific animals and objects, such as a bird and a dog.
Mutilated Pictures	The child is shown a series of pictures and is asked to determine which part is missing from each one.
Number Concepts	The child is given 12 blocks and is asked to count out a certain number of them. This is repeated for several different numbers.

variety of different abilities rather than a single general ability. In Binet's opinion, his test measured an individual's average level of mental functioning for a group of widely different capabilities (Tuddenham, 1962). Thus Binet included a large number of diverse tasks in his test. This diversity is illustrated in the sample items shown in table 5–1, taken from a recent version of the test.

Binet's view

But while Binet believed that intelligence involved a number of discrete abilities, H. H. Goddard, who translated the Binet test from French into English, did not share Binet's views. Rather, he agreed with Spearman and regarded intelligence as a unitary process. Moreover, where Binet believed that environment helped determine intellectual functioning, Goddard agreed with the English genetic stance. As a result, intelligence test scores in the United States were interpreted from Goddard's viewpoint rather than from Binet's for nearly half a century.

Goddard's view

What kind of capability comprised the mysterious and unchangeable process that Goddard described? Several theorists now hold that what used to be called *general intelligence* is largely verbal skills associated with the language patterns of upper classes of the society (Jencks, Smith, Acland, Bane, Cohen, Gintis, Hayns, & Michelson, 1972). The idea of general intelligence fits the practice of judging everyone by a single set of cultural standards, which end up looking down on groups that are different from the dominant classes.

general intelligence and verbal skills

PSYCHOMETRIC INTELLIGENCE IN A PLURALISTIC SOCIETY

Contemporary American culture is quite different from the layered society of nineteenth century England that gave birth to the concept of intelligence. For over 50 years, the ideas about intelligence that had been established during the nineteenth century dominated American thinking. However, during the last three decades or so, that attitude has been changing. As we increasingly accept and value cultural diversity, our tendency to regard cultural variations in intellectual functioning as signs of unchangeable differences in general intelligence is weakening.

genetic stance on class-related differences in intelligence

Intelligence and Social Class   It has been reliably demonstrated on many occasions that there is a significant relationship between intelligence-test performance and social class (Jencks et al., 1972). In general, people from the lower classes score lower on intelligence tests than individuals in the middle or upper classes. But although the fact that this happens is not in question, the cause of it is. Theorists such as Arthur Jensen argue that differences in social station are the *result* of differences in intelligence. Thus, Jensen (1971) writes:

> Social classes as defined largely in terms of educational and occupational status are subject to differential selection for mental abilities. Since these have genetic as well as environmental components, they are transmitted to the offspring; and because of a high degree of assortative mating for mental traits in Western cultures, the gene pools for different social classes will differ in the genetic factors related to ability. . . . It is now generally accepted by geneticists, psychologists, and sociologists who have reviewed the evidence that social class differences in mental abilities have a substantial genetic component. This genetic component should be expected to *increase* in an open society that permits and encourages social mobility. (pp. 40–41)

environmental stance on class-related differences in intelligence

Several researchers have challenged various aspects of Jensen's views (e.g., Bergan, Zimmerman, & Ferg, 1971; Guthrie, 1971; Jencks et al., 1972). Christopher Jencks and his colleagues have extensively challenged Jensen's position. Jencks and his associates admit that the relationship between intelligence and social class is probably based on genetically determined differences in IQ to some extent. However, in their view, the central question is whether the role of heredity is large or trivial. Their data have led them to conclude that only about 30% of the relationship between social status of the parents (as measured by the father's occupation) and child IQ can be traced to genetic factors. The remaining 70% can be attributed to environment. These estimates are in sharp contrast to Jensen's views regarding the importance of heredity.

Assuming that IQ has at least some effect on social class, the question of how it works remains. Jencks and his associates argue that IQ may not affect social status directly. Rather, they assert that the relationship between IQ and social class can be explained in terms of the relationship between IQ and education. People who are willing and able to stay in school for a long time have access to occupations with high social status. In Jencks' opinion, neither IQ nor educational attainment necessarily contribute directly to job success. IQ is related to school success. School success in turn provides credentials that open the way to desirable careers.

how IQ affects social class

Other contemporary theorists, while admitting that schools do serve as credential agencies, nevertheless assert that level of education may affect productivity on the job. Bowman (1974), for example, argues that schooling contributes to productivity. However, she admits that the extent of the contribution is an open question.

Intelligence and Race   In 1969, Arthur Jensen shook the scientific and professional community and the nation at large with an article entitled, *"How Much Can We Boost IQ and Scholastic Achievement?"* He argued that the frequently observed difference of about 15 IQ points between whites and blacks might be genetically based. Jensen's views created an immediate furor. The editors of the *Harvard Educational Review* published Jensen's article along with rebuttals. Shortly after the article was published, it was picked up by the *New York Times* and other media. Within a few days, members of Students for a Democratic Society were driving a sound truck across the campus of University of California, Berkely (where Jensen was and is employed), chanting "Stop racism. Fire Jensen!"

the genetic view

The Jensen article and reactions to it are a good example of the way science and society work to shape developmental views and socialization practices. As Cronbach (1975) points out, the controversy was in part created by the media. Jensen's original remarks were cautious and tentative. For example, consider the following quotation (Jensen, 1969):

> There is an increasing realization among students of the psychology of the disadvantaged that the discrepancy in their average performance cannot be completely or directly attributed to discrimination or inequalities in education. It seems not unreasonable . . . to hypothesize that genetic factors may play a part in this picture. But such an hypothesis is anathema to many social scientists. The idea that the lower average intelligence and scholastic performance of Negroes could involve, not only environmental, but also genetic, factors has indeed been strongly denounced. . . . But it has been neither contradicted nor discredited by evidence. (p. 82)

The news media's translations were far less tentative. Cronbach (1975) cites *Newsweek's* summary as an example. The summary states: "Dr. Jensen's view, put simply, is that most blacks are born with less 'intelligence' than most whites" (*"Born Dumb?"* 1969, p. 84).

Jensen still believes that current racial differences in IQ may be genetically based. For example, in an article written in 1970, he asserted that genetically based racial differences in IQ were not only possible, but probable. More recently, Jensen and Figueroa (1975) found racial differences in performance on a cognitive task related to IQ. They were unable to account for these differences in terms of environment.

environmental view

There are many critics of Jensen's view. One argument against a basically genetic view is simply that IQs in different racial groups reflect a combination of heredity and environment. Thus, it is not possible to attribute group differences mainly to genetic factors (Buss, 1975; Cleary, Humphreys, Kendrick, & Wesman, 1975).

A second argument is based on research evidence that suggests that environment may have a markedly beneficial effect on the intelligence scores of nonwhite children. For example, recently Sandra Scarr and Richard Weinberg (1976) studied black and interracial children raised in white middle- and upper-middle-class families. The average IQ among these children was 106. The average IQ for black children raised in their own homes in the same area is only 90. This finding, along with data that suggest that the characteristics of the adoptive parents and the timing of placement influence intellectual functioning, led Scarr and Weinberg to conclude that the IQ scores of black and interracial children are affected by environment.

Culture, Intelligence, and the Nature–Nurture Debate   The questions of how social class and race relate to IQ, called the nature–nuture debate, are important because the answers may affect how we allot resources to the socialization of our children. The ways we try to socialize our children may vary drastically, depending on reasons why we think different children perform differently. If we take a predominantly genetic view, then we have little reason to expand our cultural resources to reduce group differ-

implications of the genetic view

ences. The focus of our educational programs should be on adapting to unchangeable differences in capability. On the other hand, if we use an environmental interpretation of group differences, then we might see the group differences as a call for action to eliminate them.

evidence for the genetic view

For most of this century, the nature–nurture debate has been dominated by the genetic stance. The evidence comes from two major sources. One is the stability of intellectual functioning over time. Stability is generally measured by looking at the intelligence-test performance of specific children at successive ages. The results of two well-known studies, the Berkeley Growth Study (Bayley, 1949) and the Berkeley Guidance Study (Honzik, Macfarlane, & Allen, 1948), are shown in figure 5–1. These studies show a high degree of stability in intellectual functioning across most age levels. However, there is less stability during the early years of life. People who favor a genetic interpretation of the stability data point out that tests of infant intelligence usually contain many items measuring motor skills, while tests given to older children are heavily loaded with verbal questions. The lack of consistency during the early years is explained by differences in the tests rather than by differences in ability (Hofstaetter, 1954). Environmentalists argue that lack of stability during the early years shows that intelligence is particularly open to change early in life (Bloom,

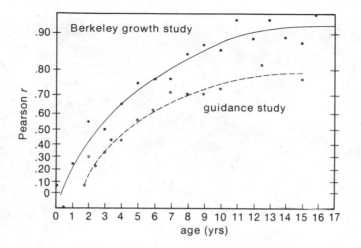
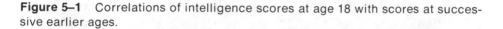

Figure 5–1 Correlations of intelligence scores at age 18 with scores at successive earlier ages.

From J. E. Jones, "The Environment and Mental Development," by J. E. Jones, in L. Carmichael [Ed.], *Manual of Child Psychology,* New York: Wiley, 1954, p. 639. Copyright 1954 John Wiley & Sons, Inc. Reprinted with permission of John Wiley & Sons, Inc.

1964). From this evidence, some researchers have drawn the idea of a critical early period when environment may have a maximum influence on intellectual development (Hunt, 1961).

The second and principal source of evidence for the genetic view comes from studies of the similarity in IQ among related and unrelated people. For example, there are data describing correlations in IQ for identical and fraternal twins reared together and reared apart. Data are also available describing IQ correlations for siblings, parents, and children, and for unrelated people.

The data from these studies have been widely distributed. For example, Erlenmeyer-Kimling and Jarvik (1963) summarized 52 kinship studies. Their work has been extensively quoted and used to support the genetic arguments of Jensen and other investigators.

But when original data are summarized, there is always a danger that mistakes will creep in. Kamin (1974) has discovered a number of inaccuracies in the reports of kinship results. For example, in the Erlenmeyer-Kimling and Jarvik summary, Kamin found that certain data were not always included. This produced an overestimation of the contribution of heredity to intelligence. The many errors that Kamin discovered led him to conclude that available summaries supporting a basically genetic explanation of intelligence cannot be taken seriously.

The problem of suspect data is not limited to research summaries. The original data also have a number of serious flaws. The most influential

Scientists are still trying to find out whether intelligence is based on heredity or environment.

data source has been the work of Sir Cyril Burt (see, for example, Burt, 1958). Burt's studies conducted over nearly half a century received such acclaim in his native England that he was knighted. His studies of twins were regarded as among the most significant ever done. They include the only available data on identical twins reared apart in dissimilar environments. Kamin (1974) has discovered several methodological short-comings, inaccuracies, and contradictions in Burt's work. For example, in studies of the relationship between the IQs of parents and children, Kamin found that Burt had estimated the intelligence of parents through informal interviews rather than through standardized tests. Burt also reported correlations that were impossible to obtain from the data presented.

Kamin's detective work revealed what could go down as one of the biggest scandals in the history of psychology. His analysis suggests that Sir Cyril may have altered his data to fit his theories (Kamin, 1974). After becoming familiar with Kamin's work, Oliver Gillie, medical correspondent for the *London Sunday Times,* probed further into the matter. He said that not only had Burt cheated in reporting his findings, but also that he had apparently invented mythical research assistants who were supposed to have worked with him (Evans, 1976). The Burt issue has not been completely resolved yet. There is general agreement that Burt's results are in error, but some people attribute his errors to carelessness, while others suspect fraud (McAskie, 1978).

Although until quite recently, the genetic view has been dominant, data favoring an environmental position have been accumulating for some time. Migration studies are one of the earliest sources of evidence sup- porting an environmental position. Otto Klineberg (1935) studied the IQs of American black children who migrated from the South to the North and found that IQ increased as a function of amount of time spent in the North. These findings were repeated later by Lee (1951).

Studies involving places that have undergone rapid cultural change are a second source of evidence favoring an environmental stance. For ex- ample, Wheeler (1932) compared the intellectual functioning of people living in isolated rural Tennessee to the functioning of people living in less isolated areas. He found that the isolated children had lower IQs. With the introduction of the Tennessee Valley Authority, new roads, and increased telephone and radio communication, their cultural isolation was reduced. The IQ discrepancies that had been observed disappeared. The change may have resulted from cultural stimulation, or from the selec- tive migration of competent people into the area.

Investigations of children raised in institutions are the most poignant evidence supporting an environmental position. Infants who were separ- ated from their mothers and placed in institutions suffered severe psycho- logical and physical damage (Spitz, 1945; Spitz & Wolf, 1947). Despite the fact that they were adequately fed and given appropriate medical care, 23 of 88 children whom Spitz studied died. Only one or two among a group of 26 children ranging in age from 18 months to 2½ years could speak more than a few words, and only three could walk. Other investigators have reported retardation in intellectual development similar to that seen by Spitz (e.g., Dennis & Najarian, 1957; Ohwaki & Stayton, 1978; Provence & Lipton, 1962).

Lack of stimulation and chance to move around may be critical causes of intellectual retardation in children raised in institutions (Thompson & Grusec, 1970). For example, in an investigation of children raised in orphanages in Iran, Dennis and Najarian (1957) note that the children re- ceived little visual or auditory stimulation and that they had very little op- portunity to move about. Several studies have shown that opportunity to move and level of stimulation may affect intellectual functioning (e.g., Casler, 1965; Dennis & Sayegh, 1965).

A fourth source of evidence is studies of interventions with children who would have been expected to do poorly on intelligence tests. For example, Heber (1969) has run a comprehensive program of extensive tutoring for infants whose mothers have IQs below 70. Scarr-Salapatek (1975) reports that by the time the infants in Heber's investigation were 3 years old, they had mean IQ scores of 120, which is well above expecta- tions. She also reports that Rynders conducted an equally impressive study with Down's syndrome children. At the age of 3 years, these chil- dren had average IQs of 85, where most children with Down's syndrome do not have IQs above 50.

What conclusions can we draw from the evidence on hereditary and environmental influences on intellectual functioning? Despite the shat- tering blows recently delivered to the genetic position, even the staunch-

*Children who grow up in isolated rural communities may miss out on some bene-
ficial experiences.*

est environmentalists (e.g., Kamin, 1974) admit that genetic factors
probably play some role in determining intelligence. However, at this
point the discredited evidence gives us no information on precisely what
the role of heredity may be. By contrast, evidence supporting an environmental explanation suggests that experience may be very important.

*intervention to
alter intellectual
functioning*

The available evidence suggests that we can develop socialization
policies and practices to eliminate some of the inequities we see among
the cultural subgroups that make up contemporary America. Yet massive
interventions have been tried and have not been successful. During the
1960s, several large-scale social programs designed to relieve the intellectual deficits of the poor were begun. These efforts generally did not
achieve their objectives. For example, in the late 1960s, the Westinghouse
Learning Corporation (1969) evaluated the massive Head Start program,

*Children from urban ghettos may also be deprived of needed opportunities for
learning.*

which had been intended to improve the intellectual functioning of poor preschool children. The Westinghouse evaluation said that the Head Start program did not have a significant long-term impact on intellectual development. However, successful small-scale programs such as the ones described above suggest that the "failures" of the social programs of the 1960s should not be blamed on the genetic inferiority of the children. Rather, the failures may lie in our inability to intervene effectively on a large scale, and in our lack of knowledge about precisely what makes an intervention effective.

The Sociological Perspective

People like Galton and Spearman, who laid the cornerstones of psychometry, paid no attention to the role of culture. They treated intelligence as an individual trait that, like eye color or hair color, could be described without a particular cultural context. But in applying psychometry in our pluralistic American society, we find increasing awareness of the relationship of intelligence to culture. Out of this awareness a new perspective on the nature of intelligence is beginning to develop. This new view, which we call the sociological perspective, holds that intelligence is a culturally created phenomenon, defined only with reference to a particular setting or context.

CHARACTERISTICS

The sociological perspective has three major characteristics. One is the view that intelligence is defined by social norms. The second is the assertion that there are social statuses defined by level of intelligence, and the third is that people assigned to ability-determined statuses are expected to play certain roles.

Definition by Social Norms Every society has norms that specify standards of acceptable behavior for the group members. For example, people in our culture are expected to be kind to their fellow human beings, to pay taxes and funeral expenses, and to eat hot dogs at baseball games. According to the sociological perspective, intellectual behavior is like other forms of social behavior; it is defined by social norms. Thus, a child who does not respond to questions, has a glassy stare, and drools may well be said to have less than normal intelligence. His actions do not meet the social standards that describe how a "normal" child is supposed to look and act.

Some of the norms defining intelligent behavior are informal. They are   informal norms
not written down and cannot easily be verified. For example, a mother watching her little girl put together a puzzle may say "You're so smart to have figured that out." Remarks like this are based on informal and obviously subjective judgments. Nonetheless, these judgments often make up standards that we use to define intelligent behavior.

formal norms

In addition to informal standards, there are, of course, highly formalized norms to define intelligence. These norms are used in intelligence tests. However, they are also used in legal documents, written guidelines prepared by government agencies, and published statements by professional organizations. For example, the American Psychological Association's Board of Scientific Affairs recently issued a report on the use of educational tests with disadvantaged students (Cleary, et al., 1975). It contains a definition of intelligence. (It is interesting that the authors recognize that what we consider intellectual capability may change to reflect significant criteria in a particular society.)

intellectual assessment

Not only are there highly formalized norms to define intelligent behavior, but also there are rigid standards for how and by whom intelligence will be assessed. We have a corps of highly skilled professional diagnosticians. They know elaborate procedures for assessing intellectual functioning in our culture (Bardon & Bennett, 1974; Kratochwill & Bergan, 1978). By setting up this group of professionals, we make sure that our social norms will be used. A diagnostician trained for several years to use accepted social norms is likely to continue to use them after his or her training has been completed.

incentives for adhering to norms

In addition to using trained diagnosticians, we sometimes use powerful economic goals to see to it that our norms for intelligence are used. For example, public schools receive federal and state money for educating the "mentally retarded." In light of these funds, it is not surprising that schools label far more individuals "retarded" than do other community agencies (Mercer, 1973).

Social Status Based on Intelligence   Societies generally define many different social positions that individuals may occupy. Teacher's pet, cub scout, and class clown are some familiar positions we associate with childhood. Some roles, such as being a child, are assigned on the basis of personal characteristics. These social positions are called **ascribed statuses.** Other social positions, such as Eagle Scout, homecoming queen, and neighborhood nuisance, are earned. These are referred to as **achieved statuses.**

ascribed and achieved status

intellectual level as an achieved status

In the sociological perspective, intelligence is one route to an achieved social status. For example, Mercer (1973) describes mental retardation as an earned social position. Her view implies that the behavioral patterns that are characteristic of retardation are learned. The biological limitations of the individual may contribute to his or her learning how to be retarded; but nonetheless the specific responses associated with retardation are acquired, not inborn.

cultural variations in status assignment

A status such as retardation may vary from society to society and from group to group within a given society. For example, in some societies there is no social group called the "mentally retarded." In these cultures people we would call "retarded" may be given other social positions. For instance, in some societies, the "retarded" are believed to have magical powers and are held in awe (Mercer, 1973). In other social groups, the "retarded" are given the status of clown and are ridiculed (Klapp, 1949).

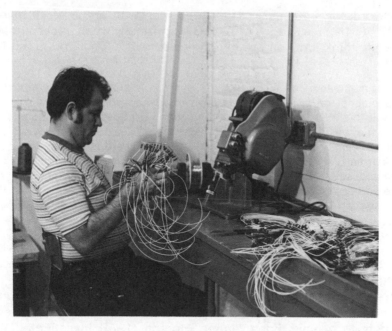

In our society, many people labeled "retarded" are able to work and be productive citizens.

Even when the same status exists in more than one social system, the ways someone is assigned to the status may be different. For example, a child may be called "mentally retarded" in school and yet act "normal" outside of school. Children like this have been called the "six-hour retarded." One story will illustrate. Sean grew up in a Spanish-speaking home and did not speak English well during his early school years. In elementary school he was tested, labeled "retarded," and placed in a special-education class. He kept that label and the special placement throughout his years in the public school. However, when he left school, he entered the Navy. There he was no longer assigned the status of retarded. He took correspondence courses in the Navy and eventually was able to graduate from high school. Upon leaving the Navy, he entered college and successfully graduated. He then entered graduate school and got a Ph.D. He is now a university professor.

situational variations in status assignment

Role Expectations   When a person has a social status, society expects him to behave in certain ways. The word "role" refers to the expected behaviors that go with a status. For example, in the role of infant, a child is expected to eat baby food, cry when he's hungry, wet his diapers, and gurgle at his parents.

role

The sociological perspective holds that people who are assigned to social positions based on their intellectual functioning are expected to act out those roles. Thus, a child who is regarded as "bright" is expected to behave like a bright child. And a child who is regarded as "retarded" is expected to act retarded.

intelligence and role expectations

The words of a 26-year-old retarded man with an IQ of 49 give us a glimpse of what it is like to try to develop normally when important people in your life think that you are handicapped and expect you to act handicapped.

I can remember trying to be like the other kids and having my mother right there pulling me away. She was always worried about me. You can't force yourself to say to your mother: "Stop, I can do it myself." Sometimes I think the pain of being handicapped is that people give you so much love that it becomes a weight on you and a weight on them. There is no way that you can break from it without hurting them—without bad feelings—guilt. It is like a trap because of the fact that you are restricted to your inner thoughts. After a while you resign yourself to it. The trap is that you can't tell them, "Let me go." (Bogdan & Taylor, 1976, p. 48)

Recently there has been extensive research on the issue of social expectations and status assignments. Most of this research deals with the ways status labels influence how teachers behave toward children and how children learn in school.

status labels and teacher expectancy

There is some evidence that labeling children according to ability or other personal characteristics does affect the ways their teachers expect them to behave. For example, Herson (1974) investigated the influence of degrading diagnoses on how teachers judge hypothetical students. Herson found that teachers rating students called "retarded" or "emotionally disturbed" assumed that the students were more handicapped than did teachers who were given only a description of behavior without accompanying labels.

Although we do have research to indicate that labels influence the expectations of adults about children's behavior, we do not yet know the extent to which these expectations affect the interactions between the adults and the children. For example, Alpert (1974) found no evidence that information about ability level influenced teacher behavior toward children. On the other hand, a number of other investigators have data that say that knowledge of ability does influence teacher behavior. For instance, Beez (1968) observed that teachers taught more to students labeled as "high ability" than to students labeled as "low ability." In contrast, Good (1970) found that low ability students were given more opportunity to respond in class than high ability students. Heller and White (1975) observed more verbal disapproval in low ability classes than in high ability classes. However, this difference may be caused by differences in the way the two groups acted.

teacher expectations and student learning

The central question is the extent to which teacher expectations lead to differences in how students learn. Rosenthal and Jacobson (1968) stimulated interest in this topic with a book that said that different expectations do produce different rates of learning. However, their research was filled with flaws in method (Barber & Silver, 1968; Thorndike, 1968, 1969). Later studies trying to duplicate the Rosenthal and Jacobson findings have had mixed results and have only clouded the picture (Claiborne, 1969; Kester, 1969; O'Connell, Dusek, & Wheeler, 1974; Rappaport & Rappaport, 1975). *At present we just don't know what effects teacher expectations may have on children's learning.*

Labels related to children's abilities may influence not only the way the teacher acts, but also the way the students themselves act. Elsa, the young girl described at the beginning of the chapter, is a perfect example. She said that she did not even try to do well in school because she believed that she was not capable of doing well. The opposite may also happen. A student may be successful because he or she believes that success is possible or probable. Rappaport and Rappaport (1975) strongly praised a group of young black children for their work on an academic task. In addition, they told the children that they would in all likelihood do very well in school. These children subsequently performed better on a reading readiness achievement test than children who were not given any special encouragement.

student expectations and learning

A SOCIOLOGICAL LOOK AT THE MEASUREMENT OF INTELLIGENCE

The sociological perspective raises a number of questions about the usefulness and appropriateness of our present ways of measuring intelligence. Today there are no clear-cut answers to these questions. Indeed, there is a great deal of controversy over them. Some feel that intelligence testing is detrimental to the interests of certain cultural subgroups. For example, George D. Jackson (1975) of the Association of Black Psychologists argues that intelligence tests have created "a cesspool of intrinsically and inferentially fallacious data which inflates the egos of whites by demeaning Black people" (p. 88). On the other hand, others assert that intelligence tests are useful in predicting the academic and vocational performance of people from varying backgrounds (Cleary, et al., 1975).

Test Norms for a Pluralistic Society   One question that is being raised more and more often has to do with the appropriateness of the ways test norms are constructed. As we saw earlier, current practice says that norms for a test will be established to represent the population for whom the test is intended. Thus individuals from diverse cultural subgroups may be treated as members of a single group and given proportional representation in the norm group. For example, a test developer constructing an IQ test for use in the United States would probably make sure that 10% of the people in his norm groups were black, since 10% of the people in this country are black.

While current practice represents different cultural backgrounds, the extent of representation for ethnic minorities is usually small. For instance, even if 10% of the people in the norm groups for a test were black, the performance of a black child taking the test would still be judged against a norm group that was approximately 90% white.

Cleary and her associates suggest that it would be useful to add norms established for particular cultural subgroups (Cleary, et al., 1975). They say that for some purposes these norms would provide more information about children's "intelligence" than traditional norms. Critics of testing suggest that even norms for individual subgroups would be of little value. They argue that it is not simply the norms but rather the tests themselves that are inappropriate (Bernal, 1975; G. D. Jackson, 1975).

IQ tests and
cultural fairness

The Cultural Fairness of Intelligence Tests   Critics of testing argue that IQ tests are unfair to nonwhites because the content of the tests is aimed at the middle class. Allison Davis introduced the idea of cultural fairness of test items in the late 1940s. He argued that IQ test items were heavily weighted with middle-class content and thus were not fair to people who grew up outside of the middle-class mainstream (Davis, 1949). Davis and his colleagues were not very successful in changing testing practices (Cronbach, 1975). However, there is growing support for the idea that IQ tests are generally not culturally fair (Horn, 1976).

Let's look at Lisa, a 16-year-old girl who was a refugee from a foreign country. She was asked to take the Wechsler Adult Intelligence Scale (Wechsler, 1955). One of the items asked her to put a set of pictures showing a burglary in order. Lisa had difficulty with this item, along with many other similar items. After the exam, she discussed this particular item with an American friend, describing in detail how she had arranged the pictures. Her friend immediately identified the flaw in the girl's "intellectual ability." Lisa had put the thief in prison before he came to trial. When the error was pointed out, she responded simply: "In my country you go to prison first. Then you are given a trial."

NONBIASED ASSESSMENT

The long-standing debate over the use of norm-referenced ability tests with individuals from diverse cultural backgrounds has led those concerned with testing to search for nonbiased assessments, that is, procedures that do not discriminate against people because of their ethnic backgrounds. One approach has been to try to eliminate the sources of bias in norm-referenced tests. For instance, it has been suggested that when IQ tests are given to Spanish-speaking children, they ought to be given in Spanish. One of us recently participated in a study on this topic (Bergan & Parra, 1978). This research revealed that bilingual children tested in Spanish scored significantly higher on an IQ test than bilingual children tested in English. However, it also showed that children tested in both English and Spanish scored even better than those tested only in Spanish.

The attempt to get rid of the bias in norm-referenced tests has not been very successful so far. For example, translating a test into Spanish doesn't eliminate bias. Questions that require knowledge of Anglo middle-class culture do not become any less culturally biased when they are asked in Spanish. The Spanish translation may help by increasing the likelihood that the person being tested will understand what is being asked. Nonetheless, cultural background will still have a strong influence on how the person responds to test questions.

A second approach to nonbiased assessment, advocated by Mercer (1973), is to supplement traditional ability tests with other tests that are not biased against particular ethnic groups. For instance, Mercer suggests that a child's ability to behave appropriately in his or her out-of-

Cleary, et al. (1975) do not agree that IQ test items merely reflect middle class behavior patterns. They say that if the tests were nothing more than collections of middle-class behaviors, the relationship between social class and intelligence would be extremely high. In fact, there are many middle-class people who do quite poorly on IQ tests. Likewise, there are many lower-class people who do quite well on IQ tests.

Cleary and her associates further suggest that you could argue that IQ tests are related to behavior patterns that the middle class values but that the majority of people in the middle class may not follow. However, they argue that it would be more accurate to say that the items relate to socially relevant criteria rather than to middle-class criteria.

The members of the Cleary group suggest another way to judge the fairness of tests. You should decide whether the tests predict performance on socially relevant tasks as well for minorities as for the majority group. They go on to point out that the available evidence suggests that our ability tests are culture-fair when evaluated against this criterion. For example, scholastic aptitude tests do predict grades in college equally well for black and white students (Cleary, et al., 1975).

Test critics point out a major problem with the Cleary definition of fair-

arguments against the charge that tests are culturally unfair

school environment ought to be considered in determining the child's ability. Unfortunately, not much is known at this time about the extent to which adaptive behavior reflects a child's ability to learn. Many people feel that if a test can't predict academic learning, it isn't of much use in school. Thus, whether or not Mercer's approach will ultimately prove beneficial in nonbiased assessment remains to be seen.

Behavioral assessment represents a third nonbiased assessment strategy. Behaviorists avoid bias by not labeling children and by not using norm-referenced tests. Their approach to assessment is to use tests to determine what a child can do and to describe precisely what the child needs to be able to do to make academic progress. At present behavioral assessment is limited by a lack of tests assessing children's skills. Also, our society has not yet accepted the idea that abilities should be described by what an individual can and cannot do. For instance, most state regulations call for a description of a child's position in a norm group to determine whether or not the child is mentally retarded for purposes of funding education programs. They do not ask what the child can do.

Today nonbiased assessment is far from being a reality. Thus, if you are confronted with test results for a child from an ethnic minority, you should realize that the test may not accurately reflect the child's capabilities. Nonetheless, significant progress has been made toward the goal of establishing nonbiased tests during the last few years. We can hope that before long, adequate nonbiased assessment procedures will become available.

ness: the choice of the measures against which the tests are validated. The Cleary view that test items are related to socially relevant criteria assumes that there are skills that virtually all people in the society agree are important. While even the most ardent critics of testing would probably agree that the skills used in test validation are highly important, many would not agree that the specific measures of those skills are appropriate for all individuals. For example, the ability to use language effectively is generally regarded as an important skill. However, several theorists question the middle-class assessment procedures and test items used to assess the language of members of minority groups (e.g., Labov, 1972). Similarly, school grades given by middle-class teachers who are not trained to recognize the behaviors and ways of thinking of children from varied cultural backgrounds are regarded as inappropriate criteria for test validation.

rebuttals to arguments supporting test use

THE FUTURE OF IQ TESTING

Amidst the furor that has surrounded testing practices since we began to look at intelligence from a sociological perspective, it is difficult to forecast the future of intelligence testing. Some suggest that testing should be either abandoned or severely cut back and regulated (G. D. Jackson, 1975; R. L. Williams, 1974). Others argue that testing should continue, but that there should be a concerted effort to make it useful in contemporary America (Bernal, 1975). Today the trend seems to be toward more testing rather than less. Recent federal legislation (P.L. 94–142) saying that the schools shall provide appropriate special-education services for all handicapped children has increased the demands for tests to identify the intellectually handicapped. Moreover, where in the past testing identifying intellectual deficits focused mainly on school-aged children, the scope of assessment has now broadened to include the identification of handicapping conditions from birth on.

The existing dissatisfaction with current testing practices and technology is a measure of the strong pressures in our society for changes in assessment techniques and test use. These pressures have already produced some movements toward change (Mercer, 1974). However, although there is pressure for change and some changes have occurred, in all likelihood it will be a long time before we see major alterations in testing. Nevertheless, if the sociological perspective has the impact in the years ahead that it has in the recent past, there may be some changes in the very near future. Socializing agents and the children whom they guide will quite probably be less and less influenced by the view that IQ tests measure innate intellectual potential. Parents, teachers, and other people involved in socialization may begin to realize that the concept of intelligence is a cultural invention—what constitutes intelligent behavior may vary from one cultural subgroup to another. Finally, people in socializing institutions such as the public schools may become sensitive to the various ways in which intellectual capability manifests itself in different cultural subgroups. Hopefully they will acquire additional skills to help them nurture the unique capabilities of children from ethnically diverse backgrounds.

Suggested Readings

Bernal, E. M., Jr. A response to "Educational uses of tests with disadvantaged subjects." *American Psychologist,* 1975, *30,* 93–95.

Cleary, T. A., Humphreys, L. G., Kendrick, S. A., & Wesman, A. Educational uses of tests with disadvantaged students. *American Psychologist,* 1975, *30,* 15–41.

Cronbach, L. J. Five decades of public controversy over mental testing. *American Psychologist,* 1975, *30,* 1–14.

Hunt, J. McV. *Intelligence and experience.* New York: Ronald Press, 1961.

Jensen, A. R. How much can we boost IQ and scholastic achievement? *Harvard Educational Review,* Reprint Series No. 2, 1969, 1–124.

Kamin, L. J. *The science and politics of IQ.* New York: Wiley, 1974.

Mercer, J. R. *Labeling the mentally retarded.* Berkeley: University of California Press, 1973.

Mercer, J. R. A policy statement on assessment procedures and the rights of children. In *Rights of children.* Cambridge: Harvard Educational Review, 1974.

Scarr, S., & Weinberg, R. A. IQ test performance of black children adopted by white families. *American Psychologist,* 1976, *31,* 726–739.

Scarr-Salapatek, S. Genetics and the development of intelligence. In F. D. Horowitz (Ed.), *Review of child development research* (Vol. 4). Chicago: The University of Chicago Press, 1975.

Williams, T. *Competence dimensions of family environments.* Paper presented at the annual meeting of the American Educational Research Association, Chicago, April 1974.

How Intellect Develops

This chapter focuses on two theories of intellectual development: the behavioral view and the Piagetian view. When you have finished, you should be familiar with both and be able to compare them. You should understand the concept of rule-governed behaviors and three views on how they are acquired. In addition, you should be familiar with some behavioral practices used to further intellectual learning.

You should also know about Piaget's concept of internal structures and the three major stages of intellectual development. You should know what kind of changes occur as a child moves from concrete through abstract thought. Finally, you should know some of the ways adults can further intellectual development in children.

To be effective and successful in America today, children need to reach a certain level of intellectual competence. Contemporary America is a technological society that thrives on the complex and specialized skills of its citizens. Adjusting to the rapid cultural change that has accompanied the advance of technology also demands intellectual ability; we need to be able to solve new problems every day. And the pluralism that surrounds us is another demand for flexibility, for the ability to be effective in varied cultural environments.

If a parent, teacher, or other child care worker is to help children grow up to meet these intellectual challenges, he or she should understand the process by which intellect develops. This chapter presents two theories of intellectual development and their implications for guiding children's development.

The Behavioral Perspective

The behavioral perspective has provided us with a great deal of scientific information about intellectual development. Let's look at the case of Irene, a second-grade child who had great difficulty learning to read, as an introduction. Irene spent 2 years in the first grade, but acquired virtually no additional skills as a result of her long-term exposure to the adventures of Dick and Jane and their canine comrade, Spot. Many specialists were called in to analyze Irene's reading problems. One was a local psychologist who got information from Irene's teacher about what the girl did during reading sessions. A particularly puzzling feature of the problem was that even though Irene was a very poor reader, she eagerly took part in reading activities. For example, during class oral reading sessions, Irene was usually the first to volunteer. Yet her performance was always an agony for everyone in the group. She made many mistakes even though she read painfully slowly.

Irene's reading problems made all the adults in her life want to help her. Her teacher worked steadily and patiently with the child; and her father, who was a busy professional with a hectic work schedule, spent all his free evenings helping Irene overcome her reading problems.

When the psychologist heard about the unusual amount of adult time and attention that Irene's reading problem provoked, he began to wonder whether or not getting adult attention was what Irene wanted. To test this hypothesis, the psychologist told Irene that he would be willing to spend some time with her working on oral reading. However, he said that he would stop working with her if she made more than five mistakes. Like the woman in the tales of the Arabian Nights who told the king stories for a thousand and one evenings to save herself from execution, Irene was soon able to read and read and read with no mistakes.

The psychologist used a behavioral perspective in deciding that Irene's reading difficulties were probably related to adult attention. In contrast to the widely held view that academic skills such as reading are determined by internal mental abilities, the psychologist assumed that reading was a behavior controlled by the environment. The assumption that intellectual skills are behaviors controlled by environment is the fundamental premise of the behavioral viewpoint.

RULE-GOVERNED BEHAVIOR

In the behavioral perspective, intellectual functioning is described as *rule-governed behavior* (e.g., Zimmerman & Rosenthal, 1974). Rule-governed behavior is behavior that conforms to a set of specifications that indicate the relationships among phenomena. For example, phonics is a rule-governed activity. Consider Jenny, a first-grade girl who is taught to read a set of similar words such as "coat," "boat," and "float." Then Jenny sees the word "goat" and identifies it correctly. Jenny's reading behavior is said to conform to a rule.

The critical test of rule acquisition is that a person who has mastered a rule must identify new instances of it. Thus the key evidence that Jenny's reading was rule governed was that she was able to read the word "goat," which she had not been taught. The use of a rule with unfamiliar examples shows that the learner is not simply responding to a set of stimulus events that he or she has learned, but rather that he or she is reacting to the common features that link those events together.

Sometimes the person who has learned a rule can specify it, but not always. For example, you undoubtedly had little difficulty reading the words "goat," "coat," and so forth but you may not be able to recite the rule that governs your behavior. Young children who are taught phonics

Children can learn to label objects in their homes by listening to their parents.

Parents can use many informal situations to reinforce their children's learning.

rules might well have little difficulty with the rule. Upon request, they could chant "When two vowels go walking, the first one does the talking."

Symbolic Representation   Rule-governed behavior is the basis for the skills that are the most useful types of human functioning. For example, the ability to use symbols to represent external reality is a rule-governed behavior. When Frank points to the small fur-bearing animal sharpening its claws on the living room furniture and says "kitty," he is probably using symbolic rule-governed behavior. If the behavior is truly rule governed, the specific animal Frank calls "kitty" will be a member of a category of creatures, all of whom will be referred to by the language symbol "kitty."

But note that Frank's rule may not be the same as the adult rule for defining that category. For instance, he might see a cow grazing peacefully by the roadside and say "See big kitty." We then might guess that his behavior was governed by a rule such as "All fur-bearing animals are called 'kitty.'"

symbolic representation and complexity reduction

The ability to use language and other symbols lets human beings simplify the information present in the environment. By grouping experiences into categories that we can respond to in the same way, we can react appropriately to much more information than if we had to react to each experience as if it were completely new. For instance, a mother can say to a child "Watch out for cars when you cross the street" and expect that the child will look out for any of the many different objects that are all properly called *cars*. This ability is particularly important in an information-heavy, technological society (Bruner, Olver, Greenfield, et al., 1966).

People who grow up in different cultural groups may use different rules to group their experiences. For example, a number of studies show that young children from societies which do not have formal schools tend to classify objects by color, while children from cultures that have schools prefer to classify objects according to shape (Glick, 1975). This is a seemingly arbitrary difference that in all likelihood comes from variations in socialization (Corah, 1964). However, even arbitrary differences like this may turn out to be important. For example, Raven's Progressive Matrices is a nonverbal intelligence test involving reasoning problems using various two-dimensional shapes (Raven, 1960). Investigators have found cultural differences in performance on this test. For instance, Shapiro (1975) found that adolescents from the Bedouin tribe in the Negev desert scored substantially lower on the Raven's test than youths of Moroccan or Eastern European descent. Bedouins have had far less exposure to Western culture than the other groups tested. Jensen (1969), in his controversial treatise on social class and racial differences in IQ (see chapter 5), used the Raven's test to support his arguments. He claimed that the test was "culture free" and that, even so, some of the largest of observed social class differences in intellectual ability occurred on it. Apparently Jensen assumed that culture would have little influence on a person's ability to use rules associated with variations in the shapes of objects. Clearly he was mistaken.

cultural variations in rule use

Problem Solving One of the most important forms of rule-governed behavior is problem solving. Problem solving requires you to discover a rule (Gagné, 1970). Because it involves discovery and therefore can lead to the production of new things, problem solving is often linked to creativity. Guilford (1967), for example, describes creativity as problem-solving activity.

problem solving

Problem solving begins with identifying the problem. This involves specifying what needs to be done to solve the problem. In some cases the nature of the problem may be obvious. For example, a high school student staring blankly at an algebra test would not need help or time to find out the nature of her problem. On the other hand, in some instances problem identification may require sensitivity and effort. Consider Mrs. George, a well-meaning grandmother who invites her son and daughter-in-law to bring their 2-year-old for a visit. Unfortunately, she leaves expensive breakable objects on tables within reach of little hands. Mrs. George's behavior suggests that she may not be sensitive to the possibility that breakable objects pose a problem for families with young children.

The second major phase in problem solving is figuring out a way to solve the problem. This often requires you to come up with several widely varying potential solutions, solutions that may need to be original. The ability to produce lots of potential problem solutions is regarded by some theorists (e.g., Guilford, 1967; Torrance, 1962) as a critical part of creativity. Some behaviorists, such as Skinner (1974), suggest that original problem solutions are the result of selective reinforcement from the environment. Others point out that you can learn innovative behaviors by observing models who are displaying creative behavior. For example, Zimmerman and Dialessi (1973) found that children could be taught to

creativity and problem solving

Table 6–1 How rules are acquired

types of rule learning	descriptions of types
Operant learning	Rules can be acquired through selective reinforcement of the discrimination of categories of stimuli.
Social learning	Rules can be learned by observing rule-governed behavior in a model.
Cumulative learning	Rules can be acquired as a result of learning sets of hierarchically related skills.

increase both the number and variety of ideas that they produced by observing a model. More recently, Belcher (1975) has shown that children can be taught to increase the originality of their responses by observing a model.

After alternative solutions have been generated, they must be tried out and evaluated. If the solutions are not effective, new solutions must be found. On the other hand, if one or more of the proposed solutions is satisfactory, the problem is solved.

HOW ARE RULE-GOVERNED BEHAVIORS ACQUIRED?

There are at least three theories about how rule-governed behaviors are learned (see table 6–1). Each theory describes procedures that adults use in guiding children's development. The way these techniques are applied, of course, may vary in varied cultures. And different rule-governed behaviors may be taught in different cultures.

rule-governed behavior acquired through operant conditioning

The Operant View   The operant view put forth by Skinner (1953, 1974) says that rule-governed actions are learned through operant conditioning. More specifically, the environment selectively reinforces behavior that conforms to a rule. For example, Howard may learn to call his mother's mother "grandma" by being smiled at and cuddled when he uses that term to refer to the sweet lady. During the early stages of learning, he may be confused in his use of the name. He may refer to the cherished grandma as "grandpa," or he may call his 25-year-old aunt "grandma." But his errors will probably not be reinforced, and thus he will stop making them. At some point Howard may be reinforced for referring to the grandmother of another child as "your grandma," and eventually he will be able to use the name appropriately for anyone deserving the title.

Through selective reinforcement, Howard learns to tell the difference between the appropriate response "grandma" and other similar but inappropriate possibilities such as "grandpa." In addition, he learns to discriminate between those situations in which his response "grandma" is likely to lead to reinforcement and those situations in which the response will not be reinforced. He also learns to generalize the response to the entire category of appropriate stimuli. When this occurs, Howard's behavior can be said to be rule-governed.

The Social-Learning View   Social-learning behaviorists point out that rule-governed behavior may be learned by observing a model (Zimmerman & Rosenthal, 1974). For instance, they would suggest that Howard might learn to identify grandmothers properly by watching other people use the label "grandma" appropriately. According to the social-learning view, a child learning a rule-governed behavior such as labeling grandmothers may learn not only to use the correct rule-governed response appropriately, but may also learn the rule that controls the response.

The rule the child learns while learning a rule-governed behavior may take the form of an internal symbol (Bandura, 1969). For example, Howard might say to himself "A grandma is the mother of a person's mother." This statement would affect whom Howard called "grandma."

Several factors may influence whether or not a child will learn rules through observation (Bandura, 1971). First of all, the child must pay attention to the behavior of the model. Obviously if the child does not see or hear or in any other way perceive the behavior to be learned, he will not learn it.

Second, children are more likely to attend to and therefore to learn from a model that they associate with pleasant consequences than they are to learn from a model toward whom they have no strong feelings.

rule learning through observation

factors influencing observational learning

One child can learn a great deal by watching another.

Some years ago Dorthea Ross (1969) conducted an interesting experiment showing the effects on observational learning of attaching positive consequences to a model. In her study, young children were shown a picture of a child named Polly. The children were told that Polly went to another school, but that she had sent lots of toys and games for the children to play with. The children were then allowed to use the toys and games, while being frequently reminded by the experimenter of where the toys came from. After several play sessions, it became obvious that the children had become attached to Polly. They brought her presents, often patted, hugged, and kissed her picture, and sought her praise and approval through the experimenter.

Following the extended play sessions, children who had learned to associate Polly with the toys and games watched her on film modeling skills such as how to answer a telephone. Other children who had not been "introduced" to Polly also observed Polly's modeling. The children who associated Polly with rewards learned significantly more from observing her behavior than the children who had no previous exposure to Polly.

A third factor influencing observational learning is the ability to remember what has been observed. According to the social-learning view, the child must recall a symbol of a behavior to be learned. The symbol may be either verbal or a mental image. For example, a child may remember the rule for finding the area of a rectangle by saying to herself "you multiply length times width." On the other hand, she might imagine that she is actually carrying out the necessary multiplications.

There are several ways to help a child remember in order to acquire a rule-governed behavior. One way is to give the learner a symbolic code relating to the rule to be acquired (Zimmerman & Rosenthal, 1974). For example, in teaching a toddler basic quantitative skills such as the ability to arrange objects by size, a mother might create a model by placing a set of sticks in order from the smallest one to the largest one. At the same time, she might say: "They are all in order now, just like stairs." This statement could help the child to symbolize and therefore to remember the rule.

In some cases to learn a rule-governed behavior, a child needs to perform rather complex physical tasks. For instance, to count objects correctly, a child must be able to point to each object once and only once during the process (Potter & Levy, 1968). This may seem to be relatively simple, but in fact very young children often have trouble pointing to each object only once.

A final factor that may influence the observational acquisition of rule-governed behaviors is reinforcement. Social-learning theorists assume that reinforcement is not necessary for learning (Zimmerman & Rosanthal, 1974). However, they say while a child learns a behavior by observing it, reinforcement can influence the extent to which the child uses the new skill (Bandura, 1969). Moreover, they suggest that reinforcement may determine the characteristics of model behavior that the learner pays attention to. It also may affect the ways the learner recalls what he or she has learned.

The Cumulative-Learning View   Some forms of rule-governed behavior are much more complex than others. For example, a young child learning to name a spoon has a much less complex task than an adolescent trying to master the laws of physics. There are obvious developmental differences in the abilities of children of varying age levels to perform complex rule-governed behaviors. One major problem faced by behaviorists has been to explain the source of developmental differences in rule learning.

Gagné (1968, 1970, 1977) argues that the differences can be partially explained by the existence of prerequisite skills. For example, to learn to add, a child must be able to count. Counting is a component of addition. Children who do not have rule-governed counting behavior are not likely to have rule-governed addition behavior.

Gagné (1968) asserts that development is in part a process of cumulative learning in which children master increasingly complex tasks. He distinguishes eight types of learning that vary in level of complexity.

Gagné's eight types of learning

The first type of learning identified in Gagné's model is **signal learning**. Signal learning is a kind of conditioning. A stimulus that occurs before a response can acquire the power to bring out the response by being paired with a stimulus that already has the power to elicit the response. For example, a young child may learn to like books by being held and cuddled as his parents read to him. Books acquire the power to provoke positive feelings when they are paired with being held.

Stimulus-response learning, the second level of learning in Gagné's model, is operant conditioning. A cue serves as a signal for a response that is then reinforced. For example, the mother wants to teach her child to respond to the cue of seeing two pennies by saying the word "two". She will reinforce the child by praising him when he gives her the desired verbal response.

The third level of learning is **chaining.** Chaining requires the child to learn a set of stimulus-response connections in sequence. Pointing to each of a set of objects, as in counting, is a good example of chaining. To count things, a child must be able to carry out an appropriate sequence. Each pointing response serves as a stimulus for the next pointing behavior in the sequence.

Verbal association is Gagné's fourth level of learning. Verbal association is chaining involving words. Reciting numbers in order from 1 to 10 is an example. Here the child chains with symbols, not concrete objects.

Multiple discrimination is the fifth category of learning. This is the ability to distinguish among individual stimuli in a set. Multiple discrimination learning occurs frequently in school, particularly during the first few years. Basic early reading tasks such as learning to identify the letters of the alphabet or arabic numerals are familiar examples of multiple discrimination learning.

The sixth level of learning Gagné identifies is concrete concept learning. What Gagné calls a *concrete concept* is a rule used to classify concrete things. Learning to name concrete phenomena is a familiar example. For instance, when a child learns to apply the label "dog" not only to her own pet, but also to other canines such as those fierce creatures she sees around the neighborhood, she has learned a concrete concept. That is, she has learned a rule for classifying a particular set of tangible things.

The seventh form of learning is rule learning. Gagné uses the term "rule" in a very limited way. In Gagné's model, rule learning refers to learning relationships among concepts. For example, consider the simple rule "birds fly." This rule is composed of two concepts, the concept of birds and the concept of flying. To understand the rule, a child would need to have mastered both of these concepts.

The final level of learning is problem solving. As we have seen, *problem solving* may be defined as rule learning involving rule discovery. In problem solving, the learner uses lower level rules to come up with a higher order rule. For instance, a child may use the rules of addition, subtraction, multiplication, and division to solve complex story problems in his arithmetic workbook.

As shown in figure 6–1, Gagné assumes that the most complex forms of learning depend upon mastery of the simpler varieties of learning. Thus, problem solving is not possible without appropriate rule learning. Rule learning in turn requires concept learning. Concept learning is based upon the acquisition of multiple discriminations. Multiple-discrimination learning may in some instances require the mastery of verbal associations and chains. Finally, multiple discriminations, verbal associations, and chains will require previous signal and/or stimulus-response learning.

Gagné's model is useful in explaining why intellectual development proceeds as slowly as it does. It also helps us see how to accelerate intellectual growth. According to Gagné, development proceeds slowly in part because it takes time to acquire the component capabilities that are

dependencies among learning types

Figure 6–1   A general sequence for cumulative learning.

Adapted from "Contributions of Learning to Human Development," by R. M. Gagné, *Psychological Review*, 1968, *75*, 182. Copyright 1968 by the American Psychological Association. Reprinted by permission.

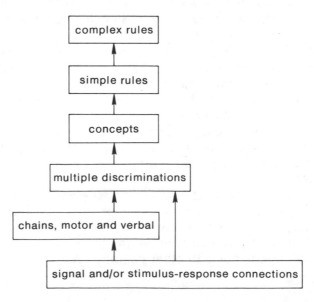

needed before complex learning tasks can be mastered. For instance, very young children cannot master complex mathematics because they have not yet mastered discriminations between numerals, basic number concepts, and simple mathematical rules. To accelerate development, we could systematically identify component capabilities and teach them.

Figure 6–2 shows Gagné's analysis of a task studied extensively by Piaget. The task requires the learner to recognize that liquid poured from a tall thin container into a short wide container does not change in volume. A glance at figure 6–2 (p. 148) shows how complex this concept is. And the expression on the child's face in the photo at the bottom of this page shows how perplexing the task can be for young children.

Piagetians believe that conservation is a capacity that children develop through the growth of intellectual structures. This internal development is based on biological make-up and interactions with the environment. Gagné suggests instead that conservation can be explained at least in part as a form of cumulative learning. In general, he finds that before children can comprehend the measurement of volume, which involves three-dimensional measurement, they must master two-dimensional measurement; and before they can learn tasks requiring measurement in two dimensions, they must be familiar with single-dimensional measurement.

SOCIALIZATION IN CONTEMPORARY CULTURE

According to the behavioral perspective, intelligent behavior is shaped by the environment in which it occurs (Skinner, 1971). The rules people use to classify their experiences, the ways they reason, the mechanisms they use to solve problems, and the intellectual skills they use to create art and other innovations are all determined by environment. Biology, of course, sets limits on intellectual functioning; but, except in cases of severe physical defects, biology does not account for the great variability we see in human intellectual behavior.

This little girl is learning about conservation of volume.

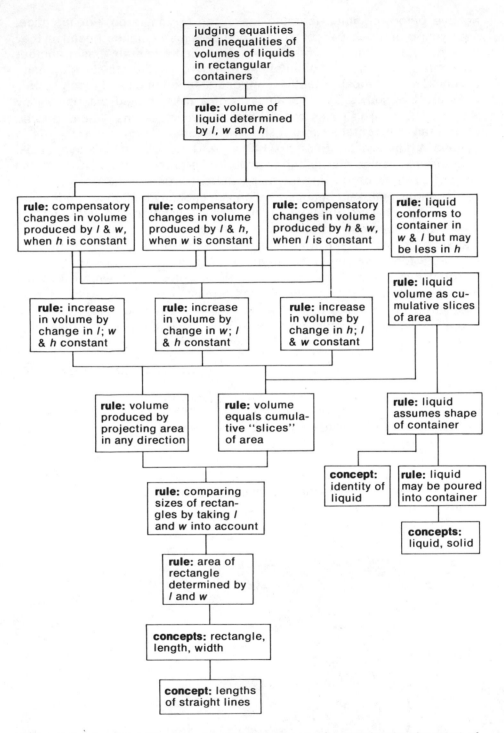

Figure 6–2 A cumulative learning sequence pertaining to the development of nonmetric judgments of liquid volume.

From "Contributions of Learning to human development," by R. M. Gagné, *Psychological Review*, 1968, *75*, 184. Copyright 1968 by the American Psychological Association. Reprinted by permission.

The Cultural Evolution of Behavioral Intelligence   Skinner (1971) asserts that the socialization practices we use to shape behavior are determined by a process of cultural evolution that is similar to biological evolution. Just as different types of plants and animals have developed physical characteristics that promote their survival (see chapter 3), so should different cultures evolve varied kinds of intelligent behavior to promote the survival of the culture. Socialization techniques that promote cultural survival are selected and maintained by being reinforced, while procedures that are harmful to the culture are not reinforced. Thus they tend to be eliminated. Research supports this expectation. Lesser, Fifer, and Clark (1965) studied verbal, spatial, reasoning, and numerical abilities among lower-class and middle-class children from different ethnic groups. Their most striking discovery was that there were distinctive patterns of abilities within the various ethnic groups. This finding is illustrated for black children and for Jewish children in figure 6–3. As shown in the figure, even though the average level of performance varied considerably between middle-class and lower-class children, the peaks and valleys were consistent within each of the two groups.

cultural survival and variations in ability patterns

Figure 6–3   Patterns of normalized mental ability scores for middle- and lower-class Negro and Jewish children.

From *Mental Abilities of Children from Different Social-class and Cultural Groups,* by G. S. Lesser, G. Fifer, and D. H. Clark. Monographs of the Society for Research in Child Development 30 (serial no. 102). Copyright 1965, The Society for Research in Child Development. Reprinted by permission.

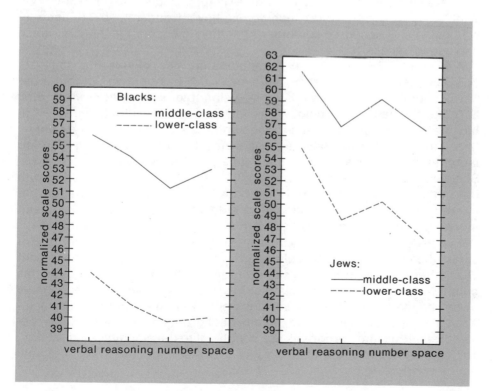

cultural variations
in the
socialization
of abilities

Recent research indicates that the varied patterns of intellectual abilities within different ethnic groups is in large measure determined by differences in socialization practices (Walberg & Marjoribanks, 1976). The particular skills that a given population wants to develop are systematically encouraged by the adults in that population. For example, in general, Jewish parents spend a significant amount of time and effort in developing verbal skills in their children. They are usually highly successful in promoting verbal skill development.

Behavioral Intervention in the Socialization Process Cultural evolution is an on-going process; new practices are continually being developed, and old ones are continually being discarded. In societies with relatively slow cultural change, the changes in environment that bring about changes in socialization are often of no particular concern and may go unnoticed. But behavioral theorists argue that in a rapidly changing society (such as ours today in America), it is vital to control our socialization practices and the outcomes of socialization.

the need for a
technology of
socialization

During the last two decades we have begun to develop an impressive behavioral technology. This technology shows promise for guiding not only intellectual development but other forms of human growth as well. But although behavioral techniques have already proved to be very useful (O'Leary & O'Leary, 1972), there are some unresolved issues related to their application. We must be sure that behavior modification is used in a way that benefits human development (Bandura, 1974). In a number of instances, behavioral procedures have been used to produce outcomes that are of questionable value. For example, according to Winett and Winkler (1972), behavioral techniques have frequently been used in schools to make children conform rather than to encourage independence and assertiveness.

the development
and control of
socialization
technology

side effects

A second question involves unanticipated side effects that may accompany behavioral programs. Willems (1974) has pointed out that a behavior modification program is an intrusion into an existing system. Just as natural science technology has led to air and water pollution, behavioral technology may also produce unforeseen ill effects. For example, Mrs. Allen, a preschool teacher, was worried that Billy was spending too much time with her and not enough time playing with the other children. She was able to solve this problem by reinforcing him for interacting with the other children and ignoring his bids for her attention. However, her strategy produced an unanticipated side effect. Billy began to spend much less time in learning activities than he had before her program.

The problem of unwanted side effects is particularly important to consider when members of one cultural group want to affect the development of another cultural group. We see programs of this kind frequently in this culture. For example, middle-class school teachers have the responsibility of promoting the intellectual development of children from lower socioeconomic groups and varied ethnic backgrounds. In many cases behavioral intervention programs are beneficial to development (e.g., Beller, 1973). Nevertheless, the possibility of unanticipated side effects should not be overlooked.

To help avoid side effects, the adults directing the program should be aware of the unique characteristics of the cultural groups they are teaching. For instance, a middle-class white teacher with black ghetto students should be familiar with the ghetto dialect. Otherwise he may unwittingly reinforce a child for using phrases that would be ridiculed in the child's own neighborhood.

One tactic that has been widely used in connection with both the goal and side effect problems is involving the children's families in program planning. For example, if families help select the goals of intervention, the likelihood is increased that the program objectives will reflect the aspirations of the individual families and their cultural backgrounds. For instance, consider an elementary school in which Indian parents were involved in curriculum planning. After reviewing the school curriculum, the parents asked if it would be possible to add tribal history to the traditional instruction in history. The parents pointed out that the standard program, while undoubtedly beneficial, did nothing to convey to the children their own background.

the control of side effects

Involving families also gives the professional some information about both limitations of the program and possible resources (Bergan, 1977). For example, the elementary school might plan a behavioral intervention program using praise as a reinforcer. But suppose that in that particular Indian culture, children are not generally praised for school work. Adequate performance of school-related tasks is considered a child's responsibility, and adults feel that there is no reason to praise children for merely doing their duty. This is a potential problem for the intervention program. Either another reinforcer needs to be found, or the planners must convince parents of the advantages of praise.

The Piagetian Perspective

One thing that is strikingly apparent to anyone who has spent much time with children is that their thinking is often quite different from that of adults. Imagine the following scene. A young mother is working on counting with her 3-year-old son Billy. Five objects are on the table in front of them. The mother begins instruction by saying: "Watch me, Billy. I'm going to count these blocks." She then proceeds with the counting while the child watches intently. Then she says: "Now you try it." He is delighted with the opportunity, and so proceeds to count the blocks. However, when he gets to the fifth block, he doesn't stop. Rather he continues, displaying his superior mathematical skill by counting all the way to 10. The fact that this requires counting some blocks more than once seems to be of no particular concern. His mother, however, objects pleasantly but firmly. She counts the blocks again and concludes decisively at the end of her efforts that there are five and only five blocks. She further points out that she has not added or subtracted any blocks from the pile. Then she asks the child to repeat the counting task. Billy responds, displaying mathematical sleight-of-hand normally attained only by accountants and tax lawyers. He counts the blocks once more and proudly states, "This time there are seven."

After repeated trials, his mother concludes that Billy does not see quantity in the same way that she does. The notion that the number of objects in a set might change without subtracting or adding any objects is not at all disturbing to Billy. Even though he can recite numbers in order and can point to objects as he counts them, he does not see the number of objects in a group as fixed when objects have neither been added to the set nor taken from it.

What accounts for the interesting, charming, and sometimes exasperating ways in which children think? Jean Piaget has devoted much of his professional life to this question.

INTELLIGENCE AS THE CONSTRUCTION OF KNOWLEDGE

Piaget sees intellectual development as an active process in which children construct knowledge from their encounters with the environment. Intellectual functioning produces internal structures that determine the way in which children use the information available to them. The internal structures are, of course, not directly observable, but we see evidence of their existence in the ways the children act.

Intellectual Functions   Piaget believes that human beings are innately programmed. Under appropriate environmental conditions, they will construct knowledge (Flavell, 1963). He identifies two types of intellectual functioning that result in knowledge construction. One is an innate tendency to organize experience rather than to react passively to stimulation. This tendency is easily seen in children's interactions with adults. For example, a father attempting to explain to his young child that the stuffed kitty that she sleeps with every night is really not alive said, "Kitty doesn't have feelings like we do." "That's all right," retorted the child. "I'll buy him some feelings." The idea of buying feelings was probably of the child's own making. An adult would not be likely to come up with this unique solution to the problem of giving kitty the gift of life.

organization in intellectual functioning

adaptation in intellectual functioning

The second type of intellectual functioning leading to the construction of knowledge is the tendency to adapt to the environment. Through adaptation, children take in new information. They gradually change their thinking patterns so that they correspond better to objective reality. Much of school learning is adaptive. For example, in arithmetic lessons, children take in new information about number concepts that they relate to their notions of quantitative reasoning.

structures and the control of thinking

Intellectual Structures   As they interact with the environment, organizing and adapting to their surroundings, children develop the internal structures that will determine how they will act. These structures may be thought of as mental mechanisms that control the child's thinking processes. For example, in explaining the basic facts of growth to Tony, a mother said: "Some day you'll grow up to be a man just like daddy, and grandpa, and Uncle Jim." The child registered no particular astonishment, but later he made a remark that showed how he had interpreted his mother's comment. "Mom," he said, "when I grow up to be three men, will I be married?" At this point, Tony's mother realized that he had understood the consequences of being an adult far differently than she had intended. What could cause a child to believe that he might grow up to be three different people? In Piaget's view, the source is the intellectual structures that the child uses to interpret his mother's statement.

Very young children can think in only the most concrete and personalized terms. Accordingly, it is not surprising that Tony would assume that his mother meant that he would grow up to be three people. Piaget's research suggests that it would be highly unlikely that a young child would have intellectual structures that would let him comprehend an abstract and objective notion such as being "like" someone. Without the structures he needed to comprehend the idea of "likeness," Tony fell back on a more concrete and personal interpretation of his mother's message.

The Behavioral Content of Intelligence   Piaget, like many other scientists, assumes that it is possible to tell something about how people think by what they say and do. Let's look at Tony again: We can make inferences about his internal structures from what he said about growing up to be three men. Of course, this remark taken alone would not provide very convincing evidence of the existence of a particular kind of intellectual structure. However, if the comment about growing up to be three persons were combined with other similar data, a more compelling case might be established.

inferring structure from content

DEVELOPMENTAL CHANGES

Piaget holds that children progress through a *fixed* developmental sequence marked by qualitative changes in thinking processes. He identifies three broad periods of development: the *sensorimotor period,* the *period of concrete operations* (which includes two subperiods), and the *period of formal operations.* Each period represents a distinct way of understanding experience. In the sensorimotor period the child deals with the environment mainly through physical acts. He understands objects in terms of the actions he associates with them. Thus, rattles are things to shake, and bottles and pacifiers are things to put in your mouth and suck. The onset of language begins the **preoperational subperiod** of the period of concrete operations. During this subperiod, the child learns to represent experiences through symbols. During the second part of the period of concrete operations, the child learns to classify concrete objects in terms of their relationships with other objects. Finally, in the period of formal operations, the child learns to represent not only concrete events but also hypothetical events with symbols.

The evolution from sensorimotor thought to formal operations involves a dramatic movement from concrete to abstract thought. We'll look at the overall changes from personalized to objective constructions and from concrete to abstract thinking below. The specific developmental tasks that the child learns during each of the three major periods will be described in chapter 7.

egocentrism

The Change from Personalized to Objective Thinking   During the early phases of development, children's thinking is highly personalized. Their ideas may be described as **egocentric;** they do not yet distinguish their personal constructions of events from objective reality (Piaget, 1954). For instance, young children often do not understand that their dreams are "less real" than events that have actually taken place (Piaget, 1954). A child's inability to understand the reality of a dream accurately is probably one reason why unpleasant dreams are often excessively frightening.

objectivity

As children develop, their knowledge of things becomes increasingly objective. According to Piaget, this objectivity develops because children become increasingly familiar with their own modes of thinking. However, as each new developmental stage begins, new thinking patterns emerge. As a consequence, additional egocentrism will come to the fore.

concrete thought

The Change from Concrete to Abstract Thinking   During the early stages of development, children's thinking processes are tied closely to concrete experiences. Moreover, when they run into abstract concepts, they generally redo them in concrete terms. For example, following a long class on religion, an adult who was steeped in the intricacies of abstract theology asked a 10-year-old to state the difference between Protestantism and Catholicism. The child responded tersely: "In the Catholic church they have big stained glass windows."

abstract thought

As development progresses, children become more sophisticated in handling abstract concepts. Eventually they can construct hypothetical realities that are far removed from concrete events. By the time they reach adolescence, they generally can handle the broad range of abstractions needed for living in a complex society. Maccoby and Modiano (1966) found that the movement toward abstract thinking is influenced by culture. They assessed children's judgments of similarities and differences among objects. For example, a child might be asked how a peach and a banana were alike and how they were different. Initially, they studied children from a rural village in Mexico and North American children. They found that Mexican children tended to classify on the basis of perceptual attributes such as color. Young North American children had the same tendency. However, older North American children used abstract concepts as a basis for classification. Thus, for instance, an older child might assert that a banana and a peach are alike because they are both fruits. In a second phase of their investigation, Maccoby and Modiano compared rural and urban Mexican children. They found that urban children raised around Mexico City behaved like the North American children. This result led the investigators to speculate that urban life fosters abstract thinking. They argue that urban children are taught to manipulate abstract concepts to control the environment.

HOW INTELLECTUAL DEVELOPMENT OCCURS

assimilation
defined

Development through Assimilation   One way that adaptation may occur is through **assimilation.** Assimilation is the process of acquiring new knowledge by relating it to existing knowledge. For example, suppose that Sara knows that if she shakes a rattle it will make a sound. Later she may learn that a box of dry cereal will also make a sound when it is shaken. At this time the cereal has become assimilated into the concept of things that make noise when they are shaken.

Much school learning involves assimilation, particularly in learning new names for previously acquired concepts. In biology, students learn that birds are warm-blooded aves and that people are homo sapiens. In geometry they are told that four-sided figures are quadrilaterals, and in chemistry they find out that water is H_2O.

Assimilation may occur in a number of ways. Behavioral procedures like modeling, cueing, and reinforcement (see chapter 2) are familiar techniques for promoting assimilation. For example, a teacher might model the use of the term "triangle" by displaying a triangular shape and saying: "This is a triangle." She then might cue the appropriate response from her students by saying: "What do we call this?" Finally, she might reinforce a correct response with verbal approval.

how assimilation occurs

Play is another means by which children may assimilate information from the environment. Piaget regards play as assimilation engaged in for pleasure (Flavell, 1963). For example, while playing with blocks, a child may build towers and learn something about principles of balance. Putting the blocks in piles may also convey information about quantity. For instance, the child may learn that one pile has more or less than another.

Play not only affords an opportunity for new learning, but also it provides an occasion for rehearsing what has already been learned. Play is often highly repetitive; children will use acquired knowledge over and over again. Thus, play serves a similar purpose to educational drill sessions. However, since children themselves, choose what to play with they are usually not bored the way they might be with classroom drill.

Development through Accommodation   A second way in which adaptation may occur is through **accommodations** to environmental conditions. Accommodations are changes in the way in which an individual acts on or conceptualizes things. For example, as discussed in chapter 4, quite early in life changes occur in eye-hand coordination that make it possible for a child to grasp objects. Grasping requires accommodation to the environment; a child must now reach toward the object he wants to grasp. Grasping not only constitutes a new way of interacting with the environment, but it also produces a new meaning for the grasped object. What was initially something to look at becomes something to touch and hold.

accommodation defined

After the earliest stages of development, accommodation generally involves changes in symbolic conceptualizations of the environment. For example, young children are quite willing to believe that bears can talk and that there is a fairy who puts money under the pillow after the loss of a tooth. However, as children develop, they become much more realistic. They accommodate to reality by exchanging their fantasies for objective ideas of things.

Piagetians argue that accommodation learning cannot generally be directly taught by adults (Turiel, 1973). For example, Jeremy asked his mother when the family was going on the picnic that they had been

how accommodation occurs

planning for some time. The mother responded: "We're going tomorrow." The next day at the picnic area the child asked: "Is this tomorrow?" The mother responded: "No, this is today." "But you said we were going on the picnic tomorrow," argued Jeremy. "Tomorrow is always the next day," said the mother. "Will it be tomorrow on Monday?" asked Jeremy. "No," said his mother, "it will be today." Pursuing the obvious problems with his mother's logic to their conclusion, the exasperated child reminded his mother that she had just said that this was today. With this remark, she decided that the concept of "tomorrow" simply could not be explained to Jeremy in words. For him, "tomorrow" had to refer to a concrete temporal event. He had no other way to think about the concept, and he was unable to make the necessary accommodation to comprehend his mother's explanation.

Piaget (1952) believes that children acquire new modes of representing experience only through a process of discovery. This process involves active interchange with the environment. For example, through repeated exposure to applications of the term "tomorrow" in different situations, Jeremy will eventually discover its meaning. According to Piaget, a child usually makes a discovery of this kind when his view of things is no longer adequate to explain his experience. A child whose way of representing reality is not suitable for handling his experience is in a state of *disequilibrium*. *Equilibrium* is restored when the child discovers a new concept that explains things adequately.

THE PIAGETIAN PERSPECTIVE AND SOCIALIZATION

As we have seen, Piaget believes that intellectual development occurs as a result of the interaction of biology and environment. The inborn tendencies to organize experience and to adapt to the environment determine how development takes place. The specific experiences of each individual set the scene for developmental progress. The result of this continuous interchange is the sequential development of sets of intellectual structures that control how experience will be interpreted.

environmental structure and discovery learning

The Construction of Developmental Environments Piagetians suggest that the principal role of adult care-givers is to structure the environment to further development. The environment should be arranged to give the child extensive opportunities to engage in discovery learning. In the early phases of development, learning must be tied closely to concrete experiences. Children should be given the chance to manipulate objects with their hands so that they can learn through direct experience how objects function in the environment. At the most advanced levels of development, the need to interact with concrete things is less pronounced than in the early periods. Nevertheless, some contact with concrete phenomena remains essential to promote development.

developmental environments and culture

In a pluralistic society, the environmental opportunities for discovery learning should be linked to the child's cultural background. This link is ensured for those aspects of socialization that occur in the home. However, it is not guaranteed for socialization that occurs outside of the home.

The everyday things that surround a child can be a source of discovery learning.

As more and more women enter the work force, institutions such as day-care centers and public and private schools are assuming a greater proportion of the responsibility for socialization. Thus the problem of finding ways to link learning to culture is becoming more important.

Discovery learning can be linked to the child's cultural background by using objects in the child's natural environment. For example, a teacher might use household objects from the children's backgrounds in teaching basic number concepts. This not only helps develop intellectual skills, but also tells the children that objects from their culture are useful and are valued by adults from different backgrounds.

The Universal Developmental Sequence Piaget says that all children progress through the same developmental sequence. The major focus of his work is a description of the ways in which children think at different levels in the sequence. In keeping with his belief in the universal character of intellectual development, Piaget places very little emphasis on individual or group differences in intellectual functioning. Accordingly, adults using a Piagetian framework are not likely to spend much time arguing about the extent of individual or group differences or about the genetic or environmental causes of such differences.

de-emphasizing individual and group differences

Some people might suggest that Piaget's position in regard to individual and group differences ignores one of the major social problems in our culture. However, Piaget's view does have the distinct advantage of not insulting the intellectual abilities of people outside of the middle-class mainstream who may receive low scores on a norm-referenced intelligence test. Moreover, his position encourages teachers to help all children to develop their intellectual abilities to the fullest possible extent.

As an alternative to concerns for differences in intellectual functioning, Piaget offers a concern for where the individual child is in the developmental sequence. From this standpoint, it is of no particular importance that one child is more or less advanced than another. What is important is to determine each child's current stage of intellectual development. This information provides the basis for constructing an environment that will stimulate discovery learning at an appropriate level. Determining a child's stage of intellectual development requires a thorough knowledge of the ways children think at different periods in the developmental sequence. This topic is a major focus of the next chapter.

emphasizing developmental level

Suggested Readings

Bandura, A. *Social learning theory.* Englewood Cliffs, N. J.: Prentice-Hall, 1977.

Elkind, D. *Children and adolescents: Interpretive essays on Jean Piaget* (2nd ed.). New York: Oxford University Press, 1974.

Gagné, R. M. Contributions of learning to human development. *Psychological Review,* 1968, *75,* 177–191.

Gagné, R. M. *The conditions of learning* (3rd ed.). New York: Holt, Rinehart & Winston, 1977.

Skinner, B. F. *About behaviorism.* New York: Knopf, 1974.

Willems, E. P. Behavioral technology and behavioral ecology. *Journal of Applied Behavior Analysis,* 1974, *7,* 151–166.

Zimmerman, B. J., & Rosenthal, T. L. Conserving and retaining equalities and inequalities through observation and correction. *Developmental Psychology,* 1974, *10,* 260–268.

Guiding Intellectual
Development

We know that children learn—that they develop intellectually. This chapter describes the sequence of that development, the impact of social institutions such as the home and the school on development, and what you can do to guide development at each of the major stages of intellectual growth. When you have finished the chapter, you should know the major periods of intellectual development and how the home, the school, and other institutions affect development. Finally you should be aware of some things you can do to guide intellectual growth during different developmental periods.

The question of how to guide development is generally thrust forcefully and abruptly on adults at the time of a child's birth. This was certainly the case for two young parents, Dick and Suzanne. Their venture into the responsibilities of parenthood began in typical fashion at 1 A.M. Dick was sound asleep, and Suzanne was nudging him gently, saying, "It's time." The message gradually seeped through, and Dick groaned: "It can't be time. It'll be time in the morning. Go back to sleep." Five minutes later Dick was carrying things to the car, the only remaining sign of his former peaceful state being the tousle of his hair.

Shortly after reaching the hospital, Suzanne went into the advanced stages of labor, and Dick was ushered into a hospital waiting room. There he sat for an incredibly long period quietly reading a dog-eared copy of *Newsweek* that he vaguely remembered seeing in a barber shop months earlier. After glancing at several articles, his half-hearted efforts to read were interrupted by a deep female voice: "First kid, huh?" Dick looked up abruptly. "How did she know?" he thought as he stammered a yes. "Hell, it ain't nothin. I got four," she said in reassuring tones. Dick agreed that birth was indeed a natural event and that he was not at all concerned by it; but in fact, of course, he was concerned. Through the long night his concerns steadily increased. He wondered why it was taking so long. He thought that something might have gone wrong, and yet he was sure that someone would have told him if there were any problems.

Shortly after dawn a nurse came into the room and called Dick's name. She was holding a small blanket. "Are you the father?" she said. "Yes," Dick replied. "Congratulations," said the nurse, "you have a fine baby girl." As the nurse pulled back the blanket revealing the infant's face, Dick could see the child's developing years flash before his eyes. He imagined his little girl in school. Then he saw her getting ready for the senior prom, and finally she appeared in a white dress marching down the aisle to matrimony. However, just as Dick was beginning to assimilate these visions, a questioning look appeared on the nurse's face and she began to pull back the blanket further. Then, with a look of surprise, she announced, "No, it's a boy."

Dick was stunned, not only by the abrupt change in the child's sex, but also by the change that he knew had occurred in his and Suzanne's lives. Yesterday, they had been a couple. Today, he was the father of a baby boy and Suzanne was a mother. How would they guide the growth of this child? Suddenly Dick realized that this was a question with which he and Suzanne would be concerned for a significant portion of their lives.

In this chapter, we shall describe the process of guiding intellectual development in relation to four age levels corresponding to major developmental periods and subperiods identified by Piaget (see table 7–1). The discussion will focus on developmental accomplishments of children of varying ages and on socialization practices we can apply to bring about those accomplishments.

The Sensorimotor Period

The newborn child is a seemingly helpless creature with an extremely limited range of abilities. Yet, during the first 2 years of life, the child will make impressive progress. Much of this progress will be in the form of a rapid increase in the ability to coordinate movements with information taken in through the senses. Advancements in sensorimotor ability will produce increased physical control over the environment. In addition, the child's new sensorimotor skills will be responsible for the development of very significant intellectual competencies.

Piaget has conducted extensive investigations of the developmental achievements of children during the first 2 years of life. His studies, based in large measure on observations of his own three children, have provided the guiding framework for much of the research that has been carried out on early intellectual growth. The major intellectual accomplishments that occur during the early years take place in what Piaget calls the sensorimotor period of development. Most achievements during this period occur before the child begins to use language.

SENSORIMOTOR DEVELOPMENT

As you might expect, the sensorimotor period derives its name from the fact that the intellectual activities that occur then require the coordination of sensory experience and movement. Sensory experience (that is, information received through the sense organs) gives children their first knowledge about the nature of objects. Movement affords them a means to manipulate things. By using their sensory and motor abilities together, children act upon the environment and observe the consequences of their actions on the things around them.

Table 7–1   Periods of intellectual development

period	major accomplishments
Sensorimotor intelligence (ages birth-2 years)	Representing concrete experiences through physical acts.
Concrete operational intelligence (ages 2–11)	Representing concrete events with symbols and rules.
Preoperational thought (ages 2–7)	Using symbols.
Later concrete operational thought (ages 7–11)	Using rules to relate concrete objects.
Formal operational intelligence (ages 11 or 12 through adulthood)	Acquiring abstract thinking ability.

Object Permanence   The central achievement of the sensorimotor period is the realization that objects have some permanence that is independent of a particular time or location. According to Piaget, newborn infants do not distinguish between objects and their perceptual experience of them. An object exists when it is perceived. When it is removed from the perceptual field, so far as the infant is concerned, it no longer exists. For example, when a ball is taken out of sight, it no longer exists for the infant. The inability to recognize object permanence is egocentric in the Piagetian sense of the term (see chapter 6). The infant does not see that there is an objective world beyond his or her personal experience. The eventual realization that objects exist independently of the child's perception of them is the first achievement of objectivity in intellectual development.

Infants do several things that are congruent with Piaget's assertion that they do not initially recognize the permanence of objects. For example, during the first 2 months of life, infants do not generally look for objects that have disappeared from view (Piaget, 1954). They are, however, able to tell when an object has disappeared. For instance, a sudden disappearance of an object causes an infant to stop sucking (Bower, 1967). They also remember objects that have disappeared. Bringing back an object will cause the infant to begin sucking again (Bower, 1967). Since infants can tell when an object has been removed from view and they do remember the object, their failure to search for it cannot be explained by the inability to recognize disappearance or to remember what was previously seen. Thus, two alternatives to Piaget's views are ruled out, while his assumption that the infant does not search because he assumes that the absent object no longer exists remains a possibility.

About the beginning of the third month of life, children start to search for objects that have disappeared (Piaget, 1952). However, they make errors that suggest that they do not recognize object permanence. For example, if an infant has repeatedly seen an object disappear behind one end of a screen and reappear at the other end of the screen, he or she will learn to look for the object where it typically has reappeared in the past. However, without a screen, infants will still look in the direction that an object has previously moved, even when the object is in full view going the opposite way. Bower (1971) conducted an experiment involving a toy train that illustrates this. As shown in figure 7-1, if the train typically moved in one direction, but on a particular occasion reversed its path, the infants tended to look in the direction toward which the vehicle *usually* moved rather than in the direction that it was *actually* going. Bower suggests that the behavior of the infants in his study was governed by this simple rule: if an object has appeared in a particular location in the past, it will appear in that location again. This rule does not require the assumption of object permanence.

At about 5 months of age, infants will begin to search for missing objects with their hands as well as with their eyes. Initially the search must be prompted by placing the hidden object in the child's hand before it is moved into the field of vision (Bower, Broughton, & Moore, 1970; Piaget, 1952). Piaget believes that the prompt is necessary because the child does not yet understand that an object has a location when it is not in view. A simpler explanation would be that the child does not have the

lack of object
permanence and
egocentrism

evidence
supporting
Piaget's findings
on object
permanence

motor coordination to conduct the search. However, Gratch (1972) has shown that infants are quite capable of retrieving objects that are not removed from the visual field. He found that 23 out of 24 6-month-old children could conduct a successful search for objects hidden behind a transparent cloth, even though infants of that age generally cannot retrieve objects placed under an opaque cloth.

A few months after children have passed their first birthday, their searching becomes highly effective. Children between the ages of 14 and 16 months can generally find a hidden object even when the object has been put inside a container and moved from one hiding place to another. At this point, the child apparently realizes that objects do have an existence in space and time that is independent of their perceptual experience.

Figure 7–1   A child's observation of a moving train

From "The Object in the World of the Infant," by T. G. R. Bower, *Scientific American* 1971, *225*, 39. Copyright © 1971 by Scientific American, Inc. All rights reserved.

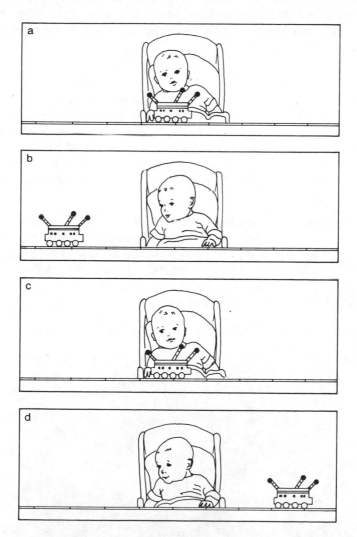

Symbolic Representation and Causality   To recognize that objects endure independently of perceptual encounters with them, the child must be able to represent objects in some symbolic form. The child's first ability to use symbolic representation is acquired during the sensorimotor period. The first symbols are motor movements. For example, a child may see one of her toys drop from a nearby shelf and then represent this event by dropping her arms to her sides. Likewise, she may see a door open and open her clenched fist to signify that event.

movements as symbols

As children learn to represent environmental happenings and acquire the knowledge that objects have an independent existence, they begin to recognize that things that occur have a cause. Piaget (1954) assumes that at first children believe that their own thoughts control the things that happen in the world around them. However, through sensorimotor interactions with the environment, this early egocentric view is replaced by the objective recognition of physical causality. For example, as children learn to reach for and to grasp objects, they can see that their actions may affect objects. A child will learn that if he shakes his crib it will move, and that if he lets go of his rattle it will fall. As Piaget (1954) observes, children take great delight in discoveries of this kind. They often insist on seemingly endless repetitions of small acts that bring about some desired effect.

causality

SOCIALIZATION

During the sensorimotor period, the child needs a stimulating and responsive environment. The principal institution responsible for giving the infant such an environment is, of course, the home. However, day-care facilities are assuming an increasing role in socializing infants. One issue of concern to many developmentalists is ensuring that increased reliance on day-care institutions will not be detrimental to infant development.

Guiding Sensorimotor Development   There is evidence that a child's early environment influences his or her subsequent intellectual development. For example, Elardo, Bradley, and Caldwell (1975) found that measures of the types of home environment provided for children at the age of 6 months are strongly related to children's performance on the Stanford-Binet Intelligence Scale at age 3. Later, Bradley and Caldwell

early home environment and intelligence

Infants learn by playing with bulky toys they can pick up and explore.

(1976) discovered that the direction of changes in intellectual functioning occurring between infancy and the early childhood years is also related to home environment.

One variable identified in research as important to intellectual growth is stimulation. The child's physical environment during the sensorimotor period should provide adequate but not excessive sensory stimulation (Appleton, Clifton, & Goldberg, 1975). A major portion of children's early intellectual development is based on sensory contact with objects. To stimulate development, infants must have a variety of sensory inputs. As pointed out earlier, the failure to have adequate sensory stimulation can have disastrous consequences. There is also evidence that extra direct sensory stimulation can be beneficial to intellectual development. For example, Rice (1977) found that premature babies who were given systematic stroking and cuddling scored significantly higher on a test of infant intelligence than infants who had not received the systematic stimulation.

the need for stimulation

During the early months, feeding is an excellent opportunity for sensory stimulation (Appleton, Clifton, & Goldberg, 1975). Being held offers varied sensations that are associated with touch and with changes in body position that occur as the child is picked up. Moreover, the face of the adult provides visual stimulation, and whatever words are spoken offer auditory experiences.

ways to provide stimulation

In addition, objects can be used to supplement the direct stimulation given by contact with adults. For example, a mobile hung over a crib gives interesting visual stimulation. And a music box can be used for auditory stimulation.

As children gain control over their motor movements, objects that can be manipulated are beneficial. They should be large enough that they will not be swallowed, since most infants immediately put all objects into their mouths. Rattles, busy boxes, and other crib toys are familiar examples of things that provide opportunities for manipulation. Crib gymnasiums made up of rings and bars that the child can grasp are also useful.

During the later part of the first year of life, children generally acquire basic locomotion skills. When this occurs, many parents are tempted to prevent them from moving about by installing gates or by using a play pen. But available research suggests that these devices should be used sparingly. For example, White (1972) found that parents who gave their infants lots of chances to move about and to explore their environments tended to have children who became highly competent during the early years of life.

In addition to providing stimulation and opportunities for manipulation and exploration, adults should be responsive to a child's behavior. Infants are born with a very limited set of capabilities to influence their environments. It is important that they be encouraged to use those abilities to produce reinforcement. In this way they learn that they can achieve some control over their surroundings (Appleton, Clifton, & Goldberg, 1975). For example, during the early months of life, the infant's principal means of affecting his environment is crying. At this stage, crying generally indicates either the need for food or some form of discomfort. When adults respond to a child's crying with food or comfort, they show the

the importance of responsiveness

child that his or her actions may have an effect. This may have a beneficial influence on development. For instance, Bell and Ainsworth (1972) found that infants whose mothers were responsive to early crying showed less distress and better communication skills than infants whose mothers were reluctant to respond to early crying.

Responsiveness to infant behavior can also be used as a basis for teaching a child specific skills. For instance, Etzel and Gewirtz (1967) increased the smiling of infants by smiling back and giving verbal approval when the infants smiled. Responsive socialization requires the adult to be alert. You cannot decide to provide instruction in a given skill at a fixed time. Rather, you must wait for the right opportunity and seize it when it comes.

Adult attempts to force instruction when the moment is not right can be frustrating for a child. For example, after hearing his infant son say "da da da" on several occasions at feeding time, one father decided that it would be useful to give this verbalization a meaning. He reasoned that the child could probably be taught to use the "da da da" as a request for food, if he were given food immediately after he said it. Consequently at the next feeding, the father waited patiently for the child to say "da da da" at which time he fully intended to offer the infant some baby food. However, even though the father modeled the desired response several times, the infant did not say "da da da." Instead he looked longingly at the food for some time and then began to cry. At this point, the patient teacher fed the child immediately and gave up further attempts at language instruction.

socialization in the family

Socializing Institutions   The major socializing institution responsible for sensorimotor development is the child's family. Accordingly, one approach to enhancing intellectual growth is to give parents research results concerning beneficial socialization practices.

Several programs have been carried out that prove that parents can be taught to further the intellectual development of their infants. For example, Gordon (1969) conducted a large-scale program in which home visitors taught parents specific child-rearing techniques aimed at fostering intellectual growth during the early years of life. The program relied heavily on Piagetian theory. The parents were instructed to perform activities that would promote capabilities such as the recognition of object permanence. For instance, parents were shown how to play a hidden object game in which a toy on a string was hidden from the child's view. By pulling the string, the child could return the object to his field of vision. The purpose of this game was to help the child see that objects that have disappeared from view may still exist. Gordon's program was effective in stimulating intellectual growth. By the time the children in his study reached 1 year of age, those infants whose parents had received home visitor training were intellectually ahead of those who had not. By the time the children reached 4 years of age, those who had participated in the program over a relatively long time period were consistently superior in intellectual performance to those whose parents had not been trained (Beller, 1973).

Although the home is the major institution responsible for guiding early development, it is likely that it will have a less prominent role in the future. As increasing numbers of women work, there will probably be greater and greater reliance on infant day-care programs. Large numbers of commercial day-care centers have already sprung into being, and the number of such centers will very likely continue to increase in the years ahead.

day care

Can day-care centers effectively promote early development? Some studies dealing with this question have produced rather discouraging results. For example, Schwarz, Strickland, and Krolick (1974) studied the behavior of 4-year-old children who had spent differing amounts of time in a day-care center. Children who had spent 2 years or more in day care were less cooperative with adults and more aggressive with both adults and peers than children who had spent only a few months in day care.

Notwithstanding these negative results, a number of studies have reported encouraging findings. For instance, Macrae and Herbert-Jackson (1976) investigated the behavior of 2-year-olds who had spent differing amounts of time in day care and found day care to be beneficial to both social and intellectual growth. Children who had spent at least 13 months in day care were better able to get along with peers, were more effective in problem solving, and were better at planning than children who had spent between 1 and 6 months in day care.

One conclusion that can be drawn from these studies is that the kind of day-care program may markedly affect the child's progress. This conclusion is especially important in light of the long debate over whether government-subsidized day care should be custodial care or care directly aimed at enhancing children's development. The prospect of widespread custodial day care is frightening. Merely meeting the infant's physical needs is not sufficient to ensure adequate development (Appleton, Clifton, & Goldberg, 1975).

Several factors should be considered to make sure that day-care facilities provide high quality developmental environments. One of these is the training of the staff (Appleton, Clifton, & Goldberg, 1975). Staff should be thoroughly trained to work with young children. They should know the basic principles of child development and should have had supervised experience using those principles with young children.

A second factor is the ratio of staff to children (Appleton, Clifton, & Goldberg, 1975). If there are too many children for staff to work with, care may quickly become routine. Attention to individual needs will suffer. Under these conditions, there is a good chance that the interactions between staff and children will become impersonal. Moreover, the staff members may become unresponsive to the children.

A third factor that may influence the quality of day-care services is the environment. Beyond the obvious requirements that the environment should provide adequate space for play, stimulating materials, opportunities for outdoor exercise, and a suitable place to nap, there is some evidence that the openness of the facility may be important. Twardosz, Cataldo, and Risley (1974) studied the effects of an open environment design for day care on the behavior of staff and children. They found that the open environment shown in figure 7–2, in which there were no walls or partitions separating activity areas, greatly increased the amount of time that children could be seen by adult staff members. Moreover, openness increased the extent to which staff activities were visible to the staff supervisor.

Twardosz and her colleagues argue that the visibility provided by the open environment increases the likelihood that the adults will be aware of children's needs and take whatever action is necessary to fulfill them. In addition, they say that staff supervision is more effective. Finally, they point out that their data showed that openness had no discernible negative effects. Children slept as well at nap time and pursued learning activities with as much attention and productivity in the open setting as in an enclosed environment.

Figure 7–2   Four views of the open environment Infant Center. Top left, view of the play, sleep, and diapering areas from the feeding area. Top right, view of the receiving and diapering areas from the food preparation area. Bottom left, view of the play, feeding, food preparation, and receiving areas from the sleep area. Bottom right, view of the feeding and food preparation areas from the play area.

From "Open Environment Design for Infant and Toddler Day Care," by S. Twardosz, M. F. Cataldo, and T. R. Risley, *Journal of Applied Behavior Analysis*, 1974, 7, 531. Reprinted by permission.

The Preoperational Subperiod

When children are about 3, they move into what Piaget calls the *preoperational subperiod* of development. According to Piaget, this phase generally lasts until a child is about 7 years old. However, some investigators (e.g., Brainerd, 1973, 1976) feel that children usually progress beyond preoperational development earlier than the age of 7. This difference exists because Piaget requires children to give verbal explanations to show their thinking patterns. In contrast, Brainerd and others judge children's developmental levels by watching them solve problems. They do not require the children to give verbal explanations. Children can solve problems before they can explain them. If you use the ability to solve problems as the critical index of development, you can say that most children progress beyond the preoperational subperiod at least 2 years earlier than Piaget's research would suggest.

PREOPERATIONAL THOUGHT

Preoperational development is a subperiod within the larger period of concrete operations. Concrete operations is a developmental period characterized by the ability to represent concrete objects with symbols (Flavell, 1963). The preoperational child cannot carry out the logical thinking that is possible later in the concrete operational period.

The Use of Symbols   The central achievement of this subperiod is the development of the ability to use symbols to represent concrete experiences. As we have seen, the first symbols the child uses are physical acts. A toddler may represent the opening of a door by opening his mouth, or he may symbolize a falling object by dropping his hand to his side.

types of symbolic behavior

Piaget believes that, as children begin to represent objects through action, they form mental images of their representations (Flavell, 1963). These are the first internal symbols the child can use for referring to concrete phenomena. For example, a small child may think of the feeding experience by imagining herself sucking.

When children have developed the ability to represent experience through action and images, they begin to attach words to their representations. Words make the child's symbols public; they involve meanings that may be shared by other people. According to Piaget (1954), words are not necessary for the child to represent experience in symbols. Language begins *after* the child has already acquired the ability to represent experience with actions and images.

Thinking Processes   As young children begin to use words, it is readily apparent that they think in quite different ways from adults or older children. Preoperational thinking tends to be highly concrete. For example, consider the scene in which a father comes to the breakfast table one morning and announces proudly: "I have lost 2 pounds." His young son

concrete thinking in the preoperational subperiod

responds immediately: "I'll help you find them." Not only is this unwanted assistance, but also it reveals a very unusual interpretation of the father's message. Even though the child has not seen the lost pounds running around, he thinks of the pounds in concrete enough terms to assume that if they have been lost, they can surely be found again.

the failure to distinguish between symbols and experience

Preoperational thought also involves the inability to distinguish between concrete experience and the symbols used to represent that experience. The following exchange illustrates this point:

"Have words got strength?" "—Yes." "—Tell me a word which has strength." "—The wind." "—Why has the word 'wind' got strength?" *"Because it goes quickly."* "—Is it the word or the wind which goes quickly?" *"—The wind."* (Piaget, 1963, p. 45)

preoperational egocentrism

In Piaget's view, the young child's failure to distinguish between the properties of symbols and the properties of concrete things is another form of egocentrism. Children make up their own personal symbols. Piaget says that children cannot tell the properties of symbols from those of concrete things because they cannot distinguish their own ideas from objective facts.

The preoperational child's egocentrism comes out in some other ways, too. For instance, these children often attach their own traits to objects that do not share those traits. We all know young children who give human characteristics such as life, feelings, and the ability to use language to their favorite stuffed animals.

USING PLAY TO FIND OUT HOW CHILDREN THINK AT DIFFERENT DEVELOPMENTAL STAGES

One way that you can gain information about a child's intellectual level is to use Piaget's intellectual tasks in play situations. For instance, suppose you want to get some idea about a child's understanding of ordered relations in a series. You might begin, as Piaget did, by getting a large set of sticks that vary in length. During a play period, give the child a set of 10 sticks and ask him or her to arrange them in order from the shortest to the longest. Then give the child nine more sticks. Say that these were forgotten and need to be inserted in the right places. Have the child count as many of the sticks as possible. Then remove those sticks that represent higher numbers than the child can count. Now point to one of the sticks, and ask how many stairs a doll will have to climb to reach that point. Then scramble the sticks and ask the same question again. This will make it necessary for the child to reconstruct the series before responding.

Children in the advanced stages of the concrete operational period will respond correctly to all of these tasks. Preoperational children will not, because they will not be able to remember that an object in a series is bigger than the object that precedes it and at the same time smaller than the object that follows it.

Another feature that distinguishes preoperational thinking from more advanced forms of thought has to do with the concept of causality. For the preoperational child, any set of events that occur at the same time may be regarded as causally related. For example, in one of Piaget's (1963) experiments, a young child said that the position of the hands on the clock determined when the sun would come up and when it would go down. The child explained the clock's remarkable powers simply by noting that the position of the clock's hands and the sun's movements were related.

preoperational concepts of causality

Children become increasingly careful in assigning causes to their experiences after they have learned that some events occur together by chance (Berzonsky, 1975). We do not know for certain how children learn this. However, the little evidence we have suggests that it comes through concrete experiences involving manipulating objects (Berzonsky, 1975).

The most important characteristic of preoperational thought is the inability to judge concrete relationships, such as equality or inequality, logically. For example, a preoperational child may think that two rows of four sticks each are not equal simply because the sticks in one row are farther apart than the sticks in the other row. Likewise, the child may say that rolling a long thin clump of clay into a small ball reduces the amount of clay.

inability to conceptualize relationships between objects

This inability to classify relationships among things logically often shows up in interactions with adults on learning tasks. For example, a teacher trying to teach preschool children basic number concepts may find that, although the children can count, they have trouble understanding the equality or inequality of sets. They may not know when one set has more than, the same as, or less than another. Even when they apparently understand these concepts, their weak grasp on them may easily be overwhelmed by a perceptual "riddle" such as the set with the smallest number being the longest.

SOCIALIZATION

During the 1960s psychologists and educators began to challenge the belief that intellectual development is largely controlled by heredity. At that time, we began to gather evidence that early experiences play a critical role in the course of intellectual growth (Bloom, 1964; Hunt, 1961). The nation was then prepared to increase the resources spent on wiping out the differences in academic performance that had always existed among different cultural subgroups. The combination of scientific evidence and a national commitment to developing the full intellectual potential of all our children led to an increase in research. This research was designed to identify environmental conditions that influence early learning. We began massive social programs aimed at increasing intellectual competence during and beyond the early childhood years. Unfortunately, these far-reaching goals of the 1960s have not been achieved. Nevertheless, the effort to achieve them produced useful information and greatly expanded our resources for guiding preoperational socialization.

Table 7–2   Some environmental factors related to intellectual functioning

name	description
Achievement press	Parents' aspirations and standards relating to intellectual achievement
Language in the home	Parents' use of language, awareness of child language, and encouragement of correct language use
Academic guidance	Parents' assistance with child's academic tasks
Family activeness	Provision of variety of learning opportunities for children
Range of social interactions	Variety of child's social contacts outside the home
Home intellectuality	Activities and materials in the home that may foster intellectual growth
Availability of adult models	Availability of models of varied occupational levels

Guiding Preoperational Development   Two students of Benjamin Bloom at the University of Chicago, R. H. Davé (1963) and R. M. Wolf (1964), pioneered in studying environmental factors related to intellectual functioning. They interviewed parents, trying to identify the kinds of socialization processes that were occurring in the children's homes that were positively related to intellectual performance. The findings of other researchers (e.g., Henderson, Bergan, & Hurt, 1972; Henderson & Merritt, 1968; Walberg & Marjoribanks, 1976) have agreed with the early findings of Davé and Wolf. They have shown that environment is related to children's intellectual performance not only during the early childhood years, but also later on.

Various groups of environmental factors have been looked at in different studies. Henderson (1972), relying heavily on the early work of Davé and Wolf, studied several conditions that represent the kinds of variables that are related to intellectual functioning. These are summarized in table 7–2.

One variable that is strongly related to intellectual performance in young children is achievement press (Henderson, 1972). *Achievement press* is the hopes of parents concerning their own intellectual achievement and the achievement of their children. In addition, it includes the standards that parents set for achievement and for rewarding education.

achievement press

A second variable Henderson relates to intellectual performance is the quality of language in the home. It includes the way in which parents use language, their awareness of how their child uses language patterns, and their efforts to encourage the child to use standard grammar.

language

A third factor that Henderson studied is the extent to which parents provide academic guidance for their children. Parents who are willing to help their children with academic tasks are far more likely to have children who do well intellectually than parents who are not willing to give academic help.

guidance

Books and other materials may stimulate intellectual growth.

The way that academic help is given would, of course, vary with the age of the child. Preschool children are often not used to the forms of teaching typically used with older children. They will generally not know how to sit for long periods passively taking in new information from an adult. Nor will they be familiar with the pattern of answering questions when it is clear that the adult already knows the answers. Because young children do not know these patterns, adults often think the children have short attention spans. This is not necessarily the case. Given strong enough incentives, preschool children will pay full attention to intellectual tasks for long time periods (Staats, Brewer, & Gross, 1970). However, we have no indication that a long time spent on a single intellectual activity is in the long run better than brief attention paid to a variety of activities. If strong reinforcement is not available, young children should usually be taught for only brief periods. To be sure that the child is interested in learning, some adults give instruction only when children request it (White, 1972). For example, a child's question may set the stage for a short lesson. The adult may increase the chance that the child will ask more questions by modeling and reinforcing question asking (Henderson & Garcia, 1973).

A fourth variable that Henderson finds positively associated with intellectual functioning is the activity of the family. Children whose families provide them with a variety of different kinds of learning opportunities both inside and outside the home tend to perform well intellectually.

activity level

A fifth variable related to intellectual functioning is the family's range of social interactions. Families that have many social contacts outside the home have children who function better intellectually than families who stick to home.

social interaction

A sixth variable identified is the intellectuality of the home. This includes such items as the kinds of toys and games that the children have to foster intellectual growth. For example, games that involve counting or identifying letters help teach young children basic skills. Children who have educational games and toys, are more likely to do well intellectually than

intellectuality

FOSTERING CREATIVITY IN CHILDREN

Our society's most precious resource is the creativity of its people. Ironically, most cultures—including ours—do much to stifle creativity. The stifling begins at different ages in different societies, but in general it is particularly noticeable during the elementary school years. Fortunately, there *are* a number of things you can do to stimulate creativity in children. Here are some of them.

1. Encourage children to try new ways of thinking.
2. Model ways to think of new ideas by techniques such as thinking of as many solutions to a problem as you can in a short time period.
3. Separate idea generation from idea evaluation. For instance, when you've asked the child to do something new, don't start off by criticizing him for the first thing he comes up with. Set aside a time to evaluate ideas only after several ideas have been generated.
4. Let children evaluate their own ideas. They will not only learn something about the quality of their work, but also how to judge their own efforts.
5. Finally, encourage children to follow through on their ideas by making creative products such as art work, stories, and simple scientific experiments.

children who do not have this kind of stimulation. The leisure activities of other family members also contribute. Parents with hobbies that involve some thought and imagination are more likely to have children who do well intellectually than parents who spend their free time sitting in front of the television set.

model availability

The final variable that Henderson finds is related to intellectual functioning is the availability of adult models who represent a variety of occupational levels. Children who come from homes that give them the opportunity to interact with adults with relatively high-status careers as well as adults with relatively low-status jobs do better on tests of intellectual skill than children from homes that do not give them the chance to see adults in a variety of different job roles.

We cannot determine the separate contributions of each of these individual environmental factors because they are highly interrelated (Henderson, Bergan, & Hurt, 1972; Walberg & Marjoribanks, 1976). What we can say is that parents who value education and encourage intellectual growth are likely to foster high levels of intellectual achievement in their children. Moreover, a favorable environment is likely to affect a child for a long time. For example, Henderson (1972) found a strong relationship between the environments of 5- and 6-year-old children and their academic performance 3 years later. McCall, Appelbaum, and Hogarty (1973) studied the relationship between parent behavior and positive changes in IQ over a much longer period. They found that positive changes in IQ from 2½ years of age to 17 years of age were related to the extent that parents actively tried to accelerate the intellectual development of their children. These changes were also related to consistent discipline.

Socializing Institutions During the early childhood years, the child is exposed to more socializing institutions that affect his intellectual development than during the sensorimotor period. The family continues to be dominant in guiding intellectual growth. However, preschool programs and television also become important at this stage.

An early training project by Gray and Klaus (1970) showed that a joint home-school program encouraged intellectual development. In this study, preschool children were taught by trained teachers during a summer program. This summer training was followed by weekly home visits during the school year. The program was designed to foster attitudes and abilities associated with success in school. The attitudes encouraged through the program included the desire to achieve success in school, interest in academic tasks, and persistence in working on academics. The abilities encouraged included perceptual discrimination skills and language development.

family
interventions

Some children in the project received training and home visits for 3 years, others for 2 years. These children were compared to groups who did not receive training or home support. The evaluation lasted for 3 years after the last training sessions. The children who had received training and home visits did consistently better than those who had not on the Stanford-Binet Intelligence Scale (Terman & Merrill, 1960). However, the children's IQs went down after the training was ended. And the early differences between the children who had received instruction and home visits and those who had not disappeared by the time the children reached the fourth grade. These results led Gray to conclude that, although early intervention programs may be beneficial, they cannot carry the entire burden of education.

Despite the current widespread recognition of the effects of the home on early learning, the major focus of early intervention programs has been in the preschools. During the 1960s, our national commitment to young children led to the massive Head Start program. It was aimed at developing the intellectual growth of low-income children. In the late 1960s, the Westinghouse Learning Corporation (1969) published an evaluation that assessed the effectiveness Head Start. The results were disappointing. There was no evidence that Head Start had any long-term effect on children's growth.

Head Start

After the Westinghouse report, the Office of Child Development (OCD) within the Department of Health, Education and Welfare sponsored an evaluation of varying Head Start programs. Head Start was implemented in many ways, according to widely different educational philosophies. OCD investigators reasoned that the overall program evaluation might not have found significant program effects because of the wide variation in the quality of individual programs. They evaluated specific Head Start programs and found that different programs produced different outcomes. Highly structured, academic programs were found to have been beneficial (Bissell, 1970). This basic finding has been corroborated in other investigations (Beller, 1973).

As children enter the preoperational phase, television becomes a force in their socialization. Of all households in the United States, 95% have one or more working television sets (Leifer, Gordon, & Graves, 1974). For families with children, more than 98% own sets (Lyle, 1972). In the average home, television sets are used for more than 6 hours each day. Children begin to watch television extensively when they are 2 or 3 years old. And they are active viewers; they have distinct program choices and viewing times.

Television can be used to encourage the child's intellectual growth. This has been demonstrated in an evaluation of the Children's Television Workshop program, *Sesame Street* (Ball & Bogatz, 1970; Bogatz & Ball, 1971). The Children's Television Workshop began to work on *Sesame Street* in the summer of 1968. Their major goal was to produce a television show for preschool children that would be both educational and entertaining. The designers of the show achieved their aims. In November of 1969, over 200 educational television stations in the United States began to broadcast *Sesame Street*. Since then, the show has been broadcast in more than 50 nations outside of the United States. Its audience over the years has run in the tens of millions.

Shortly after work began on *Sesame Street,* the Educational Testing Service (ETS) in Princeton, New Jersey, was given a contract to evaluate the program. Over a 3-year period, the ETS staff extensively studied the effects of the show on children's learning. Their evaluation showed that for children from both the lower and middle socioeconomic levels, *Sesame Street* was effective in teaching basic skills such as the ability to recognize numbers and letters. Moreover, some of these children were able to use these skills in learning other things like how to recognize words. *Sesame Street* was not effective in teaching complex skills like number concepts (Bogatz & Ball, 1971). However, those skills can be taught by television if they are broken down into small parts and each part is taught separately (Henderson, Swanson, & Zimmerman, 1975).

A particularly significant, but not unexpected, finding in the *Sesame Street* evaluation is that the children who watched the show the most learned the most. This result immediately raised the question of what controlled the viewing behavior of the children. We have no answer to this question. However, the evaluation did show that the children who spent the most time watching *Sesame Street* were the children whose parents watched the program with them.

The Concrete Operational Years

The age range for the advance concrete operational subperiod is only a general framework. According to Piaget, it begins around age 7 and ends about 12. But as mentioned earlier, some theorists argue that children have concrete operational skills well before the age of 7. There is also some evidence that, with instruction, children can move beyond concrete operational thought before they reach the age of 12 (e.g., Siegler, Liebert, & Liebert, 1973). Thus, the 7 to 12 range should not be taken as absolute.

CONCRETE OPERATIONAL THOUGHT

When children acquire concrete operational thought, they can think logically. With the aid of formal education, they can learn the basic language and quantitative skills they need to be effective in the adult world. Although many children have impressive logical powers during this phase, their thinking tends to be highly concrete. That is, they use logic to think about concrete things rather than abstract possibilities. Moreover, when they are faced with abstract concepts, they generally think about them in a concrete way.

Classification and Conservation   The principal intellectual achievement in the advanced concrete operations subperiod is the acquisition of the ability to classify objects in terms of their relationships to other objects. Let's look at an example. A young boy who returned from play was looking forward to his usual snack when his mother appeared with a glass of milk and a cookie. The child, with disappointment written across his face, complained: "I want two." "Oh," said the mother, while breaking the cookie in half. "Here, now you have two." The boy's smile showed his obvious delight with this response. A child in the advanced stages of concrete operational thought would certainly not have responded in this way. He would have understood that the number of pieces into which the cookie was broken does not change the total quantity available to him. Because of his ability to relate the parts of the cookie to the whole, he would have immediately recognized what was going on and probably would have protested.

> the ability to judge relationships

The child learns to classify relationships among objects by developing what is called *conservation of the whole*. The concept of **conservation** refers to the fact that a whole remains unchanged despite how its parts are arranged. For example, a child who can conserve realizes that changing the distance between the sticks in a row does not change the number of sticks that there are. Similarly, the child would know that rolling a ball of clay into a sausage shape would not change the amount of clay available.

> conservation

When children learn conservation, they move from their egocentric thinking patterns to a new level of objectivity. Unlike preoperational children, children in the advanced level of concrete operations can tell the difference between their symbolic representations of things and reality. Thus, they no longer believe that teddy bears can talk, that words have magical powers, and that dreams are as real as actual events.

Conservation is highly significant in children's intellectual development. It is the basis for important verbal and quantitative skills that they learn in middle childhood. For instance, understanding conservation lets children understand the basic arithmetic operations of addition, subtraction, multiplication, and division. Arithmetic equations require the ability to see that a whole does not change despite the quantitative rearrangement of its parts.

The importance of conservation in children's development has been supported in several research studies. For instance, Kuhn (1976) has found that conservation ability is significantly related to IQ. Haynes and

Kulhavy (1976) and Prawat and Cancelli (1976) report that conservation is related to verbal memory.

knowledge of compensation

Factors Affecting Conservation   Piaget believes that, for children to be able to conserve, they must take into account all of the elements that make up a whole at the same time. For example, to understand that changing the length of a row of sticks does not change the number of sticks in the row, a child must see that changes in overall length are compensated for by changes in length between the pairs of sticks in the row. When the overall length is increased, the length between each stick and the next stick in the row is increased.

A recent experiment by Brainerd (1976) casts doubt on Piaget's beliefs about what children must know to conserve. He found that it was not necessary for children to understand that changes in one dimension are compensated for by changes in other dimensions in conservation problems. For example, it would not be necessary for the child to recognize that a change in the overall length of a row of sticks is compensated for by a change in the distance between the individual sticks to profit from conservation training.

language

One factor that has been found to underlie conservation is language skill. Children who can do conservation tasks generally must know the meanings of words such as "same" and "more." For instance, a child may be asked whether a row of sticks that has been spread apart has the "same" number of sticks or "more" sticks than it had previously. Harasym, Boersma, and McGuire (1971) and LaPointe and O'Donnell (1974) have found a relationship between the ability to conserve and knowledge of relational words.

perceptual task characteristics

The perceptual characteristics of the task also influence conservation. Pufall and Shaw (1972) have shown that young children tend to base their judgments on the perceptual features of conservation tasks. In judging the equality of two rows of dots, children who did not conserve based their judgments either on the overall length of the rows or on the distance between the dots in the rows. Miller, Heldmeyer, and Miller (1975) have shown that conservation can be encouraged by changing the perceptual features of the tasks. For example, conservation tasks that involve judgments concerning the equality or inequality of two sets are affected by the distance between the two sets. When the two sets are placed close together, the children can judge their equality more easily.

skill application

A third factor that influences conservation is how well the child uses his conservation skills. For example, Baron, Lawson, and Siegel (1975) found that even though children can judge the equality of two rows of things on the basis of the number of things in each row, they do not always do so. Rather, they may use the perceptual features of the rows just as nonconserving children do.

SOCIALIZATION

There is a great deal of controversy over the socialization practices used to promote intellectual development during the advanced stages of the period of concrete operations. Some theorists favor the use of discovery-

Hobbies provide a vehicle for discovery learning during the elementary school years.

learning techniques; others prefer strategies such as modeling. But regardless of how socialization is accomplished, most theorists agree that the school now has much of the responsibility for guiding intellectual growth. However, as we shall show shortly, the family continues to be very influential.

Guiding Concrete Operational Development Piagetians and behaviorists have been the principal opponents in the debate over strategies to guide concrete operational development. Piaget argues that concrete operations can only be developed through discovery learning. Children cannot learn to think logically simply by being told how to think. Rather, they must discover logic for themselves. According to this view, adults should provide chances for discovery to occur. Behaviorists, on the other hand, say that the skills associated with concrete operational thought can be learned through behavioral techniques such as modeling and corrective feedback.

the discovery-learning approach

The discovery-learning approach is usually begun by identifying the child's current stage of development. To do this, most people simply observe the child informally. The child is put in several situations that require the use of concrete operational thinking processes. For example, a teacher might evaluate a child's readiness to learn certain number concepts by playing number games with the child. During the games, the teacher could put two rows of blocks in front of the child and then ask if both rows are the same or if one has more. If the child responds that both rows are indeed the same, the teacher can make one row longer by spreading the blocks apart. Then he could again ask the question of equality versus inequality. If the child responds correctly to questions of this kind sometimes, but not others, the teacher might decide that the child is ready to discover the number concepts being taught. As a result, the teacher would set up some situations for discovery learning to occur.

Piagetians hold that discovery learning can be promoted by putting a child in a situation that places two or more of the child's beliefs in conflict. A study done several years ago by Smedslund (1961) illustrates one way this conflict can be produced. Smedslund was interested in teaching young children that stretching or compressing a ball of clay does not change the amount of clay in the ball. To help the children understand this, he put two of their beliefs about the clay in conflict. The first was the belief that changing the length of the ball (for example, stretching it) increased the amount of clay available. The second was the belief that if some clay were taken off the ball, there would be less clay in the ball. To place these two beliefs in conflict, Smedslund stretched the length of the ball and at the same time removed some of the clay. This procedure was effective in helping the children understand the amount of clay in the ball.

WORKING WITH A HYPERACTIVE CHILD

Marsha and Allen Bowman are the parents of a bright-eyed 7-year-old named Jeffrey. Jeffrey seems intelligent, but he has had great difficulty in school, mainly because he can't sit still long enough to learn anything. His energy has created problems not only for him, but also for the other children in his class. He often bothers his classmates when they are trying to work. Occasionally he becomes so active that, without meaning to, he hurts children by jamming into them or bumping them as he twirls in a circle.

Recently the Bowmans have been told that Jeffrey is "hyperactive" and their physican has prescribed a drug (Methylphenidate, commonly known as Ritalin) to control Jeffrey's behavior. When Jeffrey takes his first pill, he will join over 150,000 other American children who are on medication to control school learning and/or behavior in school (Sroufe, 1975).

What should the Bowmans expect from drug therapy for their son? First, they should know that even though their son's problem is that he is too active, research has shown that prescription of a sedative or tranquilizer would probably not be beneficial (Sroufe, 1975). On the other hand, prescription of a stimulant such as Ritalin will probably have desirable effects (Stroufe, 1975). For example, Jeffrey's tendency to do things that are not relevant to the task at hand might be reduced through appropriate drug treatment.

The behavioral approach relies on the use of procedures such as modeling and feedback (Zimmerman & Rosenthal, 1974). For example, to teach a child number concepts such as we described earlier, a teacher might arrange two rows of blocks in front of the child and then say that each has the same number. The teacher might then spread the blocks apart and model the correct judgment by saying once again that the two rows of blocks both have the same number. The teacher might then ask the child to tell her whether two different sets of blocks were equal. If the child answered correctly, the teacher might praise him. If he responded incorrectly, she might give corrective feedback. She could indicate that, although the rows seemed to be different, each one still had the same number of blocks.

Several studies have shown that it is possible to teach concrete operational tasks using behavioral techniques (Brainerd, 1976; Charbonneau, Robert, Bourassa, & Gladu-Bissonnette, 1976; Halford & Fullerton, 1970; Rosenthal & Zimmerman, 1972; Zimmerman & Rosenthal, 1974). Much of this research has shown the effectiveness of modeling. For example, Zimmerman and Rosenthal (1974) used modeling to teach children several concrete operational skills that Piagetians had argued could be acquired only through discovery.

the behavioral approach

It was once thought that the beneficial effects stimulants can have on activity level were limited to hyperactive children. However, research now suggests that this is not true. For example, normal adults respond to stimulants in essentially the same way that hyperactive children do (Weiss & Laties, 1962).

Another idea from the past that has recently lost support is that children's excessive activity is caused by "minimal brain dysfunction" (Sroufe, 1975). We have no clear evidence of a tie between brain injury and hyperactive behavior. However, some authorities continue to believe that minimal brain injury underlies hyperactivity.

Although the Bowmans can expect that the drug therapy will improve their son's behavior, they should not assume that Jeffrey will necessarily do better in school as a result. However, they can take some encouragement from the efforts of Ayllon, Layman, and Kandel (1975) to improve the academic skills of hyperactive children. These researchers found that reinforcement is effective in controlling the learning of hyperactive children. Furthermore, as learning increases, hyperactivity decreases, even when the children are not on medication. One option the Bowmans might consider is to place Jeffrey on medication for a brief period to reduce his activity level. They could then replace the medication with a behavioral program to control Jeffrey's activity level and his learning.

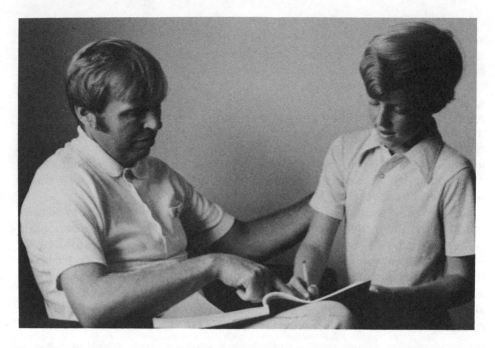

Parents play an important role in guiding intellectual development during the period of concrete operations.

Piagetians (such as Turiel, 1973) have criticized the behavioral research on grounds of method. For example, they have argued that the children being trained may have already learned the necessary skills through discovery. They have also suggested that the learning may be temporary and that the children may revert to their former ways of thinking very quickly when the training stops. Although this controversy has not been resolved, the evidence today suggests that concrete operational skills *can* be learned through procedures such as modeling (Charbonneau et al., 1976). This view is important because it suggests that socialization efforts need not be restricted to a discovery-learning approach.

Socializing Institutions   As in the earlier phases of development, the family is dominant in influencing intellectual development during the advanced stages of the concrete operational period. Their role has been described in a number of studies. For example, Walberg and Marjoribanks (1973) studied the relationship between home environment and ability test performance by 11-year-old children. They found the environment to be strongly related to both the children's verbal and numerical abilities.

There is some evidence that the make-up of a family affects the environment for intellectual growth. For example, Blanchard and Biller (1971) report lower IQs in third-grade boys from homes with absent fathers than in homes with fathers present. However, findings on the effects of the absence of the father on intellectual functioning are not consistent. Some studies have not shown any ability differences associated with father absence (Hess, Shipman, Brophy, & Bear, 1969). A close look at several of these studies suggests that the relationship between father absence

family influences

and ability has other causes (Herzog & Sudia, 1973). For example, in a fatherless family, the mother often has the major responsibility for earning a living. This often takes time away from the home and may lessen her opportunity to work with her children. Whether or not the father is present, outside employment of the mother is associated with decreased intellectual ability and lower school performance (Gold & Andres, 1978).

During the concrete operational years, the school should and does play an important part in the child's intellectual development (Shea, 1976). Nevertheless, the schools have not met some of the educational needs that we expect them to meet. One of the cornerstones of American education is the idea that all children should have an equal opportunity to develop their intellectual potential. This view recognizes that individual students have different abilities. Thus all students will not reach the same level of competence at the end of their schooling. But although the idea of equal educational opportunity implies *individual* variations in achievement, it does not imply *group* differences in achievement. Indeed the fact that these differences exist is used as a sign of inequality of opportunity (Jencks et al., 1972). There are substantial differences in intellectual achievement among children from different cultural subgroups, and the schools have not been effective in eliminating these differences (Shea, 1976).

school influences

The group differences in intellectual achievement received widespread attention in the 1960s. During that time, the nation took a comprehensive look at the extent to which school systems across the country provided equal opportunities for children from varying social strata. It included not only information on the facilities, materials, and qualifications of teachers, but also data on the effectiveness of the schools in promoting intellectual growth. The study, under the direction of Dr. James Coleman of Johns Hopkins University, collected data from 4,000 schools involving 60,000 teachers and 570,000 children. The results of the investigation were published in 1966 in a two-volume work that has come to be known as the *Coleman Report* (Coleman, Campbell, Hobson, McPartland, Mood, Weinfeld, & York, 1966). To the shock and amazement of social theorists and educators, they found that, although children from all socioeconomic levels received the same quality of education, children from the lower levels did not profit as much from their schooling as children from the upper levels. Moreover, the schools became less and less effective in eliminating social class and ethnic group differences as children progressed. They concluded that family is a far more important factor in school achievement than the school itself.

The Coleman report was compiled under heavy pressure of time, and many theorists have challenged its validity. One persistent question is whether or not the quality of schooling actually has little impact on eliminating discrepancies in achievement among different cultural subgroups. Theorists who have looked at this question have, for the most part, supported Coleman (Shea, 1976).

Although the Coleman investigation said that schools have had little impact on group differences in achievement, there is evidence that individual teachers do affect the achievement of both poverty level and middle-class children. Veldman and Brophy (1974) studied the effects of 275 teachers on the academic performance of over 1,000 second- and third-grade children. They found that some teachers are significantly more effective than others in promoting student achievement. We do not yet know the sources of the differences, but this question is being studied right now.

The Period of Formal Operations

As children approach adolescence, their concrete operational skills become increasingly refined. They gradually become aware that there are certain situations in which concrete operations do not do the job. According to Piaget, at this point they are once again prepared to make a sharp, qualitative jump in intellectual functioning.

FORMAL OPERATIONS

Piaget uses the term *formal operations* to describe the thinking of the adolescent. Formal operations are thinking patterns that involve the full range of possible conditions for a given situation. With formal operations, we can think up and test hypotheses about the results of potential conditions. For example, consider Jason, an adolescent in a basic science course who is given the problem of finding out what controls the swing of a pendulum. If Jason had reached the period of formal operations, he would be able to name all the possible factors that might influence how long it takes for the pendulum to swing back and forth. He would very likely test them one at a time. Thus, he might begin with a guess that the weight of the pendulum bob controls the swing. To test this assumption, he might build a pendulum and then replace the first bob with a lighter or heavier one. If he were to do this, he would see that the time it takes for the pendulum to swing back and forth would not have changed. So he would select another hypothesis and test it. Eventually Jason would see that lengthening or shortening the string would affect the time it took.

The central difference between formal operational thought, as illustrated with Jason, and concrete operational thought is that Jason used logic to test hypotheses systematically. For instance, he was not told to change the weight of the bob without changing anything else. Rather, it was his job to figure out that a change in the weight of the bob was a possibility that could be systematically looked at. The experiments of Inhelder and Piaget (1958) demonstrate that children in the period of concrete operations do not make up hypotheses and systematically change one factor at a time to test them.

Formal Operational Abilities   Formal operational thought is shown in a number of different abilities. We will not consider all of them, but rather will look at some examples.

One hallmark of formal operational thought is the ability to imagine all possible combinations of things that might occur in a situation. Inhelder and Piaget (1958) studied the use of different combinations of chemicals. The children in their study were given four flasks with different colorless, odorless liquids that looked exactly the same. In addition to the four flasks, there was a small bottle with a fifth chemical. The experimenter showed the children that, by combining liquids, a yellow solution could be made. The experimenter poured drops from the small bottle into two additional flasks containing liquids. In one flask, the liquid turned yellow. In the other, it stayed clear. The experimenter then asked the child to use all or any of the four flasks plus the bottle to produce a yellow solution. To solve this problem, the child had to think up all the possible ways that the five solutions could be combined. Young children could not solve the problem. However, a number of adolescents were successful in systematically combining the chemicals to produce the yellow solution. *the ability to conceptualize combinations*

A second ability that develops during this period is called **propositional thinking.** It involves the ability to make up propositions that describe the implications of a particular set of conditions. Inhelder and Piaget (1958) studied propositional thinking in a number of experiments. In one, children were allowed to play a billiard game (see figure 7–3) in which a plunger was used to shoot a ball toward a wall so that it would rebound and hit a target. The child's task was to state a proposition that would explain how to hit the target. The correct solution was that the angle at which the ball struck the wall would be the same as the angle at which the ball was reflected from the wall. For example, if the ball struck the wall at a 45° angle, it would bounce off at a 45° angle. The young children in the study were quite good at making the ball hit the target, but could not explain the rule. On the other hand, the older subjects could correctly state the rule. *the ability to create propositions*

The ability to test hypotheses by holding all factors except one constant is also acquired during the formal operational period. This ability was illustrated in the example of Jason. Jason tested hypotheses by varying one feature of the pendulum at a time while holding the other features constant. *hypothesis testing*

School-Related Abilities   There are some findings that suggest that formal operational thought is related to IQ test performance and other ability measures stressed in school. However, the research on this issue has been somewhat inconsistent. For instance, Keating (1975) and Keating and Schaefer (1975) found that children who got very high scores on a standardized achievement test and on other measures of ability learned formal operational competencies earlier than children who got average ability scores. In contrast, Kuhn (1976) was not able to find a significant relationship between formal operational competencies and IQ.

There are a number of possible explanations for the difference between the Kuhn and Keating findings. One is that the two studies measured formal operational competencies and ability in different ways. Although the findings so far have not been consistent, the reports suggest that at

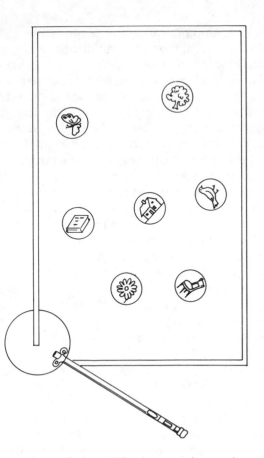

Figure 7–3 The principle of the billiard game is used to demonstrate the angles of incidence and reflection. The tubular spring plunger can be pivoted and aimed. Balls are launched from this plunger against the projection wall and rebound to the interior of the apparatus. The circled drawings represent targets which are placed successively at different points.

From *The Growth of Logical Thinking: From Childhood to Adolescence,* by Barbel Inhelder and Jean Piaget, translated by Anne Parsons and Stanley Milgram. © 1958 by Basic Books, Inc., Publishers, New York. Reprinted by permission.

least some of the competencies identified by Piaget are probably important for academic learning during adolescence. Some support for this view comes from cross-cultural studies that have shown that formal operations develop earlier in societies with formal schooling than in societies that do not have formal educational systems (Neimark, 1975).

Egocentrism   Although the period of formal operations is the highest phase of intellectual development Piaget identifies, it includes its own form of egocentrism. The impressive logic that adolescents learn leads at first to an inflated view of their intellectual capabilities. As Inhelder and Piaget (1958) remark,

The adolescent goes through a phase in which he attributes an unlimited power to his own thoughts so that the dream of a glorious future or of transforming the world through ideas (even if this idealism takes a materialistic form) seems to be not only fantasy but also an effective action which in itself modifies the empirical world. (pp. 345–46)

As adolescents have new experiences interacting with the adult world, their idealistic egocentrism fades. They develop a more realistic view of the limitations of thought in guiding human affairs. The typical change is illustrated in a classic Mark Twain story about a young man who, on his 21st birthday, remarked that when he was 14 his father had been quite stupid, but that the father had learned a truly remarkable amount in the short span of 7 years.

SOCIALIZATION

The controversy over what socialization practices to use to guide concrete operational development extends to the question of socialization techniques for promoting formal operational development. And there is no immediate solution to the controversy in sight. The schools have been no more effective in promoting formal operational development than in stimulating concrete operational growth. Indeed, the discrepancies between groups observed during the concrete operational period are even more pronounced in the formal operational period. Thus, it is not possible to advocate any particular socialization strategy because it has been proven to be effective.

Guiding Formal Operational Development   Piagetians, as might be expected, again believe in using discovery learning to guide formal operational development. Barratt (1975) shows that discovery learning can help promote adolescent intellectual development. He used it with a group of secondary school students. For instance, they were given this problem: the guests at a party were given food from only four bowls. One contained rice, one chicken, one tomatoes, and one mushrooms. Everyone took some of the food. Some took just one kind of food. Others took two kinds, others three kinds, and one person gorged himself on all four kinds. Everyone took a different mixture of foods. What is the largest number of people who could have been at the party, and what did each of them have to eat?

discovery-learning approach

While you are trying to solve the problem, let us tell you how Barratt helped the students solve it. He gave them mimeographed booklets with a series of similar problems that ranged from easy to hard. They were asked to solve each problem and then to check their answers against answer sheets at the backs of the booklets. Later the students who participated in this activity were better able to solve similar problems than students who had not had that chance.

Although discovery learning can be effective in stimulating formal operational development, it is not the only effective procedure. Behavioral

behavioral
approach

theorists have used direct instruction to help students with problem solving. For example, Siegler, Liebert, and Liebert (1973) used direct instruction to teach 10- and 11-year-old boys and girls to solve the pendulum problem we described earlier. The children were first taught to identify the dimensions (such as weight and length) that might be involved in the experiment. The experimenter then pointed out that each dimension could include different levels. For instance, a ball measured in terms of weight might be either heavy or light. Following the discussion of dimensions and levels, the children were given a rule to use. Specifically, they were told that if a change in the level of the dimension caused a change in the event, then that dimension was important in determining the event. For example, the children were shown that a heavy ball made a scale move more than a light ball. They were also shown that changing the color of the balls had no effect on the movement of the scale. From this demonstration, they were taught that weight is an important dimension in the movement of the scale but color is not.

Children who received direct instruction were better at discovering that the length of the string determined the swing of a pendulum than children who had not received direct instruction. This result was particularly striking in light of the ages of the children in the study. Piagetians do not expect 10- and 11-year-olds to have formal operational thought. Siegler and Atlas (1976) have recently shown that direct instruction can teach elementary school children formal operational abilities even more complex than those required in the pendulum problem.

Socializing Institutions   One fear of many parents is that when their children reach adolescence, their ability to guide the children's development will greatly diminish because the children are influenced by their peers. Complaints such as "He just won't listen to me anymore" or "I feel that I have completely lost control" are common among the parents of adolescents. School personnel also may feel frustrated because they cannot counteract the powerful forces of the peer culture. In part because of peer group influences, teachers may feel that, if a child does not have well-established learning patterns by the time he reaches adolescence, little can be done to help him. Thus, some teachers may make comments like *"There is a real need to solve learning problems before children get to high school,"* or *"By the time I get a hold of a child if he hasn't learned how to learn he's generally so far behind that I can't help him,"* or *"It's really the other kids that influence behavior in high school, not the teachers."*

peer influence
on intellectual
functioning

To what extent do the family, the school, and the peer culture influence intellectual growth during the adolescent years? Many years ago Coleman (1960) conducted a classic study on this question. He studied the attitudes of male and female students in 10 midwestern high schools. Each male student was asked how he would like most to be remembered: as a star athlete, as a brilliant student, or as the most popular student. Their responses showed that boys preferred to be remembered for their athletic skill rather than for their scholarly ability or popularity. Girls were asked whether they would rather be leaders in extracurricular activities, brilliant students, or popular students. The girls preferred popularity to scholarship.

Coleman also found that student attitudes toward scholarship influence their academic achievement. Social forces draw the most able students into nonscholarly pursuits. In all but one of the schools that he studied, Coleman found that high-ability students achieved academically at lower levels than expected. Coleman concluded:

> The implications for American society as a whole are clear. Because high schools allow the adolescent subculture to divert energies into athletics, social activities, and the like, they recruit into adult intellectual activities people with a rather mediocre level of ability. (1960, p. 345)

Shea (1976) summarized research on adolescent peer influence on attitudes toward academics. For example, the likelihood that a high school student will decide to attend college is affected by the attitudes of his or her friends toward college degrees. Shea (1976) also found some support for teachers' fears that they have little effect on student attitudes. The Shea summary shows that teachers do influence student aspirations. However, teachers have much less influence on adolescents than other important people in a student's life.

In contrast to popular beliefs, research does suggest that a child's parents have a strong influence on intellectual growth during adolescence. For instance, Shea (1976) reports that parents' attitudes toward college are very significant in determining an adolescent's educational goals and the likelihood that he or she will go beyond high school. Moreover, although the findings are by no means conclusive, there is some evidence that parents have more influence on the educational aspirations of their children than peers do. Kandel and Lesser (1970) asked mothers to name the highest educational level they would like their children to reach. In addition, the children's friends were requested to guess the highest level that they thought would be completed. The children's own goals corresponded more closely to their parent's desires than to their friends' expectations.

parental influences

In Sum

Not only during adolescence but during every phase of growth, a critical need is to make it possible for parents to be more effective in guiding their children's intellectual growth. At least two things must be done to meet this need. One is to make psychological information more readily available to parents (Bergan, 1977). The second is to increase the coordination between the home and the school and other socializing institutions responsible for guiding intellectual growtn. There are signs that we are moving toward accomplishing these tasks. Research on early parent intervention programs attests to this movement. Recent research interest in the problem of home-school coordination also reflects our increased concern for finding ways to help parents be more effective as socializing agents. During the past few years, the issue of home-school coordination has been a major national research priority. It is much too early to tell what benefits we may reap from this research. Nevertheless, we may hope that we will move closer to accomplishing our long-held goal of helping youngsters from every segment of society realize their full intellectual potential.

Suggested Readings

Appleton, T., Clifton, R., & Goldberg, S. The development of behavioral competence in infancy. In F. D. Horowitz (Ed.), *Review of research in child development* (Vol. 4). Chicago: University of Chicago Press, 1975.

Barratt, B. B. Training and transfer in combinatorial problem solving: The development of formal reasoning during early adolescence. *Developmental Psychology*, 1975, *11*, 700–704.

Beller, E. K. Research on organized programs of early education. In R. M. W. Travers (Ed.), *Second handbook of research on teaching*. Chicago: Rand McNally, 1973.

Bower, T. G. R. The object in the world of the infant. *Scientific American*, 1971, *225*, 30–47.

Charbonneau, C., Robert, M., Bourassa, G., & Gladu-Bissonnette, S. Observational learning of quantity conservation and Piagetian generalization tasks. *Developmental Psychology*, 1976, *12*, 211–217.

Coleman, J. S., Campbell, E.Q., Hobson, C. J., McPartland, J., Mood, A. M., Weinfeld, F. D., & York, R. L. *Equality of educational opportunity.* Washington, D.C.: U.S. Department of Health, Education and Welfare, 1966.

Elardo, R., Bradley, R. H., & Caldwell, B. M. The relation of infants' home environment to mental test performance from 6 to 36 months: A longitudinal analysis. *Child Development*, 1975, *46*, 71–76.

Henderson, R. W., Bergan, J. R., & Hurt, M. Development and validation of the Henderson Environmental Learning Process Scale. *Journal of Social Psychology*, 1972, 88, 185–196.

Inhelder, B., & Piaget, J. *The growth of logical thinking from childhood to adolescence.* New York: Basic Books, 1958.

Piaget, J. *The child's conception of the world.* Paterson, N. J.: Littlefield, Adams, 1963.

Twardosz, S., Cataldo, M. F., & Risley, T. R. Open environment design for infant and toddler day care. *Journal of Applied Behavior Analysis*, 1974, *7*, 529–546.

How Language Develops

This chapter describes the behavioral and structural perspectives on language development. When you have completed the chapter, you should know the two behavioral positions on language: the social-learning view and the operant view. In addition, you should understand two structural positions: Noam Chomsky's transformational grammar and the new cognitive view of language development based on Piaget's work. You should also understand the influence of culture on language development. More specifically, you should know some social class differences in language patterns, and some of the problems involved in guiding the language development of bilingual children and children who speak nonstandard dialects such as Black English.

The likelihood that a child growing up in America today will be socially and economically successful is strongly tied to his or her ability to use standard English, to speak and understand the language that most Americans use. Any deviation from the accepted language patterns can lead to negative consequences for the child. A child whose speech varies from the norm may be labeled unintelligent, lazy, and even dishonest (Ervin-Tripp, 1972). Language has life-long effects on a child. The ability tests often given to school children are heavily loaded with items that depend on basic English language skills; children's scores on these tests are associated with the amount of schooling they ultimately go through. Schooling, in turn, is associated with eventual income level. Given these realities, it is critical for people who work with children to know something about how language develops and about the relationship of children's language to their culture. These are the topics covered in this chapter.

Perspectives on Language Development

New parents sometimes wonder if their children are ever going to learn to talk. Later they wonder if these same offspring will ever stop talking. The learning and flowering of language in the young child is truly remarkable. Theories of language development try to explain what it is that children learn and how they learn it when they acquire language.

BEHAVIORAL PERSPECTIVES

Behaviorists believe that language development depends on the conditions in the child's environment. There are two versions of the behavioral position. One is the operant view, which assumes that language development involves learning behaviors that are reinforced. The second is the social-learning or cognitive view, which holds that language development involves learning language rules, primarily by observing how others use them.

The Operant View   B. F. Skinner (1957), the principal architect of the operant viewpoint, says that in the course of language development the child learns a complex set of verbal behaviors (often called *operant responses*). When a child makes a sound and that sound is followed by reinforcement, the likelihood is increased that the child will make the sound again. For example, if Tim happens to utter "da da da da" and the sound is followed by smiles and caresses from his obviously pleased father, the likelihood that Tim will say "da da da da" again increases.

reinforcement
effects

A number of studies have shown that verbal behavior can be influenced by reinforcement. For example, several years ago Rheingold, Gewirtz, and Ross (1959) found that the sounds made by infants as young as 3 months old could be influenced by positive consequences. At first, the experimenters counted the number of sounds infants made without reinforcement. Then the experimenters started reinforcing the sounds by smiling, saying "tsk tsk tsk," and touching the children lightly on the abdomen. These reinforcements distinctly increased the number of sounds the infants made.

Operant research conducted with children of a variety of ages and intellectual levels has consistently produced similar results. For instance, several studies of severely retarded children have shown that it is possible to teach them to use a broad range of grammatical structures by using appropriate reinforcements (e.g., Guess, Sailor, Rutherford, & Baer, 1968). This research is particularly impressive because the children involved typically had very limited language. In many cases, before the study it was not at all certain that they would be able to learn language by any means.

Although operant theorists base their view of language acquisition on the idea that language learning is controlled by reinforcement, they also recognize the part played by other environmental conditions. One condition of particular importance is modeling. A child who has a model of language behavior available can learn language much faster than a child who has to learn language on the basis of reinforcement alone. A child can learn solely by reinforcement only when he or she makes a good response or something close to that. For example, a parent cannot reinforce a child for saying "da da da" unless the child says it first. To learn by imitation of a model, the child does not have to make the response on his own. The response can be brought about directly and immediately by modeling it.

modeling effects

By being reinforced for coming close to being right, young children can learn new words.

Despite the fact that reinforcement and modeling have been used effectively to teach language, there is still some question whether or not language is actually learned naturally in the way that operant researchers describe. For example, Chomsky (1957) argues that the system of language rules that a child must learn is far too complex to be learned on the basis of reinforcement.

Operant theorists recognize how complex language is and the problems of assuming that children learn language by learning specific responses through reinforcement. To try to explain complex language learning, they say that children learn not a set of specific and unique responses, but rather a set of response *classes* that can be used under a range of circumstances. For example, Guess and his colleages (1968) taught a severely retarded child to form the plurals of several words by using modeling and reinforcement. The child learned more than just the specific responses that they taught. She was able to generalize to words that had never been taught. For instance, after learning to form the plurals of words such as *cup, cap,* and *truck* by adding -s, she was asked to form a series of plurals that did not call for the addition of -s. She responded to the new words in the same way that she had reacted to the words that were specifically taught. Thus, when forming the plural of *man,* she said *mans.* The fact that she followed the same strategy in forming the plurals of words not included in training sessions and that she used this strategy even when it was inappropriate was taken as evidence that she had indeed learned a generalized class of responses.

Skinner (1953) says that a child learns to use response classes because of common characteristics among sets of stimuli. For instance, the common characteristic signaling the plurals in the Guess study was multiple numbers of objects. Whenever the child was shown more than one object, she added an ending -s to the name of the object.

If you listen to children at home, in school, and around the neighborhood, you can find charming examples that show that children learn response classes rather than specific verbal reactions. For instance, one of mother playing with her child held him briefly with his head toward the floor and said: "Now you're upside down." The child protested immediately: "No upside down; make John upside up."

Operant theorists explain complex language learning not only by showing that children can learn response classes, but also by showing that they may learn things that will help them learn to speak while they are learning to understand language. It is well known that children understand language before they can produce it (Frazer, Bellugi, & Brown, 1963). For example, a child may learn to follow a direction such as "Pick up the spoon" before he can say those words himself. While learning to understand speech, children have the chance to listen to countless examples of speech by adults and other children. Operant research suggests that comprehension learning of this type may help the child speak later on. Mann and Baer (1971) taught 4-year-old children to understand nonsense words like *"lir," "kob," "jad," "qad," "pes," and "vuz"* by reinforcing the children for pointing to objects to which the words referred.

response class
learning

comprehension
and production

Children learn language by observing their parents.

After this training, the children were asked to repeat these nonsense words along with other nonsense terms that had not been associated with objects. The children did a much better job of imitating the words to which they were exposed during comprehension training than of repeating the new words.

The Social-Learning View The social-learning view holds that children learn language primarily by listening to people talk. Parents are generally the child's most significant language models. They often spend countless hours talking to their children. Parental language modeling starts during the earliest days of life and continues as the child grows up.

There is evidence that a child's language development can be affected by the kinds of social-learning opportunities parents provide. Wulbert, Inglis, Kriegsmann, and Mills (1975) studied children who were slow in developing language and children who developed language at a normal rate. They looked at how both sets of parents reared their children. The investigators found a number of differences in how mothers and children interacted in these groups. The mothers of children with language delays were less responsive to their children, both verbally and emotionally, than the mothers of children with adequate language. And the mothers of language-delayed children spent less time with their children than did the mothers of children with acceptable language.

social-learning influences on language

According to the social-learning position, children learn language by cognitively representing the language patterns they hear. For example, a child might form a mental image of a language pattern she heard. Later, the child might speak and imitate the language she had heard. This would demonstrate that she had learned something earlier.

cognitive representation of observed language

Social-learning theorists say that children learn rules that control how we use language while they learn language skills (Zimmerman & Rosenthal, 1974). For example, according to the social-learning position, when children learn to form the plurals for words by adding -s, they learn a language rule that lets them make words plural in appropriate situations.

reinforcement and
language learning

Social-learning and operant theorists debate the role of reinforcement in learning language imitation. The operant position says that reinforcement is essential for a child to learn new language responses. By contrast, social-learning theorists say that reinforcement is not necessary for language learning (Zimmerman & Rosenthal, 1974). A child may learn new language patterns simply by observing a model.

This debate raises significant questions for adults working with young children. If reinforcement is necessary for learning, then it is essential for the adult to be around to reinforce the desired language when it appears. But if language can be learned through observation alone, then a socializing agent would not always be needed to reinforce language. Thus children could increase their language skills through media like television without having direct contact with a parent, teacher, or other socializing agents.

We have found that young children can learn language rules by watching television programs in which models performed behaviors that conformed to the rules to be learned (Henderson, Swanson, & Zimmerman, 1975). In this study, preschool Papago Indian children living in an isolated reservation were taught certain question-asking skills by televised models. The children watched the models asking questions about cause involving phrases such as "why" or "what would happen if." As a result, the children's causal questions increased. And the questions that they asked did not simply mimic those of the televised models. The fact that they asked causal questions but did not repeat the specific questions they had seen suggests that they learned a rule.

As we have seen, research does show that children can learn language both by having their verbal behavior reinforced and by observing models. However, how much these procedures account for the development of children's language has not yet been established.

STRUCTURAL PERSPECTIVES

Structural perspectives on language development are in sharp contrast to the behavioral viewpoints we've just discussed. Structural theorists believe that language behavior is controlled by mental structures (Chomsky, 1959; Lenneberg, 1964). Unlike behavioral theorists, they do not think that language learning is a direct function of environmental influences. Rather, they think language is controlled by a combination of innate and acquired mental characteristics.

attack on the
operant viewpoint

Transformational Grammar   During the 1960s the dominant structural position was the transformational grammar view, developed by Noam Chomsky (1959, 1968). He (1959) attracted wide attention among linguists and psycholinguists through a devastating criticism of the operant position. Chomsky argued that the creative use of speech we see in everyday language could not possibly be accounted for by simple reinforcement as advanced by Skinner (1957). Following his successful attack on the be-

NOAM CHOMSKY (1928–   )

Born in Philadelphia, Chomsky received his bachelor's, masters, and doctoral degrees from the University of Pennsylvania. In 1957, he published *Syntactic Structures*, in which he proposed a radically new theory of linguistics. Chomsky's theory is based on the idea of innate grammatical structures. It has been both controversial and provocative. Chomsky also has been involved with New Left politics and the anti-war movement, and has written on both. He is a professor at the Massachusetts Institute of Technology.

havioral position, he put forth his own view that language learning is based on a system of language rules born into human beings, but not into other species (Chomsky, 1966, 1968).

Chomsky hypothesizes a language acquisition device (LAD) that he says is made up of the rules that govern language behavior. The LAD is thought to be made up of a universal set of rules that control speech in *all* languages. Chomsky also says that a separate set of rules is involved in learning the special features that distinguish one language from another. These special rules are determined by learning rather than by inborn structures. the LAD

Chomsky (1968) cites several characteristics of language that suggest the existence of the LAD. One is the fact that there are an infinite number of possible verbal combinations within a given language. He finds it impossible to believe that all of the many different kinds of things that people can and do say could be learned. In his opinion, there simply isn't time during the brief span of a lifetime for people to learn all the verbal behaviors that they use as adult speakers.

The creativity in everyday speech is a second language characteristic that suggests the existence of the LAD. People can talk for hours without ever saying the same thing twice. Even those aging speakers who often repeat stories of bygone adventures are not likely to spin their yarns in exactly the same way two times in a row. Thus, the child who says "Grandpa, tell me the one about the time you were surrounded by enemy soldiers" is not likely to hear exactly the same version he heard before. Chomsky claims that this creativity cannot be accounted for by reinforcement learning.

A third factor that leads Chomsky to believe in the LAD is that learners are not taught all the language rules they use. Thus, it is hard to understand how we learn the rules that we use as adult speakers. For instance, consider the following sentences:

"John is easy to please."
"John is eager to please."

These sentences have the same grammatical form. Yet they are constructed in quite different ways. Look at this transformation:

"It is easy to please John."
"It is eager to please John."

Chomsky has shown that there are rules that tell why the first transformation makes sense while the second one is not acceptable. Virtually all English speakers—even young children—know that the first transformation is acceptable, and the second is not. Chomsky argues that it is not reasonable to assume that we learn rules like this through imitation or reinforcement, especially considering how soon in life we learn them.

grammar

The inborn rules that make up the LAD and the special acquired rules of a specific language make up the grammar for that language. Chomsky describes grammar as a system of rules that specify how sound and meaning relate in a language. Grammars have three parts: the rules that govern how sound is used, the rules that assign meanings to words, and the rules that govern how words are strung together into larger units of meaning. Again, we use these rules without being consciously aware of them.

deep and surface structure

Chomsky believes that grammars are composed of two types of syntactic structure. One is called the *deep structure;* the other the *surface structure.* We need two structures because the surface appearance of a chain of words may not always be clear. For example, the sentence "They are visiting consultants" can be interpreted in two ways. It may be that the people referred to have gone to visit some consultants. On the other hand, the sentence might mean that the people referred to are consultants who have come for a visit.

The deep structure of a sentence relates the surface structure to meaning. For instance, the deep structure associated with our example would relate the sound patterns of the sentence to a clear meaning. The surface structure would transform the sentence into the specific sequence in which it was finally spoken. Chomsky's theory is called *transformational grammar* because rules of transformation are applied to change deep sentence structures into surface structures.

Chomsky's impact

Chomsky's theory has had a major impact on developmental studies of children's language learning (Bloom, 1975; McNeill, 1970). Before Chomsky, research focused on counting the kinds of utterances that children make at different age levels (e.g., McCarthy, 1954). For instance, there were studies of the percentages of adjectives, nouns, and so forth in children's speech. With Chomsky's influence, the focus shifted to the kinds of rules that children use to understand and to speak. Table 8–1 shows some data from research of this sort. The search for grammar continues to be the major focus of language research. However, the theoretical basis for the search has been changing.

The Cognitive Perspective   In the early 1970s, some researchers who were trying to describe how children acquire language decided that it could not be completely explained by Chomsky's sets of rules. Their reservations stemmed from at least two sources. First of all, research on whether or not people actually use rules of formation and transformation was not able to support Chomsky's ideas (Johnson-Laird, 1974). Second, further research suggested that cognitive factors that Chomsky did not recognize also influence language acquisition (Bloom, 1975).

Table 8–1   Acquisition of complex syntactic structures

structure	difficult concept	age of acquisition
John is easy to see.	Who's doing the see-ing?	5.6 to 9 years*
John promised Bill to go.	Who's going?	5.6 to 9 years*
John asked Bill what to do.	Who's doing it?	Some 10-year-olds still haven't learned this.
He knew that John was going to win the race.	Does the "he" re- re-fer to John?	5.6 years

*All children 9 and over know this.

From "Language Development after Six," by C. Chomsky, in C. S. Lavatelli and F. Standler (Eds.), *Readings in Child Behavior and Development* (3rd ed.). New York: Harcourt Brace, 1972.

Piaget's view that language development follows intellectual develop- ment has had a significant influence on cognitive research. To review briefly, Piaget believes that children develop intellectual structures that let them represent their experiences in symbols. The first symbols are physical actions. For example, a child may represent her bottle by suck- ing. As children develop, they use language along with the early action symbols. Thus, when she is relatively advanced, the same child might use words to represent an infant's bottle, saying that "A bottle is something that a baby sucks to get food."

Piaget's influence

An implication of this position is that children's language should reflect their current thinking processes. Sinclair-de-Zwart (1969) studied this issue. She looked at the language of two groups of children at different Piagetian developmental levels. The children in the lower level group were in the preoperational subperiod. They tended to describe objects in absolute terms. For instance, they made comments like "This one is big, this one is little." Children in the higher level group were in the period of concrete operations. They tended to describe objects in relative terms. Statements like "This one is fatter, but shorter than that one" were common among the higher level group. A major difference between the preoperational child and the child in the advanced concrete operational period is that the preoperational child does not understand relationships accurately. The Sinclair-de-Zwart study shows that this difference in the way children think shows up in the ways in which they talk.

Bloom's (1975) studies of very young children further support Piaget's views. She found that children who are just beginning to talk use words and phrases that reflect the intellectual achievements of the period of sensorimotor development. As we have seen, during this period children come to understand the idea of object permanence, that objects that have disappeared from view may still exist. Bloom finds that when children learn to talk, they learn to use words to discuss object permanence. For example, a child may say "bear gone" when a teddy bear has been taken out of the room. When the bear is returned, he may say "more bear."

meaning and
syntax

These studies suggest that language development reflects cognitive development. They have led to a new look at the way children learn language. Researchers influenced by Chomsky emphasize syntax, the ways children put words together to form larger units of meaning (e.g., McNeill, 1970). Cognitive research suggests that our theory of language development should not necessarily rest on syntax since it is determined at least partially by cognition. Young children put words together in a certain way largely because of the meanings that they want to convey rather than because of rules of structure. As a case in point, Bloom (1975) reports that young children use word combinations before they learn the necessary structures to represent their meanings. For example, children may use the word "no" to mean either that an object does not exist or that it does not fall within a particular classification. Thus, Cindy may point to her mother's apron and say "no pocket." She means that the apron has no pockets. Likewise, she may look at a particular toy and say "no truck." Now she means that this toy does not fall into the category of objects which she calls "truck."

Some theorists are now trying to construct grammars that connect syntax with categories of meaning. For example, rather than describing a sentence as being composed of a noun and a verb, we could describe it as a word for an agent who acts upon the environment and a word for the action taken by the agent (Brown, 1973). The words "agent" and "action" are categories that reflect meaning, while "noun" and "verb" refer only to syntax structures.

Although this strategy is promising, it cannot entirely replace the more traditional categories we use to describe language development (Bloom, 1975; Brown, 1973). Certain facets of children's speech cannot be easily described this way. For example, transformational grammars can describe a broader range of language structures than the grammars that link syntax to meaning (Bloom, 1975). Thus, today theorists are using a combination of grammars that emphasize both traditional structures and descriptions based on meaning (e.g., Brown, 1973).

Language Development and Culture

So far we have discussed language development independent from its cultural context. But of course, language development is not independent of culture. Indeed, one of the most obvious characteristics of our pluralistic society is that the people of the different subgroups of this country talk differently. Cultural differences lead to variations in speech patterns. In addition, culture influences the ways we react to linguistic differences.

LANGUAGE AND SOCIAL CLASS

Social class plays an important role in influencing peoples' language. For example, the use of a dialect (that is, a nonstandard form of a language) is class related. Thus, black speakers from the middle socio-economic class are less likely to use the Black English dialect than are black speakers from the lower socio-economic class. Similarly, Mexican American speakers from the middle class are less likely to adopt Chicano as their basic style of speech than are lower-class Mexican Americans. Aside from the obvious variations in language we associate with ethnic dialects, a number of investigators have found substantial difference in the speech patterns of people from middle-class and lower-class groups (e.g., Blank & Solomon, 1968; Hawkins, 1969).

Bernstein's Restricted and Elaborated Codes   Basil Bernstein (1968, 1972) has developed a theory that describes class-related differences in language development and tries to account for such differences. Bernstein describes these differences in terms of two linguistic codes: the restricted code and the elaborated code. He has concluded that lower-case speech follows the restricted code, while middle-class speech tends to follow the elaborated code.

There are several features that distinguish the restricted code from the elaborated code. One is that speakers using the restricted code tend to use concrete rather than abstract words in their conversations. For example, lower-class families emphasize the accomplishment of physical tasks. The lower-class speaker, in Bernstein's view, is more likely to talk about the outcome of a local sports event than about an abstract matter like the economic indicators that govern the stock market.

A second difference between restricted and elaborated speech is that a speaker using the restricted code usually does not consider the motives and intentions of others. For instance, a lower-class mother is more likely to say to a child "Stop teasing your sister" than she is to say "You shouldn't criticize your sister's hairdo because it will hurt her feelings."

A third distinction between the restricted and elaborated codes is that the restricted code tends to stress social status as a standard for guiding behavior. For instance, a lower-class mother may try to stop her son from crying by saying "Boys don't cry" where a middle-class parent might say "Your father will be unhappy if he sees you crying." The idea that a child should not cry because he is male depends on the idea that the status of being male ought to determine the child's conduct.

Bernstein suggests that these social-class differences in language exist because of differences in the purposes language serves in middle- and lower-class families. Because people from the lower socio-economic classes tend to have jobs and hobbies that involve physical labor rather than management, they have less need to use abstract terms or to use language to describe motives and feelings. By contrast, people from the middle class, because the kinds of jobs and hobbies they have, do need abstractions and are more likely to talk about the feelings and motivations of other people.

Bernstein's theory is one of several theories that describe differences in language between middle-class speakers and members of various cultural subgroups. These theories have been the subject of extensive controversy. Some theorists (e.g., Bereiter & Engelmann, 1966) argue that various lower-class groups have *deficient* language development. Other theorists, such as Baratz (1973), Cazden (1966), and Labov (1970), argue that, while the language of lower-class groups is *different* from middle-class language, it is not inferior to middle-class language. For

distinguishing features of the restricted and elaborated modes

class differences in language functions

differences versus deficits

example, Labov (1970) says that the language of lower-class blacks is every bit as rich, varied, and complex as the language of middle-class speakers. However, the lower-class black uses different linguistic structures to communicate than his middle-class counterpart.

Instruction to Develop an Elaborated Code   Bernstein's theory suggests that it might be possible to teach a child to use an elaborated code. Gahagan and Gahagan (1970) have investigated this possibility. They developed an educational program to teach children from low-income families to use an elaborated linguistic code.

The Gahagan program focused developing skills such as explaining a set of procedures to another person and describing the feelings of another person. For instance, a child sat on one side of an opaque screen and had to tell a child on the other side of the screen how to build something. The speaker was told to build an object and then to explain how it was built so that it could be put together by the person on the other side of the screen. Children were also asked to describe the feelings of people shown in pictures.

Children in the program did especially well on a number of tests of language skill. They were given standardized language tests and tests specifically designed to assess the restricted and elaborated codes.

LANGUAGE AND ETHNIC DIVERSITY

Stand in a major airport in this country and listen to the people around you. The linguistic variations you will hear come largely from people of many different ethnic backgrounds. While English is the dominant language in our culture, Americans speak many languages other than English. Among them are Spanish, French, Chinese, Japanese, Hawaiian, and a number of Indian tongues. In addition to the many formal languages

Schools must adapt instruction to meet the needs of bilingual children.

we speak, there are a variety of dialects being used. Cajun (a version of French spoken mainly in the deep South), Chicano (made up of speech patterns spoken by Mexican Americans), and Black English (a dialect used by blacks living for the most part in urban ghettos) are examples.

Bilingualism   Many children in the United States do not speak English as their first language. Most of these speak Spanish, but a variety of other languages are also used. The word "bilingual" is generally used to refer to people who speak two languages. However, children are sometimes labeled *bilingual* for educational purposes even though they may not actually speak more than one language. For example, young children in American public schools who speak only Spanish are often called *bilingual.* Similarly, Mexican American children who speak only English may be called *bilingual.* The major reason for this is administrative. For instance, if a school has a bilingual program for children who speak Spanish and English, the administration may think that placing a Spanish-speaking child there is the best available educational option for the child.

bilingualism defined

Bilingual children often have serious educational problems, including mastering basic academic skills such as reading. In many cases the first day of school is the bilingual child's first contact with the dominant culture. In the first few years of schooling, the child may be expected not only to learn all the standard basic skills, but also to learn a new language and become familiar with a new culture and new customs. These tasks may pose quite a challenge to the child. In addition, the child may have his or her own language and cultural heritage down graded by members of the dominant culture. The chances that the child will become discouraged and angry, that he will not master all the basic skills, are high.

educational problems

At least two strategies have been suggested for dealing with the early educational problems of the bilingual child (Engle, 1975). One is to begin schooling with oral instruction in the dominant language. Only after the child has mastered the dominant language, is instruction in reading and other academic skills begun. The second approach is to teach basic academic skills in the child's first language. After the child has learned the basic academic skills, instruction in the dominant language begins.

Research on how best to teach the bilingual child has had mixed results. Engle (1975) summarized research by Modiano (1968) suggesting that the first language instruction ought to occur in the child's first language. Modiano studied Indians living in the Chiapas highlands of Mexico. The children from this area attend two kinds of schools offering different early instructional programs. Children attending state or federal schools are first taught to speak the dominant language, Spanish. After a period of being taught oral language, they are taught basic academic skills in Spanish. The other children are educated by the National Indiginest Institute. They are first taught academic skills in their native Indian tongue. Then they are taught academic skills in Spanish. Modiano found that the children taught at first in the Indian language were later better able to read in Spanish than the children who had received their first instruction in Spanish.

Although this study does suggest that beginning instruction in the child's first language may be beneficial, there is other research that indi-

These children in a bilingual classroom are practicing for a holiday observance.

cates that initial instruction in the language to be learned at school may also be effective. Engle (1975) has also summarized findings of investigations by Lambert and his colleagues working in Canada. Lambert and his associates studied a program where children who were native English speakers received all of their early school instruction in French. Their achievement was compared to that of children who were native French speakers and to children who were native English speakers receiving instruction in English. The children in the experimental program did not

HOW JUAN LEARNED TO SUBTRACT

Juan was an 8-year-old Mexican-American boy. He was classified as bilingual in the school records, but he knew almost no English when he first came to school. He had learned a great deal of English in the two years that he had been in school. However, he was still far from being fluent in the language. Juan had experienced many learning problems which his teachers had initially thought were related to his lack of fluency in English. Currently he was having a particularly difficult time learning subtraction. He was able to do simple problems that did not require regrouping, but he just couldn't seem to grasp the regrouping concept. His present teacher had finally come to the conclusion that he was probably retarded and had referred him to a school psychologist.

In their first meeting, the psychologist asked Juan to tell her about his difficulties with subtraction. Juan responded that he knew how to subtract, but that his teacher confused him. The psychologist then asked Juan to work some subtraction problems, including the following one:

834
−529

achieve the language facility in French of native French speakers. Nonetheless, they were only slightly behind the French-speaking group. And they scored as well on English achievement tests as the English-speaking children. Finally, they showed a more positive attitude toward learning French than the children who had not been intensively exposed to the language during the early years of schooling.

Although there are no definite answers to the question of how best to teach the bilingual child, a number of useful conclusions can be drawn from the existing evidence (Engle, 1975). Among these is the fact that bilingual education does not in any way damage children's language learning or school achievement. It also seems likely that teacher training and cultural background may influence the effectiveness of a bilingual program. Finally, the success of a bilingual program is influenced by a complex web of factors involving issues such as the cultural values assigned to each of the languages.

Because of the influence of culture on the educational achievements of the bilingual child, many educators and social theorists advocate bilingual-bicultural education. These programs are designed not only to provide bilingual children with basic academic skills, but also to give them a cultural identity and further their cultural traditions. Children in a bilingual-bicultural program learn to speak in two languages and to understand and appreciate the cultures of each group.

Nonstandard Dialects: Black English   Nonstandard dialects are variations of the standard form of a language. To some extent nonstandard

nonstandard dialects defined

Juan said, "That's an easy one." Then he began to work the problem out loud. "Nine plus what makes fourteen," he said, writing the 5 in the appropriate place. Then rather than crossing out the top 3 and replacing it with a 2 as an Anglo child would have done, he placed a 1 beside the bottom 2 saying, "Three plus what equals three." He then wrote down the 0 and proceeded to the final column of digits. "Five plus what equals eight," he said, and wrote the 3 in its proper place.

The psychologist watched in amazement as Juan carried out these operations. As she watched, she began to realize that Juan did indeed know how to subtract, but that he was using a method that she had never seen before and that he had certainly not been taught in school. "Where did you learn this?" she asked. Juan responded proudly that his mother had taught him. Later the psychologist learned that subtraction was taught Juan's way in many Mexican-American homes and that some children, like Juan, became confused when they were required to subtract the teacher's way. Seeing Juan subtract made the psychologist realize for the first time that the problems of educating bilingual children cannot be solved simply by teaching them to speak English.

Table 8–2 Some syntactic differences between standard English and Black English

variable	standard English	Black English
Linking verb	He is going.	He goin'.
Possessive marker	John's cousin.	John cousin.
Plural marker	I have five cents.	I got five cent.
Subject expression	John lives in New York.	John he live in New York.
Verb form	I drank the milk.	I drunk the milk.
Past marker	Yesterday he walked home.	Yesterday he walk home.
Verb agreement	He runs home.	He run home.
Future form	I will go home.	I'ma go home.
"If" construction	I asked if he did it.	I ask did he do it.
Negation	I don't have any.	I don't got none.
Indefinite article	I want an apple.	I want a apple.
Pronoun form	We have to do it.	Us got to do it.
	His book.	He book.
Preposition	He is over at his friend's house.	He over to his friend house.
	He teaches at Francis Pool.	He teach Francis Pool.
Be	Statement: He is here all the time.	Statement: He be here.
Do	Contradiction: No, he isn't.	Contradiction: No, he don't.

From "Teaching Reading in an Urban Negro School" by J. C. Baratz, in J. C. Baratz and R. W. Shuy (Eds.), *Teaching Black Children to Read*. Washington, D.C. Center for Applied Linguistics, 1969. Used with permission.

dialects are regionally determined. However, culture also plays a role. The nonstandard dialect that has been of most concern to American educators and researchers is Black English, a dialect used mainly by black speakers from urban ghettos. Table 8–2 summarizes some of the major characteristics of Black English. Among them are the omission of linking verbs as in "He goin," the omission of the possessive marker as in "John cousin," and the omission of the plural marker as in "I got five cent."

educational problems

Like the bilingual child, speakers of Black English often have serious educational problems. For example, Cohen (1969) reported that in New York City, 83% of black children from low-income families were from 1 to 3 years behind in reading by the time they reached the third grade.

Two theories have been offered to explain the educational difficulties of speakers of Black English. One is that they suffer from a cultural deficit that must be corrected before they can be expected to do well in school. The second is that Black English is different from, but not inferior to, standard English. According to this view, speakers of Black English have trouble in school because the language the teacher uses (standard English) is different from their language. This explanation suggests that these students need to learn the relationship between Black English and standard English, perhaps by being taught in the Black English dialect.

The prevailing view is to reject the idea that speakers of Black English have a cultural deficit (Harber & Bryen, 1976). However, most theorists are also reluctant to teach basic academic skills such as reading in the Black English dialect. Teaching in Black English presents both social and technical problems. There is evidence that parents, educators, and community leaders may resist a Black English curriculum during the early school years (Wolfram, 1970). Black parents, for example, may object to having their children taught ghetto language in school. They may feel that school time should be spent on standard English, which the children will need for success in the dominant culture. In addition, to teach in Black English would require elaborate educational materials that do not now exist. Furthermore, there are many unanswered questions about the form such materials should take. For instance, it is not entirely certain that Black English could be accurately written with the standard English alphabet. Constructing a suitable new alphabet would be a difficult task. And at some point it would be necessary to relate the new alphabet to the standard one to allow the child to learn standard English.

Black English is the primary dialect many children learn.

The obstacles to teaching in Black English would be worth overcoming if it were certain, or at least probable, that the program would be beneficial. Unfortunately, we are far from certain that that would be the case. There is no definitive evidence on the extent to which speaking Black English interferes with learning to read in English (Harber & Bryen, 1976). There are studies that show that there is a relationship between speaking Black English and reading problems (Bartel & Axelrod, 1973). However, the specific ways that speaking Black English may affect reading are not known. We do not know whether speaking Black English *causes* reading problems, or whether the two simply seem to occur in the same children.

As in the case of the bilingual child, the problem of how best to teach the child who comes to school speaking Black English has not been solved. What we do know is that, as with the bilingual child, sociocultural factors affect how speakers of Black English learn. We must develop educational programs that value rather than down grade the language and culture of the black child. Also, black children must be able to believe that they can have access to and acceptance in the middle-class society that uses standard English. As Richards (1972) has pointed out:

> Nobody can be expected to learn the language of a social group if at the same time he is denied the means by which he can become a member of that group. . . . Acknowledgment of the social basis of consequent educational problems should lead us to reject weakly conceptualized pedagogic answers to problems which basically require social, economic, and political solution. (p. 253)

As we have seen, there are no simple answers to the question of what promotes language development most effectively among the different ethnic groups in this nation. In the next chapter we will look at how to guide language development. While we are far from having clear-cut solutions, there is much useful information available. Determining how to use the information we do have will require your most careful judgment.

Suggested Readings

Baratz, J. C. Language abilities of black Americans, review of research. In K. Miller & R. Dreger (Eds.), *Comparative studies of blacks and whites in the United States.* New York: Seminar Press, 1973.

Bernstein, B. A socio-linguistic approach to socialization with some references to educability. In J. J. Gumperz & D. Hymes (Eds.), *Directions in sociolinguistics.* New York: Holt, Rinehart & Winston, 1972.

Bloom, L. Language development review. In F. D. Horowitz (Ed.), *Review of child development research* (Vol. 4). Chicago: University of Chicago Press, 1975.

Chomsky, N. *Language and mind: Enlarged edition.* New York: Harcourt Brace Jovanovich, 1968.

Engle, P. L. Minority language groups. *Review of Educational Research,* 1975, *45,* 283–326.

Harber, J. R., & Bryen, D. N. Black English and the task of reading. *Review of Educational Research,* 1976, *46,* 387–406.

Labov, W. The logic of nonstandard English. In F. Williams (Ed.), *Language and poverty: Perspectives on a theme.* Chicago: Markham, 1970.

McNeill, D. *The acquisition of language: The study of developmental psycholinguistics.* New York: Harper & Row, 1970.

Skinner, B. F. *Verbal behavior.* New York: Appleton-Century-Crofts, 1957.

Guiding Language
Development

This chapter describes the sequence of language development, including preverbal communication, and ways of promoting language growth. When you finish the chapter, you should know Brown's stages of language development. You should be familiar with the sequence that children go through in learning how to use language to communicate, how parents can help guide language development, and the effects of structured intervention programs on language growth.

After just a few short years, most children have a remarkable grasp of language. Not only can they use complex linguistic forms, but also they can use words to assign new meanings to the objects, conditions, and events they meet up with. As a case in point, let's look at 7-year-old Julie, who can use language to help understand an unfamiliar situation. The setting was the family's evening meal. Julie sat quietly, staring past her brothers and sisters across the table. She had not taken a bite of food, though no one had noticed except her mother. Finally the concerned mother asked: "Julie, what's the matter?" "Mom," the child said, without responding to the question, "what do you call it when a child doesn't have a mother or father?" Julie's mother, caught off guard by this new topic, asked: "What do you think it is called?" After a thoughtful silence, the little girl responded: "I think it would be called a loneliness."

What is the sequence children go through to master language so impressively? How can parents and other adults who work with children help them learn language skills? These questions are addressed in this chapter.

The Origins of Language Development

Children learn a great deal about language before they can speak. In the first few months of life, they learn to distinguish among speech sounds. Toward the end of the first year, well before they are capable of speaking intelligibly, they learn to understand basic language forms. Parents, of course, play a major role in encouraging children to develop preverbal language skills. However, the parents' behavior is influenced by the children, as well.

BEFORE LANGUAGE

Very young children do many things that seem to be related to later language learning. From the moment they are born, infants communicate by crying. During the first few months, they begin to make the sounds that they will eventually use to construct speech. Finally, toward the end of the first year, they begin to understand language. Table 9–1 summarizes infants' prelanguage behaviors.

Preverbal Communication   Infants can communicate long before they
can speak. At first, crying is their most effective means to convey information to their parents. Infants can communicate different messages by varying the ways in which they cry. Analyses of the cries of infants have shown distinct types of cries in newborns (Wolff, 1969). Adult care-givers can soon distinguish among these variations and can respond to them in different ways. For example, a mother will probably be able to tell if her 2-month-old child is crying because he is uncomfortable or because he wants attention.

crying as
communication

When they communicate by crying, babies have the opportunity to learn that the sounds they make can influence other people. This lesson is limited by how adults respond to the child's communication efforts. Bell and Ainsworth (1972) studied this assumption. They found that the children

Table 9–1   Early achievements in language development

Sound production

Differential crying	Spectograph analyses indicate distinct cries in infants. Crying may convey discomfort, anger, or the need for attention.
Cooing	Children emit simple vowel and, by 2 months, consonant sounds.
Babbling	Strings of vowel-consonant combinations appear between 3 and 6 months.
Inflection imitation	Babbling gradually becomes imitative; infants mimic themselves and then, around 8 months, the intonations of adult speech.
Early words	By the 12th month, children replicate sounds more often; and some words are spoken. Early words include "mamma," "dadda," "bye bye." By the 18th month, children have a repertoire of between 3 and 50 words.
Repertoire expansion	By 24 months children have a vocabulary larger than 50 words and spontaneously construct two-word phrases. The greatest increase in the verbal repertoire occurs around the 30th month. By then all babbling has disappeared, and speech is definitely used for communication. Children construct long phrases and some sentences, both of which vary from adult grammar forms. By 3 years, the vocabulary includes approximately 1,000 words, most of which can be understood even by strangers. By 4 years, language is well established, although it varies in style from adult patterns.

Sound discriminations

Consonant sounds	Distinction between voiced and unvoiced consonants is made as early as 4 weeks of age.
Voice differences	Distinction between voice of principal caregiver and unfamiliar voices can be made as early as 4 months of age.
Syllables	Distinction between syllables varying in only one letter can be made as early as 5 months of age.

Language comprehension

Response to words	By 10 to 11 months children can learn to react to words more quickly than to other sounds.
Recognition vocabulary	During the second year, children develop an extensive recognition vocabulary. By 12 to 18 months they respond to simple requests (e.g., "Show me the bear's ear"; "Bring Mommy the book").

Adapted from: T. Appleton, R. Clifton, & S. Goldberg, "The Development of Behavioral Competence in Infancy, in F. D. Horowitz and E. M. Hetherington (Eds.), *Review of Child Development Research* (Vol. 4). Chicago: University of Chicago Press, 1975; and from E. H. Lenneberg, *Biological Foundations of Language.* New York: Wiley, 1967.

This infant is fascinated by the sound of his father's voice. He responds with sounds of his own.

whose mothers were the most responsive to their communications in the first few months of life cried less and were more effective in communication toward the end of their first year than children whose mothers tended to be unresponsive to their early crying.

Early Sounds   The first sounds infants make are vowel sounds. However, they begin to use consonants regularly during the first 2 months of life. These early simple squeals, bleats, and gurgles are often called *cooing*. When children are between 3 and 6 months old, they begin putting together strings of consonant-vowel combinations (McCarthy, 1954). The word "babbling" is generally used to describe these strings.

As children develop, their babbling begins to be imitative. At first children imitate their own sounds and then the sounds of adult language. Shirley (1933) and Leopold (1939-1949) found that infants babbled sequences that sounded assertive, interrogative, and exclamatory. The inflections were expressive and they occurred in the correct context; however, they were not communication in that they did not convey a particular meaning the way words do. Infants from middle-class homes make more sounds during this period of imitation than infants from lower-class homes. This suggests that the greater amount of adult speech in the middle-class home may influence the amount that infants babble (Rheingold, Gewirtz, & Ross, 1959).

babbling and
language learning

Despite the fact that babbling involves using sounds that will later be used in meaningful communications, its role in fostering language development is not clear. Children who cannot make speech sounds and therefore do not babble may still be able to understand complex language (Appleton, Clifton, & Goldberg, 1975; Lenneberg, 1962). In addition, deaf

children, who do not learn to speak normally, babble in spite of their handicap (Appleton, Clifton, & Goldberg, 1975). These facts suggest that babbling is neither necessary nor sufficient for future language learning.

Although babbling is not necessary for language development, it does
give adults the chance to promote the child's use of speech sounds (Bijou
& Baer, 1965). For example, a parent can reward a child for making sounds
that are similar to those the child will need to use to communicate in
words. Rewarding the child for producing specific sounds may increase
the chance that the child will make these sounds again in the future (Skinner, 1957).

How much children learn to produce language by being reinforced for
making speech sounds is a matter of some controversy. Operant theorists believe this kind of learning is a basic part of learning to speak. Other
theorists do not believe that reinforcement of speech sounds plays a major role in language acquisition. Research has not yet answered the question.

Early Language Discrimination and Comprehension   Children learn to
discriminate among speech sounds very early in life. Infants as young as 4
weeks old can tell the difference between **voiced consonants** like *b* and
unvoiced consonants like *p* (Trehub & Rabinovitch, 1972). By the time
they are only a few months old, their speech discrimination abilities are
quite sophisticated. For example, children as young as 5 months old can
tell the difference between syllables such as "bah" and "gah," which differ in only a single sound (McCaffrey, 1972).

> discrimination of
> language sounds

Not only can very young children tell differences in the sound patterns
that make up speech, but they are also able to distinguish among the
voices of the different people who talk to them. For instance, at 4 months
of age, some infants will smile consistently when they hear their mothers'
voices, but not when they hear unfamiliar voices (LaRoche & Tcheng,
1963). Similarly, in another study 10-month-old infants tended to look at
their mothers after hearing a tape recording of the mother's voice, while
they looked at the experimenter after hearing an unfamiliar voice (Tulkin,
1971). In addition, the infants made more sounds after hearing their mother's voice than after hearing a stranger's.

> voice
> discrimination

During the second half of the first year of life, infants begin to understand
language. By the time they are between 10 and 11 months old, they can
learn to respond to new words much faster than they can learn to respond
to other types of sounds (Appleton, Clifton, & Goldberg, 1975). When they
are between 12 and 18 months old, they can respond to simple commands
such as "Bring me the toy" or "Come here." Once they are a year old, they
develop rapidly. In particular, they rapidly expand the list of words they
recognize.

> comprehension

As we learned in chapter 8, the ability to comprehend language comes
before the ability to produce it. For example, children pass through a stage
of learning to talk during which they tend to leave out articles, prepositions,
and other words that affect the meaning of a message. Shipley, Smith,
and Gleitman (1969) found that children who did not use these types of

words (called modulators) in their own speech still responded more appropriately to messages that did use modulators than to messages that left them out. For instance, they made more accurate responses to a well-formed command like "Throw the ball" than they did to "Throw ball," even though the latter was closer to the children's own speech patterns.

GUIDING PREVERBAL DEVELOPMENT

It is generally agreed that preverbal language behavior development is largely controlled by heredity (Appleton, Clifton, & Goldberg, 1975; Lenneberg, 1964). For example, how soon a baby begins to babble during the first 6 months is thought to be basically determined by genetic factors. If this were not so, deaf children would probably not babble. But deaf children do babble. Thus babbling must not be learned mainly by hearing sounds in the environment.

Although heredity undoubtedly plays an important role in determining preverbal language behavior, parents and other adults may also influence it. For instance, parents may affect the amount that their children babble. Likewise, they may affect the kinds of comprehension skills that the children develop. The influence of adults on preverbal children is in part determined by the goals and skills of the adults and in part by the responses of the children.

Socializing Influences in the Preverbal Period   Adults may directly affect language-related preverbal behavior by using behavioral techniques. Moreover, the influence of adults on early language behavior may determine the communication skills the child develops later. For instance,

Encourage preschoolers to talk to their "friends."

the kinds of interactions that a baby has with his or her mother may affect the child's language skills (Appleton, Clifton, & Goldberg, 1975).

Adults may work on preverbal communication in a number of ways. For example, they can use social reinforcement. Rheingold, Gewirtz, and Ross (1959) found that smiling could increase the frequency with which infants made sounds. Weisberg (1963) found that using social reinforcement was more effective than using comparable nonsocial reinforcement in increasing the amount that infants babble.

reinforcement

Modeling can also influence the frequency with which infants make sounds. Dodd (1972) studied infant babbling under three conditions. In one, the experimenter made babbling noises while playing with the infant. In the second, the experimenter and the baby played, but there was no modeling. In the third condition, the child heard a tape recording of the experimenter babbling. The child's babbling increased only when babbling was coupled with play. At this point, we do not know why the combination of play and modeling was effective and tape-recorded modeling was not. It may be that the physical presence of the adult has some effect on the amount of sounds the infant makes. On the other hand, play might act as a reinforcer for the children's imitations.

modeling

Although we have some evidence that adults can increase the frequency of infants' sounds, research has not shown that the number of different sounds infants make changes because of adult efforts. For instance, in the same Dodd study, there was no discernible increase in the range of consonants and vowels used by the infants.

Recent research indicates that there are marked individual differences in what adults do in working with preverbal children. For example, Cohen and Beckwith (1976) studied the way mothers talk to their infants at different age levels. They examined the interactions between infants and mothers in their homes when the infants were 1 month, 3 months, and 8 months old. There were significant variations in how much and how the mothers talked to their children. For example, some mothers said nothing at all to their children, while others talked most of the time that they were being observed. The individual differences between mothers tended to be the same at all 3 age levels. That is, if a mother talked a great deal to her child when the infant was 1 month old, she continued to talk more than the average mother as the infant matured.

variations in socialization practice

Both how much the mothers talked to their children and how often they made positive remarks rather than reprimands were related to the mothers' educations. Parents with more schooling talked more and made more positive comments than mothers who had relatively little schooling. These findings suggest one possible explanation for the early language superiority we find in children born into highly educated families. It may be that these children develop good language skills at an early age in part because they hear lots of language as babies (Cohen & Beckwith, 1976).

Child Influences on Socialization Practices   Children may influence the adults' socializing practices related to language in a variety of ways. For example, at different ages children may do things that affect how much

child age and
socialization

their parents talk to them. In the Cohen and Beckwith study (1976), they found consistent variations in how the mothers talked to their children at the three different age levels. The mothers spent less time talking to their children and made relatively fewer positive comments as the children grew older.

child behavior
and socialization

The experimenters point out that the infants acted different as they matured, and that these differences could have led to the changes in how the mothers acted. For instance, infants smile often at about 3 months of age. The babies' smiles were probably rewarding to the mothers, and may have encouraged the mothers to talk more. But at 8 months, infants are becoming mobile. As a result, they can do a host of objectionable things like putting metal objects into wall sockets, swallowing buttons, and knocking prized porcelain knickknacks off tables. Cohen and Beckwith argue that mothers are likely to respond to these acts with negative, controlling statements.

family position
and socialization

Cohen and Beckwith found that not only child behavior, but also the position of the child in the family is associated with the way mothers talked to their children. Mothers of first-born children talked more to their children than mothers who already had other children. New mothers also used more praise than mothers who had more than one child. We often find strong language skills in first-born children. Cohen and Beckwith suggest that this may be partially accounted for by the difference between how and how much mothers talk to first-born and to other children.

The Growth of Language Skills

After their first birthday, children begin to develop language skills rapidly. During their second and third years, children learn many new and complex language structures. At first, they have some trouble choosing words to fit the meanings they want to communicate. For example, a 2-year-old boy who had just cut his finger looked at his mother with fear in his eyes and said: "Are you going to put education on it?" Notwithstanding these charming mistakes, children soon acquire highly sophisticated language skills that they continue to refine as they grow up.

STAGES IN LANGUAGE DEVELOPMENT

Roger Brown (1973) has extensively studied language development in young children. He has concluded that they master language in discrete developmental stages. Brown believes that children pass through these stages in a fixed sequence, although there may be marked variations in the *rates* at which individual children progress. So far he has conducted research on only two of the stages of language development that he has identified. We will look at how Brown defines the developmental stages, and the two stages for which we have research evidence.

Sentences and Stages in Language Development   Brown defines stages in language development in terms of different kinds of sentences. As children progress, their sentences become more and more complex.

Brown's first stage is called *semantic roles and grammatical relations.* He uses this name because he has found that children's first language achievements involve learning to use meanings to convey the concepts of people and things in sentences. They also learn a simple grammar to communicate the relationships among the meanings they want to express. Children vary greatly in the age when they enter Stage I. One of the children in Brown's research entered Stage I before she was 18 months old, where the others did not use Stage I skills until they were 27 months old.

definition of Stage I

Stage I is characterized by the ability to put two words together to form what we might call a primitive sentences. Utterances such as "More tickle," "All gone," and "Mommy dress" are examples. They can be translated into sentences like "Tickle me again," My cereal is all gone," and "That is mommy's dress."

Before entering Stage I, a child's utterances are made up of single words. There is some evidence that even during this period, children begin to understand grammatical relations (Brown, 1973). For example, a child may say "dada" not only to name his father, but also to convey the idea of possession. Thus he may point to his father's hat and say "dada," apparently indicating that the hat belongs to his father. However, even though the child uses certain basic grammatical relations during this period, it is not until he begins to put two words together that we have clear evidence that he can express grammatical relations. It is at this point that Stage I begins.

Table 9–2   Two-term relations acquired in Stage I

two-term relations	relations described	examples of relations
Agent and action	A person initiates a process.	Adam pull.
Action and object	A process affects someone or something.	Break cup.
Agent and object	An instigator and object interact.	Adam ball (as in Adam kicks the ball).
Action and location	Action leads to a change in place.	Put table (as in Put it on the table).
Entity and location	Something in a place.	Lady home (as in The lady is home).
Possessor and possession	A relation between a being and that which belongs to the being.	Daddy chair (meaning Daddy's chair).
Entity and attributive	Specification of an attribute of something.	Yellow block.
Demonstrative and entity	Name of an object.	See ball.

The words in the Stage I sentences each play a specific role. Brown has described the kinds of roles that words may play. Examples include agent, instrument and location.

Stage I roles

To put together their two-word sentences, children use a set of meanings related to the roles occupied by what they are describing. For example, the sentence "Mommy dress" involves the roles of possessor and possession. The child's mother is the possessor, and the dress is her possession. By putting the two words together, the child conveys a specific relationship. Thus, by saying "Mommy dress," the child links the role of possessor to the role of possession. Table 9–2 summarizes the kinds of two-term relations between roles that children express in Stage I.

definition of Stage II

Brown's second stage is called *grammatical morphemes and the modulation of meanings*. A morpheme in a language is the smallest unit of sound that has meaning. It may be a word ("cat") or a sound (the -*s* that makes "cats"). During Stage II children learn to change the meanings of their sentences by using small grammatical units such as articles and prepositions.

Children enter Stage II when they begin to use three-word rather than two-word sentences. For instance, at some point, the child will begin to say "Throw the ball" rather than "Throw ball." The word *the* modulates the meaning of the sentence; we would get a slightly different meaning if the child said "Throw that ball." The ages when children enter Stage II vary considerably. One of the children that Brown studied was just 21 months old when she began to use Stage II constructions. Other children were between 2½ and 3.

the relationship between Stage II and Stage I

To use Stage II constructions, the child must have mastered Stage I constructions. Children learn to use grammatical morphemes after they learn to express the relations characteristic of Stage I. That is, they must be able to communicate meanings before they can be expected to modulate them.

modalities

In Stage III, children learn to use word order to change their meaning. They can express the difference in meaning that adults use word order for before they can use the correct sentence structures. For example, a young child might say "Mommy sock" indicating that her mother should put on her sock. This sentence would be imperative. By contrast, the child might say "Mommy sock" meaning "That's my Mommy's sock," in which case the sentence is declarative. Not until they have reached Stage III do children actually use word order to express these differences. For example, a Stage III child might correctly say "Are you going" and "You are going."

embeddings

During Stage IV, the child learns to make sentences more complex by embedding one clause or sentence within another. For example, a child might say "I would like a hamburger." After she turns her back to her plate, and to her dog who has been sitting patiently by the table, she might protest "Whoever ate my hamburger should get me another." The second sentence is more complex than the first because it uses an embedded clause ("whoever ate my hamburger") as the subject, while the first subject is the single word "I."

Although the ability to embed a clause in another sentence lets a child use more complex sentences, it does not apparently add to the range of

**STIMULATING
LANGUAGE DEVELOPMENT
DURING THE SCHOOL YEARS**

Parents and teachers can do much to encourage language development during the school years. It is important to realize that language teaching need not be limited to formal instruction. Language skills are acquired to a large extent in the course of everyday activities. Parents and teachers should seize opportunities to provide instruction in language whenever the chance comes up. Here are some guidelines that may help you to encourage language learning.

1. Model language skills that you hope to foster in the child.
2. When other people use language effectively, call attention to it.
3. Arrange the child's environment so that effective language will be rewarding. For instance, in responding to a child's requests, encourage her to make her needs explicit. Thus, if a child says "I'd like the whatchamacallit," ask her to name the thing she wants.
4. Finally, praise the child for instances of language growth. For example, if a child has been saying "sugetti" and then pronounces the word *spaghetti* correctly, praise him.

roles that children's sentences describe. For example, the clause "whoever ate my hamburger" indicates the role of agent. As we have seen, the role of agent can also be a part of sentences in which the subject is single word.

Finally, during Stage V the child learns to combine simple sentences or prepositions using coordinating conjunctions such as *and* or *but*. This ability lets children describe many relationships among things. For instance, a child can try to explain his own behavior by relating it to the behavior of another child, as when he says: "It's true that I pushed George, but he pushed me first."

clause and sentence combinations

If learning language does, in fact, require a child to learn certain skills in a fixed sequence, we have a reason for why young children do not directly imitate the language they hear from their parents and other adults. Brown and Fraser (1963) studied this several years ago. They found that 2- and 3-year old children who were asked to repeat adult language simplified the sentences they were asked to copy. They left out articles, prepositions, and other little words that affect the sentence meaning. However, they usually kept the key words that conveyed the basic meanings of the sentences. For instance, to imitate the sentence "I showed you the book," one of the children said "I show book."

As we will see, many parents are aware of and take into account the differences between adult language patterns and those of their developing offspring when they are teaching language skills. A summary of the normal growth pattern of language skills is shown in table 9–3.

Table 9–3 The growth of language skills

One word utterances	During this phase, which can occur during the first year of life, the child uses a single word to convey a message. For example, "up" can mean "pick me up."
Two-word utterances	In this phase, which can begin as early as 18 months or not until after the start of the third year, the child uses two words to show a relationship between roles. For example, "break cup" shows a relationship between an action (break) and an object (cup).
Multiword utterances	The children enter this phase when they begin to utter three-word sentences. This may occur before 2 years of age or not until after the third birthday. Articles, prepositions, and adjectives are included in the sentence structure at this point. The sentences are grammatically correct but differ from adult structures.

GUIDING LANGUAGE GROWTH

At first, parents are the principal social influence on their children's language. However, as children grow up, they are exposed to more and more social stimuli. Sources outside the home begin to have some effect on their language learning. As during the preverbal period, the ways in which adults interact with children is influenced by the children's characteristics. Thus, for example, a father will use different speech patterns when talking to a 2-year old than he will use with the same child when she is 3.

parent effects on language

Parental Socialization We have evidence that the general quality of the interaction between parents and children can have a significant impact on language development. A study by Wulbert, Inglis, Kriegsmann, and Mills (1975) illustrates this point. They looked at mother-child interactions of children with language delays and children with more standard language skills. The most striking finding was that the mothers of language-delayed children were less responsive to their children, both emotionally and verbally, than mothers of the children who had acquired language at a more usual rate.

Studies like this suggest overall kinds of relationships between parents and children that may affect language learning. Recently research has begun to focus on specific verbal interactions in an effort to identify precisely how parents guide language development. For example, Moerk (1975) analyzed tape recordings of mother-child interactions to find the specific strategies that mothers use to promote language.

length of mother and child verbalizations

Moerk found that mothers spend a considerable amount of time teaching their children language. About 25% of the comments the mothers made were associated with language instruction. They use at least two basic strategies to guide their children's language development. One is to link the length of their comments to the length of the utterances used by their children. Mothers seem to feel that the number of words a child strings to-

TREATING SELECTIVE MUTISM IN CHILDREN

There are some children who seem to have normal language skills at home but develop communication problems when they begin school. Alicia was such a child. She was obviously bright. When she was 2, she could recognize many letters, and by the time she was 5 she could read. However, she was now almost 7, and as far as anyone knew she had not said one word since she had entered school.

The term *selective mutism* is used to describe children who can speak but do not do so in certain situations in which you would expect them. The problem is common. Although it may disappear by itself, there are times when it requires treatment. This was certainly the case for Alicia. She had not spoken in preschool, kindergarten, or first grade. Her first-grade teacher was very concerned because the child wasn't making friends or enjoying school. Moreover, it was very difficult to tell whether or not she was learning anything. Needless to say, Alicia's parents were concerned too. They wanted her to act "normal" in school. They were afraid that if she didn't start talking soon, the other children would permanently brand her as being odd and would avoid her. In addition, they assumed quite reasonably that Alicia could not do well in school if she didn't say anything.

What could Alicia's teacher and parents do to encourage her to speak? Case studies and research provide some suggestions (Bergan, 1977; Kratochwill, in press). The adults should make sure that they were not unknowingly encouraging Alicia to communicate nonverbally rather than verbally. For example, suppose that Alicia went up to her teacher and pointed to some building blocks. Perhaps the teacher said "Would you like to play with those?" and then Alicia smiled. The teacher might feel good about figuring out what Alicia wanted. On the other hand, Alicia would have learned that you don't need to talk to get the things you want in school. Another thing that Alicia's parents and teacher should do is gradually demand that she talk and reinforce her for talking. For example, to get her to talk to people outside the family, Alicia's parents might praise her for talking at home when someone outside the family is present. Then they might reinforce her for talking to the outsiders. Finally, they might encourage her to respond to questions from the outsiders. After she has been taught to speak to nonfamily members in her own home, she might be taught to talk to other people such as her teacher and her classmates outside of her home but with a family member around. Finally, she would be reinforced for talking at school when her parents were not there.

gether is an important dimension of language learning. They seem to reason that a child who uses two- or three-word strings will learn better from a parent who uses relatively short sentences than from one who uses long, complex forms. However, although they recognize that they need to relate the length of their sentences to the length of the child's, they *invari-*

ably challenge their children by using sentences that are somewhat longer than those used by the children. Through this practice, mothers give their children language experiences that are always more advanced than the children's current abilities.

The second strategy that mothers use in guiding language development is to relate the *kinds* of verbal interactions that they use with their children to the kinds of utterances the children use. In the early stages, mothers often model specific sentences for their children to imitate. For example, a mother may look at a picture book with her child and talk about the pictures in the book. Thus, she might say "See the bunny." The child then might imitate by saying "bunny."

modeling

Another technique that mothers sometimes use is to expand on what the child has said. For example, if a child were to say "black horsey," her mother might respond "Yes, that is a black horsey." Interestingly, Seitz and Stewart (1975) found that mothers do not use this kind of expansion before their children have shown that they are able to imitate language. However, as the children learn to imitate, their mothers encourage them to use language by expanding on the children's words.

expansion

As children become more sophisticated, their mothers' language shifts to develop the child's new skills. Thus, mothers move from modeling and expanding to techniques such as giving explanations and answering the child's questions (Moerk, 1975; Reichle, Longhurst, & Stepanich, 1976).

explanation

Structured Interventions   Because language plays such an important role in children's overall intellectual functioning, a number of programs have been designed to alter children's language development. One such program was established by Genevieve Painter (1971). This was a tutorial program intended to promote linguistic and cognitive growth in children from low-income families. It was founded on the assumption that structured intervention beginning during infancy could prevent the language deficits that often appear in children from low-income homes.

the Painter program

In the Painter program, female tutors trained children for a period of 1 year. Training began at the time that a child uttered his or her first word. The first step was an active attempt to teach the child to imitate adult behavior through a variety of techniques. For example, tutors played the familiar bye-bye game in which an adult waves to a child and says bye-bye. If the child waves back, the adult smiles and praises the child. To teach children to imitate sounds, the tutors imitated the children's babbling. Painter assumed that the children would get the idea that they could imitate adult sounds just as the adults imitated theirs.

When the children were about 14 months old, they were encouraged to learn to identify objects by such means as pointing to them and naming them. For instance, a tutor might ask a child to find a spoon. Or the tutor might ask the child the name of a particular object.

At about the age of 16 months, the children were encouraged to talk about the things that they needed or wanted. Thus, if a child tried to ask for something by pointing to it, the tutor would encourage him to use a verbal request.

As the children began to use sentences, they were encouraged to do so. One of the techniques used was to ask the children to tell stories about various things.

When the children were about 24 months old, they were taught to use internal dialogues that could be applied to solve problems. For instance, they were taught to verbalize the steps required to put a puzzle together.

Painter found a 10-point IQ advantage for children who had received this training as compared to a control group of children who had not had any special training. As you will recall, IQ test scores reflect verbal skills. This IQ test score advantage could have resulted in part from language training. However, the program also included cognitive training. Thus both cognitive and language instruction could have contributed to the increased scores.

The Painter program indicates that early intervention may be effective in promoting language and cognitive growth. Osborn (1968) described a program that suggests that intervention during the school years may also be effective. This program was designed to teach language skills to black children from low-income homes. Osborn used a "pattern drill" approach. Language concepts were taught using incomplete sentences like the following:

the Osborn program

    This is a _____ .
    This is not a _____ .

Picture books can provoke verbal responses in young children.

The instructor modeled correct answers for the child and reinforced correct responses.

As with the Painter program, Osborn found a significant IQ test score advantage for the children who had been in the program as compared to children who had not been involved.

Although these programs produced desirable outcomes, they were both founded on assumptions that many theorists question. Specifically, both programs began with the assumption that, without intervention, the language of the child from lower-class homes was going to be inferior to the language of middle-class children. As pointed out in chapter 8, many contemporary language theorists feel that this assumption poses a threat to children's pride in themselves, pride in their language, and pride in their cultural heritage. In a pluralistic society such as ours, there are many different ways to speak. Although learning to speak the standard English of the middle class is obviously useful, there is no reason to assume that the speech patterns used by people outside of the middle class are inferior.

The Painter and Osborn programs do prove that powerful techniques such as modeling and reinforcement can be used effectively to promote language development. Many theorists now believe that, for these techniques to be used to meet the socialization needs of our pluralistic society, they must be linked to programs that value the language and cultural heritage of children from widely diverse backgrounds.

Suggested Readings

Bell, S. M., & Ainsworth, M. D. S. Infant crying and maternal responsiveness. *Child Development*, 1972, *43*, 1117–1190.

Brown, R. *A first language: The early stages*. Cambridge: Harvard University Press, 1973.

Moerk, E. L. Verbal interactions between children and their mothers during the preschool years. *Developmental Psychology*, 1975, *11*, 788–794.

Osborn, J. Teaching a teaching language to disadvantaged children. In M. A. Brottman (Ed.), *Language remediation for the disadvantaged preschool child*. Monographs of the Society for Research in Child Development, 1968, *33*, 36–48.

Painter, G. A tutorial language program for disadvantaged infants, In C. S. Lavatelli (Ed.), *Language training in early childhood education*. Urbana: University of Illinois Press, ERIC Clearinghouse on Early Childhood Education, 1971.

Rheingold, H. L., Gewirtz, J. L., & Ross, H. W. Social conditioning of vocalizations in the infant. *Journal of Comparative and Physiological Psychology*, 1959, *52*, 68–73.

How Emotions and Self-Concept Develop

This chapter describes how children learn emotional responses. When you have finished the chapter, you should understand how emotional responses are influenced by culture and how they can be learned by conditioning. The chapter also discusses Freud's concept of personality structure. When you have read it, you should know what the id, the ego and the superego are and how they interact. You should know about psychosexual stages and defense mechanisms.

You should also understand several explanations of motivation and motivation systems, as well as the needs for achievement and affiliation. Finally, you should understand the idea and importance of self-concept and self-esteem.

As they grow up, people develop characteristic ways of responding to others and to their own thoughts and feelings. The ways people respond to others in social situations, and the way their responses change over time and according to circumstance, are the topics of chapters 12 and 13. We often use the word "personality" to mean all those social responses that we can see in other people. We cannot see the part of personality that involves responses to internal thoughts and feelings as well, but it is an equally important element. In fact often it is nearly impossible to separate the social and emotional parts of personality.

People's typical emotional reactions, the ways they evaluate how they act and how valuable they are, the ways they manage their impulses and guide their behavior, are all extremely important aspects of personality development. In this chapter we will refer to these aspects of personality formation as *affective development,* because they all involve feelings and subjective judgments about the self.

Emotional Development

Close your eyes and picture a child—any child. Was the child smiling, playing, expressing joy or delight? Or did you imagine the face of a sad-eyed child like those in the ads of the Save the Children Foundation? Chances are you pictured a happy child, because in America today we think of childhood as a time of joy and happiness, punctuated now and then by the temporary hurt of a skinned knee or a lost friend. Most of us are quite pleased with ourselves for having come so far from the child abuse that Dickens described so vividly in his nineteenth century novels. But in spite of our wealth and the real improvements in the quality of life for children, we do not serve up equal helpings of happy times for all children. Many children go to school hungry. Others have their lives made miserable by teachers who think that learning must be at least a little painful if it is to have any value. And a surprisingly large number of children are abused and neglected by their own parents.

Most psychological theories agree that, over a long period of time, both positive and negative conditions may have long-range effects upon people's emotional development. The theories even agree particularly frightening single events may have long-range implications. But these theories differ in the specific processes they say affect emotional development. In this section we will explore some of the similarities and differences between two of the major psychological theories that try to explain emotional development.

LEARNING PROCESSES

Many people believe that children are born with the full range of emotions built in, just waiting to pop out at the appropriate time. We know now that this is not the case. Even the belief of the pioneer psychologist Watson (1919), who thought that newborns come equipped with the three basic emotions of fear, rage, and love, has been shown to have no foundation. When newborns come up against some very unpleasant stimuli they will respond with excitement; they move around and cry. But it is impossible to associate their excitement with any specific emotion such as fear or anger. The newborn infant does not distinguish between emotions. Unless observers already know what specific stimulus excited a baby, they cannot agree on whether the emotion being expressed is fear, anger, or something else (Sherman, 1927a, b). It is only through experience that babies learn to differentiate emotions.

Differentiation of Emotions   When people feel strong emotions, their bodies react and they have certain physical responses, but there is not a different set of responses that goes with the different emotions such as fear, anger, jealousy, ectasy, and sorrow. The physical response associated with joy is about the same as that associated with grief.

What happens when someone is badly frightened? The heart rate increases and the muscles become tense, and that is also just about what happens when an emotion like joy is experienced. One of our favorite stories to illustrate this point comes from one of our children when he was 7 years old.

common characteristics of emotional responses

The children were looking forward to the arrival of their grandmother, who always brought gifts on her infrequent visits. Before leaving for the airport on the evening of her arrival, the 7-year-old said, "Dad, I'm just so excited I can hardly wait. It feels like my heart is going to come out of my chest." The boy described his feelings in very similar words on another night when he woke up to see a huge, shadowy figure at the foot of his bed. It turned out to be a plastic jack-o-lantern on his dresser.

Children learn to differentiate their emotions on the basis of experiences with their environment.

Pets can help teach their owners loyalty and affection.

This example shows what psychological studies have found. No matter what emotion the person feels, the different emotions cause a common kind of physical arousal. This raises an interesting question: How then does a person know what emotion he or she is experiencing? The evidence shows that we identify our emotions primarily by external events, not by our internal states (Bandura, 1969). If you think that a situation signals danger, you will interpret the knot in your stomach as fear. If someone or something stands in the way of your achieving some goal, then you will probably experience your flush and pounding heartbeat as anger. And while the situation differs from one family to another, most mothers still think they are crying tears of joy rather than sorrow at their daughters' weddings.

cognitive influences on emotional experiences

In brief, physical arousal is an important component of emotions, but social and cognitive factors are more important in determining the specific emotion the individual feels on any particular occasion. These variables also affect the intensity of the emotion. One frequent characteristic of children's emotional responses is that they seem to adults to be out of proportion to the events that caused them. As people grow up and learn about their society, their emotional responses come to "fit" with events. An adult who cannot match emotional responses to the social situation is considered immature, and is likely to have trouble dealing with people.

differential cultural meaning of emotional responses

The same set of circumstances may have very different meanings for members of different cultural groups. When a Chinese school boy is scolded, he smiles to show his respect for his critic. Navajos and Apaches lower their voices to show anger, rather than raising them as their Anglo neighbors do (Opler, 1967). As a result, when people from different cultures interact, they may have misunderstandings because of the differences in the cultural meanings of certain acts.

Classical Conditioning   Some kinds of stimuli will produce a reaction the first time a child comes in contact with them, "no experience necessary." Touching a hot stove will cause any youngster to pull his finger back very quickly, and a puff of air on the eyelid will make a newborn blink. Stimuli that produce their effects without the person having to learn anything are called **unconditioned stimuli.** The response that follows an unconditioned stimulus is an **unconditioned response.** People would not get very far if they had to do it on the basis of their unconditioned responses alone. There must be ways to learn new ways to act on the basis of experience. Classical conditioning, which we looked at in chapter 2, is one of the ways that new responses are learned. To review briefly, if a stimulus that causes no response (called a **neutral stimulus**) occurs at the same time as an unconditioned stimulus, the neutral stimulus will eventually produce the same response that the original unconditioned stimulus did. The neutral stimulus becomes a **conditioned stimulus.** It can evoke the same response—perhaps fear or withdrawal—that was produced earlier by the unconditioned stimulus. If a child hears the word "hot" at the same time she touches a hot stove, eventually she will feel the same excitement and fear that the burn produced in the first place.

unconditioned stimuli and responses

conditioned stimuli and responses

A classic example is the story of Albert, who was conditioned to be afraid of a rat. Albert also generalized this fear to a wide range of objects that all had something in common. Albert's fear was produced and later removed as an experiment. Often people acquire similar fears quite accidentally, when a neutral event occurs at the same time as an event that already produces a fear response. Because we often are not aware of these circumstances, the fears that result may appear to be irrational.

A generalized fear, such as Albert's fear of rats and other furry things, is called a *phobic reaction.* Many young children have **phobias** specific to dogs or snakes, or even particular places or situations. An adult may have an irrational fear of cocktail parties or sorority dances for the same reason. A response may be several steps removed from the stimulus that first produced it, and the origin of a phobia may be difficult to trace.

phobic reactions

People usually try to avoid or withdraw from situations that make them feel afraid. Once someone has learned an avoidance behavior through conditioning, it is very difficult to get rid of naturally. The reason should be apparent when you think about it. If you are irrationally afraid of certain things or situations, you will stay away from those things as much as possible. As long as you avoid the situations, you have little chance to learn through experience that there is nothing to be afraid of.

persistance of avoidance behavior

Fortunately, conditioning can also link new situations to stimuli with pleasant associations. When you encounter a sight or a sound that you have associated with pleasure in the past, that sight or sound can produce the kind of physical arousal and mental images that you interpret as "happy feelings."

Operant Conditioning   In classical conditioning, responses are controlled by the things that happen just before the response. Responses may also be controlled by the events that follow them, through the process of operant conditioning. We were introduced to this process also in chapter 2. Recall that when a behavior is followed by a reinforcing event, the behavior will be strengthened. By definition, a reinforcer is a consequence of an action that is favorable to the individual. Because different cultural groups attach different values to different outcomes, we see great variability from one person to another in events that act as reinforcers.

operant principles in daily life

Operant conditioning influences the strength of all sorts of different behaviors, from voluntary actions to subtle physical responses (Bandura, 1971). Many people think of operant conditioning as something that happens primarily in a psychological laboratory, but this is a misconception. Operant principles are at work all around us every day, and often we condition responses that we really do not want. A child's temper tantrum, for example, is largely an emotional response. When a parent gives in to a child who throws a tantrum, the parent is reinforcing that kind of emotional outburst. The tantrum may be reinforced merely when the parent pays a lot of attention to the child while she is throwing her tizzy.

Vicarious Conditioning   Many emotional reactions are developed through

REDUCING FEARS

Many children develop extreme fears. To some parents it may not seem important if a child trembles with fear at the sight of a dog, for example. But being unreasonably or "irrationally" afraid of certain objects or situations severely restricts the things the child can do and the places he or she can go. For instance, some children with whom he/she might want to play might have a dog at home.

It is very hard for children to lose an irrational fear "naturally," because they avoid situations in which they might learn that there is usually nothing to fear from a dog, so long as certain precautions are observed. It may do more harm than good to confront the child with the feared object in a "sink or swim" philosophy. The following suggestions, derived from learning theory, hold greater promise for the adult who wants to help a child get over a debilitating fear:

1. A child who is afraid of dogs will generally not be afraid if the dog is a good distance away. When you are with the child, and see other children playing happily with their dog, call your child's attention to the scene. Call specific attention to the ways the other children show their pleasure. A parent might say, "Look how those children enjoy their dog—do you hear them laughing? They seem to be having a very good time playing catch with the dog. That dog must really love children. Did you see how she licked their hands?"
2. Don't rush things. Gradually try to find opportunities to observe dogs and children playing from a closer vantage point. You can judge how

direct experience, either through operant or classical conditioning or a combination of both. But it is not essential to have direct experience to acquire all emotional responses. Some responses may be learned vicariously, by observing how others react. How else could you explain how a child comes to be afraid of snakes, or even mice, when he has had no direct experience with these creatures? If a child sees his mother respond by shrieking and running away from a mouse that runs across the kitchen floor, the child will quite likely come to share his mother's fear of rodents, although no mouse has ever harmed him, or the mother either for that matter. The mother probably learned her fear through the same vicarious process. And if a child sees someone who is important to him look pleased—smiling, talking happily, and so on—these expressions may teach the youngster something. On future occasions he may feel the same pleasant feelings again in response to the kind of situation that he saw produce those responses in the model.

modeling influences

Children may be more likely to learn emotional responses vicariously by watching people who are close to them than by watching people who are strangers, but the evidence is quite clear that they also learn emotional responses by watching models on television or in movies. Emotional responses may even be conditioned when they are only presented in words and printed media (Bandura, 1971).

close is appropriate by watching for signs of tension in the child. If you see those signs, back off a bit and watch for the anxiety to disappear.

3. You don't have to wait for situations with real dogs and real children to come along. Vicarious experience can also help.

   a. Find books that show happy interactions between a child and his dog. If possible, find a book in which the main character is the same sex as your child. Read these books as bedtime stories, or at some other time when the child is likely to be very relaxed. As with the real-life situations, take time to call attention to expressions of pleasure.

   b. Don't overlook the possibilities of television. Watch your local television guide. Some communities still have reruns of the Lassie series, the Benji movies, and so on. These will be more effective if you watch along with the child, and call attention to the acts of friendship and loyalty between dog and owner.

4. Move gradually into the introduction of a real dog. When that dog comes, choose a nonthreatening introduction. A very docile large dog or a calm small dog will fit the bill. The last thing you want to do is to undo your months of preparation by introducing the child to a 40-pound German Shepherd puppy who will jump on the child and shower a tearful face with wet kisses.

These suggestions can be adapted for any object of "irrational" fear.

DEALING WITH CHILDREN'S TANTRUMS

Many parents become frustrated when they can't deal successfully with tantrums. The following suggestions may help:

1. Remember, there is generally nothing "wrong" with children who throw tantrums. They throw their screaming and kicking tizzies because they have learned that it is a good way to get what they want. Tantrum behavior is very distressing to most adults, and often they give in and give the child what he wants rather than endure the outburst.

2. When the parent gives in, it is very likely that the child will use the same means of getting what he wants the next time the parent says "no."

3. Remember that sometimes the issue under question really isn't very important anyway. If a parent realizes that the conflict really isn't very important, it probably just won't seem worth the hassle to continue insisting on having your own way. Therefore, before you say "no," think about whether you have a good reason. Some parents get so taken with their own concerns that they say "no" or "don't" almost automatically—without thinking about it. A good first step in dealing with, or avoiding, tantrums is to be careful not to be too negative in response to your child's requests.

4. It is not easy to get rid of tantrum behavior once it has started. In a typical case, a parent may be very determined "not to give in this time." But when the usual kicking and screaming does not produce the desired result, the child will try harder. If loud crying got results in the past, this time she may cry louder and longer and lie on the floor, kicking and pounding her fists. At that point, many a determined parent gives in. Kids soon learn that this tactic works particularly well when there are other people around, so mother or dad

THE CASE OF CARLOS

Carlos was the oldest child of a middle-class family living in a suburb of a Southwestern city. He had only been in junior high school for a few weeks, and so far it had not been a happy time for him. His first problem was his health. Carlos was generally healthy, with nothing more serious than some very troublesome allergies that usually bothered him during the springtime, but this fall his allergies were giving him even more problems than ever before. This was the first time they had ever come on in the fall.

Even worse than the allergies was the school. Carlos had begun junior high with enthusiasm. He and his friends had been planning for school for weeks, and Carlos was even looking forward to meeting new friends and to changing classes and having different teachers for every subject. He was a good athlete, and the sports program would also be a new adventure. But his enthusiasm was soon dampened. Most of his classes left a lot to be desired; history and English were the worst, and that came as a real surprise. In elementary school he had enjoyed social studies and reading will be embarrassed into surrender. "Round two goes to the kid."

5. Sometimes the parents will hold out, and sometimes they will give in. This makes the behavior even harder to deal with, because it is being maintained with an intermittent schedule of reinforcement. Extinction becomes very difficult.

6. Is there anything a poor, beleaguered parent can do? Fortunately, yes!

   a. Before you say "no" or "don't," think about it. Does it really make sense to say "no?" Is the issue important?

   b. If it is important, try to provide an acceptable alternative. Just saying "no" does not teach the child what *is* acceptable.

   c. If the issue is really important, explain your reasons. Point to the consequences of the forbidden act, if that is the question. If the alternative you offer is not acceptable to the child, quietly stick to your guns. Don't argue.

   d. Ignore the tantrum behavior, unless the child is in danger of injuring himself.

   e. If you have given in to tantrums in the past, don't expect immediate results when you begin to ignore them. Things will get worse before they get better. Remember, if this tactic has worked in the past, the child is going to try a bit harder the first few times it doesn't produce results.

   f. If the child is in danger of injuring herself, quietly carry her, kicking and screaming if necessary, to a safer place.

   g. Don't jump to the conclusion that the child is "willfully" opposing your authority. He is only responding to a general law of behavior that influences all of us. Concentrate on finding interesting and constructive things to occupy the child.

about famous men and women and writing reports on their parts in history. But at this school, history was different. There were long passages to be memorized and chapters to be outlined. Carlos could manage that without much trouble, but the teacher never made it clear what the students would be tested on, or when; and sometimes the questions were so confusing it was almost impossible to answer correctly even if you knew the right answer. Carlos was doing failing work for the first time, and he could not figure out why. Before long he began to get a sinking feeling inside whenever he stepped into history class.

History class wasn't the worst either. Carlos liked to write stories and poems, and he was an avid reader. But there was no room for that sort of thing in this English class. Every day was the same. The teacher said there was no sense in doing creative writing until the students had mastered the fundamentals of grammar, so every English period the students worked at filling in blanks and underlining words in a workbook. Then there were spelling words to be memorized, which wasn't so bad, and homework nearly every night. It was the homework that caused Carlos the most worry, because the assignments were often unclear, and you could never be sure if an assignment was just for practice or for a grade. Carlos seemed to misunderstand the assignments a good deal of the time; and in this class once you made a mistake there was no way to make it okay by doing better next time. Each bad grade stayed there to haunt you and pull down your good marks, so even when you did well you had the feeling that you were going to fail in the long run.

There was no way to win, and the school counselor wasn't much help. Carlos had gone to her for advice about how to improve his grades, but the counselor didn't seem to think it was very serious. She casually dismissed the case by explaining to Carlos that he had two very demanding teachers, and he should set aside a special time to do homework each evening. Carlos was already doing that, but the counselor did not seem to believe him.

As if history and English were not enough for a 12-year-old to bear, the allergies continued to complicate life. At the beginning of the school year he was having trouble breathing and was awake coughing most of the night. That made him tired in school, which might have explained why he had trouble getting his work done in class and keeping the assignments straight. It might also explain some of the foolish mistakes he made, which looked like carelessness to his teachers. When his parents took him to the doctor, they learned that his allergies had developed into seasonal bronchial asthma. The doctor explained that many people with allergies were having unusual trouble that fall.

The doctor prescribed medication that relieved the discomfort and coughing, but it also made Carlos groggy when he had to take it during the daytime. So he was back where he started—sluggish if he did not take the medicine to let him sleep, and sluggish if he had to take it to keep from coughing in school.

Meanwhile, something else began to happen that Carlos couldn't understand. All fall he had felt embarrassed by not being able to control his coughing in classes. But by now that should have stopped. The pollen count was down, and he no longer needed the medicine to let him sleep at night. The cough that had bothered him all these weeks was almost gone; but when he went to history and English classes, he found himself short of breath and the cough returned. It seemed to happen only in those two classes, and his relationship with those teachers went from bad to worse. The junior high experience he had looked forward to with such high expectations had become a nightmare for Carlos and his family.

Do you have any hunches about how the learning processes we have discussed may have led to Carlos' asthma even after the pollen-producing plants had gone dormant? A school psychologist was asked to look at Carlos' case, and she had a hunch after gathering the information we have just summarized.

The school psychologist knew that researchers had found that asthma could be conditioned to occur in response to neutral stimuli by exposing an asthmatic patient to the neutral stimuli and at the same time to the allergens that brought on the asthma symptoms (Dekker, Pelser, & Groen,

aversive school practices

1957). As the psychologist put the clues from the case together, she came up with the hypothesis that a very complicated set of relationships between some unseasonably late rains and Carlos' negative school experiences had led to his psychosomatic attacks of asthma during English and history classes.

Fortunately, what learning principles can do, they can also undo if skillfully applied. In Carlos' case, two things had happened at the same time. His failures in English and history had led him to learn to have anxiety reactions to those classes. At the same time, his asthma attacks had become conditioned to occur during these same two classes because they were scheduled immediately after P.E., when Carlos had just been exposed to high levels of allergens. Stranger things have happened. One pair of researchers analyzed psychosomatic asthma attacks and found that the stimuli that brought on the attacks included such a diverse range of stimuli as goldfish, waterfalls and even radio speeches by politicians (Dekker & Groen, 1956, cited in Bandura, 1969). Many people believe that asthma attacks are provoked by emotions, but they may actually be due to the fact that an aversive stimulus is paired with an unconditioned and asthma-producing stimulus, as in Carlos' case.

The school psychologist decided to work on the anxiety reactions to English and history classes first. Fortunately the school district policy permitted minority group students to change schools if their new choice would improve the ethnic balance of the new school. Carlos was moved to a new and more progressive school. Before he began English and history classes in the new school, the school psychologist put him through a program to eliminate his anxiety. The procedure was complex. In brief, the first step was to find out which aspects of English and history classes provoked the greatest anxiety and which were least anxiety-provoking. They were arranged in order. Carlos was then taught to relax, because you cannot be anxious and relaxed at the same time. Handing in homework assignments was the thing that caused Carlos the most trouble, so it was at the top of the list. Studying vocabulary words provoked relatively little anxiety, so that was at the bottom. Next, he was trained to relax deeply while imagining that he was studying vocabulary words. Once he could do this, he moved to the next least threatening step in the sequence, and so on. Eventually he was able to imagine himself being relaxed and turning in homework assignments, and finally actually doing an assignment made up by the psychologist and turning it in. While he did homework assignments and turned them in, he was given pleasant experiences to "countercondition" his earlier reactions.

intervention procedures

During this period, Carlos did not attend either English or history class at his new school. He spent those periods in the school library. When he had completed his counterconditioning program, he was assigned to English and history classes that were different from those at his previous school. Luckily he started those classes at a time when allergens in the air were at a low level, so his new experiences began with neither the natural responses to allergens nor the conditioned ones that had bothered him before. Carlos enjoyed his new chances to do creative writing, analyze current events, and debate politics.

We need to add a postscript to this brief summary. Most school psychologists are busy giving intelligence tests for program placement recommendations. The school psychologist who worked with Carlos was in private practice; she was not employed by the school district. If Carlos' parents had not been able to afford this service, the ending to this story would probably have been quite different.

inadequacy of school services

PSYCHOANALYTIC THEORY

A second major explanation for how personality develops is provided by psychoanalytic theory. This theory, developed by Sigmund Freud, is considerably different from social learning theory. Freud devoted the major part of his career to treating people with emotional disorders and developing a theory to explain his observations. Although his observations were based upon a group of fairly similar upper middle class people from Vienna, he did not hesitate to assume that his theory could explain the emotional development of people from any time or place. His ideas have had a significant influence on psychological theory and on research on human development, and they have probably had more influence on the man on the street than any other personality theory.

Personality Structure   Freud saw personality as a three-part structure—an id, an ego, and a super ego. Of these parts, only the id was thought to be present and working at birth. The id is dominated by the desire for pleasure principle, and it is directed at immediately satisfying instinctive desires. These instincts are basically of two types: sexual and aggressive. The character and personality of each person are shaped as the id's attempt to gratify instinctual desires is molded by all the things that happen outside of the person.

id

ego

The ego is the second structure of the personality to develop. The id has no knowledge of the outside world. While it may work to an infant's advantage to be controlled by instinctive impulses, someone older who is governed entirely by the id would continually be in trouble for violating the customs of society. To avert this trouble, the ego develops out of the structure of the id. The ego's task is to test reality and to decide on the proper time and place for the id's energies to be released. Thus the ego not only delays the gratification of the id's instincts, but it also determines the form of the energy release and the appropriate objects or people toward which it is directed.

super ego

The last part of the personality structure to develop is the super ego. This structure represents the standards and values of the society in which an individual grows up. Adults in the child's environment, especially parents, represent the standards of society. The norms and values that the child learns from these adults are incorporated into the super ego and thus become part of the personality system. In everyday terms, the super ego serves as the conscience. From Freudian viewpoint, it is the super ego that lets us resist temptation and exercise self-control.

The conscience is actually only one subsystem of the super ego. Children learn standards of conduct from their parents in two ways. First, they punish actions that violate social norms, and the child learns to avoid doing those things that would call for punishment. The subsystem operating in this case is conscience. But there are also positive acts that children learn to perform by being rewarded. These become incorporated into the super ego as standards for the kind of person one would like to become. These standards form the ego ideal, the second subsystem of the super ego.

development of conscience

How the id, ego, and super ego interact affects both social and emotional development. Here we are primarily concerned with how this interaction affects emotional development.

The possibilities for conflict between the three parts of the system are obvious. On the one hand, there is the id, eager to express its sexual and aggressive instincts. At the other extreme there is the super ego, trying to abide by social rules and conventions. Since the desires of the id and the duties of the super ego often conflict, the ego has to act as a go between for outside realities, the primitive impulses of the id, and the super ego's often unreasonable expectations. This is a decision-making task of no small proportions. The ego acts as the executive of the personality, to find socially appropriate ways to satisfy instinctive needs.

intrapsychic conflict

Freudian theory assumes that early childhood experiences are very important to long-range psychological health because they influence the basic structure of the personality. Personality characteristics that develop because of early experiences are assumed to be very stable across time and from one situation to another. A person's actual *behavior* may change from situation to situation; but (according to psychoanalytic theory) once the personality is formed, the behaviors will be motivated by a relatively stable personality.

importance of early experience

Younger children are likely to act on the urgings of the id and end up running afoul of social norms and expectations. As the child becomes more socialized and as the personality structures are formed, conflict shifts from confrontations between the individual and the environment to conflict among the personality components. This internal conflict produces anxiety that the individual feels as painful tension. Anxiety plays an important role in development, because people adopt characteristic ways to reduce or avoid anxiety.

Psychosexual Stages The kinds of adjustments people have to make change with age. According to psychoanalytic theory, these changes are largely governed by biology. Freud believed that at different ages, the needs for physical pleasures become centered in different erogenous zones. These changes lead to a sequence of psychosexual stages. Each stage has a unique set of requirements for the developing person to cope with. Each stage offers its own unique chances for gratification, but at the same time each one has conditions in which the urge for pleasure may be frustrated. Thus the individual's adjustment task changes from one stage to the next.

fixation

The first stages of development are considered decisive in the formation of personality. At any stage, development may become *fixated* if the sexual impulses of that stage are not satisfied. Moving from any stage to the next also produces some anxiety; and if that anxiety is too great, the individual may have trouble moving on to meet the challenges of the next stage. And when faced with a frightening experience, an individual may

regression

also go back, or *regress*, to an earlier stage. Usually, regression is determined by earlier fixations. If a person does regress, it will most likely be to a stage at which there was an earlier fixation.

The first three stages of development in Freud's scheme—the oral, anal,

oral stage

and phallic stages—are all critical. The first of these is the oral stage. During the first year of life, the mouth is the center of pleasurable sensation. First the child gets pleasure through sucking and later through biting and chewing. If the child's need to satisfy these urges is not adequately met, he may fixate at that stage. As an adult, his behavior will show clues to this early frustration.

The adult traits that reflect early frustrations are often exaggerated in literature and in characters in the popular media. Edith, the long-suffering wife of Archie Bunker on *All in the Family,* is such a creation. A true believer in psychoanalytic theory might well think that Edith was frustrated during the first part of the oral stage, because at that point oral needs are dominant. If the needs of that period are frustrated, the adult may be gul-

According to psychoanalytic theory, one outcome of frustration during nursing could be later gullibility.

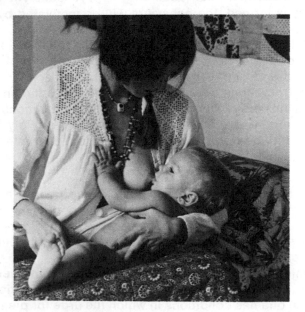

lible, like Edith. Symbolically, the gullible person is easily taken in (Mischel, 1976). But frustration during this period could also result in a personality pattern quite different from gullible Edith. Presumably, a character such as Silas Marner could also have been frustrated during that period. Silas Marner is an almost perfect example of the sort of miser that psychoanalytic theory would say could result from early oral fixation.

If frustration occurs later in the oral stage, when the child's pleasure is centered on biting and chewing, the child may become a sarcastic adult or one who is "bitingly" argumentative (Mischel, 1976). Television has exaggerated such traits in characters such as Fred Sanford of *Sanford and Son,* and Ed of *Chico and the Man.*

During the oral stage the infant is completely dependent upon others. He has little need to control his impulses. The first pressure to control his impulses comes during the second year, when the anal area is the primary center of bodily pleasure. During this **anal stage** the child gets pleasure   anal stage
by defecating. But in most western cultures, the child is now faced with a demand to postpone this gratification. Toilet-training practices vary greatly from one culture to another. Since psychoanalytic theory predicts that toilet training will have long-lasting effects on personality, many anthropologists and psychologists have looked for relationships between the toilet-training customs of different cultures and typical personality characteristics of those cultures. From the vantage point of psychoanalytic theory, we would expect that a child may learn to hold back her feces if her parents use strict and severe practices to train her. The long-lasting effects of this treatment might be expressed by "retentive" personality characteristics such as stinginess, precision, and orderliness. Dickens might well have had such a childhood in mind when he invented Scrooge for *The Christmas Carol.* In contrast, other children whose parents use stern methods of toilet training might rebel and release their feces at inappropriate times. In adulthood, these individuals might be messy, bad-tempered, or even cruel. These two contrasting outcomes of anal frustration were developed in the main characters for *The Odd Couple.*

While some parents try to toilet train their children with sternness and reprimands, others praise their children for producing feces at the proper time and place. In this event the child may look at producing feces as a very important activity. This way of adjusting may be symbolized later in life by creativity and productivity.

From the third through about the fifth year, the important events in psychosexual development center around the genital organs. This period is called the **phallic stage.** At this point gratification is achieved largely   phallic stage
through masturbation and fantasy. A drama of critical importance to future development begins to unfold. Freud thought that during this period little boys begin to love their mothers. This love is not a simple bond of affection; it is a sexual kind of attraction. At this stage, boys resent their fathers because they are rivals for their mothers' affections. In Freud's   Oedipus complex
view, little boys develop an incestuous desire for their mothers, but by this

time they are well enough socialized to know that these desires must not be expressed. Freud believed that boys at this stage come to be afraid that they will be castrated by their fathers, acting in response to the child's fantasies. These fears are presumably due to the boy's perception of the female as a castrated male, and from direct threats of castration as punishment for masturbation.

What is a little boy to do in such a spot? Freud thought that they reduced their anxiety by repressing their sexual desires for their mothers and trying to be like their fathers. By identifying with the father, boys achieve some vicarious satisfaction of their desire for their mother. Freud called this drama the *Oedipus complex,* after the character in Greek mythology who unknowingly killed his father and married his mother.

Events that take place during the Oedipal conflict have a long-lasting influence on the personality, according to Freudian theory, and resolving their anxieties is considered essential to healthy emotional development.

Freud did not give as much attention to the development of girls during the phallic stage as he did to boys. He did describe a parallel set of conflicts that he called the *Electra complex* for the character in Greek mythology who avenged the death of her father by persuading her brother to kill their mother. Freud felt that the mother is the first object of affection for both boys and girls. However, with girls this love is transferred when they discover that boys have protruding organs where they have only a space. This discovery leads to penis envy in girls, and they redirect their love from mother to father, because they want to share the organ that is the object of envy. They are not afraid of their mothers as boys are of their fathers. Their sexual desires are merely modified again because of social barriers to incest.

As the phallic stage draws to a close, sexual instincts subside and overt expressions of sexuality decline. Freud described this stage as a **latency period,** and gave it relatively little attention in his writings.

Until this time, love interests are directed primarily towards the self. Through the course of normal development, love impulses become rechanneled, and during adolescence people become capable of altruistic love. This final stage, which includes adolescence and adulthood, is called the **genital stage.** Besides being characterized by mature sexuality, it is a time when people can feel love and concern for other people's feelings. In this conclusion Freud's theory is similar to Piaget's ideas about the point when people become capable of altruism. The two points of view differ, however, in their explanations for the development of altruism. As we shall see soon, social learning theory differs from both of these points of view, both in its explanations for the development of empathy and in its conclusions about the age at which children become capable of empathetic responses.

Electra complex (margin)

latency period (margin)

genital stage (margin)

anxiety (margin)

Defense Mechanisms   Anxiety is a state of tension that warns the ego of impending danger (Hall & Lindzey, 1970). People may become anxious when they are afraid that their instincts will get out of control and lead to punishment. Anxiety may also be a direct result of threat from the environment. When he feels anxious, the individual is motivated to do something to cope with the threat. When a situation is so threatening that the ego cannot deal effectively with the resulting anxiety, the person has a **traumatic experience.** If the ego cannot deal with the situation rationally, it must resort to unrealistic solutions called **defense mechanisms.** Let's look at several widespread examples.

People sometimes deal with their unacceptable feelings by thinking that someone else has those feelings. For instance, if Roger feels aggressive toward Pat, he may reduce the anxiety created by this unacceptable impulse by believing that Pat feels aggressive too toward him. This lets Roger express his originally unacceptable feelings when he defends himself against Pat, his "enemy." This mechanism is called *projection.*

projection

Very young children may use such a similar defense mechanism when they are confronted with information that is too threatening to accept. They may simply deny the unacceptable impulse or knowledge. For example, a child who feels strong attachments to his father may convince himself that, even though everyone says so, his father has not really robbed a grocery. This mechanism is called *denial.* It is more difficult to use as the child matures and is less able to ignore reality (Mischel, 1976). The child may then use *repression,* where the child "forgets" the troublesome information. The information is not lost, but rather remains in the unconscious where it may cause emotional difficulties.

denial

repression

A person may also deal with unacceptable impulses by replacing them with the opposite feelings. Interest in sex, for example, may be replaced with disdain for such matters. This form of ego defense is called *reaction formation.* Take the case of Annabelle, a young lady with a strict moral upbringing who is active in antipornography campaigns. A psychoanalytic interpretation could be that she cannot accept her own interest in erotic materials. As a defense, she conducts an all-out assault on anything sexually provocative.

reaction formation

This same behavior could be interpreted quite differently from the perspective of social learning theory. It might be reasonable to expect that Annabelle had been reinforced by her family and by fellow church members for her disapproval of erotic materials. Through this experience, Annabelle would come to expect to be reinforced for any expression of social and moral concern about erotic materials. Moreover, she would probably learn to approve of her own antipornography campaign, so self-reinforcement would keep the behavior strong even if others no longer commented. Thus, reaction formation and most of the other behaviors that Freudians interpret as defense mechanisms could be explained quite differently from a social learning perspective.

Sometimes people have impulses that they cannot ever bear to think about. These impulses are usually sexual. To avoid the anxiety of dealing directly with the impulse, the individual may *sublimate,* or transform the drive into a socially acceptable form. Through sublimation, a person may transform sexual energy into productive pursuits such as hobbies, a career, or athletics.

sublimation

regression   *Regression* is a defense mechanism that we have already discussed. When a child does things that were acceptable earlier but have now become inappropriate for his age, he is regressing. Regression is one of the most common defense mechanisms used by children.

Mark was 3½ years old when his baby sister arrived. For a few weeks, his parents had been telling him that he would soon have a new baby brother or sister. Then one day his mother was taken to the hospital. A few hours later Mark's father told him that he had a new sister, and that mother would be bringing her home in 2 or 3 days. Sure enough, 3 days later Mark's mother returned home with the new infant, and for Mark home just wasn't the same any more. The baby required a lot of care, and demanded the time and attention of both mother and father. The baby kept Mark's parents from sleeping well, so they were often irritable and short-tempered with him and his requests. Whenever the baby cried, someone went to her and held her, or changed her diapers, or gave her a bottle. Neither of Mark's parents had much time left to play with him or to read stories to him at bedtime.

Before long, Mark's parents had another problem besides a new baby on their hands. Mark began to cry for a bottle, and sometimes he even took bottles prepared for the baby from the refrigerator and drank from them. Even more annoying was the fact that he began wetting the bed—which he had outgrown several months before. By reading a child-care book, Mark's parents learned that he was going through a period of regression. He probably felt displaced by the baby sister, but he also felt that it was not acceptable to express his resentment. His feelings of resentment produced anxiety. To deal with this anxiety, he adopted old behaviors that had once been comforting.

Again, it is possible to interpret Mark's regressive behaviors quite differently from a social learning point of view. Behaviors like taking a bottle had been appropriate at an earlier point in Mark's development; but as he grew older his parents encouraged him to give up the bottle and praised him for drinking from a glass or cup. Before the baby came the parents expressed their approval when Mark acted "more mature." But there wasn't much time for that after the baby came. Mark received less attention than he did before because the infant required so much care. His new patterns of independence no longer earned him approval and attention. At the same time, Mark observed his baby sister receiving a great deal of attention for dependency, like for being fed with a bottle. Bottle feeding was a behavior that Mark still knew, but it had stopped being functional. Now that his more mature behaviors were not getting him any attention, he began to use old behaviors that used to be satisfying, and that he now saw earning his sister the attention of his parents. In brief, Mark merely reverted to an old habit when his new behaviors no longer seemed satisfactory. Moreover, he had observed that immaturity produced benefits for his baby sister.

Just as learning principles may explain the development of patterns that parents never intended, so can they be used to avoid the kinds of problems Mark's parents ended up with. Perhaps even more important, these principles may be used to prevent anxieties like Mark's before they develop. Try to devise some procedures that could be used for this, and see if your plans agree with the suggestions we offer in the next chapter.

Rationalization is one of the best known and most commonly used ego defense mechanisms. Unacceptable motives can be justified and the anxiety they lead to reduced if we can convince ourselves that there are socially acceptable reasons for our behavior.

rationalization

Displacement is a means of redirecting emotions from their original objects to other, less dangerous ones. A frustrated child may want to hit his mother, but even to let himself feel that impulse would heighten his anxiety. Besides, most children know that it is not very safe to hit someone who has as much power and authority as a parent. The child may therefore hit a safe object such as a dog, a ball, or a younger brother. Some psychoanalytic theorists believe that pent up aggressive or sexual energy must be released in some form. For a child who has a great deal of pent-up hostility, therapists sometimes deliberately try to use displacement by giving him an object such as a punching pillow, so he can release his aggression freely. We will have more to say about this practice when we discuss aggressive behavior in chapter 11.

displacement

Few people today admit to subscribing completely to Freud's original theory. Nevertheless, it continues to have a strong influence upon many psychologists' and psychiatrists' interpretations of behavior. It also has an influence upon helping professions such as psychiatry, education, and social work.

Regulatory Processes

MOTIVES AND ACTIONS

Think about the things you did last night. Did you spend the evening watching the latest television serial when you should have been studying for a test? Or did you study when you would rather have been watching a movie or seeing a friend? At any particular time, the range of things an individual *could* be doing seems almost limitless. But, as Thoreau observed, we tend to march to different drummers, or at least many of us like to think we do. Why do we choose one activity over another, even when we know that our choice is not the most rational one? What accounts for differences in motivations among individuals? And can parents and teachers deliberately influence the motivational development of their children?

The factors that determine choices seem much easier to sort out for children than for adults. The younger the individual, the more clear-cut the influences on behavior appear to be. At first, physical needs determine behavior; but as people grow up, they develop more social needs that hide their motives. In this section we will look at how a person's motives develop through social experience.

Drives as Instigators of Action   Behavior may be motivated by physical drives. If you are hungry or thirsty, the physical arousal will direct your behavior. This basic fact is widely acknowledged in psychological theories; it is a focus in **drive reduction** theories of learning.

physiological needs and primary drives

Primary drives are inborn physiological needs for the basic necessities of life, including food, water, oxygen, and sexual activity. Drive reduction theories suggest that all human motives come from the tensions created by these drives, or from secondary drives that are learned while satisfying primary drives. The primary drives are affected and changed by the child's social experiences. The primary drives are altered, and secondary drives develop, according to the learning principles we have already discussed. Neutral events that occur at the same time that the primary drives are satisfied become secondary drives.

secondary drives

According to the drive reduction theory, secondary drives such as the need for love and affection develop because events which are originally neutral occur at the same time that primary drives are satisfied. According to this point of view, most babies learn to love their mothers because the mother is regularly present when the child's hunger is satisfied. Over time, the child comes to feel comforted by the presence of the mother alone, and this response gradually generalizes to other people as well. The drive reduction point of view is also compatible with psychoanalytic explanations for emotional development.

Needs as Instigators of Action   Some investigators have tried to identify those human needs that seem to be essential. Years ago, Murray (1938) listed a total of 38 needs that do not directly satisfy physical drives, but that operate in some form across a broad range of different cultures. These *psychogenic needs* include achievement, affiliation, aggression, and autonomy. The trouble with lists like Murray's is that you can generate new needs as long as you can think of new categories. These lists do little to tell us why these needs are expressed the way they are in different cultures. A great deal of effort has also gone into identifying the social influences that lead people to need achievement and affiliation. We will return to those considerations later in this chapter.

psychogenic needs

Interrelationships Among Needs   Many psychologists feel that drive reduction theories do not completely explain the forces that guide and maintain behavior. One such psychologist was Abraham Maslow (1943, 1968). Maslow acknowledged that physiological drives do lead people to certain actions, but he argued that in most cultures the basic physical needs are satisfied regularly and reliably. If these needs are regularly satisfied, then their influence on behavior is relatively insignificant. The helpless and unsocialized infant is influenced in most of what she does by physiological needs; but as the child grows and develops, less and less of her behavior is directed by these biological drives. Maslow believed that the ultimate motivation is a desire on the part of each person to reach his or her own potential—to become as good and accomplished a person as you are able to become. He developed a theory to explain the relationship between the physical needs at one extreme, and the need to become what he called *self-actualized* at the other, with several levels in between.

Maslow's need hierarchy

physiological needs

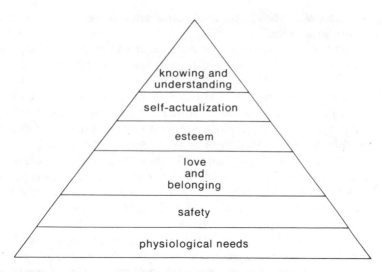

Figure 10–1   Maslow's hierarchy of needs.

Maslow's model for human motivation may be thought of as a series of steps. At the base of the steps are the physiological needs. These needs direct behavior until they are reasonably well satisfied; then needs at the second level begin to direct behavior. The needs at each level have greater power than the needs at the next higher level. Only when the more basic needs have been relatively well satisfied can needs at the next level begin to influence behavior.

Maslow's second level consists of safety needs. The need for safety can be expressed in many different ways. It is especially easy to see in young children. Young children like a certain amount of order and routine. When things are done according to some schedule, the world is more predictable. This desire for a predictable world is an expression of the child's safety needs. If a child has been separated from his mother, he may cling tightly to her when she is finally found. This is yet another expression of the operation of safety needs in young children. This need does not direct adult behavior very often, because it is satisfied regularly for most of us, and because its expressions may be more subtle than with children. But when disaster strikes, or seemingly unsolvable problems must be tackled, many adults turn to religion, even if it has not been a part of their daily lives. Maslow would say this is an expression of safety needs. For other adults, science may fulfill safety needs. *safety needs*

If the safety needs are well taken care of, the individual may be motivated by the need for love and belonging, which follows safety needs. Needs at this level are not primarily related to sexual gratification. Once people are well fed and safe, they search for satisfying affiliations with social groups. They also need a range of affectionate relationships with others. *love and belonging*

The next level is occupied by the need for esteem. Before people can be influenced by needs at the next higher level, they must be convinced that they are respected and well regarded by others. They must also develop a high regard for their own value. Once this is accomplished, ac- *esteem* cording to Maslow's model, the individual should be well on the way to becoming self-actualized.

self-actualization

The need for self-actualization stands near the apex of human needs. The term *self-actualization* means different things to different people, but basically it refers to a state when the individual is directed by his or her own inner convictions and interests. A self-actualized person would not do something just because other people are expected to do it or because it is the "proper" thing to do. Unfortunately, the model does not make clear just where self-actualization leaves off and selfishness begins.

knowledge and understanding

Some of Maslow's writings discuss a level of needs one step beyond self-actualization. This is the need for knowledge and understanding. A person directed by the needs of this level would presumably look for knowledge for its own sake, for new relationships among existing bits of information. He would try to put all his knowledge together.

Maslow's model of needs describes a systematic relationship among various needs. It has proved useful to teachers and others in the helping professions. For example, a teacher who is familiar with it might realize that the child who comes to school hungry can scarcely be motivated to seek knowledge for its own sake, while a less informed teacher might well attribute the youngster's lack of attention to some "character deficit" in the child. Similarly, the supervisor of an adolescent just beginning her first job would understand that she cannot perform at her best unless the supervisor gives her feedback that conveys respect and positive regard for the employee and for the specific things she is doing well.

limitations of Maslow's hierarchy

While this model can provide some useful insights, it is not always clearly stated. Because the levels are not described in terms of behaviors, it can be difficult to plan systematic programs for changing a child's motivation.

influencing the environment

Motivation for Competence   Harvard psychologist Robert White proposed that human beings are motivated by a fundamental desire to have an effect on their environment. Children do countless things that cannot be explained on the basis of Freud's ideas or drive reduction theory. What drive is reduced by an infant's efforts to crawl and later to walk? Why do children skip rocks across ponds? Can you explain the exploratory behavior shown in the grasping and sucking of the infant on the basis of what these behaviors do to reduce physical drives? White thought not, and many child psychologists agree.

White (1959) pointed out that when an infant learns to reach for and grasp an object, he makes purposeful and persistent movements. They are not random, and they cannot reduce drives until he almost perfects the final behavior. White believes that behaviors like this have a common biological meaning. By playing and exploring, the child learns to interact effectively with the environment. This motive must have been essential in the evolution of humans and other "higher animals," because they have so much to learn in order to survive.

Exploratory behavior helps children develop the skills they need to interact effectively with their environment.

Cognitive Motives White's theory does not explain why some children seem to be more curious than others, or why one child will explore a new environment, while another child may ignore the things around him in the very same environment. J. McV. Hunt (1961) has drawn upon Piaget's observations to explain individual differences in motivation. He has proposed that the act of processing information can be motivating. According to his view, as the child interacts with his environment, he forms sets of ideas of things that fit together, called **schemata.** As the child runs into objects or events that fit the schemata he already has, he readily adds the new experience to the existing structure. But if the objects or events he encounters are so unfamiliar that they cannot be put into an existing schema, the child will not be interested in the new item. If the discrepancy between an event and an established schema is great enough, the child is likely to be frustrated. Like other kinds of frustrating situations, the child will try to avoid it. motivation and experience

A child will also lose interest if an object or event is always identical to those that he already knows. If there is no novelty, he gets bored.

The key to motivating children, according to this view, is to give them experiences that have enough in common with things they are already familiar with for the task of accommodation to be manageable. If the experience is not different enough, an event may be readily added to the child's background, but it will not arouse her curiosity. If the difference presents too great a challenge, frustration and "negative" motivation may result. Hunt calls this the problem of the "match." problem of the match

Hunt's notion was widely circulated among educators involved in designing certain education programs in the mid- and late 1960s. These programs were intended to compensate for holes in the children's compensatory education

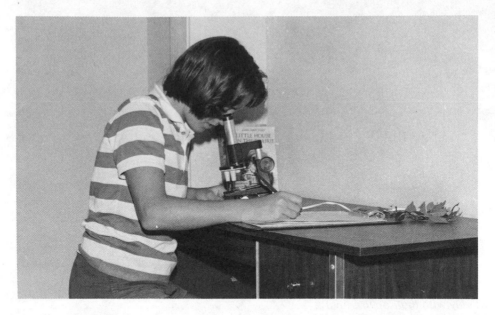

According to cognitive theory, curiosity may depend upon a gap between what a child knows and what new things he experiences.

backgrounds. In programs such as Head Start, many children showed little interest in the kinds of activities that attracted middle-class children. When Head Start children did not respond to the materials and methods that had been used for years in middle-class preschools, educators often said their lack of interest was caused by "deficits" in their home lives. Programs were devised to make up for these deficits. But during this same period ethnic pride began to grow. As parents and community groups learned about school programs and the reasons behind them, many objected to this interpretation.

deficit
interpretations

This interpretation was unfortunate, because it focused upon deficiencies in the child, rather than upon making the schools fit the pupils they were supposed to serve. Hunt's ideas do not dictate a "deficit" theory, even though that interpretation has been the most frequently given explanation for the poor performance of children from minority and economically disadvantaged homes.

The variability we see in the motives of children may well be caused by the different experiences of children from different cultural backgrounds. Minority children learn different things in their homes and communities than their middle-class counterparts. Schools have been run primarily by middle-class Anglo-Saxon origin Americans, and school programs have reflected their values. Some steps have recently been taken to make children's entering skills and motives and the methods of their schools fit better through multicultural programs. It is too early to evaluate these efforts objectively.

SOCIALLY DETERMINED MOTIVES

All human motives are shaped to some degree by social forces. Even the ways we express basic drives such as hunger and sex differ from one culture to another. There are, however, some motives that are especially important in the development of children and adolescents. Like other motives, they are the products of the children's socialization. These are achievement motives and affiliation motives.

Achievement Motivation   Traditionally, Americans have placed a very high value upon achievement. Many parents have high hopes for their children to do well in school, and later in business or a profession. Many people believe that children are motivated to achieve if their parents train them to be independent and reinforce them for achievement behavior. Some psychologists assume that this motive, generally called need achievement (*n Ach*), depends upon how the child internalizes standards   *n Ach* of excellence. One well-known study showed that the mothers of boys who scored high on a measure of *n Ach* demanded independence at an earlier age than did mothers whose sons scored low. Furthermore, mothers of boys with high *n Ach* scores were more prone to respond to their sons' accomplishments with physical affection, like pats or hugs, than were the mothers whose boys scored lower (Winterbottom, 1958).

Most of the recent evidence, however, indicates that it is direct training for achievement rather than independence training that contributes to *n Ach* (Zigler & Child, 1973). Parents of children with high *n Ach* seem to have high hopes and expectations for their sons' achievement. But   parental mothers and fathers differ in the ways they teach their sons. Fathers of   Influences boys with high *n Ach* stress both independence and achievement; while the mothers reward successful achievement and punish failure, but are more dominant and expect less self-reliance from their sons than mothers whose sons scored low on achievement motivation (Rosen & D'Andrade, 1959). Recent work with academically talented adolescents suggests that achievement motivation may depend more upon the models parents provide than upon direct training (Viernstein & Hogan, 1975).

The ways achievement motivation develops are undoubtedly compli-   development of cated, but having models available and reinforcing successful achieve-   *n Ach* ments are clearly important. With models and reinforcement, children are likely to have pride in their accomplishments.

If a parent is reasonably consistent in reinforcing some accomplishment,   success a such as academic success, the success itself may become reinforcing   secondary through the conditioning process. The parent or another significant per-   reinforcer son is not always there to cheer when the child succeeds. Therefore, under natural circumstances, reinforcement is delivered only intermittently. As we have seen, this would help maintain the behavior over long periods of time when it is not reinforced. To the observer, it would certainly seem that the child's efforts were guided by an internal standard of excellence, and that the activity was intrinsically motivated.

BIRTH ORDER

Some psychologists and school counselors believe that you can predict a lot about a person's behavior and personality by knowing his or her ordinal position in the family. Actually, the research on this question has produced fairly inconsistent results, but a few findings do seem to hold up. For example, first children and only children usually develop language skill quickly. They generally try harder than children who are born later to please their parents and other adults by being obedient and trying to live up to the adults' expectations. However, they are often less self-confident and secure than later arrivals in the family. Here the first child differs from the only child, who is less likely to be fearful of failure. Perhaps this is because only children do not have the experience of being "displaced" by younger siblings.

Children in later ordinal positions tend to seek out the company of their peers. They are often very outgoing, while being less successful scholastically than the first born.

One theory (Zajonc, 1976; Zajonc & Markus, 1975) seems to explain why first-born children are more successful on intelligence and achievement tests than their later-born brothers and sisters. Robert Zajonc claims that the intellectual growth of each member of the family depends upon all the other members. The ratio of growth depends on the number of people in the family and the size of the time interval between children.

The theory can be explained with some arbitrary numbers. Suppose the intellectual level of each parent is 30. Imagine that this score represents the amount of absolute knowledge and intellectual skill of the person—not an IQ. The level of a newborn baby would be zero. Using Zajonc's formula, the intellectual value of a home environment with one newborn child would be mother's score (30) plus father's score (30) plus baby's score (0), with that total divided by the number of people in the family. Thus 30 plus 30 plus 0 equals 60, divided by 3 equals 20. If a second baby comes along before the first one has developed a very high intellectual level, the home environment will be less stimulating than one in which the first child had developed to a higher level before the second baby was born. When both the number of children in a family and the spacing between them is taken into consideration, birth order drops out as a significant factor.

However, when we look at real data, only children do not do as well as the formula would predict, and last borns also tend to have relatively low scores. Zajonc's theory explains this too. Neither an only nor a last child has a chance to share his or her knowledge with younger siblings, and teaching is a good way to consolidate your knowledge.

Zajonc has also taken care to say that intellectual performance is not the only important characteristic for children to develop, and there may be important social and emotional qualities that are best developed in larger families. This is an important question that has yet to be pursued. What are the essential elements of social competence, and are these elements all promoted by the same kinds of home environments?

If parents reinforce academic success, success itself may become a reinforcer for future academic work.

Affiliation Motivation Many social observers feel that our young people are guided less and less by a need for achievement. Sociologists such as David Reisman (1954) suggest that we are becoming a society in which people want to "fit in" and to be accepted by their peer groups. Reisman calls this being "other directed."

Some societies tend to be more "other directed" than our own. Even within our society, there are ethnic groups who stress consideration for the group over individual achievement. Many theorists assumed that the *n Ach* and the need for affiliation (*n Aff*) are somewhat in conflict. There is some support for this opinion in reports of a relationship between the achievement motives of a society, as expressed in folklore, for example, and the actual achievements of members of the society (McClelland, 1961).

n Aff

Some recent research suggests that the *n Aff* need not be contrary to the motivations that make accomplishment possible. Most concepts of achievement are economic and neglect successful human relationships. This concept leaves out some of the important differences in values among various groups of Americans. If motivation has only an economic frame of reference, Hawaiians, for example, would be considered affiliation rather than achievement oriented, because they would honor a commitment, help another person, or seek good fellowship (Gallimore & Howard, 1968; Gallimore, Boggs, & Jordan, 1974) before they would seek economic gain for themselves. Does this orientation interfere with their achievement? Apparently not.

culture and motivation

It seems likely that neither *n Aff* nor *n Ach* is a constant disposition that people carry around inside them. They probably operate in quite specific ways in given situations. External cues may merely activate behaviors that are culturally preferred in a certain situation (Gallimore, Boggs, & Jordan, 1974).

IMPULSE CONTROL

Motives regulate and give direction to behavior. Each cultural group emphasizes certain motives while others have positions of less importance. A principal aim of socialization is to teach the developing child the kinds of motives and skills that are valued in the culture. Other regulatory processes are equally as important. These are processes that let people resist temptation and put off satisfying a desire in order to achieve greater returns later. The popular term for these processes is *will power*; some psychologists call it *ego strength*. Newborn babies quite obviously lack will power or ego strength. How then do we develop the ability to control our own impulses? What form does self-regulation take? The ability to delay gratification is one form of self-regulation.

will power and ego strength

Gratification Delay   Any good thing can be carried too far. When a person becomes so obsessed with postponing his gratification that the day to enjoy the fruits of his efforts never comes, his impulse regulation has obviously gotten out of hand. But even though the Protestant ethic can easily be carried too far, it is difficult to imagine how a person could be successful without being able to forego certain immediate rewards in order to reach more distant goals with greater returns.

the Protestant ethic

The first problem in finding out how a child learns to delay gratification

DEVELOPING POSITIVE MOTIVATION

Very few human motives are inborn. Even those that are, such as the need for nourishment, sex, and avoidance of pain, become richly expanded and overlaid with motives that develop from social experience. Anthropologists have shown that failure to satisfy biological needs may cause fewer daily sorrows than the failure to "get ahead of the Joneses" among many middle-class Americans, or to wear the appropriate number of dog teeth in Manus Society (Mead, 1939).

These motives are learned through interactions with parents, peers, teachers, and from TV and other popular media. While parents cannot control all these influences on their children, they need not leave the development of their children's motivational systems to chance.

1. Modeling by parents and others influences the development of motivation. Children enjoy doing the things they see others do. This is particularly true when there are positive feelings between the child and the model. A child who sees her parent reading a book will "pretend" to do the same. Give your child (or your pupils) a chance to see you doing things you want them to learn to value. The teacher or parent who preaches about how important it is to learn to read will not be very convincing if he never does it himself.

2. When your child does imitate the acts you model, acknowledge that response; show the child that you value it. Your comments should be very specific so the child can recognize the behavior you approve of. The behavior may be looking at books, asking good questions, help-

is to decide how to measure it. We may all have some idea of which of our friends have will power and which have not, but we may not agree about it. One method of measurement is based on psychoanalytic theory. It assumes that ego strength is tucked inside the individual, but that the personality may disguise it as a defense. One way to get past the defenses of the ego is to use projective techniques such as Rorschach or Thematic Apperception Tests. These tests present unclear pictures to a subject. The subject is not supposed to be aware that in interpreting the pictures he is projecting and revealing his own personality. Unfortunately, information taken from these tests has not been very effective in predicting how people will behave in real-life circumstances (Mischel, 1968).

approaches to assessment

Certain other kinds of tasks measure children's ability to inhibit an impulse more directly. A child may be given a motor task and some instructions to follow. The task may be to draw a line slowly, and the time taken to draw a line from one point to another may be used as an indication of motor inhibition. Or the child may be instructed to pull a toy truck tied to a string slowly. The problem with these measures is that the child's performance on the task may have little or no relationship to his ability to keep from kicking another child or his ability to stick to a task and see it through. People who work with children are generally more interested in these practical forms of impulse control than in how slowly the child can draw a line or pull a toy truck.

ing to care for a baby brother or sister, whatever. A parent might say something like, "Susan, you'll learn a lot by reading books," or "Billy, I can finish making dinner when you help take care of your little brother like that."

3. When your child (or a pupil in your class) is successful at an academic task, reward him. For most children, social praise is the most convenient and appropriate feedback for good work. Before long, just knowing he has done a good job will be its own reward. A little praise, attention, and encouragement will still help, but once in a while should be sufficient.

4. The old saying that "nothing succeeds like success" has a sound psychological basis. Arrange for children to take on tasks they can do successfully. The task should provide some challenge, but success should be within reach. Children who succeed take on new tasks, expecting to succeed again. They are usually willing to assume some risk by trying to do something new. On the other hand, children who have experienced more failures than successes learn to expect to fail. They may be afraid to take the risk involved in trying a new task. They may develop feelings of "learned helplessness."

5. Setting standards for oneself is an important part of motivation. If you set high, yet reasonable, standards for yourself, and model this clearly for your child, he is likely to set his own standards reasonably high.

When you get right down to it, the behaviors that we might think reflect ego strength or will power are only slightly related to one another. We have little evidence to suggest the existence of a general property of personality that we could call ego strength or will power.

Walter Mischel (1974) has studied will power by offering children the chance to choose between a small but immediate reward, and a larger one for which the child will have to wait. He has found that some children prefer the immediate small reward, while others choose the larger, delayed reward. He has also found that the children who prefer larger, delayed rewards tend to be higher on achievement motivation, brighter, more trusting, and more socially responsible than those who opt for the immediate reward. This "Puritan character structure" is most often found among children from the middle and upper socioeconomic classes and among people from cultures that stress achievement. However, he has also found that the situation has a lot to do with which kind of reward a person chooses. A study conducted in Trinidad is particularly revealing here.

Mischel found that blacks in Trinidad usually preferred a small immediate reward over a more substantial but delayed reward offered by a white man. In this culture, immediate gratification was commonly modeled and rewarded. As it turned out, however, this did not mean that the people were not able to postpone their gratification. Under a different set of circumstances, when given the chance to plan ahead for future events such as religious festivals and feasts, they were quite capable of delaying their immediate gratifications. These findings show the danger in drawing conclusions about the self-regulation of a group of people on the basis of a single measure.

There was probably another critical factor here. Mischel noted that blacks in Trinidad had plenty of experience with broken promises offered by whites. It only makes sense to accept a small but immediate reward from a promise giver who cannot be trusted to deliver a more valued reward later. But the activities for which the black Trinidadians did delay gratification were events under their own control. It appears that trust is extremely important in the delay of gratification. An individual's ability to delay gratification is influenced in part by her history of reinforcement for waiting, but it is also influenced by trust. Trust in a particular individual or in a group of people depends again upon the individual's history with particular promise givers.

Experiences that influence delay of gratification need not be direct. As with other behaviors, children again are influenced by what they witness in models (Bandura & Mischel, 1965). By watching a model, children learn some of the possible consequences of waiting for a reward. They come to expect positive consequences for waiting if that is what they witness with the model.

In a continuing effort to discover what experiences lead to the ability to delay gratification, and what children do to delay their impulses when they feel temptation, Mischel and his colleagues (Mischel & Ebbsen, 1970), put children in situations where both the immediate and larger reward for which the child must wait were in plain view. A disguised tape recorder

(margin notes)
multidimensional characteristic

cultural differences

influences on gratification delay

called "Mr. Talk Box" was put in the room with the children as they tried to wait to receive the larger reward. The tape recorder introduced itself and announced in a cheerful voice:

> "Hi, I have big ears and I love it when children fill them with all the things they think and feel, no matter what." (p. 267)

The children invented a variety of techniques to help themselves resist the temptation. They sang songs, played games with their hands and feet, and even tried to go to sleep. Pursuing the case further, other children were put in a situation with favorite foods, such as marshmallows or pretzels, tempting them. They were instructed to think of certain things as they waited for their rewards. When the children thought about such fun things as finding frogs, they could wait much longer than when they were not instructed to think of distracting things. It has also been found that children can wait longer by thinking of happy thoughts than by thinking of something sad (Mischel, Ebbsen, & Zeiss, 1972; Moore, Clyburn, & Underwood, 1976). Perhaps this is because a happy child can examine the alternatives rationally, and decide which one is better. On the other hand, a sad child may want any immediate satisfaction to help make him feel better. His immediate need may keep him from looking at the long-range consequences of his choice (Moore, Clyburn, & Underwood, 1976).

distraction techniques

Children have also been told to concentrate on different characteristics of objects that were going to be rewards to see how their delay of gratification is affected. When children were told to think about things like the salty crunchiness of the pretzels or how chewy and sweet the marshmallows would be, they could wait hardly at all. But when they were instructed to think of the pretzels as brown logs, or the marshmallows as puffy white clouds, they could wait a very long time indeed. (See figure 10–2.) In fact, they could outwait the graduate students assigned to conduct the experiment (Mischel & Baker, 1975).

Figure 10–2. Learning to delay gratification.

The essence of all this is that while personal traits such as intelligence, social maturity, and cognitive style may influence a child's ability to delay gratification, it is also influenced by several situational and cognitive variables.

Cognitive Style   From these conclusions it should be clear that cognitive processes and affective development are highly related. Most studies of cognitive development have measured the extent to which certain intellectual abilities are developed by a certain age, and how this development differs among groups and individuals. Another aspect of cognition is the social and motivational preferences people develop for approaching certain kinds of tasks in specific ways. These individual differences in the approach to cognitive tasks are called *cognitive style*.

One dimension on which cognitive style may vary is in the degree to which a problem is approached slowly and reflectively or quickly and impulsively. Some children tend to be reflective. They approach problems with care and thought. Other children tend not to consider alternatives.

impulsivity and reflectivity These impulsive children tend to make more errors than reflective children.

Impulsivity and reflectivity are usually measured with a test that requires a child to deal with uncertainty. The most commonly used measure is the Matching Familiar Figures Test (Kagan, 1965a) (see figure 10–3). The child is shown a picture of a familiar object and requested to identify which of several smaller pictures is identical to the first. Responses are scored both for the time a child takes in responding and for the number of errors. The test has been shown to predict some academic skills, including reading recognition (Kagan, 1965b).

Reflective children approach the Matching Familiar Figures Test by excluding nonmatches. They make systematic comparisons with the standard or with other variations. Impulsive children do not use either of these strategies (Wagner & Cimiotti, 1975).

It is tempting to think of impulsivity and reflectivity as a general personality dimension. To teachers or parents, these terms are likely to suggest a child's ability to control impulsive aggression or to keep from talking out in class (Block, Block, & Harrington, 1974, 1975). But there is no evidence that the impulsivity-reflectivity dimension of cognitive style is at all related to a general disposition to control impulses.

Differences in impulsivity and reflectivity may be influenced by individual differences in biological tempo. But in large measure, these styles are learned. Since different cultural groups are different in this way, it seems reasonable that certain parts of the socialization practices used in different cultural groups may influence the children's style. It has also been

influences on cognitive style demonstrated (Ridberg, Parke, & Hetherington, 1971) that children's cognitive styles may be changed through modeling. An especially interesting finding is that it may be easier to change a child's style from impulsive to reflective than vice versa. This may be because the reflective style is more successful in problem solving, and reflective children's success may increase their self-esteem. Children with high self-esteem appear to be less susceptible to modeling influences than children with lower self-esteem.

Figure 10–3.   Type of item used in the *matching familiar figures test.*

Expectations and Self-Control The ability of individuals to regulate their own behavior depends in part on their perceptions of their control over their own destinies. Some people think that they have little control over the things that happen to them. They see what happens to them as largely the result of fate or luck. Others generally believe that there is a relationship between their own efforts and their rewards or punishments. This dimension of individual differences has been called *locus of control* (Rotter, 1966).

Those who see a connection between their own behavior and its consequences are said to believe in internal control. Those who feel that their destiny is subject to fate believe in external control. When the relationship between children's behavior and things that happen to them is not clear or consistent, they are likely to believe in external control.

locus of control

parental
influences

Children's locus-of-control orientations are fairly well established by third grade (Crandall, Katokovsky, & Crandall, 1965). This suggests that the child's early experiences contribute to these perceptions. One influence on locus of control seems to be the directiveness of parents. Boys who develop external locus of control are more likely than their internally regulated peers to have had very directive parents (Loeb, 1975). Directive parents make the child's decisions for him and regulate his behavior. Excessive directiveness may interfere with the child's development of independence.

Children's beliefs about locus of control influence how they work toward goals. It makes a difference, however, whether the anticipated goal is positive or something to be avoided. If locus of control affects how a person approaches a goal, the goal is likely to be very specific (Mischel, Zeiss, & Zeiss, 1974). We cannot generalize too much, however, on the effects of locus of control. Certain groups of people, such as the poor and blacks, tend to have external locus of control. But that is what you would expect if you looked at the questions on the tests used for measuring locus of control. Most of the questions relate to outcomes like school grades or influencing bureaucratic policy. Given the obstacles to minority groups having any influence on policy, and given the poor record of the schools in effectively instructing the poor and ethnic minorities, their perception that much of what happens is beyond their own personal control seems quite rational. As with most of the concepts discussed in this chapter, perceptions of locus of control are affected by situation.

Self-Perception and Assessment

PERCEPTION OF SELF AS CONCEPT FORMATION

As a child grows up, he forms an idea of the kind of person he is. This idea includes beliefs, attitudes, feelings, and personal qualities that the individual comes to feel are his most important traits (Coopersmith & Feldman, 1974). Many people think of self-concept as a unitary trait. Teachers may often be heard to say such things as, "Sally has a good self-image," or "Billy has a poor self-concept." But it is unlikely that any child thinks of herself along just a single dimension (Shavelson, Hubner, & Stanton, 1976). Sally may recognize that one of her best traits is her athletic ability. She knows that she plays sports well, and her feeling is confirmed because she is always the first one chosen for team sports. But she is also realistic enough to know that mathematical skill is not one of her better abilities. Her judgment is borne out by her grades and by the fact that she is not eagerly sought out by her friends for group projects in math class.

multidimensional
self-concept

The concepts we develop about our own characteristics develop largely as a reflection of how we think other people see us (Mead, 1934). But our perceptions of how others see us are not always quite accurate. The eighteenth century Scottish poet Robert Burns recognized this fact as he watched a louse on a lady's bonnet in church—the lady thought she looked very fancy indeed to the churchgoers whom she assumed were admiring her.

Nevertheless, feedback from the environment gives the child important information about the kind of person he is. In our example, Sally's classmates gave her different feedback concerning her abilities in sports and math. Young children are very aware of remarks made by their parents and other adults, as they comment on the clever things their children do.

There is only so much information a person can process at once. Since every bit of information cannot be stored and called upon separately, the feedback we get is sorted into categories. Early experiences are important because they serve as the basis for the categories people use as they sort and classify the feedback they receive throughout life. Into Sally's category of "athletic" may later go specific feedback information, such as "well-coordinated" and "fast runner."

efficiency and information processing

There are two important things to remember about environmental feedback relating to the self. First, the earliest images of one's self tend to bias future information, because we tend to select the information that fits the categories that are already formed. Second, the number of categories a person has available will influence the selection and storage of feedback about the self (Mischel, 1976). Children's early impressions tend to be quite general. As they mature, they develop more categories, and their self-impressions become more differentiated (Mullener & Laird, 1971).

Sometimes people get feedback that is inconsistent with the self-images they have already formed. We have already indicated that one way of dealing with this information is to ignore it by not paying attention to it. This information may also be reconciled by reinterpreting the facts to make them more consistent with one another. If Sally is not chosen for the soccer team because the team captain says she is not good enough, Sally may conclude that she is really so good that she would show the captain up. Thus, she may decide that the real reason she was not chosen was because she was actually so superior a player that she would threaten the team captain.

self-image and selective attention

There are many instruments designed to measure self-concept. For example, one test (B. Brown, 1966) shows a child a photograph of himself. When the child agrees that it is his picture, he is asked to assess the child's attitudes and feelings about his appearance, general ability, physical status, affective tone, and fears. Tests used with older children dispense with pictures and depend entirely upon verbal statements. The Lipsitt Self-Concept Scale, for example, asks children to judge the degree to which a number of adjectives apply to them (Lipsitt, 1958). The adjectives include the words *friendly, happy, kind, brave, honest, likable, trusted, good, proud, cooperative, cheerful,* and so on, for a total of 22 traits. These adjectives are intended to get the child to describe her per-

ceptions of herself. They are not necessarily identical to the child's evaluations of her self-concept.

SELF-EVALUATION AND SELF-ESTEEM

self-esteem and
self-concept:
a distinction

Sometimes the term *self-esteem* is used interchangeably with *self-
concept*. The two ideas are closely related, but there is an important
distinction. Self-esteem involves a judgment about the self-concept. The
case of Maria illustrates the relationship between self-concept and self-
esteem.

Maria lived with her family in a barrio within one of the larger cities in
the Southwest. Her days were spent pleasantly playing with neighbor
children and imitating the household chores she saw her mother do.
Things were still pleasant when she went to Head Start. The children all
came from her own neighborhood, and Maria could talk freely with them
because most of them spoke Spanish. The teacher and the aide could
also speak Spanish. Some of the children were already bilingual in Spanish
and English, and Maria was gaining confidence in her own ability to speak
English. Her teacher encouraged her to learn as much English as possible,
but she also made Maria feel proud to speak Spanish. Often in class the
children would help to prepare Mexican food or learn about Mexican customs. At this point Maria's concept of herself probably included the fact
that she spoke Spanish, among other characteristics. But at the time Maria
graduated from Head Start, her family moved into a new house in another
part of town. Her skills in speaking English were still not nearly as well
developed as her Spanish when she entered first grade, but that would
have been all right because she could communicate fairly well. What did
sadden her was that the other children teased her about her accent and
even about the kind of food she brought in her lunch. The teacher told her
that she should not speak Spanish to the few other Mexican-American
children in the school because they were all living in the United States;
English, she explained, is the language of the United States.

This treatment caused Maria to evaluate herself negatively as a
Spanish-speaking child. She also came to feel ashamed of the traditional
Mexican foods she had grown up with, and she wanted her mother to put
sandwiches in her lunch instead of tortillas. Maria's self-concept may not
have changed much, since she still thought of herself in terms of about
the same characteristics as she had before, but her evaluation of that
self-concept surely did change.

self-esteem and
achievement

Many educators and some psychologists assume that high self-esteem
leads to higher school achievement, while negative evaluations of the self
lead to failure and underachievement (Coopersmith & Feldman, 1974).
The available evidence on the relationship between achievement and
self-esteem does not provide firm conclusions concerning whether low
self-esteem causes poor academic performance, or whether academic
failure leads to lowered self-esteem. However, the bulk of the evidence
strongly suggests that differences in self-esteem develop in reaction to
experiences of success and failure in school rather than the other way
around (Bandura, 1969; Bridgeman & Shipman, 1975; Mischel, 1976).

Another common assumption is that children from minority groups have low self-esteem. The reasoning goes something like this. Children from minority groups generally do not perform as well academically as children from white middle-class families. Since minority children come from "disadvantaged" backgrounds, they probably have low opinions of themselves when they come to school. Their self-esteem may be responsible for their poor performance on academic tasks.

The facts simply do not support this argument. Comprehensive studies of Head Start children show their initial self-esteem to be almost uniformly high. Neither do there seem to be differences in the levels of self-esteem of children from different social classes or races. The differences reported in some studies probably reflect differences in level of development and environmental contexts rather than differences in the self-evaluations of the children (Bridgeman & Shipman, 1975).

self-esteem in Head Start

In this chapter we have looked at some of the processes involved in the affective development of children. We have also seen some of the environmental circumstances and experiences that can influence that development. In chapter 11 we will follow these processes further by seeing how they apply to children and adolescents at different points in their lives, and we will suggest some things that parents, teachers, and other adults can do to foster sound emotional growth.

Suggested Readings

Crandall, V. C., Katokvsky, W., & Crandall, V. J. Children's belief in their own control of reinforcement in intellectual-achievement situations. *Child Development*, 1965, *36*, 91–109.

Gallimore, R., Boggs, J. W., & Jordan, C. *Culture, behavior, and education*. Beverly Hills, Calif.: Sage, 1974.

Gordon, I. The beginnings of the self: The problem of the nurturing environment. *Phi Delta Kappan*, March, 1969.

Kagan, J. His struggle for identity. *Saturday Review*, December 7, 1968.

Mischel, W. On the future of personality measurement. *American Psychologist*, 1977, *32*, 246–254.

Mischel, W. Toward a cognitive social learning reconceptualization of personality. *Psychological Review*, 1973, *80*, 252–282.

Rosen, B. C., & D'Andrade, R. The psychosocial origins of achievement motivation. *Sociometry*, 1959, *22*, 185–218.

Yamamoto, K. (Ed.), *The child and his image: Self-concept in the early years.* Boston: Houghton Mifflin, 1972.

11

Guiding Emotional Development

This chapter describes the stages children go through in emotional de-velopment. When you have finished the chapter, you should be familiar with infants' states of activity, and with how stimulation can affect them. You should be able to describe Erikson's psychosocial stages, and the type of crisis he associated with each stage. You should then be able to suggest ways parents, teachers, and other adults can help children progress through these stages. You will also know the pros and cons of breast and bottle feeding, and you should be able to recommend the con-ditions under which each would be preferred.

Psychoanalytic and social learning theory provide conflicting compet-ing explanations for regression. When you have finished this chapter, you should be able to describe and compare these explanations. You should also be able to compare Erikson's view of self-evaluation and standard-setting with the explanation offered by social learning theory.

You should know how children's experiences can affect their motivation to achieve and their feelings of competence or inferiority. You will also see some kinds of experiences that can influence how children learn to set their own standards.

Childhood seems to be getting shorter; and adolescence, longer. This chapter describes some social circumstances that affect this trend. You should be able to identify and describe how an adolescent develops an identity and how adults can help young people move from adolescence to adulthood smoothly.

Most people feel a sense of awe and wonder when they see a newborn child in the hospital nursery. What kind of creature is this? What does the infant "know" and experience in this new environment? Are its previously protected senses offended by the sights and sounds and smells of this new world? What are the baby's capabilities at this early age?

No matter what child you go to see, it always seems that the infant is either sound asleep or crying at the top of his lungs. Viewing a new baby can be uncomfortable as well as awe inspiring. From the looks on the faces of the infant's proud family, you know that they expect you to make some comment, but what can you say? The baby is red and wrinkled and has flaky patches on its skin. Can you tell the child's family that the baby is handsome, or that it resembles the father's side of the family—or the mother's? Americans do not have convenient conventions for reacting in this situation. Some people sincerely believe that new infants are cute, or even beautiful, but those who don't are hard put to make an honest statement that will satisfy the child's parents. A Trobriand Islander, for example, could merely say "how baby," which is certainly the truth, and offends no one (Lee, 1960).

But first impressions not withstanding, the newborn baby is more than a red and wrinkled organism that sleeps and cries its way to greater maturity. The human infant is highly complex. To the casual observer it may seem that infants cannot do very much, but from the earliest moments of life the child's behavior is highly organized, and there is a rhythm to its varied responses.

The First Two Years

Some characteristics of infants are common to all human babies; others differ from one child to another. Most child psychologists believe that the experiences the child has during the first two years are extremely important to future adjustment. Many people find this view easy to accept. A view that is less self-evident is that the infant influences her caretakers as much as they influence her.

INTERACTIVE INFLUENCES IN SOCIALIZATION

Over the years, intellectual and religious leaders and psychologists have been pretty active in giving parents advice about how to raise their children. John Locke, the nineteenth century philosopher, taught that reward and punishment were the "spurs" and "reins" by which parents could guide and mold their children. He felt, as modern behaviorists do, that praise for deeds well done was a more effective influence on the child than blows or criticism (Kessen, 1965). Cotton Mather, a Calvinist minister of Colonial times, warned parents to develop honesty, industry, and piety in their children. Early in this century, G. Stanley Hall advised parents to

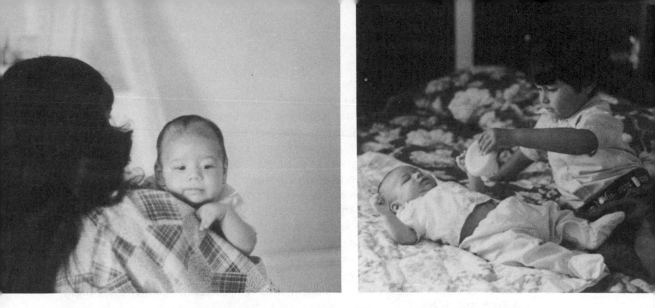

(Left) An infant can explore the environment from his mother's shoulder during a state of alert inactivity. (Right) A baby in a state of waking activity may enjoy playing with older brothers or sisters.

keep out of nature's way and allow their children to develop. By intervening, Hall believed, parents could only damage the child's natural development. Freud's clinical observations convinced him that parents often unwittingly damage the emotional development of their children. He influenced parents to give up certain repressive practices that unduly keep children from expressing their natural instincts.

All these views, and many others, assume that parents shape the child's character. They suggest that this influence goes only one way, with the parents molding the child. We now know that the process is not that simple. Influence is not one-sided. There are noticeable individual differences among infants from the moment of birth, and these differences lead to different responses from parents (Bell, 1968). A parent is not likely to respond in the same way to a calm and quiet baby as he will to an irritable one.

Some of the differences we see in young infants may be the result of differences in temperament (Bell, 1968). These differences may influence the development of social relationships, which will be discussed in chapter 13. Neonates also differ in their behavior patterns, which we call *states*.

BEHAVIORAL STATES IN INFANCY

To a casual observer, there seems to be little variety in the behavior of young infants. For the most part they just eat, sleep, and cry. But systematic observation shows that all infants go through several different behavior patterns during an average day. Obviously there are times when the baby is more alert and more responsive than others, but the behavioral states do not simply reflect differences in alertness (Hutt, Lenard, & Prechtl, 1969).

Types of States The infant's behavioral states occur over and over again for each individual. Children do not move rapidly in and out of different states. Instead, they are stable, remaining in one state for a period of time. Interestingly, the things children do in a given state are similar for different children, but the relative amount of time they spend in each state varies a great deal from one infant to another.

The states range from sleep at one extreme to crying at the other. In *regular sleep* the infant's eyes are closed, breathing is slow and regular, and there is no movement except for sudden generalized startle responses. There is a second form of sleep called *irregular sleep*. In irregular sleep, the eyes are closed; breathing is irregular and faster than in regular sleep. Movement is generally confined to small muscular twitches. A major difference between regular and irregular sleep is that rapid eye movements (REM) occur during irregular but not during regular sleep. In adults, dreaming occurs during REM sleep. We do not know the exact role of REM sleep in the newborn infant, but it may help stimulate the development of the infant's central nervous system (Roffwarg, Muzio, & Dement, 1966).

regular and irregular sleep

rapid eye movements

Between sleep and crying there are other states that occur regularly. An infant may lie quietly with eyes open for a while and then closed for a while. In this state of *drowsiness,* his breathing is regular but faster than during regular sleep. At other times the infant will lie quietly, making very few movements, but with eyes wide open, bright, and alert. This state has been called *alert inactivity.*

drowsiness and alert inactivity

Just because the infant is active does not mean she is also alert. In the state of *waking activity,* the infant's entire body is involved in rather random movements. Breathing is irregular; and while the eyes are open, they do not appear alert. They seem dull or glazed.

waking activity

The state of *crying* involves both making noise and vigorous and diffuse movements of the body and limbs (Wolff, 1966). Infants have different cries to communicate hunger, anger, and pain. Most mothers think that they can tell the difference in their children's different cries, while people

crying

MAKE THE MOST OF ALERT INACTIVITY

Many child psychologists believe that infants learn a lot from the things available for them to watch while they are quietly alert. Here are some things a parent might do to take advantage of these opportunities for learning:

1. Decorate walls near the baby's crib with colorful pictures that capture his or her attention.
2. Hang a mobile just out of the infant's reach. The color and patterns of the pieces of the mobile and their movement will give the baby something interesting to watch. Mobiles can be made easily from things you find around the house.
3. When the baby is quiet and alert, give him a chance to watch the other family members. You can prop the infant up where he can see you doing household work or where he can watch other children at play nearby.

who are not familiar with a baby cannot make these distinctions. There is evidence that the mothers' belief is correct. Mothers show signs of distress when they hear the cry of pain, but they show less concern at the sound of other cries (Wolff, 1969).

Relationships to Maturity and Environment   The amount of time infants spend in each state varies between individuals and changes as they mature. On the average, a newborn baby spends about 17 to 20 hours a day sleeping. About 75% of that time is spent in irregular sleep. The baby is awake and quiet for 2 or 3 hours a day, and awake and active for an hour or 2. The rest of the time is spent crying or fussing. The newborn baby sleeps from 45 minutes to 2 hours at a time, alternating between 10- to 20-minute periods of regular sleep and 20- to 45-minute periods of irregular sleep. Of course these are only averages. They vary considerably depending upon factors such as the temperature of the room. In colder rooms, infants spend less time in regular sleep and more in motor activity (Hutt, Lenard, & Prechtl, 1969).

state patterns

As the infant matures, the periods of sleep and waking both become longer. By the time most children are a year old they sleep through the night. Diet also seems to influence sleep patterns. Infants who eat solid food before going to bed in the evening are more likely to sleep until morning than infants on a liquid diet.

States and Stimulation   Even during wakefulness, there are some times when the infant profits by being stimulated by the things available around him, and other times when the sights and sounds around him have little influence. A baby who is fretful or crying does not pay attention to the little things that could help him develop.

Some infants spend more time than others in a certain state. Those who spend a relatively large part of their time in alert inactivity have more chances to learn by visual exploration (Korner, 1972). During this state the infant may watch the mobile above his crib intently, or watch her mother working nearby or an older brother playing with his toys.

Since being in the state of alert inactivity is important in the child's early learning, it is interesting that some ways a caretaker can quiet a baby are more effective than others in shifting the infant from crying or sleeping into alert inactivity. Because the caretaker will only rarely want to interrupt the infant's sleep, we will look at activities that soothe the crying infant.

Stimulation and Shifts in State   Change from one state to another takes place quite naturally. But even though there are natural rhythms in an infant's changes in state, there are times when a caretaker wants to speed up the process—particularly when the child is crying. There are few sounds in the world that can rattle a harried parent quite like the crying of a baby.

When Mrs. Green wants to quiet her infant, she cradles him in her arms and rocks him back and forth. She holds her baby horizontally, in a nursing position. Mrs. Redd generally tries to soothe her infant by holding

quieting techniques

Rocking is a time-honored way to quiet a crying infant.

him up to her shoulder, in a vertical position. She supports his head with her hand. Mrs. Brown holds her child in an upright position at her breast.

These three techniques for quieting the infant are not all equally effective. All may help soothe the baby, but Mrs. Redd's habit of holding her son to her shoulder with his head upright may have added advantages. It is more effective than the other techniques in leaving the child alert so he can attend to the visual environment (Korner, 1970; Korner & Thoman, 1970).

rocking   Parents soothe infants with other time-tested methods as well. Rocking is effective. Mothers the world over comfort their infants by rocking them. Some mothers like to rock their infants from side to side. Others rock them up and down, and still others use a head-to-toe motion. Most mothers probably use some combination of these, and research has shown that it does not really make any difference. One motion is as effective as another. However, the *speed* of rocking does seem to make a difference. One study showed that a rocking motion of 60 cycles per minute led to less infant activity than rocking at 45 cycles per minute (Pederson, 1975). No doubt not very many mothers will use a clock to set the pace for rocking their baby, but faster rocking does seem to be more effective than slow rocking.

swaddling   In some cultures swaddling is a common practice. It involves wrapping the infant rather tightly in cloth strips or in a blanket. This practice is common in Russia (Erikson, 1963), and in times not long past it was widely used among certain native American groups, such as the Hopi (Dennis, 1940). From an adult's point of view, common sense would suggest that being snugly wrapped up so that you couldn't move would be very frustrating. In this case, the facts defy common sense. Swaddling does have a soothing effect (Lipton, Steinschneider, & Richmond, 1965).

Last but not least, feeding is often an effective means of quieting a fussy infant. Moreover, infants often soothe themselves by sucking.

Parents are not always immediately successful in quieting crying infants, but being able to soothe the baby is important both to the infant and to his family. Infant crying is aversive to adults. It is a good thing that it is, too, because crying lets an infant get adults to attend to his needs, where behaviors that are less irritating to adults might be ignored. Crying is the infant's main means of communicating with his caregivers. Many psychologists believe that the ways the caretaker attends to an infant's needs and relates to him have long-lasting effects on the child's learning and personality development.

THE DEVELOPMENT OF TRUST

Freud believed that a child's very early experience is exceptionally important in his future emotional adjustment. He focused on different psychosexual stages (discussed in the last chapter). According to Freud, the sexual instincts that motivate people are concentrated in different zones at different ages. The patterns by which these instincts are gratified or frustrated are important in the child's adjustment.

Erikson, a neo-Freudian, also believed that development proceeds through a number of stages. However, he emphasized social influences on psychological development more than Freud did. Erikson called his stages *psychosocial* rather than psychosexual. He believed that there are certain basic psychosocial crises that are characteristic of each stage. These crises result both from biological changes and from the expanding social relationships with which children must cope as they mature. These stages, "The Eight Stages of Man," are called the oral-sensory, muscular-anal, locomotor-genital, latency, puberty and adolescence, early adulthood, young and middle adult, and mature adult stages.

psychosocial crises and stages

Oral Incorporation   The first period of development in Erikson's scheme is the oral-sensory stage. During this stage, which lasts for roughly the first year of life, the child develops a basic attitude of trust or mistrust toward the world. Erikson sees trust as a desirable outcome, and mistrust as an unhealthy one. Whether a child becomes trusting or not depends on whether or not his needs to "take in" what the environment has to offer through his mouth are regularly satisfied. During this period, Erikson believes the infant "lives and loves with his mouth; and the mother lives through and loves with her breasts" (p. 72). This is an interdependent relationship, because the mother's own self-esteem depends on how well the baby nurses.

Biting and Symbolic Grasping   In the second substage of the oral-sensory period, the child's approach to her world shifts from taking in to biting. This shift takes place as the child develops teeth. In a more general way, this stage is associated with "taking hold of things." The eyes can now grasp and follow specific objects in the environment. The child also learns to localize sounds and to grasp objects with her hands. She is learning to use her environment.

Trust and Mistrust If the infant's needs are regularly met, she will develop a sense of social trust. This trust will be reflected in optimism as she grows up. Erikson believed that the infant's first social achievement was to let her mother out of sight without feeling undue anxiety. This achievement indicates trust. In chapter 12 we shall see that other theorists think that cognitive structures rather than emotional attachments govern this process.

If the infant's needs are not well met, she will become mistrusting. In its most extreme form, a child who does not have basic trust may be an infantile schizophrenic. A life-long pattern of depression may be an adult expression of mistrust and lack of optimism (Erikson, 1963).

The Breast versus the Bottle Some people have interpreted Erikson's ideas about the oral-sensory stage to suggest, among other things, that mothers should breast feed their infants. Years ago breast feeding was very common in the United States, and only the very rich used artificial means of feeding. It was not uncommon for mothers to nurse their babies while talking with friends and family. For many years breast feeding was on the decline in this country, although it is becoming more popular once again. Mothers who breast feed today usually go off by themselves to

social and cultural variations

nurse their infants in privacy. This change is probably attributable to cultural changes in standards of modesty. It can make breast feeding very inconvenient. What does a mother do when her infant wants to be fed while she is on a shopping trip or while traveling on public transportation? You can imagine the embarrassed reactions of fellow passengers if a contemporary American mother were to breast feed in a crowded airport. Naturally some mothers have given up breast feeding in favor of the "more convenient" bottle. Others wear clothing or shawls that allow them to breast feed in public while being modest. Still others breast feed in complete privacy in spite of the inconvenience, because they believe that breast feeding is better than bottle feeding.

considerations of convenience

Many mothers today have little choice. They have jobs outside the home, and it is quite difficult to find a wet nurse. But if you have a choice, which is best? Is breast feeding or bottle feeding better for the infant? Like most matters relating to child rearing, there is no simple "either-or" answer to this. To decide you must weigh the advantages and disadvantages of one method as compared to the other. Artificial nursing, or bottle feeding, is convenient. A baby sitter can feed the infant as well as the mother can, if the baby is on a bottle. But on the other hand, this convenience is strictly a function of social customs that inhibit breast feeding in public. Otherwise, breast feeding would be more convenient. The "equipment" is completely portable, as long as the mother is the caretaker. And there is no need to worry about refrigerating the milk or warming it at feeding time. In addition, mother's milk provides the infant with some protection against certain allergies, colds, respiratory diseases, and other contagious diseases (Baum, 1971). This protection is obviously to the child's advantage, but undesirable substances may also be passed on to the infant through mother's milk. Tobacco, alcohol, and other drugs taken by the mother may be passed on to the infant; and some of these substances, including some prescription medications, may be harmful to the baby.

transmission of harmful substances

What about the psychological benefits of breast feeding? Once again, the answer is not simple. In the best of situations, feeding provides for body contact between mother and infant. After all, a mother cannot prop her infant up with his dinner and go about her business if she is breast feeding. Other things being equal, the tactile stimulation of body contact is advantageous. On the other hand, bottle feeding allows the father to participate in feeding, to cuddle the baby while he is being fed. This can help strengthen the bonds between father and infant, and help avoid the common feeling among new fathers of being "left out."

tactile stimulation

There are several reflexes involved in nursing. One is the infant's reflex of turning the head toward the breast (in the direction of the pressure against him). The sucking reflex is another. The other reflexes are the mother's. One is the nipple erection reflex, which makes the nipple easy for the infant to suck. Another is the "let down" reflex. When the infant sucks the nipple, sensory impulses are carried to the pituitary gland, which releases a hormone into the blood. This hormone travels to the breast, where it causes contractions in the structures that hold most of the milk. As these structures contract, the milk is squeezed into a larger duct, where the infant may obtain it by more sucking (Newton, 1958).

nursing reflexes

The let down reflex does not operate as well in some mothers as in others. It may be inhibited if the mother is anxious, or if she does not like to nurse. When the reflex is inhibited, nursing is likely to become frustrating for both mother and child. Even if the let down reflex is not inhibited, breast feeding is frustrating for some mothers and their infants for other reasons. Breasts differ in shape, and some are not well designed for nursing. If an infant cannot get the nipple well back in his mouth, the mother is likely to hold him to her breast a bit harder to give him a better hold. This may result in the upper lip going up over the nostrils or the breast covering the nostrils. Usually the mother cannot see this happen; and in any case, the infant's oxygen is shut off. In reaction, the infant will fight the mother with his fists (Gunther, 1961). The mother is likely to feel rejected by her infant, making it impossible for her to feel the self-esteem that Erikson says she should as she nurses her child.

nursing and frustration

In each of these situations, the infant and mother are both frustrated. Besides that, the infant is likely to not receive enough milk, and he will become hungry and cross again soon. This further contributes to the tension between mother and child. The most important factor in feeding is the quality of the relationship rather than the shape of the container. If the mother enjoys breast feeding and communicates her relaxation and pleasure to the infant, then it is probably wise to breast feed because of the benefits of mother's milk. But if breast feeding makes the mother tense, and if she approaches feeding feeling unhappy and resentful, then bottle feeding may well be best. It may let her relax and enjoy feeding her baby.

BOTTLE OR BREAST

Not long ago it was considered the modern thing to feed babies by bottle. Somehow that practice seemed to fit with the theme of efficiency that came with industrialization and technology. Now the tide seems to be swinging the other way among many young parents. Advocates of "natural childbirth" are often equally enthusiastic supporters of mothers' milk. And most popular book stores are well-stocked with paperbacks describing the virtues and techniques of breast feeding.

It is true that breast feeding may have certain advantages for mothers and their infants. Some advocates say it helps to develop the bond of affection between mother and infant. It also helps stimulate a rapid return to normal for the mother's body after pregnancy. Moreover, the infant may get some antibodies to help protect against some diseases through the mother's milk. But there are some cases where it would be better to bottle feed. Mothers who take any drugs should not breast feed. Naturally this applies to mothers who use narcotic drugs. But it also includes those who are regular users of prescription drugs or over-the-counter medications. It also includes mothers who smoke.

Mothers who find that they cannot feel comfortable and relaxed during breast feeding may be able to have a more positive relationship with their babies if they bottle feed. If they can cuddle the baby affectionately and if the baby responds by relaxing and making eye contact with the mother during bottle feeding, an important basis for the mother-child relationship may be formed. And it is a relationship fathers and babies can share too. The quality of the relationship between the parent and infant is the most important consideration.

THE DEVELOPMENT OF AUTONOMY

Autonomy versus Shame and Doubt   Erikson's theory of psychosocial development says that the major conflict the child needs to resolve during the second year of life is *autonomy* versus *shame* and *doubt.* The crisis centers around toilet training. During the first year of life, caretakers generally go out of their way to meet the infant's biological needs. But in many Western families, a dramatic change takes place in the caretaker-child relationship some time during the second year. The child begins to be pressured to control his physical responses—those of elimination of body waste. Children who resolve this conflict successfully should develop a sense of autonomy. They learn to control themselves and their environment. Children who are overly frustrated in their toilet-training experiences, according to Erikson, feel shame and self-doubt.

toilet training and adjustment

Alternative Interpretations   It is not necessary to agree with Freud or the neo-Freudians to believe that a child's early experiences set the pattern for later emotional development. If early relationships between an infant and his caretakers are unpleasant and full of stress, a pattern for later reactions may be established. If parents are not reinforced in their inter-actions with their baby, they are likely to develop negative attitudes. Parent and child may both come to expect that their future interactions will be unpleasant. As time goes on, the parents and child may avoid each other, which decreases the parents' chances to influence the child's development positively. A vicious circle of action and reaction may be established very early.

Unlike psychoanalytic interpretations, however, social learning theory believes that early interactions do not result in the development of deep-seated personality traits that are very difficult to change. If social cir-cumstances can be appropriately arranged, the developing child's responses can be changed, and the effects of unfortunate early experi-ences can be reversed.

Early Childhood

By the time children are 2 years old, they have an amazing range of capa-bilities. These advances are particularly impressive when you compare them to the helplessness and dependency of the newborn infant. By their 24th month, most children are reasonably well toilet trained. They have a sizeable vocabulary of 50 or more words. Many 2-year-olds can name virtually every object in their everyday surroundings, and all the things in their picture books as well. During the next few years their vocabulary increases at a spectacular rate.

Young children are very occupied with learning to deal with and control their environments. One well-known characteristic of 2-year-olds is negativism. At this point in their development, children seem to discover *negativism* that one way they can control their environment is to refuse to do what they are told. One of the most often used words in the young child's vocabulary is "no." This feature lead some descriptive psychologists to characterize this period as the "terrible twos." However, their conclusions were based upon young children from a very limited range of back-grounds, and we are not at all certain that negativism is a universal characteristic of young children.

THE DEVELOPMENT OF INITIATIVE

The child's growing abilities to control her own body and influence others through language are important features of early childhood development. Just as important, however, are the child's new and rapidly developing powers of locomotion and thought. This development of initiative is the next stage in Erikson's model.

In Erikson's view, one way to distinguish between a child involved with developing autonomy and one working on developing initiative is to look at how the child expresses jealousy. Let's look at the experiences of a *jealousy* typical young middle-class family to see how jealousy can show up in the child who is still trying to become autonomous.

A CASE OF SIBLING RIVALRY

Gloria was 2½ years old. Her parents had told her that she would soon have a baby brother or sister. She was looking forward to having someone to play with, and she anticipated the new arrival much as she would have a new doll. Then one day her mother went to the hospital, and a few days later returned home with Gloria's new baby brother.

It was an exciting but very demanding time for the young parents. Soon the responsibilities of parenthood became even more demanding because Gloria became more difficult. She was toilet trained and reasonably able to feed herself. But a few days after the arrival of the new baby, she began to regress. She frequently wet her pants these days, and she often cried for a bottle, especially at bedtime. And while she often seemed to express affection for her infant brother, she could not be left alone with him because she sometimes tried to hurt the baby. Naturally, Gloria's parents were concerned.

Erikson might explain this turn of events by saying that children often express their autonomy by trying to keep rivals out. Autonomy, therefore, "can lead to jealous rage most often directed against encroachments by younger siblings" (Erikson, 1963, p. 256). Freud might explain Gloria's demands as an example of regression to a form of gratification that is characteristic of an earlier developmental stage. Gloria's regression would be regarded as a response to the frustration of having a rival for her mother's affection. Parents who have been influenced by Freudian ideas would be apt to give Gloria a lot of attention when she wet her pants or demanded a bottle.

Social-Learning Explanations of Regression   Learning theorists are just as familiar with these situations as the Freudian or neo-Freudians, but they would consider it very poor to pay attention to Gloria's "regression." They would also offer quite a different explanation for it. Some learning theorists would suggest that before the new baby came, drinking from a bottle and wetting her pants had been replaced in Gloria's responses by new and more mature behaviors. Before the baby brother came, Gloria had received a lot of attention from her parents; much of that attention had come in the form of approval for her independence. But with the new baby to attend to, Gloria's parents, without realizing it, began to spend less time reinforcing Gloria. Since her newly developed appropriate behavior no longer "paid off," she reverted to earlier actions that had received attention. Moreover, she could see that these "immature" behaviors got attention for her baby brother, so she was also being influenced by a model.

This situation will eventually pass for Gloria and her family, but in the meantime it distresses the parents. Is there any way to avoid it? Many parents have found that it can be avoided to a large extent. The parents who do manage to prevent this kind of situation do so, whether they know it or not, by using learning principles.

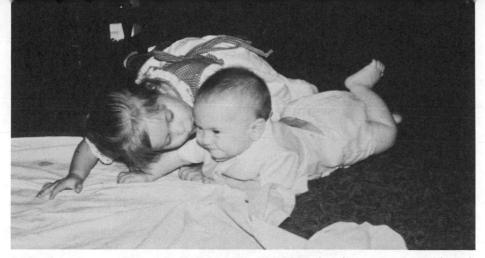

Sibling rivalry may be reduced if the older child has the chance to play with and help care for the new infant.

Applying Social-Learning Principles   One approach that often helps is to prepare the child for the arrival of a new baby by explaining that the baby will belong to the whole family, and that each member will have an important part in taking care of him because he will be very helpless. This may help pave the way for the parents to name specific positive behaviors for which they can reinforce the older child when the new baby arrives. It is important for parents to continue to pay attention to the older child for her own accomplishments. The older child will be able to accept the newcomer more easily if the baby's presence does not "cost" her some of the love, attention, and reinforcement she has previously had from her parents. And it will be easier yet if she receives praise and attention for her efforts to contribute to the baby's care. The amount of attention the older child receives should not be reduced, but it should be directed toward mature and "responsible" acts instead of immature ones.

reinforcement of nurturant behaviors

Erikson's view of the psychosocial crisis of the genital-locomotor stage is derived from Freud's theory. According to Freud, preschoolers turn the jealosy and rivalry younger children directed at siblings (as in Gloria's case) toward their parents. Especially in boys this rivalry turns into the attempt to compete with the father for the position as mother's favorite. The conflicts of this Oedipal situation may lead to guilt and anxiety if they are not resolved. This point of view is a striking contrast to the social-learning perspective.

Self-Evaluation and Standard Setting   Erikson believed that this period brings a uniquely human crisis. On the one hand the child is excited about his developing powers and potential, while at the same time he feels inhibited because he is internalizing his parents' standards. The child is more aware of his own actions, controls them better, and punishes himself more. He may feel guilty about his thoughts and physical impulses. In the best possible case, he can develop a sense of moral responsibility and get some insight into the roles and functions of social participation. He can enjoy manipulating the environment or "manipulating meaningful toys—and in caring for young children" (Erikson, 1963, p. 256).

Erikson's ideas were drawn from his observations of children and his interpretations of childhood experiences in various cultures. But we also

When models in the child's environment set high standards for their own performance, children are likely to set high standards for themselves.

have evidence of the development of self-evaluation and self-regulation in early childhood.

modeling of standard setting

Children see models setting up guidelines in many forms. Parents both let their children see them setting achievement standards and also talk about the rules they use themselves and the things they expect from others. The achievement standards of a particular culture are even worked into the kinds of stories that are read or told to children. These stories reflect a culture's achievement values and provide symbolic models that help the child form values and standards. Considering research that shows that symbolic models can influence children, we can conclude that parents who want to influence their children's standards of achievement might be smart to think about the stories they read to make sure they represent the values they want their children to develop.

developing pride in accomplishments

A direct and effective method parents can use to help their children develop achievement motivation is suggested by Winterbottom's (1958) research. If parents want their children to feel pride in their own accomplishments, they should reinforce them for specific achievements. Reinforcing children's accomplishments seems to come naturally to some parents, while others do very little of it. If a child is praised for her successful accomplishments, she is likely to feel satisfied with future accomplishments even when no one is around to reinforce her success.

A child's achievement motivation is also affected by the home environment and the opportunities it provides for early learning (McClelland, 1958). By the time they are 5 years old, children differ from one another substantially in how much they care about achievement (Crandall, Preston, & Rabson, 1960), and these differences increase as time goes on.

According to Erikson (1963), the ideal outcome of the psychosocial crisis of this period of early childhood is to develop goal-directedness and a sense of purpose.

The Middle Years

The middle years of childhood roughly correspond to the years of elementary school. The child's range of experiences increases dramatically during this period, and the differences among individual children become magnified as they develop specialized and diverse interests and talents. The middle years correspond to the latency period in both Freud's psychoanalytic theory and Erikson's Eight Ages of Man. But Freud paid very little attention to this period. He thought that the strong sexual energies that were so important in his view of personality were dormant at this time. By contrast, Erikson saw that the child's social environment expands during this stage, making this a period of significant change.

latency period

THE DEVELOPMENT OF AMBITION AND COMPETENCE

By the time he has passed through Erikson's locomotor-genital stage, the child who has successfully met the challenges of the previous stages is ready for "entrance into life" (Erikson, 1963, p. 258).

School as Preparation for Life   According to Erikson, the first part of life is "school life." It prepares the child to become a worker and provider. In technological societies, schooling is highly formal, while informal classes serve as "schooling" in simpler societies. In either case, children from all cultures are provided with some systematic instruction around this time of their development. The children learn the fundamentals of technology from adults who have been given the duty of instruction.

Children undoubtedly learn as much from older children and from their peers as they do from adults. In societies with very formalized systems of education, a critical job of schooling may be to bring children together. School is a place where they have an opportunity to interact with peers and with older children. In an age-graded society many children have few such chances. This situation stands in contrast to Hawaiian and other Polynesian societies. There much of the job of rearing young children is in the hands of older children. Even in contemporary Hawaiian communities, the group of all the children in a family is an important unit with functions that are separate from those of the adults in the family. Membership in this group of children is not restricted to brothers and sisters from a single nuclear family. Often it also includes children from neighboring or related households (Gallimore, Boggs, & Jordan, 1974).

Technological cultures are very complex and specialized. This specialization has implications for development during this period. The aim of schooling in technological cultures is to teach children to read and cal-

According to Erikson, success during middle childhood leads to an attitude of industry.

culate and prepare them for the greatest possible number of careers. The problem with this arrangement is that in complex cultures the "eventual goals of initiative" that Erikson wrote about are rather vague and far away. The schools tend to become cultures of their own (Erikson, 1963). They contain their own goals, achievement opportunities, and disappointments for children that often have very little relationship to life outside the school.

goals of initiative remote from school life

Failure in School and Feelings of Inferiority In Erikson's view, the major danger of this period is that the child will feel inadequate and inferior instead of adequate and industrious. If a child's efforts meet with success, he will become interested in working more. If a child's efforts are continually met with frustration and failure, he begins to feel inferior. Industry and ambition presumably lead to competence.

failure and inferiority

Parents and teachers are important in determining the developmental outcomes of the middle years. Some children fail in school over and over because there is no connection between the motives and skills they learn in their home environments and those required in school. To solve this problem, teachers and other school personnel must work together with parents and others who care for the children outside the school. On the one hand, school personnel must teach in a way that builds upon the skills the child already has. This is a challenge the schools have not yet met effectively. Schools in general have been especially ineffective in dealing with the differences between the skills of children from minority backgrounds and the expectations of school curricula. It is important for children to have tasks that they can do successfully if they are to want to continue to work in school. Teachers may need to teach basic skills so the children can perform the tasks assigned. And parents need to recognize the signs that their children are failing more than being successful in school.

When school becomes an unpleasant experience, children frequently talk about not wanting to go to school, or being afraid. Their worry about school may intrude into their relationship with their parents and friends. They may become moody and irritable. If children act this way, their parents should look into the child's school experiences as a possible source of the problem. Fear of school is a common problem. Parents themselves often contribute to fear of school because they are trying to maintain the child's dependence on the mother (Hetherington & Martin, 1972), but fear of school may also be learned through conditioning.

signs of school anxiety

Paving the Way for Competence Children are likely to be more successful in school if their parents teach them to value and enjoy activities that are associated with schoolwork. For example, one study of Papago native American children and their parents (Swanson & Henderson, 1976) found that parents wanted their children to value traditional Papago skills that are useful on the reservation. But they also wanted their children to be interested and competent in basic school skills such as reading. Papago homes generally have few reading materials, and the children see few adults reading. Since the parents in the study wanted to help encourage their children to read, procedures were established to help them. Mothers were taught to use books as the basis for warm and supportive interactions with their first graders. The materials were selected so that mothers could either use the text or pictures, or both, as the basis for their interactions.

parental influence

Effective teachers build on the skills children bring to school with them.

Children learn to enjoy school activities through interaction with their parents.

The mothers were also trained to allow the children to make choices regularly. They were given materials to take home for this purpose. At scheduled times, the child had free access to reading materials and to other attractive items that were selected to compete for the child's attention. At these times the child could select any of the available activities; but whenever he selected the reading activities, the mother paid attention to him and clearly reinforced him. During the program, the frequency that the children chose to read increased. This effect also generalized to the classroom. Children whose mothers had reinforced their reading selected reading during free-choice time in school significantly more often than children whose mothers did not carry out the reinforcement program.

This study offers concrete evidence that when parents reinforce certain of their children's activities, the children are likely to pursue those activities, even when their parents are not present. Thus, parents can influence their children to develop motives and preferences that will help them acquire school skills.

External Evaluation and Intrinsic Motivation   Parents and teachers try in many ways to make children eager to perform school tasks. Evaluating children's accomplishments is a chief means used to motivate them to do well in school. But many teachers are overly concerned with motivating children to finish assignments and learn specific information. They often forget that it is just as important, or maybe even more critical, to encourage children to use what they learn in school outside the classroom (Maehr, 1976). Until recently, this issue was as neglected by psychologists as by teachers. Now some researchers are trying to find out what kinds of experiences help develop continuing motivation, also called *intrinsic motivation* (Maehr, 1976; Hoffman, 1977).

One thing researchers want to know about intrinsic motivation is how it is influenced by evaluation. The schools routinely use grades as reinforcers for academic performance, and many parents, educators, and psychologists are concerned that this practice might make children interested only in grades, and not in learning and applying new information. Some of the research suggests that "there is, indeed, cause to worry" (Salili, Maehr, Sorensen, & Fyans, 1976, p. 85). The research shows quite consistently that when their work is evaluated externally, as with grades, children are less likely to work on similar activities on their own.

incentives and continuing motivation

Some people assume that the effects of teacher evaluation on intrinsic motivation might differ depending on the cultural context of schooling. For example, children in an adult-centered and authoritarian society might respond differently to external evaluation than American children. It turns out that this is not the case at all. Iranian school children, whose culture is very authoritarian, respond to external evaluation just as their American counterparts do (Salili, Maehr, Sorensen, & Fyans, 1976).

cultural context of schooling

This information has important implications for educators who have the important role of guiding children's development. One reason that children seem to lose interest in an activity when external "motivators" are used is that they feel that they are working for rewards rather than because they enjoy the activity (Hoffman, 1977). Another possibility is that the child whose actions are motivated by grades thinks that someone else is responsible for his learning. Luckily, we have ways to shift the focus of this responsibility.

There is a well-developed body of research showing that we can teach elementary school children to take increased responsibility for guiding their own learning (McLaughlin, 1976). If they are taught to set their own goals and assess their own progress toward those goals, they are more likely to think of learning as their own responsibility. And equally important, their interest in learning may be increased rather than destroyed.

Vicarious Learning of Standards   Parents and other adults influence the standards children in the middle years set for themselves. This fact has been demonstrated in several experiments. In one typical study (Bandura & Kupers, 1964), children 7 through 10 years old watched a model performing a task. Some children saw a model who used a high standard. In this situation the model reinforced himself and praised himself out loud when he reached the standard he had set. When his performance fell short of his standard, he denied himself reinforcement and criticized his own behavior. Other children watched a model who set relatively low standards for himself. The results of this and similar studies (Bandura, 1969) show that children who watch models who set low standards for self-reinforcement are satisfied with mediocre performance in themselves. Children who watch models who set high standards tend to set high standards for themselves.

These findings suggest that children will learn to set high standards if the models they see are demanding of themselves. At the same time, it is

setting realistic
standards

important for parents to help their children in setting standards to make sure they do not set impossibly hard goals. Children's own standards must be realistic, or they will fail all the time. And repeated failure will interfere with the child's development of the sense of competence that Erikson says is the desired outcome of development during the middle years.

Adolescence

puberty

There is no magic age at which a child becomes an adolescent. Erikson's theory suggests that adolescence is ushered in by two events. The timing of these events will vary for different individuals. The first event is biological. Childhood ends with the advent of puberty, and adolescence begins. Along with the onset of puberty comes a major task facing adolescents: adapting emotionally to "the physiological revolution within" (Erikson, 1963).

establishing new
roles

The second challenge confronting the adolescent is social. The adolescent is faced with the task of connecting the skills and roles he has learned as a child with the adult responsibilities that lie ahead. Both tasks of adolescence involve establishing new roles. They include developing new ways to act and new emotional responses to members of the same and opposite sex. They also include facing the demands of future career roles.

Establishing your own identity is the major psychosocial task of adolescence.

THE DEVELOPMENT OF IDENTITY

Erikson believed that a primary concern of adolescents is how they appear to others and how that compares to their self-image. Faced with developing a sexual and occupational identity, the major crisis of this period is role confusion. Young people are likely to go through an identity crisis in which they must establish who they are and what they want to become. If they are unsuccessful, they face role confusion. If the conflict is resolved successfully, the adolescent will develop a sense of devotion and the basic virtue of fidelity (Erikson, 1963). *self-image and role confusion*

Role confusion may result either from unfortunate experiences or from oppressive social circumstances. In some cases a poor identity may seem thrust upon an adolescent. Elkind (1976) reports just such a case involving a "delinquent" girl. He reports a court case: *negative identity*

> in which the defendant was an attractive 16-year-old girl who had been found "tricking it" in a trailer just outside the grounds of an Air Force base. From about the age of 12, her mother had encouraged her to dress seductively and to go out with boys. When she returned from her dates her sexually frustrated mother demanded a kiss-by-kiss, caress-by-caress description of her evening's activities. After the mother had vicariously satisfied her sexual needs, she proceeded to call her daughter a "whore" and a "dirty tramp." As the girl told me, "Hell, I have the name, so I might just as well play the role." (p. 228)

In our culture, psychosocial identity may be particularly difficult to achieve for females and for members of minority groups who have been discriminated against. Sometimes this role confusion can extend well beyond the period generally regarded as adolescence. A graduate student who was simultaneously working on his doctoral dissertation in English and undergoing an identity change (described as "becoming a Chicano") has given a vivid description of some factors that may lead to role confusion in members of ethnic minorities (Rodriguez, 1975).

When this young man was a boy, his parents were encouraged by nuns from his school to speak English at home. They complied and gave up speaking to the children in Spanish. Spanish was "the language that formed so much of the family's sense of intimacy in an alien world" (p. 103). He became fully committed to the culture of the classroom and came to share fewer and fewer interests with members of his extended family. By the time he completed his doctoral dissertation, he had come to realize that he had lost as much as he had gained through education. The new hope that excited him was to discover what it meant to be a "Chicano intellectual," terms that he had grown up thinking could not be used to describe the same person. *ethnic identity*

This story reminded Dr. Sheldon White (1976), a Harvard psychologist, of the classic legend of Doctor Faustus. Doctor Faustus sold his soul to gain riches and honor during his life on earth. White raises the question, "Do we offer some children in our society a Faustian bargain?" (p. 105). And if we do, must it continue to be so?

Children do not have to come from a minority group to go through such identity conflicts. Rodriguez recognized this in his comment that children often feel a sense of loss like he did "as they move away from their working-class identification and models" (p. 103).

Social Change and Identity   These are times of rapid social change. Young people are confronted daily with values and life styles that differ from those their families approve of. They come up against these influences in face-to-face interactions with their peers. They also see vivid models of alternative life styles on television and at the movies. In his book *Future Shock,* Alvin Toffler (1970) observed that the media gives modern Americans a problem of "overchoice." Faced with this array of conflicting alternatives, it is difficult for some adolescents to put together what they learned as children and what they experience during their teens (Elkind, 1976). This discrepancy may lead young people to seek meaning and direction in their lives by joining causes (as they did in great numbers in the 1960s) or religious "cults" (as many do today). In part, such discrepancies are the stuff that alienation is made of. Being kept out of the decision-making processes that influence their lives is another ingredient of adolescent alienation.

Decision Making and Alienation   During the past two decades or so, we have gradually come to acknowledge that some groups have traditionally been treated as second class citizens. We recognized this first in regard to racial and ethnic minorities, and more recently to women. (There are, of course, still people who hold, privately if not publicly, that this is as it should be—that it is the natural order of things). As a society, we have yet to acknowledge that adolescents of both sexes and all racial and ethnic backgrounds are also second class citizens. In a democracy, people can exercise some control over the events that affect their lives. But in the United States, youth are not given access to the political process. Consequently, like all other groups who are kept from making decisions that govern their lives, youth are likely to become alienated from the dominant society (Pearl, 1972). Some adolescents rebel actively; others use passive resistance; still others merely submit. The schools, which Erikson believed should prepare children for the demands of adult life, generally do little to prepare them to make important decisions and take part in the democratic process.

Some groups have tried to connect classroom life to real life by establishing their own schools. For example, The Black Panther Party operated an Intercommunal Youth Institute in which they tried to teach children that the world is their classroom when they were as young as 2½ or 3 years old. Their students spent 60% of their time working in community activities and only 40% of their time in classrooms. Students in the Institute helped set the policies that governed them, and they had meetings to work through mistakes and to talk about problems that children and youth are generally sheltered from in conventional schools (Seale, 1976).

alternative life styles

alienation and political process

Isolation and Identity Establishing a satisfying identity is particularly difficult in technological societies. In many less complex societies, *rites of passage* help the child move from one developmental status to another. Rites of passage are ceremonies that celebrate important events in the life cycle, such as birth, puberty, and marriage. The rites of passage associated with puberty are ceremonies that communicate messages regarding sexual and generational identity to the person who is being initiated (Levy, 1974). In nontechnological societies, this message usually conveys certain rights, privileges, and responsibilities of adulthood that take effect immediately after the ceremony. In American society there is no such clear-cut line between the status of child and adult. Some groups have kept the remains of the rites of passage (the Jewish Bar Mitzvah is one example), but these ceremonies usually do not lead to very substantial changes in duties and rights.

    Instead of a clearly marked point at which an individual changes from child to adult, American society provides a long period of adolescence separating the two. During this time the adolescent is likely to be unsure whether he or she is a fish or foul—child or adult. On the one hand, adolescents are expected to give up "childish" behavior. On the other hand, even though they may have the sexual powers and physical maturity of adults, they are prohibited by social convention and circumstances from assuming adult responsibilities.

    In some rural areas there is still a tendency for adolescents to feel immediate pressure to assume adult responsibilities. One group of researchers (Whiting, Chasdi, Antonovsky, & Ayres, 1974) found this to be the case among Mormons and Texans in small communities in the Southwest. In these communities boys were encouraged to get jobs or to help in the economic enterprises of their fathers rather than pursuing higher education. Girls were preoccupied with getting a husband.

    Nevertheless, while the step from childhood to adulthood may still be a short one in some cultures and in some communities, adolescence is getting longer and longer in American society in general. One observer (Weiss, 1974) has compared adolescence to a poorly written book. He asserts that "Culture and biology are conspiring like a bad writer to make the middle too long." The fact that adolescence is "overly long in the middle" results from two sets of events. The first is biological and the second is cultural.

    For the past century, puberty has been coming earlier and earlier. This is probably because nutrition has improved. In Norway, for example, the average age of onset of menstruation declined from 17 in 1844 to less than 14 in 1940. In the United States the average age of the first menstruation is now 12.8 years, which is about 1½ years earlier than it was near the turn of the century (Weiss, 1974). As a result, childhood is becoming shorter, and adolescence is coming earlier.

    The second set of factors working to extend adolescence is cultural. Not so long ago adolescence ended when an individual got a job or got

Right margin notes:

rites of passage

prolonged adolescence

period of childhood shortened

married or both. One survey showed that today almost half of all high school graduates go to college, and approximately one-third of those who go to college live with members of the opposite sex (Weiss, 1974). To a significant degree, the alienation of modern youth may be caused by this extended period of uncertain status between childhood and adulthood. Many young people do not understand the concerns and pressures faced by their parents. They are not at all familiar with the lives of people whose work is markedly different from the academic chores of the student.

reducing the gulf
in life experiences

Both the Russians and the Chinese have taken steps to eliminate this tremendous gap in values and life experiences between students and workers. In China, for example, children are involved in productive labor from kindergarten on. By the time they reach middle school, children may spend part of their time working in a factory, and college students are required to spend regular periods working in the fields and learning from the peasants. This practice is intended to maintain an "open door" between the lives of students, workers, soldiers, and peasants (Kessen, 1975). In contrast, U.S. public education institutions make no systematic attempt to provide work experiences for all students. The tremendous gulf between the life experiences of different groups of Americans is fostered by the very nature of our schools. Surely these institutions contribute to alienation between generations, and between the academic and working class groups of the population.

Erikson did not have much to say about what parents might be able to do to help their offspring through the developmental crisis of adolescence. He is probably correct when he says that parents can make a major contribution by helping their children through earlier periods. If a child has emerged from the earlier periods with a sense of trust, an attitude of industry, and with initiative, he has a good chance of developing a meaningful identity as an adult (Elkind, 1976). But as we noted in the opening chapter of this book, many of the forces that influence our children today are outside the family. This is especially true of adolescents, but this is not to say that the family cannot help the adolescent through this period. Maintaining open communication within the family probably helps, but it

assisting the
transitions of
adolescence

Adolescence is prolonged in America today.

must begin before the child reaches adolescence. Providing a range of recreational and work experiences may also be helpful. Unfortunately, this option is more easily available to families with money than those who are poor. And a family tradition of involving children and adolescents in the decisions that affect their lives may help to prevent intergenerational rifts. But for youth in general, families in a complex society probably cannot do the job alone.

Adolescents would probably benefit from early and varied work experiences that help them connect their academic experiences and life in the outside world. To provide this experience would require major social changes and revisions in our schools and colleges. In the United States we also need to acquaint youth with the life experiences of other groups in the population. When we consider the pace of our progress in eliminating segregation, it seems likely that the social changes that would be needed to break down the isolation of one age group from another, and one ethnic or social-class group from another, may take some time in coming.

Suggested Readings

Bronfenbrenner, U. Childhood: The roots of alienation. *The National Elementary Principal,* October 1972. Reprinted in S. White (Ed.), *Human development in today's world.* Boston: Little, Brown, 1976.

Elkind, D. Erik Erikson's eight ages of man. *The New York Times Magazine.* Reprinted in S. White (Ed.), *Human development in today's world.* Boston: Little, Brown, 1976.

Erikson, E. *Identity, youth and crisis.* New York: Norton, 1968.

Jelliffe, D. B. Culture, social changes and infant feeding: Current trends in tropical regions. *American Journal of Clinical Nutrition,* 1962, *10,* 19–45.

Klatskin, E. H., Lethin, A. G., & Jackson, E. B. Choice of rooming-in or newborn nursery. *Pediatrics,* 1950, *6,* 878–889.

Lewis, M., & Rosenblum, L. (Eds.), *The effect of the infant on its caregiver.* New York: Wiley, 1974.

Newton, N. Battle between breast and bottle. *Psychology Today,* 1972, *6,* 68–70, 88–89.

Pearl, A., Grant, D., & Wenk, E. (Eds.), *The value of youth.* Davis, Calif: Responsible Action, 1978.

How Children Develop
Social Skills

This chapter discusses how children learn to interact with other people. When you have completed the chapter, you should be familiar with the idea of attachment and several theories of how and why children become attached to other people. You should be able to discuss several topics affecting how children relate to others—fear of strangers, fear of separation, dependency, egocentrism.

One way children learn social skills is through play. When you have finished the chapter, you should be familiar with several types of play and how they relate to social development, including learning to share.

You should also come to understand sex typing and how children develop sex-role stereotypes and identities. Finally, you should recall Piaget's and Kohlberg's stages of moral development.

The scene is a kindergarten classroom. The children are singing and dancing for a group of visitors. A small girl announces the number. Another girl, who has the starring role, then plays the part of a monitor. She has been assigned to hand out apples to a group of her friends. She gives out all of the apples except the last two; and there are now only two children left without apples: herself and one other. At this point she comes to the front of the stage and explains her dilemma to the audience. One of the apples she has left is larger than the other; and she has to decide which apple to give to the other child and which to keep for herself. She then remembers the thoughts of one of her country's leaders and the deeds of one of its chief culture heroes. With their words and examples in mind, she cheerfully gives the larger apple to her friend and keeps the smaller one for herself.

This play is put on regularly for visitors and for parents in kindergarten classes throughout China. The thoughts of Chairman Mao and Lei Feng, a soldier who is admired for his service to his country, are enacted in many songs and dances. They are worked into the stories told to children as examples of correct action. Through colorful posters and stories, children begin to be introduced to Mao's thought in the nurseries just before they are 3 years old (Kessen, 1975).

Human Competence and Human Values

Every culture values certain human traits, and adults try to promote these qualities in children. In some cases they take a subtle, unobvious approach. In other instances they are crystal clear, as in the example just cited.

cultural variation

Within the United States, different ethnic groups value a wide range of different qualities. Even within the mainstream of the American people, there has always been a question of what characteristics should be most valued. Intellectuals have valued intellectual accomplishments over interpersonal skills. And Americans have relied heavily on the intellect in improving the quality of life through technology. On the other hand, the general population has a long-standing anti-intellectual attitude.

Earlier in American social history, there was greater agreement about what qualities should be promoted in children. The Horn Book used in colonial schools and McGuffey's readers, which were popular in the late 1800s, tried to teach piety, cooperation, and helpfulness. Today there is less agreement about what values should be taught in social institutions such as the schools. As a result, where social values are taught, the treatment is generally less direct than it used to be. For the most part, schools today teach only academics. They say, of course, that they teach social behaviors such as citizenship and cooperation, but these aims are rarely approached with actual instruction. What *citizenship* and *cooperation* generally mean in school is that the child does what the teacher says and does not make any trouble.

When educators think about competence, they usually think in terms of intellectual accomplishment, as shown in IQ and achievement test scores. After all, the main task of the schools is to prepare children to become successful, contributing members of society. It is becoming more and more clear, however, that competence in reading, writing, and arithmetic does not insure success in adulthood. There are various ways we can judge a person's success. Traditionally, one way has been by occupational status; and recent evidence indicates that neither occupational status nor success within an occupation depend primarily upon intelligence (Jencks, et al., 1972). There are some minimum skills needed before you are allowed into educational programs required for some occupations with high status. However, given some minimum education, success seems to depend to a large degree on motivation and differences in individual interpersonal skills (Jencks et al., 1972).

inadequacy of IQ as index of competence

Social skills and motivation are clearly important in a practical sense. In addition, people who can interact effectively with others can probably derive more personal satisfaction than people who are less effective. And for many people, occupational status is not a very important criterion for life-success anyway. Therefore, it is important to understand as well as we can how children develop socially. In this chapter we shall look at how these qualities develop and some of the skills involved in social relationships, as well as the conditions that influence their expression. Chapter 13 will then discuss social maturity at successive points in the child's development.

social competence and life accomplishment

Attachment

DEVELOPING BONDS OF AFFECTION

Although we might like to think so, infants do not instinctively love their mothers. And the police records are full of accounts of people who were apparently unable to feel affection toward any other human being. How do babies learn to love their mothers or other caretakers? As they grow and develop, how do they learn to feel affectionate towards friends, spouses, and their own children? Psychological theories offer a variety of explanations.

Drive Gratification Theories   Psychoanalytic theory says that a child becomes attached to its mother because the mother nurtures the child during the oral stage of development. According to this view, the attachment develops because the child's primary drives for food and shelter are satisfied. This explanation is compatible with drive-reduction learning theory. It suggests that the infant's physical drives, especially hunger and thirst, are satisfied when the mother is present. When the baby is uncomfortable, he finds that his mother is there at the same time that the distress caused by hunger, wet diapers, or whatever, is reduced. He therefore comes to associate pleasant feelings with the mother's presence alone.

formation of attachment bonds

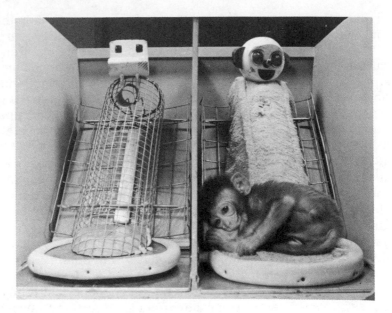

Figure 12–1.   Wire and cloth mother surrogates.

From "Affectional Responses in the Infant Monkey," by H. F. Harlow and R. R. Zimmerman; *Science*, 1959, *130*, 422. Reprinted by permission.

If a baby forms a satisfactory attachment with his mother or other principal caretaker, he will later be able to generalize and feel affection toward other people.

Research has not generally supported the assumption that attachment is an outgrowth of drive reduction (Cohen, 1976). Professor Harry Harlow has done some interesting experiments with Rhesus monkeys, trying to find better explanations for attachment.

Contact Comfort and Attachment Formation   Harlow and his associates (Harlow & Harlow, 1966; Harlow & Zimmerman, 1959) tried to learn how baby monkeys learn to love their mothers. They also wanted to find out what happens when the monkeys are deprived of the conditions that help them develop ties of affection. First they looked at the theory that the affection between a baby and its mother is based upon the reduction of physical drives during feeding. They constructed two different kinds of substitute mothers for infant monkeys. One mother substitute was made of wire, and was designed to hold a feeding bottle in the center of its chest. The second substitute mother was identical, except that it was covered with a soft terry cloth (see figure 12–1).

Both mothers were available to all the infants all of the time, but half were fed by the cloth mother and half by the wire mother. Since one evidence of attachment is that the infant wants to be near the object of the attachment, infants would be expected to spend more time near the mother that fed them than the mother who did not. That was not the case. The infant monkeys did just the opposite. They spent more and more time

attachment to
substitute mothers

attachment
criteria

Figure 12–2. Typical response to cloth mother.

From "Affectional Responses in the Infant Monkey," by H. F. Harlow and R. R. Zimmerman; *Science*, 1959, *130*, 422. Reprinted by permission.

on the cloth mother, even if they were fed on the wire mother. This finding suggests that the infant monkeys felt stronger affection for the mother who provided comfort than for the one who fed them.

To test the strength of the bond between the baby monkey and its mother substitutes, Harlow showed the babies a number of different objects that were designed to frighten them. At first, the baby monkeys always ran for comfort to the cloth mother, even if a wire mother had fed them. After clinging to their cloth mother for a while, their fear was visibly reduced. Their muscles relaxed, and they worked up enough courage to become curious about the new object. They approached it and in some cases examined and touched it. The infant monkeys took no such comfort from their wire mothers (see figure 12–2).

Some monkey infants were never exposed to a cloth mother, only to a wire one. For them the cloth mother offered no comfort at all when they were afraid. It seems that if young monkeys are deprived of the comfort of contact during their very early development, they may never develop attachment bonds. We do, however, now have some evidence that monkeys who live in isolation for their first 12 months may develop some social behaviors through intervention with "therapist" monkeys (Novak & Harlow, 1975). It is risky, to say the least, to draw conclusions about people from studies of laboratory animals. Nevertheless, Harlow's findings are interesting.

Ethological Interpretations   Ethologists are scientists who study animals in their natural environments. They sometimes relate their findings to human behaviors. There are ethological theories to help explain both aggression and attachment in humans. This interpretation suggests that the roots of attachment are biological (Ainsworth, 1973; Bowlby, 1969; Stayton, Ainsworth, & Main, 1973). It suggests that attachment is designed to help the child survive by keeping the parent nearby.

Imprinting is a process nature uses to keep babies near their mothers. Certain birds, such as Greylag Goslings, approach, follow, and become attached to the first moving object they see after they are hatched. This phenomenon is called *imprinting*. Other species have more specific requirements for the objects to which they will become attached. Mallard ducklings, for example, will accept as parents only creatures who, among other things, sound like adult mallards. Whatever the specific requirements of the species, those animals that imprint will do so only if they have the chance within the first few hours after birth. With mallards it must happen within 13 hours of hatching. Once imprinting has taken place, the duckling will avoid anything that is different from the object on which they have imprinted (Lorenz, 1952).

imprinting

Studies of imprinting demonstrate that an animal must have certain experiences at a particular point in its development. The animal will not develop certain behaviors or abilities unless the conditions are right at a very specific point. These points when certain events will have the most impact on development are called *critical periods*. We know that there are critical periods in prenatal physical development, when certain things will definitely affect the unborn child. The evidence is less clear that the idea of critical periods applies to psychological characteristics.

critical periods

We do know that infants who do not get enough attention may have trouble forming attachments later on (Yarrow, 1964), but the effects of lack of early attachments are not necessarily irreversible (Ausubel & Sullivan, 1970).

As infants develop, they go through a series of fairly typical social stages that seem to be involved in forming attachments (Cohen, 1976). At first the responses of the infant are undifferentiated; that is, she responds the same to mother (or other caretaker) and strangers alike. Later, the infant begins to respond differently to the mother and to other people. She continues to respond to her mother and to strangers, but she will smile and make noises more readily to her mother. Then the child shows a very strong attachment to the mother, and later on forms attachments to other familiar people. Two characteristic patterns of attachment that have been studied extensively are called *fear of strangers* and *separation protest*.

development of differential responses

Fear of Strangers   Many proud grandparents have had their feelings hurt when they held their grandchild and were greeted by sobs from the infant. The sobbing quits just as soon as the child is returned to its mother. If a father has not been around much to take care of the baby, he may receive the same kind of treatment, and this apparent rejection can just as easily be directed toward the mother if she happens to work outside while her husband attends to housekeeping. This significant development in the child's relations with other people usually happens sometime between

This 9-month-old infant is afraid of a bearded stranger who looks nothing like her smooth-shaven father.

the eighth and tenth month (Morgan & Ricciuti, 1969). For that reason it is often called *eighth month anxiety* (Spitz, 1965).

eighth month anxiety

Psychologists of the psychoanalytic school interpret this as evidence of the attachment between the infant and its mother. However, not all children who are strongly attached to their mothers are afraid of strangers, which casts doubt on that interpretation (Ainsworth, 1973). Cognitive psychologists have a different explanation. They believe that the difference between the visual appearance of the mother and the unexpected appearance of a stranger may frighten the child.

psychoanalytic and cognitive interpretations

Separation Protest   Beginning at about 10 to 12 months of age and reaching a peak at about 15 to 18 months of age, babies develop *separation protest*. They cry and show other signs of distress when their mother leaves the room. In psychoanalytic theory, both fear of strangers and separation protest are regarded as aspects of attachment. However, while the two patterns occur closely together, they develop independently and they do not begin at the same time (Ainsworth, 1973). As in the case of fear of strangers, cognitive theorists have offered an alternative explanation. According to this point of view, a child goes through separation protest after the fourth sensory motor period. At that point he is mature enough to have an idea where his mother has gone, but he cannot act upon that idea and do anything to bring her back (Lester, Kotelchuck, Spelke, Sellers, & Klein, 1974; Spelke, Zelazo, Kagan, & Kotelchuck, 1973).

psychoanalytic and cognitive interpretations

In fact, most children do not simply cry helplessly when their mother departs. Most children who are able make an attempt to follow her (Stayton et al., 1973).

alternative responses

When a child develops the concept of object permanence, she may try to find the parent who has disappeared from her view.

cultural
variations   How strongly children react to separation from the mother varies from one culture to another, and so does the time when the pattern appears. Infants in both Guatemala (Lester, et al., 1974) and Uganda (Ainsworth, 1967) generally show separation protest earlier than children in the United States. In Guatemala, children are usually reared in a one-room house where they are near their mothers most of the time. In Uganda, infants are carried on their mother's backs most of the time. In these cultures, then, it is very unusual for the infant to be separated from his mother. Separation protest might develop earlier than in American homes because separation is such an unusual event.

Temperament and Attachment   Some infants do not go through separation protest. Even among those who do, there are notable differences in how intensely they react. At this point, cognitive interpretations seem to explain fear of strangers and separation protest better than psychoanalytic theory does, but cognitive explanations do not explain differences in individual reactions. An additional influence is **temperament** (Paradise & Curcio, 1974). We use *temperament* to mean biologically determined characteristics that may have an overall influence on behavior. Infants who are easily upset by startling events during the first 3 or 4 months of life may have more intense reactions to strangers when they are older.

Clearly, attachment is a complex process, and we still have much to learn about how an infant's experiences influence his or her later abilities to form relationships with other people. Nevertheless, the information we do have has implications for child care, and these issues will be addressed in chapter 13.

Dependency

Lupe was 5 years old and had been in kindergarten for about 3 months. She was a friendly and attractive child, and her teacher had become very fond of her. But there was one thing about Lupe that especially concerned her teacher. Lupe would not let the teacher out of her sight. No matter what the class was doing, Lupe found a way to stay near the teacher. She never finished a task without coming, not once but several times, to seek approval and reassurance that she was doing the job correctly.

Lupe: A case example

In talking with the other teachers, Lupe's teacher often expressed concern that this charming little girl was so *dependent*. This conversation always resulted in volunteered opinions that the child would simply "grow out of it," or that the school psychologist should be called in to see if he had any suggestions. As you read this chapter and the next one, see what you would do on the basis of the information presented.

Lupe's behavior in the classroom is very similar to the attachment that infants show for their mothers. In fact, the terms *attachment* and *dependency* are often used interchangeably (Cohen, 1976). While both terms refer to similar patterns, *attachment* is usually used to describe infants. It also suggests a particular emotional bond that grows out of ways a mother satisfies her infant's needs.

similarity to attachment

FORMS OF DEPENDENCY

Dependency is often discussed as though it were a simple, single trait, just as most people think of high blood pressure as a single symptom. They are inaccurate in both cases. Actually, dependency takes several forms (Kagan & Moss, 1962). *Emotional dependency* involves seeking the approval, affection, and nearness of another person. The emotionally dependent child looks for attention and comfort from someone who is significant, just as Lupe did with her teacher. On the other hand, children may look for help to accomplish specific tasks. This is called *instrumental dependency*.

emotional and instrumental dependency

Children can do lots of different things to bring adults to them or to get attention (Sears, Raux, & Alpert, 1965). They can get attention through "negative" methods, like misbehaving. Or they can ask for reassurance, protection, or comfort from an adult or friend. Or a child may take a positive approach, and try to get attention by behaving well. Some children seek actual physical contact by touching or holding onto another person, while others just "hang around" a person whose affection they value. Almost any child who has a younger brother or sister, and who has tried to entertain his or her own friends at home, can tell you more than you probably want to know about these last two forms of dependency.

It is tempting to assume that a child who shows one form of dependency will show other forms as well. This is not necessarily the case. For example, a child may frequently ask for approval for good school work, but seldom try to have physical contact with the parent or teacher. Professor Robert Sears (1963) demonstrated this in a well-known study where he observed

situational specificity of dependency

Dependency takes many forms. Emotional dependency involves seeking body contact of nearness for security. This child meets an unfamiliar situation by seeking contact with her mother. Instrumental dependency involves seeking help or attention for accomplishment. This boy calls his mother's attention to his ability to name the letters of the alphabet.

nursery school children. He recorded each time each child negatively sought attention, positively sought attention, touched or held another person, was near the teacher, or sought reassurance. He found that most of these behaviors were not related to each other.

ANTECEDENTS OF DEPENDENCY

Why are some children more dependent than others? And why does a child show one type of dependency but not another? At present, we have no completely satisfactory answer to these questions. The reason that there is no clear-cut answer is certainly not because no one has looked for it.

socialization of dependency

Developmental psychologists have looked for the origins of dependency in parents' socialization practices. Many of these studies have examined very general parental attitudes, such as warmth versus hostility, and permissiveness versus restrictiveness (Cohen, 1976). These studies have not been as fruitful as we might hope, but they have yielded some useful information. For example, some studies have shown that parents who are warm and demonstrative with their children are somewhat more likely to have dependent children than other parents. On the other hand, there is also some evidence that if a parent rejects a child or withdraws his love, the child may end up being dependent (Cohen, 1976). Is it possible that such different practices could lead to similar outcomes, or are the studies simply wrong?

It *is* possible that a given response in children, such as dependency, could originate in different ways. From learning theory studies, we know that when a child has received very little or infrequent reinforcement, he is likely to try exceptionally hard to be reinforced. Most children find attention from important adults very reinforcing. This might be what happens in those cases where rejection is associated with dependency. On the other hand, children who have warm and loving parents probably develop strong ties of affection that lead them to want to be near their loved ones.

It seems obvious that the general characteristics of caregiving, such as warmth, permissiveness, or rejection, are much too vague to provide a full understanding of how dependency develops. We need much more specific information before we can understand how the many components of socialization produce dependent relationships.

As we will see in more detail later in this chapter, there are significant differences between the dependency of boys and girls. These differences are undoubtedly largely due to cultural influences. In our culture, dependent behavior is more often approved and rewarded in girls than boys. Boys are often punished for being dependent, and sex differences in dependency are part of most of the role models available to girls and boys. Thus, principles of reward and punishment and observational learning may account for many children's dependent behaviors. We will return to these questions when we discuss sex typing.

sex differences and cultural influences

Early Developmental Milestones and Processes

Play is valuable for young children. It provides experiences that stimulate them and let them practice and refine cognitive, motor, and social skills. Playful relationships often begin at home, but there are striking differences in how much parents play with their children. Among modern middle-class families, most parents find it fun to play with their infants. Fathers and mothers bubble their lips against the infant's skin to make him smile and laugh. As the infants get old enough, parents play peek-a-boo, enjoying the baby's laughter and expressions of anticipation, wonder, and delight as much as the child himself seems to enjoy the game. Some parents even toss their children into the air and catch them in the spirit of play. This behavior is certainly different from what the pioneer American behaviorist, John B. Watson, would have suggested. He advised parents not to joggle or unnecessarily stimulate their children during early infancy. Members of many other cultures follow similar advice. Traditionally Japanese parents soothe their infants rather than stimulating them. The nurseries that care for the children of Chinese workers comfort children when they are distressed, but otherwise see no particular need to stimulate them with any sort of games (Kessen, 1975).

variation in attitudes toward stimulation

By watching young children at play, we can get information about what social responses they are capable of and prefer as they develop. Even in early infancy children respond to each other, although at first they are more responsive to adults than to each other. Children are probably more responsive to adults than to other children for quite some time because adults feed and comfort them and are more likely to respond to the child's needs than other infants (Hartup, 1970).

By the time a child has learned to walk, he is ready to start learning new social skills by interacting with his peers. Toddlers' initial encounters with their peers are likely to involve conflict, perhaps because so many of their early interactions center around toys and other objects (Ames, 1952). One toddler is often trying to get for his own use some toy that another child feels a claim to. Be careful, however; these conclusions are based largely upon children in university nursery schools. Children may behave quite differently depending on their environment and the resources provided. We do not know if we would see these conflicts among children who play with sticks, stones, and other objects that are in plentiful supply. Neither do we know if there would be conflict if there were ample resources—a tricycle, a set of blocks, and so on for every child—in nursery schools or child care centers. Frankly, it does not seem likely that under those circumstances children would have as many conflicts over objects as the studies have suggested.

During the second year of life, children who have been raised in nuclear families seem to turn less and less to their mothers in new play settings and more to inanimate objects and then to peers (Eckerman & Whatley, 1975). When the mother is present while the child is playing, she seems to act as an attachment object, like the cloth mother monkeys in Harlow's experiments. The mother's presence seems to give the toddler the confidence he needs to explore.

Research shows that children are socially responsive to each other from *at least* the time they are 10 months old (Eckerman & Whatley, 1977). But they also change their social behavior in different situations. When toys are a factor, their interactions definitely change.

By the time they are 2 years old, children who have been raised at home seem to play freely with other toddlers they have never met before. At this age children smile, laugh, gesture, and "talk" to one another. They offer toys to each other and play together. In fact, they act toward each other as they used to act toward their mothers. This suggests that even as toddlers, children generalize from interactions with their mothers to interactions with their peers.

These children are involved in associative play.

influence of toys

unrepresentative samples

reciprocal interaction with peers

Teachers may encourage role playing to develop cooperative play.

In group situations, toddlers do several different things. They may simply play alone or watch other children as they play. These activities are called *solitary play* and *on-looker behavior*. Sometimes they do not even watch the other children. They appear unoccupied, being attracted by momentary interests, standing around, following the teacher, or randomly looking around the room. Some children engage in *parallel play*, where they play next to the other children and use the same materials, but play essentially independently of the other children. Two children may play beside one another with blocks, for example, but they build different structures rather than working together. Children also play with other children without assigning activities or differentiating roles. This interaction is called *associative play*. A group of children may enjoy each other's company. Perhaps they all ride tricycles or wagons, but their play is not organized or focused. Children's conversations at this age sometimes follow a pattern like parallel or associative play. They respond to each other by talking on the same topic, but neither child responds to the other's actual messages.

Cooperative play is organized. They have some goal, or they dramatize some aspect of adult life. Different roles are taken by members of the group, and one or two children act as leaders.

As children mature, they spend more time in more sophisticated types of play. However, some researchers have suggested that television and elaborate toys that encourage children to play alone may be slowing down today's children's social progress (Barnes, 1971). The possibility that some children may lose out on chances to develop social skills because of our popular entertainment is something to think about.

forms of playful interaction

LIMITS ON EARLY SOCIAL COMPETENCE

The development of social skills goes along with the development of other capabilities. Children do not have complex social relationships until they reach a certain point of biological maturation and have certain knowledge and skills. All of this takes time. For example, a child cannot participate in certain groups of play activities until his motor skills are sufficiently developed. Young children often think they can play the same games as their older brothers and sisters. The older children understandably resist the pleas of a younger child who wants to join them, because his lack of skill ruins the game for the rest of the players. For instance, a youngster may watch his older brothers and their friends swimming in races, while all he is capable of doing is a dog paddle.

The generally short attention span of young children and their incomplete command of language limit their social skills. Because they have not had the opportunity to fully learn the rules and norms of social interaction, they cannot participate in certain activities (Hartup, 1970).

egocentrism
Another factor that limits the range and quality of social interaction of young children is their egocentric orientation. According to Piaget, a young child cannot discriminate between herself or her actions, experiences, and ideas on the one hand, and the external environment on the other. Since they do not distinguish themselves from the environment, young children are not likely to be aware of the needs and feelings of others, and they do not understand group expectations. Therefore, they cannot put themselves in someone else's place and see a situation from that person's perspective (which may explain some of the conflict over toys we see in toddlers).

This feature of young children often comes out in their language. Darren may say to his mother, "I'm not going to play with him anymore. He cheats." Darren has apparently been thinking about some particular playmate. In commenting to his mother, he does not realize that she has no access to his private thoughts, and that she therefore has no idea what "him" Darren is talking about.

A POSITIVE VIEW OF DEVELOPMENTAL MILESTONES

It is important to understand the factors that limit young children. If we know what a child of a certain age can or cannot do, we can set realistic goals for him. On the other hand, the traditional preoccupation with what children *cannot* do seems to have diverted attention away from what they *can* do. Professor Harriet Rheingold (1977) has questioned the emphasis on the dependency and egocentrism of young children. Her own observations show that by the age of 12 months, or even earlier, children begin to share. By 18 months they often take the initiative in getting their mothers to play with them. They often do this by sharing.

early forms of
sharing
Children of this age engage in three forms of sharing. Sometimes they *show* an object to their mother; other times they *give* an object to their mother; still other times they *play* with an object while the mother still has it. These forms of sharing are not restricted to children and their mothers.

Giving an object to a parent is an early form of sharing.

Toddlers also share with their fathers and even with strangers. If it were true that children of this age cannot distinguish between themselves and the external environment, would they engage in even such a simple form of sharing as showing? If a child finds a sight delightful, and then points and calls his mother's attention to it, he must have some understanding of the difference between his own experience and that of his mother.

According to Rheingold, developing these sharing behaviors is an important milestone in children's social lives (1977). Sharing is a valued response in virtually all human cultures. We do not yet know just what kinds of experiences help children learn to share. Modeling and reinforcement probably play some role, and adding things like colorful mobiles or posters to the child's environment apparently increases the amount of showing a child does. But while young children seem to share naturally, without assistance from parents, these responses begin to decline in a year or so— at least among white middle-class children. By the time children enter preschool, we find teachers trying to teach them to share again. Thus we have a puzzle: What conditions in our culture lead to the decline of a practice that seems to come quite naturally to very young children?

influences on sharing

Role Taking

A major task of socialization in any culture is to prepare children to fill all the different roles that are essential in the society. Role-taking ability also seems to be related to children's ability to be cooperative or unselfish. To

perspectivism as task specific

assume different roles depending upon the situation, the child must be able to put himself in another person's place. Only if the child can do this can he understand other people's feelings. Piaget and his followers think that children remain too egocentric to do this until middle childhood or early adolescence (Piaget, 1952; Chandler & Greenspan, 1972). Other psychologists disagree with this point of view (Borke, 1971, 1972). Their point of view is supported by evidence that children have only seemed to be so egocentric because the tasks used in the studies were too difficult for such young children.

The idea that young children can act out roles if the tasks are appropriate for them has received considerable support in recent years (Hetherington & McIntyre, 1975; McIntyre, Vaughn, & Flavell, 1973). Some of this support is found in studies of children's communications. By age 4, children can adjust their speech and vary both form and style for different listeners (Gleason, 1973; Shatz & Gelman, 1973).

role taking in children's speech

SEX TYPING

Sex typing is the process by which children come to value and learn the behaviors that are considered characteristic of and appropriate for the child's own sex. Some actions are approved of for one sex, while they are ridiculed and disapproved of when done by members of the opposite sex. The behaviors that are associated with one specific sex are called *sex-typed behaviors.*

differential reinforcement of sex-typed behaviors

Almost from the moment of birth the child is bombarded with signals that deal with sex typing. American boy babies get blue blankets, while pink is the color for little girls. Parents show obvious pleasure when their boys demonstrate independence or stand up for their rights, and girls get approval for being compliant and helpful. There are marked differences in

Girls have relatively few chances to see female models in nontraditional roles.

the kinds of toys parents give their boy and girl children (Rheingold & Cook, 1975).

You can generally tell at a glance just by looking at the things in a child's room whether the child is a boy or a girl. The child develops an idea of his or her masculinity or femininity in the same way other concepts are developed (see chapters 8 and 9). Another influence on a child's notions concerning how members of each sex act is the observation of models. Live models in the child's life may or may not reflect the range of roles available to males and females in the society. Often the models a child sees present a more restricted range of sex-role options than are available. Sex-role models on television and in movies also influence children. Taken all together, these models usually provide a distorted picture of acceptable sex-role options, especially for women. Even when women are shown in reasonable jobs that have been traditionally reserved for men, they are usually portrayed as passive and dependent.

modeling influences

media influences

Sex-typed behavior is established well before children go to school. They show their preferences in the kinds of toys they choose. Boys choose sports objects and mechanical things, while girls select objects associated with the home and babies. Girls, however, cross sex lines in their choice of toys more freely than boys do. This may indicate that sex-role stereotypes are not as rigid for girls as for boys. On the other hand, it could be just that male activities have traditionally been given more prestige than activities associated with female roles. Many girls express the wish that they could be boys, while boys are likely to scorn girl's activities (Kagan, 1964). It will be interesting to see if this pattern changes as a result of the women's rights movement.

SEX-ROLE STEREOTYPES

The cultural expectations about the typical patterns that are supposed to be characteristic of a given sex are called *sex-role sterotypes*. There are some striking exceptions to the traditional sex-role stereotypes, both within cultures and between cultures, as Margaret Mead's exotic studies have shown (Mead, 1935). Nevertheless, these dramatic exceptions are relatively rare. Popular sex-role stereotypes are widely shared within American culture and among different cultures. Beatrice Whiting and Carolyn Edwards (1974) studied the sex-typed behavior of children between the ages of 3 and 11 in several different cultures. These children lived in Kenya, Okinawa, the Phillipines, Mexico, and the United States. They intended to look at certain sex-role stereotypes and compare them across cultures. Here are some of the stereotypes they examined, and what they found.

definition

cross-cultural comparisons

Dependence Stereotype "Girls Are More Dependent Than Boys." The results showed that this depends on the form of dependency you are looking at and the age of the child. The stereotype turns out to be true to a certain extent, but only for the younger girls. The younger girls sought help and physical contact much more than boys. Seeking attention by boasting or by doing things to gain praise or blame were male forms of dependency. They were well-established by the time the boys were 7 to 9 years old.

Passivity Stereotype   "Girls Are More Passive." When insulted or physically attacked by other children, girls were more likely than boys to withdraw from the situation. Boys were more likely than girls to respond with counteraggression. Girls were also somewhat more compliant to the wishes of others than were boys, and older boys seemed to show more initiative than the older girls. The researchers judged initiative on the basis of how often the children did what they wanted compared to how often they responded to others. This picture is clouded by the fact that girls receive more direct instructions than boys do, and they are expected to be compliant.

SEX ROLE CUES

The increasingly popular field of sociobiology suggests that there may be a genetic basis for many human social behaviors and personality characteristics. Predispositions toward certain social behaviors may be prevalent because those characteristics have survival value in human evolution. Sociobiology suggests that there may be genes for qualities such as altruism, deception, creativity, and an assortment of other kinds of behavior. Sociobiologists also suggest that some social behaviors may have had a survival value for males, while different behaviors better served the adaptive needs of females. Thus, they think biological differences account for sex differences in characteristics such as cognitive style (males tend to be field-independent while females display more field dependence) and for differences in sex-typed behavior. For example, they claim that there is a genetic basis for the fact that men tend to be more assertive than women.

While there are quite obvious biological differences between men and women, most developmental psychologists feel that sex-typed behaviors result from the fact that even very young children learn which behaviors are considered appropriate for women in their culture and which are considered appropriate for men. One prominent physical anthropologist has recently argued that even genetics supports the beliefs of social scientists better than the claims of sociobiologists (Washburn, 1978).

In any culture there are many clues that alert children to the activities that are considered appropriate for each sex. These cues persist long after movements such as women's liberation have begun to influence formal public policies, such as affirmative action. Here are a few of those cues. You can probably think of many others.

Toys   A quick glance around a child's room usually lets you know whether a boy or girl lives there. Girls' rooms or play areas generally contain dolls and toys reflecting a homemaker. Even older girls' rooms are often filled with stuffed toys, which may encourage nurturing atti-

Nurturance Stereotype "Girls Are More Nurturant Than Boys." This stereotype did not hold for children 6 years old or younger, but it did for the older age group. At about the age of 7, girls showed a marked increase in the tendency to offer help and support to others. This finding clearly does not suggest that sex differences in nurturance are biologically determined.

Aggression Stereotype "Boys Are More Physically Aggressive Than Girls; Girls Are More Verbally Aggressive." Boys engaged in more rough-

tudes. In contrast, a boy's room is likely to contain sports equipment, mechanical devices, and electronics build-it-yourself kits.

Home   Males most often model outside-the-home career orientations. Even children whose mother works outside the home are most likely to think of her role as homemaker. Parents often encourage submissive, dependent behavior in their daughters and assertive, independent behavior in their sons. The ways parents dress children make a difference too. Wearing a frilly dress to school implies the approval of different behaviors than the jeans commonly worn by boys. Jobs such as babysitting, dishes, and vacuuming are most often assigned to daughters, while lawn mowing and car washing are given to sons.

School   Most teachers in the elementary grades are still women. They tend to favor the generally more submissive and compliant behaviors of girls and actively discourage the active, physically assertive behavior of boys. Girls who are assertive are also discouraged.

Textbooks portray boys in more active and interesting roles than girls. Boys take the lead in activities presented in the readers used in many schools.

Most school principals and other administrators are male models, while women hold most of the subordinate positions (teachers, aides, secretaries).

Community   Within the child's community, women hold most of the less prestigious jobs—store clerk, doctor's receptionist, hotel maid. Men hold the positions of power and prestige that children see. The few women who hold executive or professional positions are not very visible to children.

Television   The sexes are presented differently in television fiction. For every women character, there are three men. Usually the women characters are shown in the home rather than in jobs. When they have jobs, the occupations are poorer and of lower status than those filled by males. And women are seldom found in adventurous situations (Simmons, Greenberg, & Atkin, 1977). The lot of women seems particularly dreary, and perhaps more than a little silly, as presented in television commercials.

and-tumble play than girls; but contrary to popular stereotype, they also engaged in more verbal aggression—insults and such—than girls.

The general conclusion from this study was that sex-typed behaviors are fairly consistent across a wide range of different cultures. Nevertheless, they are shaped by the socialization practices of these groups. As the authors concluded:

> The differences in many of the types of behavior seem to be one of style rather than intent, for example, seeking help ("feminine") rather than attention ("masculine"), and justifying dominance by appealing to the rules ("feminine") rather than straight egoistic dominance ("masculine"). (p. 200)

These differences in style seem to be learned. They conform to the norms of the society in which a child is raised.

IMITATION AND IDENTIFICATION

formation and
function of
ego ideal

In chapter 10 we saw that in psychoanalytic theory the superego is conceived of as two subsystems, the *conscience* and the *ego ideal*. The ego ideal includes the standards and the goals that represent the kind of person the child wants to become. Freud believed that the child's emotional ties with his parents were critical in the formation of the ego ideal and that the ego ideal sets the child's sex-role standards. By identification, the child feels that he actually has some of the characteristics of the people with whom he identifies. When things happen to a boy's father, he feels as though it happened to himself. In this way the boy shares his father's joys, sorrows, victories, and defeats (Kagan, 1964).

types of
identification

Freud conceived of two types of identification: *anaclytic identification* and *identification with the aggressor*. Anaclytic identification is based upon the intense dependence children develop upon their mothers. This relationship is considered especially important in leading girls to identify with their mothers.

The principal mechanism of identification for boys is identification with the aggressor. There is no comparable mechanism for girls, and Freud had much less to say about identification in females than in males. Both types of identification depend upon strong emotional ties between parent and child. But in the case of identification with the aggressor, the boy's love for his father is mixed with hostility because of the Oedipal situation. Boys resolve their fears of castration by identifying with their fathers and imitating their behavior.

The child may learn several different aspects of the father's behavior and personality through identification.

imitation as a
reciprocal process

Psychoanalytic psychologists feel that identification is more significant and subtle than imitation. They regard imitation as a simple type of copying. Social learning theorists disagree and see no reason to distinguish between identification and imitation. They see imitation as a reciprocal process in which adults, especially parents, and children influence each other. Influence does not simply flow from parent to child. In hair and clothing styles especially, it is obvious that preferences of middle-aged people are influenced by the up-coming generation.

Children do adopt the behaviors of people who are important to them. People who care for a child or who have power over resources that are important to the child have a better chance of influencing early development than strangers do. But parents do not simply do things to be imitated by their children. They also reward those behaviors they value and punish those they disapprove of. They also use warnings and instructions in guiding their children to meet their standards of conduct.

imitation as a selective process

By watching models in various settings, children learn what kinds of consequences are likely to follow certain behaviors. They see a variety of different models, and adopt some aspects of one model's behavior and some from another. In large measure these selections are probably made on the basis of what the child expects to result. Moreover, even a single model is not completely consistent from one time to another, or from one situation to the next. Consistency, or the lack of it, does affect the behaviors a child will adopt, and both adults and other children can be influences (Brody & Henderson, 1977).

Moral Development

Freud thought that identification explained both the adoption and internalization of sex roles, and moral development as well. But if moral standards are an internalized part of the personality, we would expect them to be consistent in how they influence a person's moral conduct. The evidence does not support this prediction. For example, the moral conduct of preadolescent children may differ considerably depending on the situation. One group of these children made quite consistent statements on moral issues, but when they were given tests on which they could cheat, there was great variation in their honesty, depending upon whether the test was given in the classroom, at home, or in a Sunday school (Hartshorne & May, 1928). Research with younger children agrees that whether or not children cheat depends more upon the situation factors than on a general trait of honesty or dishonesty (Rau, 1965). One factor that children consider is the likelihood of being caught.

situational influences

Many cognitive theorists do not completely discount Freud's theory, but they believe that moral judgments are based more on the child's decision-making abilities than upon a conscience or an ego ideal. They say that children go through a predetermined sequence, making different kinds of moral decisions as their cognitive abilities develop. While this sequence is fixed, the child's ability to deal with moral issues is stimulated by social interaction, and especially by role-taking within his peer group.

PIAGET'S STAGE THEORY

Piaget is one of the principal theorists who have tried to describe and explain how children develop morally. He has not dealt much with children's actual moral or ethical behavior. Instead, he has centered his attention on the kinds of judgments the child makes about morality, ethics, and justice. He believes that developmental changes we see in children's moral judgments are determined by the same processes as all other forms of rational thinking. The moral ideas told to them by parents and other adults are not simply included in the child's thinking as they are handed down. The child tends to accept the moral principles his parents tell him, but he simplifies and distorts them in his mind. The child's view is again egocentric, and only by sharing perspectives during social interaction with peers can an individual develop his own moral philosophy. Thus children cannot have their own moral philosophies until they are beyond egocentrism and capable of abstract thought.

Rules have little influence in the lives of children in the first stage of moral development. Then they enter a second stage where they regard rules as external and unchangeable laws handed down by parents or even higher authority. At this stage the child believes that rules are absolute and eternal. Nevertheless, children at this stage violate the rules quite regularly, seeming not to notice the gap between what they say is the proper thing to do and what they actually do.

rules as absolute

Finally the child enters a third stage in which he realizes that rules can be changed, and that they can remain in force only if people agree to abide by them. Although the child at this stage realizes that rules are relative, he is much more likely to obey them than the younger child (Flavell, 1963).

relativity of rules

According to Piaget, when children are about 3 through 8 years of age, they decide how serious an act is on the basis of its objective consequences. This simply means that if two children do some damage, a third child who is told about it will judge the harm done by the amount of damage. If one child breaks two eggs while another child breaks a dozen, a third child who is told about it will say that the child who broke the most eggs committed the worst act. In making this judgment, the child will not consider the intentions of the children who committed the damage. At about age 8 the child enters a stage of subjective morality, in which intentions are given more weight than the objective outcomes of the act. You can test this out for yourself, using stories and questions like those Piaget has employed. Tell the following story to a 5-year-old and then to an 8- or 9-year-old.

> Once there were two boys, Carl and Jimmy. Now this is what Carl did. Carl had been shopping with his mother and he was helping her carry the groceries into the house. While he was carrying a bag of groceries, he dropped the bag and all 12 eggs in a carton broke. That is what Carl did.
> Now this is what Jimmy did. His mother told him not to eat any pie before dinner, but when she was out of the house he got into the refrigerator to get the pie. When he was getting it out he knocked two eggs onto the floor, and they broke. That is what Jimmy did.

After you have told the story to each child, ask the question, "Which child do you think was naughtier? Which one did the worse thing?" Usually the older child will think that Jimmy was naughtier, because he intended to disobey his mother. Younger children will usually say that Carl did the worse thing, because he did more damage.

The children's reactions are fascinating, but Piaget's interpretation is not the only one possible. It could also be that the younger children pay more attention to consequences than to intentions because the consequences are always mentioned last. Younger children may not remember what they were told about intentions in the beginning of the story. When the last information presented has more influence than earlier information, we say a *recency effect* is operating. There is some evidence that a recency effect or some other difference in cognitive abilities may produce the interesting results in young children's moral judgments that Piaget describes. To make subjective moral judgments, children must consider two kinds of information at the same time—intentions and consequences. Younger children are not as capable of managing this two-part task as older children (Nummedal & Bass, 1976).

alternative interpretations

KOHLBERG'S STAGES OF MORAL DEVELOPMENT

Kohlberg agrees with Piaget's basic assumptions about moral development, but he has extended and elaborated them. He believes that the development of a moral philosophy follows a progression of fixed stages, although few adults ever make it to the highest stage. Kohlberg outlines three levels of moral reasoning, and each of these levels is subdivided into two stages (Kohlberg, 1963; Kohlberg & Turiel, 1971; Turiel, 1973).

In Kohlberg's first, or *preconventional level*, a child judges an act simply on the basis of cultural standards of good and bad. A behavior is judged according to what the child expects to happen as a consequence. According to the standards of his culture, would the behavior deserve punishment or reward?

preconventional moral judgment

In the first stage of the preconventional level, the child believes in unquestioning obedience to authority. His basic aim is to avoid punishment. At the second stage of this level, he judges an action "right" if it is likely to result in a reward. The child has a sense of fair play at this level, but it is based on the notion that "you scratch my back and I'll scratch yours," rather than loyalty, gratitude, or justice.

When the child reaches the *conventional level*, he feels that a sense of loyalty to family, group, or nation is more important in resolving a moral question than immediate consequences. In stage 3, the initial phase of this level, children make judgments that fit their notions of a "good boy" or "nice girl." At stage 4, law and order is the theme. Good behavior consists of showing respect for authority and doing your duty for its own sake.

conventional moral judgment

The next advance in the progression of moral judgments is to the *postconventional* or *autonomous level*. The child operating at the fifth level defines his own moral values, apart from the standards of other groups or people. He recognizes that personal values are relative, and he will stress the procedures for arriving at concensus.

postconventional moral judgment

The sixth and highest stage is dominated by the *universal ethical principle orientation*. Moral judgments at this stage are based on justice, equality of human rights, respect for justice, respect for the dignity of human beings as individuals, and fair play.

Kohlberg and his followers have tested this model in a number of different countries, and they claim that it is valid across cultures. People reach each stage at earlier ages in more developed countries than in underdeveloped countries, and urban cultures seem to be more advanced than rural ones. They suggest that children in complex cultures feel more conflicts and questions in their social interactions than children in "simpler" cultures. These experiences stimulate the development of the internal cognitive structures that the child uses to make rational moral judgments.

LIMITATIONS OF COGNITIVE STAGE INTERPRETATIONS

Cognitive stage theorists believe that changes in moral development result when children get themselves into social situations that pose moral questions (Turiel, 1973). They try to resolve their conflicts by making moral decisions. This point of view assumes that children in "simple" societies or from families with low socioeconomic status have fewer moral conflicts than economically advantaged children. This assumption has not been proven. In fact, anthropologists have found very complex kinship, religion, and other subsystems in societies with extremely primitive technology. Furthermore, studies involving 10 different groups of American Indians show marked exceptions to the sequence of moral stages (Havighurst & Neugarten, 1955). It seems obvious that culture influences the kinds of moral judgments children make.

cultural influences

It also seems unwise to assume that the moral judgments characteristic of American and Western European children and youth represent the highest form of moral reasoning. By that same line of logic, you can argue that the judgments of other people are always inferior to the extent that they differ from your own. This line of reasoning seems somehow unconvincing when we consider, for example, that the moral philosophies of many American Indian groups account for the mutual interrelationships among people *and* nature.

ethnocentric reasoning

Most social learning theorists would probably agree that moral judgments are based at least in part on cognitive decision making. However, they would not agree that the sequence of moral stages is universal for all cultures. Neither would they say that children's moral judgments develop because they have to resolve conflicts. Cognitive-stage theorists say that parents do not have much influence on the development of moral reasoning in their children, but we have ample evidence that they do indeed have an influence. Parents can influence their children with reasoning and explanations and by calling the child's attention to other people's feelings (Aronfreed, 1961; Hoffman & Saltzstein, 1967). Children are also influenced by models who make judgments and state a reason for them. There is also some evidence that adults who make consistent moral judgments and who give a reason for their judgments have more influence on the moral judgments of first graders than other children (Brody & Henderson, 1977).

parental influences

Assessment

During the course of our history the importance of social development has often been debated. Just after the Soviet Union launched the world's first satellite, critics charged that our schools were neglecting instruction in the sciences and spending too much time attending to students' social adjustment. We hear similar criticisms today, except the concern has shifted to the basic skills, including reading and mathematics. The debates seem to assume that social and intellectual skills develop separately. But it is now clear that to be effective in today's world requires both kinds of skills, and they are highly interrelated. There is also a growing awareness that in their concern for academic achievement, "mainstream" Americans have often failed to see what effective and supportive social relationships can contribute to the quality of life. Certain subcultures within the United States have always emphasized important aspects of life that the dominant culture has given only secondary priority, if they have been recognized at all. Mexican-Americans, for example, have traditionally emphasized openness, warmth, and mutual interdependence. Among the most important qualities a person can have are sensitivity to the feelings and the needs of others and skill in relating to others. As Mexican-Americans become used to the customs and priorities of Anglo culture, their emphasis on these qualities often decreases (Ramirez & Casteneda, 1974). It seems important to find ways to help people preserve these important qualities, and to even share them with people from other ethnic groups. The developmental implications of these issues will be examined in the next chapter.

There are clearly many influences on social development and no easy answer to what parents and educators should do to have the most favorable impact on their children. Nevertheless, the knowledge we have does provide many valuable insights into how parents and social institutions can influence the social development of the children in their charge. We shall now turn to those influences.

Suggested Readings

Bandura, A. *Social learning theory*. New York: Prentice Hall, 1977.

Benedict, R. Continuity and discontinuity in cultural conditioning. *Psychiatry*, 1938, *1*, 161–167.

Bronfenbrenner, U. Freudian theories of identification and their derivatives. *Child Development*, 1960, *31*, 15–40.

Harlow, H., & Harlow, M. H. Learning to love. *American Scientist,* 1966, *54,* 244–272.

Johnson, M. M. Fathers, mothers, and sex typing. *Sociological Inquiry*, 1975, *45*, 15–26.

Maccoby, E. E., & Jacklin, C. N. *The psychology of sex differences*. Stanford, Calif.: Stanford University Press, 1975.

Mead, M. *Sex and temperament in three primitive societies*. New York: Morrow, 1935.

Mischel, W. Sex-typing and socialization. In P. H. Mussen (Ed.), *Carmichael's manual of child psychology* (Vol. 2) (3rd ed.). New York: Wiley, 1970.

Sutton-Smith, B. Children at play. *Natural History*, December 1971. Reprinted in S. White (Ed.), *Human development in today's world*. Boston: Little, Brown, 1976.

Washburn, S. L. Human behavior and the behavior of other animals. *American Psychologist,* 1978, *33,* 405–418.

13

Guiding Social Development

This chapter covers the stages children go through in social development, from infancy through adolescence. When you have finished the chapter, you should know something about current child care including the most important qualities of good environments for infant care. You should also know the characteristics of authoritarian, authoritative, and permissive socialization and their outcomes. You should be able to compare Freudian and social learning viewpoints on imitation, identification, and sex-role development. It should be possible for you to describe the development of perspective-taking, altruism, and empathy.

You should also understand and be able to evaluate Freudian, social learning, and drive reduction explanations of aggression. Further, you should be able to describe some practices adults can use to control aggressive behavior in children.

You should be able to identify various influences on the cooperation and competition of children, including how schools can influence these and related social behaviors.

You should also be aware of how family, peer, and society affect adolescents. Specifically, you should be able to recommend practices that could help develop positive relationships between parents and adolescents and to ease the transition from youth to adulthood.

Finally, you should be able to identify characteristics of social maturity at each age level, from infancy through adolescence, and describe how you would use your knowledge of psychology to help children develop social skills.

Everyone places a high value on certain qualities they see in both children and adults. And we each have our own ideas about the kinds of experiences that will help children develop the qualities we value. Every boy and girl who wants to become a scout must memorize a list of the characteristics the scouts value—A Boy Scout is helpful, friendly, courteous, kind, obedient, cheerful, brave, clean, and reverent. Psychologists have studied how characteristics like these develop. They have been interested in how these characteristics change with age, and how social institutions such as the school, the family, and the peer group influence the child's social development. In this chapter we will discuss some of the changes in social skills that are associated with age. We will also look at some of what is known about how adults can help stimulate the development of social skills. Obviously, our age groupings are somewhat arbitrary. For instance, we look at the development of cooperation in connection with middle childhood. But cooperation is not confined to the period of middle childhood. We have simply placed each topic in the sections where it seems most useful.

Infancy

CHILD CARE IN A CHANGING SOCIETY

changing needs
for child care

As our society becomes more urbanized, and as more and more mothers work, we need new child care arrangements to substitute for a mother's daily and personal care of her infant. True, a few families have adopted a new life-style where the father stays at home to care for the house and children, while the mother goes out to earn the family income. This makes good copy for Sunday newspapers; we have no reason to believe that a father's care is any less adequate than a mother's, and mothers can sometimes find jobs when fathers cannot. Nevertheless, this arrangement is still rare in the United States. Other kinds of child care are needed.

Traditionally, mothers who worked outside the home had relatives or neighbors who would provide child care and *caring* during the day. But with the growth of industry and movement to the cities, families have been separated from their relatives and from trusted and concerned friends. As a result, even though informal child care is the most common form of child care, the nature of these informal arrangements seems to be changing. Often the care provided is not adequate. We need new ways to provide quality care and support for the young children of the mothers who are joining the labor force.

Alternative Forms of Day Care   There is no doubt that a nation that says it is concerned about its children should provide better quality care than we presently do. There are many forms of day care in practice today (Steinfels, 1974). While it is hard to group them, we can look at two kinds: custodial and developmental.

Inadequate funding makes it impossible for most families to have access to good day care.

Custodial programs simply try to keep children out of harm. Those programs that try to provide for more than minimum safety needs are called *developmental day care.* They try to support a range of children's developmental needs. Some of these programs are staffed by trained caretakers who get the children involved in experiences designed to encourage intellectual and social development. These centers provide a range of toys, books, and games. Usually they have a nutrition program as well. Good programs of this type may be adequate for some families, but not for all.

custodial vs. developmental day care

Children from low-income families may need *comprehensive child development programs.* Comprehensive day care provides the education and nutrition offered by developmental day care. In addition it should include medical and social services. Sometimes diagnostic services are also provided (Feeney, 1973), and some programs involve parents.

comprehensive day care

There is little doubt that good quality day care is needed. Thousands of children are now cared for in inadequate or even dangerous programs. But if parents must choose between caring for their children at home or sending them to a day care center with high standards, which should they choose? The question is not as simple as it seems, and the "experts" are by no means in agreement.

Outcomes of Home and Professional Care   Some psychologists (for example, Caldwell, 1973) believe that the day care provided by trained professionals can be as good or better for the child as home care by the parents. There are others who believe that separating the child from the mother (or mother substitute) may have bad effects on the child's social

dangers of
parent-child
separation

and emotional development. Some authorities believe that children who do not spend lots of time with their mothers will suffer from *maternal deprivation* and will have trouble forming the usual bonds with their mothers. Children who do not form these ties as infants may later suffer from the life-long inability to "establish and maintain deep and significant interpersonal relations" (Ainsworth, 1973, p. 53).

This possibility has important implications, and we must take it seriously. We must also consider the effects of putting children up for adoption or placing them in foster homes. Several people who do take this issue seriously have studied the effects of infant day care. Obviously, infants who are placed in day care are separated from their primary caretakers (few would argue that it must be the natural mother). Does this separation lead to emotional insecurity and difficulties in forming social relationships? Once again, the experts do not completely agree.

Syracuse study

One study on this topic was carried out at the Children's Center at Syracuse University. Children who had been in full-day infant day care for about 3 years were compared with children who had not been in infant day care. All the children were enrolled in a new day-care center at the time of the study. The children's behavior was rated. The researchers found that children who had already been in day care showed more positive emotions, were less tense, and scored better on social interaction than children reared at home (Schwarz, Krolick, & Strickland, 1973). But don't be too quick to decide that center care is better than home care.

Syracuse
follow-up

The same researchers did a follow-up study (Schwarz, Strickland, & Krolick, 1974). This time they compared the social behaviors of 4-year-olds who had spent 2 or more years in infant day care with another group of children who had spent their infancy at home. Now the results showed that the children who had been in day care were less cooperative with adults than home-reared children. That meant that they were less inclined to do as they were told. The children who had already been in day care also were more aggressive toward their peers and adults than the children who were attending day care programs for the first time. They were also more inclined to run around a lot, rather than sitting in one place, than the new children. Thus infant day care seems to have both advantages and disadvantages.

There are several possible reasons for these results. One has already been mentioned: The child's socialization may be disrupted if he or she is separated from the mother (Bowlby, 1973). Another possibility is that children in formal settings such as day-care centers are exposed to lots of different adult expectations. This may teach them to resist to adult pressure for conformity (Bronfenbrenner, 1970a).

Kansas study

Once again, we should not draw conclusions too quickly. Another pair of researchers (Macrae & Herbert-Jackson, 1976) studied a younger group of home-reared and center-reared children in Lawrence, Kansas. The two groups of children were compared on tolerance for frustration, cooperation with adults, getting along with peers, spontaneity, aggression, motor activity, successful problem solving, ability to abstract, and planning. The day-care children scored significantly higher than the others on ability to get along with peers, problem solving, ability to abstract, and planning. None of the findings were the same as those from the Syracuse study.

By now it should be clear that there are no easy answers to hard questions. Why the differences in the outcomes of these studies? Do the inconsistencies suggest that scientific studies are of little value? Certainly not! But they do show how little we know about day care (Schwarz, Strickland, & Krolick, 1974). The methods of the studies were not exactly the same, and the children were of different ages. And of course, the home care of all the children could have varied greatly. Beyond that, another point is very important. The two programs were different. Perhaps different programs have different outcomes, and therefore it may be possible to design programs to achieve specific goals.

conflicting findings

Certainly, we cannot reject day care just because some programs may produce undesirable effects. But both the Syracuse and Lawrence programs were good ones. If day care may have positive or negative outcomes, depending upon the quality of the program, we surely want our children in well-structured programs rather than thrown together ones.

Limitations of Contemporary Child Care   One major problem of many day care programs is that the staff members have little or no training. In many cases the pay is so low that not only is it impossible to attract trained people, but it is also difficult to keep them. If we believe that the first year of life is critical in the formation of social bonds, it may be very important to have the same people working with the children from day to day and month to month. Infants adapt well to being left with baby-sitters now and then. But these minor separations are quite different from the major separations we associate with group day care.

staff training

On the other hand, the home care that many children receive is far from the best. Ainsworth (1973) has said that "there is at present no known substitute for a family environment for child-rearing" (p. 77). But while it is heart-warming to think of a warm, supportive, and intellectually stimulating family, for thousands of children this romantic ideal is far from their reality. For some children almost any kind of developmental day care would be an improvement over their present circumstances.

ESSENTIAL QUALITIES OF ENVIRONMENTS FOR INFANTS

Caretakers   Several characteristics seem essential for infant day care (Ainsworth, 1973). The children should be active and have physical contact with their caretakers. The caretakers should respond to the infants. Each one should be responsible for only a very small number of infants so they can respond and be attentive. And very importantly, the caretakers should be assigned on a long-term basis so the children do not have to deal with a large number of adults who come and go unpredictably. But this goal is not likely to be reached as long as pay, status, and opportunities for career advancement for day care workers are low.

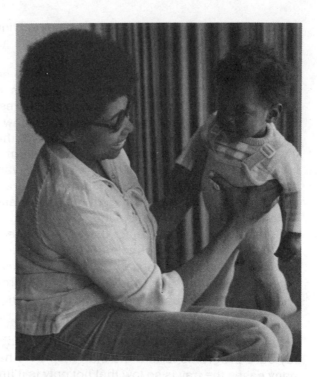

Responsiveness is an important quality in infant caretakers.

Facilitating Social Responsiveness   When parents and other caretakers respond to an infant's behavior, they can influence the child's responsiveness. An example illustrates how this can work.

responsiveness
exemplified

In this program day-care center aides came to a university for training. Those aides were to return to the centers in their own communities to train other aides. Most, but not all, of them had passed a high school equivalency (GED) test. None had any formal education beyond high school. But they were bright, dedicated, and experienced.

The aides were taught to use learning principles to strengthen or weaken certain responses of the infants. After watching modeling demonstrations, they practiced with infants who were brought into the Early Childhood Center at the university. They learned to define their targets and to keep objective records on the progress of the infants toward those goals. At the Early Childhood Center they saw rather dramatic changes in response to their efforts. This experience convinced them that the principles were effective and made them feel competent.

Following the practice period, the aides returned to the centers in their own communities to apply their new skills before returning for the next phase of their training. They quickly noticed that one infant got most of the attention in one of the centers. This particular baby had a winning smile. He smiled at adults when they came into the room, and almost invariably it drew them to him—visitors, director, and aides alike. The trainees decided that the adults were being reinforced by this infant's smile whenever they approached or played with him. The trained aides concluded that the other infants would get more attention if they smiled more.

To some extent readiness to smile seems to be biologically determined (Freedman, 1965), but we also know that very young infants can be conditioned to smile more often (Etzel & Gewirtz, 1967). Therefore, the plan formulated by the trainees seemed reasonable.

During the week they were in their home centers, the aides played with the other babies and gave them a lot of attention whenever they smiled, even ever so slightly. In doing this, they were using the shaping procedures of behaviorists. They also did the things that mothers do to make their babies laugh. They talked to them in a high-pitched voice, tickled them or bubbled their lips against their skin, and moved their faces about, first coming near the baby's face, then drawing away, and then coming face to face again. By the end of the week they reported that the infants were now smiling more, and that visitors to the infant room found it more fun to play with them.

PATTERNS AND STANDARDS FOR CHILD CARE

There is still a short supply of good quality child care arrangements in the United States. Even though everyone seems to agree that the early environment has a deep influence on children's intellectual, emotional, and social development, the most common arrangement is still informal family care. Small groups of children are cared for in a neighborhood home. The caretaker often has no special training for this responsibility, and care is usually only custodial. Fortunately, training programs for family day care are now available in some communities. There is generally no regulation of basic necessities like physical care and safety. In many cases this kind of care is the only choice available to low-income families (Steinfels, 1974).

predominant child-care arrangements

A more acceptable alternative to informal family day care is licensed home day care. Here minimum health and safety standards can be set by the government. However, in most states, the standards are low and poorly enforced, and the caretakers only rarely have special training.

Even in day-care centers created for the purpose of caring for children, most programs provide little more than custodial service. It is easier to enforce standards in these centers than in day-care homes, but the staff still generally have very little training. Often they see their roles primarily as providing for the safety of the children. Sometimes even that task is carried out without commitment or enthusiasm. We recently talked with the owner/director of one center about a research project. No matter what we talking about, he repeatedly complained about the minimum standards set by local agencies. Even though the standards for how many adults worked with how many children and for physical facilities seemed extremely low to us, he regarded the rules as unjust meddling that had the effect of reducing his profits.

It would be comforting to think that this was an isolated incident, but it is not. On another occasion we were training day-care workers for a Migrant Opportunity Program. The day-care facility in one rural community was rented from the local church. One trainer insisted several times that she could smell natural gas in the infant room. But the minister said that was impossible, and he refused to have the space heater checked by a repairman. It seemed that he may have been more interested in the children's souls than in their physical welfare. Only when the program director threatened to move the center to a different place did the minister-landlord agree to have the facility checked. The heater did leak.

We can conclude by saying that, in spite of our limited knowledge and spotty enthusiasm, formal day care is clearly going to be more and more common. Those of us interested in guiding the development of infants must look carefully at how programs can best serve babies and their families. Lots of stimulation and attention from the same people, room to move around, and lots of materials to work with seem to be minimum needs.

Early Childhood

The home is still the primary place where young children are socialized, although more and more American children spend a significant part of their waking hours in day care. While parents and children influence each other's behavior, different parents have different styles of interacting with their children. These styles influence both the child's social and cognitive development. Another significant feature of the social life of young children is that children begin by being egocentric. Later, they can assume different roles in different situations. They have learned some complex interpersonal behaviors. In this section we will look at how adults can affect this process.

THE DEVELOPMENT OF COMPETENCE

philosophies of child rearing

Even if they've never bothered to describe them in words, parents have distinct philosophies of child rearing. Parents' ideas about the nature of children and the kinds of practices that will produce the kind of children they want will influence their actual practices. Some parents do not have a very consistent philosophy of child rearing, which can also influence the relationship developed between parent and child. Over several years, Diana Baumrind and her associates have been trying to find out how child-rearing philosophies and patterns of child rearing influence children (Baumrind, 1966, 1971, 1973; Baumrind & Black, 1967).

alternative outcomes of child rearing

First, consider the qualities you think are desirable for children to develop. Suppose you could deliberately choose between procedures that would produce different outcomes. Suppose further that one set of practices would probably lead to the qualities of self-reliance, assertiveness, self-control, a liking for other children, and a gay, cheerful spirit. Another set could result in a child who is discontented, withdrawn, distrustful, and generally unhappy. This child might also not show self-reliance and self-control. Which pattern sounds better to you? These characteristics

WHO SHALL RAISE THE CHILDREN?

Modern child psychologists and educators are fond of saying that our children are our most valuable resource. This is not a new idea; Ecclesiastes (11, 30) says "Never call a man happy until he is dead: His true epitaph is written in his children."

But families are changing faster than we are finding ways to provide new ways to nurture and develop this precious resource. One profound change is in the number of children who are raised by a single parent, who has to devote a good deal of time to activities other than child rearing.

Most single-parent families are headed by women, and the number is growing rapidly. The number of families headed by women is growing at twice the rate of two-parent families. Many people think this change is taking place mostly among poor families; but in fact, the increase in the number of families with children headed by women is more rapid among the middle class than among poor families. And the change is not restricted to minority families. The great majority of single-parent families are white. And only a very small proportion of such families are headed by unwed mothers. Most are due to divorce or separation.

Put this together with the fact that an ever-larger number of women are seeking work outside the home for stimulation and self-fulfillment, and we arrive at the logical question, "Who will take care of the children?" (Solnit, 1976).

What long-range solutions would you propose?

describe some of the differences Baumrind and her associates found in children whose parents had different approaches to child rearing. These relationships are important, and like most important things they are quite complex. Baumrind assumed these characteristics are aspects of social skill. She called the elements of social skill *social responsibility, independence, achievement orientation,* and *vitality.* Each of these characteristics is defined by a number of behaviors.

According to the definitions Baumrind uses, children who have social responsibility tend to be friendly rather than hostile toward their peers. They are more likely to help or encourage the work of others than to disrupt them. They cooperate in activities led by adults; and as they grow up they develop objectivity and self-control.

social responsibility

Children who are identified as independent are assertive rather than submissive. They are more likely to make their own choices than to conform to others' wishes. And they do not act aimlessly. Rather, their behavior is purposeful and goal directed.

independence

Achievement orientation means seeking intellectual challenge. Children with this quality approach a problem with persistence and efficiency. They do not try to solve problems with impulsive guesses.

achievement orientation

A child who has vitality has lots of energy and looks vigorous in his activities.

vitality

measurement of
socialization
practices

Baumrind and her associates also looked at different socialization practices to see how they related to the characteristics they had identified. They watched parents during a 2-hour structured teaching session with their child, interviewed both mothers and fathers, and made two visits to the children's homes. These visits took place during the 2 to 3 hours just before dinner until just after bedtime. This time was used because there is a good chance of seeing conflicts between the wishes and impulses of children and the desires of their parents. With the information from these observations and interviews, the researchers examined *parental control*, *maturity demands*, *clarity of parent-child communication*, and *nurturance*.

parental control

Parental control refers to the things parents do to influence their children, and the steps they take to modify the children's dependent, aggressive, or playful behavior. It also includes the things parents do to get their children to adopt the parents' standards. It does not reflect how restrictive the parents are, or how much they intrude into their children's activities. Essentially, it is a measure of strictness in discipline.

maturity demands

Some parents pressure their children to perform up to the level of their ability. These are maturity demands, and they relate to intellectual, social, and emotional expectations. These demands for the child to perform up to his or her ability are called *independence training*. A less important aspect of maturity demands is independence granting; that is, the amount of room parents give their children to make their own decisions.

clarity of
communications

Clarity of parent-child communications is another important part of parent-child relationships. It refers to the extent to which parents use logic to influence the child to do what they ask. It also refers to the degree to which the parent asks the child's opinion, asks about his feelings, and uses direct measures rather than subtle manipulation to control the child's behavior.

nurturance

To some extent all parents try to ensure the well-being of their children, but the kind of care giving differs greatly from one parent to another. Thus, the category of nurturance includes the behaviors and attitudes that parents use to express love and to assure the child's emotional and physical well-being. A parent can express her or his compassion and love through sensory stimulation, through words of approval, and through tender touches and words.

involvement

Involvement is another aspect of the parent-child relationship. It refers to the pride and pleasure parents take in their children's accomplishments. Pride and pleasure are shown through praise and interest in the child's activities. Involvement is also shown through the things the parents do to protect the welfare of their child.

mature children

Baumrind and her associates found that nursery school children had certain clusters of characteristics. These clusters were related to the child-rearing patterns used by parents. One group of children was labeled "mature." These children were high on vitality. They showed a lot of self-control and self-reliance, and tended to approach rather than avoid new situations.

dysphoric and
disaffiliated

A second group of children was called "dysphoric and disaffiliated." They did not seek out their peers, and they were low on vitality. They were

Children with lots of vitality often come from authoritative homes.

more likely to avoid than to seek out new situations. The third group of children was considered "immature." They were not very self-reliant and had poor self-control. Like the dysphoric children, they avoided new situations.

These three patterns of child behavior were associated with three different patterns of child-rearing practices. These patterns were called "authoritative," "authoritarian," and "permissive."

The "mature" children tended to have authoritative parents. These parents were quite controlling, but they also had warm relationships with their children. They communicated more clearly with their children than the parents of any other group. They used physical punishment more than permissive parents; but on the other hand, they used ridicule, love withdrawal, and attempts to frighten the child less. Although they did punish their children when they felt they had to to make the child obey, they used positive reinforcement more than they used punishment. They put consistent pressure for mature and obedient behavior on their children, and in turn the children were socially responsive and assertive. The best way to summarize the child-rearing practices of authoritative parents is a combination of a lot of control over the child's behavior, coupled with a good deal of positive encouragement of the child's independence. They seemed to use control to train their children in the skills needed for independence, and then give them the chance to use that independence.

authoritative parents

The parents of "dysphoric and disaffiliated" children also used a lot of control with their children, but their procedures depended less on reasoning and more on coercion. Also unlike the authoritative parents, these authoritarian parents did *not* encourage their child to express himself when there was a disagreement. Compared with authoritative parents, authoritarian parents were more detached and less warm in their relationships with their child.

authoritarian parents

The parents of the "immature" children generally fell into the permissive group. These parents were less controlling than either of the other

permissive parents

groups of parents, and their households were not as well organized. Neither parent placed many demands on the child, and fathers in this group did not provide much reinforcement. These parents did not provide much training for independence, but they did tend to give in to the child's demands to be independent. Compared to the other groups, they used more withdrawal of love and ridicule as control measures and used less physical punishment and reasoning.

The most striking distinction between parents of "dysphoric-disaffiliated" children and "immature" children was that parents of the "dysphoric" children used a lot of control and little nurturance, while parents of immature children were high on nurturance and low on control.

permissive vs. nonconforming parents

These findings were repeated in a second study. In addition, the second study tried to look at parents low in control, but distinguished between those whose lack of control was the result of a belief that children should have a good deal of freedom and those whose lack of control was the result of laxness or neglect. In this study permissive parents were distinguished from "nonconforming parents." Nonconforming parents did use firmer control and were less passive in their relationships with their children. They tended to have antiauthoritarian attitudes. An interesting sex difference was discovered when the children of these different types of parents were compared. Nonconforming parents had sons who were more achievement-oriented and independent than sons of the permissive parents. In contrast, the daughters of nonconforming parents were less achievement-oriented and independent than the daughters of permissive parents. The nonconforming mothers of these girls were somewhat am-

The meaning of certain child-rearing behaviors differs among various cultural groups.

bivalent about their own roles, and the authors felt they might not have provided strong models for independence and achievement.

Some families did not fit any of these patterns. One such group was called "harmonious." The observers could not rate these families on their use of firm enforcement; because although these parents never seemed to *exercise* control, they appeared to *have* control. Their children seemed to be able to tell what their parents wanted them to do, and then they did it. The parents placed a higher value on honesty, harmony, justice, and reason in human relations than they did on things like power, achievement, control, and order. They recognized differences among family members due to experience and personality, and took these differences into account in their relationships.

harmonious families

Daughters from harmonious families had exceptionally high IQs, and they were more friendly and achievement-oriented than the girls in all of the other categories combined. This was not true of the boys from these families.

All of these findings were based on studies of white middle-class parents and their children. Baumrind and her associates also studied several black families, and found that authoritarian patterns were associated with different outcomes. Black girls reared in authoritarian families were more independent and aggressive than white girls with similar experiences. These conclusions were based on observations of only a small number of middle-class black families, but they do suggest that it is important to look at social background. The strict control and demand for obedience in the black families may help the black girl survive in her culture. Furthermore, the child probably interprets these practices as supportive. She may see them as reflecting her parents' love and concern. In the middle-class families, the same parental behaviors might be interpreted as cold and dogmatic. Moreover, in upper middle-class white families, dogmatic attitudes might be seen as emotional coldness. In this setting, the authoritarian practices would not be seen as necessary, and they are probably not the usual practice. It is important to remember that parents' behaviors that appear the same may be interpreted quite differently by children from different backgrounds, and thus they may be associated with different outcomes. Even within the same culture, a given pattern of parents' behavior is likely to be interpreted differently at different stages of the child's development.

socialization outcomes in black families

Obviously, the relationship between child-rearing practices and the characteristics children develop is very complex, but we can derive some guiding principles for parents from the studies we have just summarized. For several years now it has been popular to assume that children should be made to feel that their parents are happy with them no matter what they do. Baumrind's work suggests that this is false. Parents who do not set standards and use control with their children may think they are encouraging independence, but they are more likely to do the opposite. Children who become independent seem to have parents who demand independence, train them in the skills they need to act independently, and then grant independence so the child can practice the skills.

limitations of unconditional positive regard

ENCOURAGING MATURITY AND COMPETENCE

Competence may be defined in different ways, depending on the behaviors you value in one's cultural background. Among the characteristics that many Americans would consider part of competence are self-reliance, appropriate assertiveness, good self-control, friendly attitude, cheerfulness, and curiosity. Parents whose children display those characteristics are likely to be authoritative. Adults who value these qualities might do well to use some of the socialization practices that seem to be effective for authoritative parents.

Clear communication is important. Make sure the child understands what you expect, and why. Expectations should be communicated with warmth and understanding—in a way that lets the child know you are concerned with her welfare and development. To do this, use reasoning; don't hand down arbitrary orders. Let the child know why you think a given behavior is important, and point out the natural consequences of various options. Give the child a chance to offer her opinions, and let her tell you how she feels about a given topic. If you feel strongly about a given standard of behavior, be explicit about your expectations and the consequences you will attach to different behaviors on the child's part. Don't manipulate the child.

Be consistent. If you say you are going to take away some privilege if the child doesn't do this (or if she does that again), follow through every time. Don't try to frighten the child to get her to do what you want. Instead, provide a lot of positive reinforcement for the child's "good" behaviors and accomplishments.

Be specific about identifying the behaviors you consider to be mature and want to encourage. Use consistent encouragement and guidance to help the child accomplish those behaviors. Also, be consistent in encouraging independence. But encouragement is not enough. Teach the skills the child will need to be independent, and then provide the opportunity to use those skills.

Perhaps the most important point to remember is not to be passive in your relationships with children you care about. Take an active role. That does not mean you should take over the child's life and direct everything she does. It means to be responsive, to share your point of view with the child, while encouraging discussion of her ideas and feelings, too. Finally, make sure the child knows you care about her and her welfare. This will increase your success in passing your values—whatever they are—on to your child.

punishment
in context

There is good reason that psychologists have urged parents to avoid using punishment. It can easily be misapplied. Many parents use it along with unrealistic expectations. They may want the child to do things beyond his present level of development. It can be dangerous, and may have undesirable side effects. But in fact most parents use some form of punishment, and the context in which it is used seems to make more difference than the punishment itself. Punishment may not have undesirable effects if the parents are warm and supportive and if they use punishment infrequently compared to reason and positive reinforcement. The use of threats, fear, sarcasm, and ridicule are likely to produce undesirable effects.

Parents who have strict standards of control, are cool in their relationships with the child, and use excessive punishment without reasoning often think that these practices will help their child to develop self-control. The opposite seems to be the case. These children are more likely than those reared in authoritative households to lack self-confidence and self-control.

In the last analysis, the child's interpretation of the parents' behavior is probably one of the most important things to consider. If the child thinks that the parent is not behind his efforts and not concerned about him, the outcome is not likely to be favorable. This probably accounts for the fact that children reared by permissive parents develop less social skill than those reared in authoritative homes.

cultural meaning of parental behavior

SINGLE-PARENT FAMILIES

Things change faster than we realize. Take the typical American family for example. According to the definition used by the Bureau of the Census, a family is "a group of two or more people related by blood, marriage, or adoption who live together" (Bell, 1977, p. 19). While there are obviously various kinds of families, most of us still think of the typical American family as a man and woman and two children. The support for this "average" family is provided by the husband/father. Our tax structure and many business decisions are based on this image of the typical family. For evidence, just watch a few TV commercials.

Just how typical is this family today? Not very! In fact, only 3.3 million of the 56 million families in the United States fit this particular pattern. That constitutes only 6% of the total (Bell, 1977). What implications do these statistics hold for child-rearing? More than 1 out of every 6 children in the United States is reared in a home in which there is only one parent—usually the mother. Thus there is growing interest in a subject that has already received a good bit of attention. For a long while there has been interest in the effects of father absence on the development of children. Most of this attention has focused on boys, because Freudian theory holds that the father plays a critical role in the emotional and sex-role development of boys. The successful resolution of the Oedipal situation is supposed to have long-term consequences for development; for in order to pass successfully through this critical period a boy supposedly must have a father figure with whom he can identify.

Freudian perspective

Actually, the word "identification" has been used in several different ways in psychoanalytic literature. It sometimes refers to similarities between a child's behaviors or motives and those of some adult who is significant in the child's life (Bronfenbrenner, 1960). Thus, when a child judges his own behavior by standards like his parents', it is assumed that he has absorbed his parents' standards through the process of identification. On the other hand, often children seem to feel that they have some of

identification

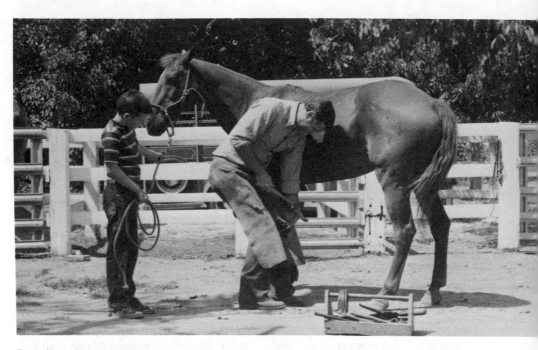

Freudian theory suggests that the father plays a crucial role in the emotional and sexual development of boys.

the characteristics of powerful people who are close to them. Through identification, a boy might believe he is as masculine as his father. Or when a parent has a triumph or a defeat, a child may feel as though these things happened to him personally (Kagan, 1964). But there is a flaw in this reasoning. Parents share their children's joys and sorrows just as though they had experienced them themselves. Does this mean that the parent identifies with the child? Psychoanalytic theory does not recognize that sharing of experience is a two-way process (Mischel, 1970).

According to psychoanalytic theory, the process of identification is somewhat different for girls and boys. For girls, identification is based upon their intense dependence on the mother. This is called **anaclytic** **identification**. The concept that anaclitic identification is more common in girls than boys has been criticized, because differences in dependency between boys and girls do not generally develop during the early years that are supposed to be so important in identification processes (Mischel, 1970).

anaclytic identification

For boys *identification with the aggressor* is the primary mechanism of identification. During the Oedipal crisis, boys are thought to feel an incestuous desire for their mother. They are afraid that their fathers will punish them for these unacceptable thoughts, and so they try to avoid punishment and to share what the father has by trying to "be like" him. Their anxiety is therefore reduced by identifying with their father, who they see as an aggressor.

identification with aggressor

Some psychologists who support the idea of identification believe that the process is much more subtle and complex than simple imitation. They see identification as responsible for sex-typing, self-control, feelings of guilt, conscience, and many other personality characteristics (Sears, Rau, & Alpert, 1965). Social learning theorists point out that these characteristics do not necessarily appear together (Mischel, 1970). In fact, a child may have some forms of dependency but not others (Sears, 1963). And a child may be dependent in one situation and not in another.

Social learning theorists also believe that imitation is not a matter of simple copying. Children adopt some behaviors from one person and other behaviors from someone else. They selectively add to their own repertoire things they see done by various models. They learn that different behaviors may lead to different results in different situations, and they are able to change their behavior to fit these expectations. Moreover, they do not learn sex roles simply from their parents. Children are also influenced by other children (Mischel, 1970; Brody & Henderson, 1977) and by media such as television, movies, and books.

Research on sex-role development does show that boys who are raised by their mothers or other women without any close association with a single adult male often develop habits and mannerisms that are generally considered feminine. This finding is in line with psychoanalytic predictions, but it is also what social learning theory would expect.

sex-role development

The effects of father absence may also differ depending upon whether the absence is temporary or permanent, and whether it occurred early or late in the child's development. Children who know that the absence is only temporary are likely to keep up their father's presence in their fantasies (Baker, Fagan, Fischer, Janda, & Cove, 1967). Children who must face the fact that the separation is permanent because of death or divorce are less likely to do so (Herzog & Sudia, 1973).

permanent and temporary separations

Single parents, whether they are fathers or mothers, usually have an especially difficult task in rearing their children. Since the one parent must both earn a living for the family and care for the children, the time available to pay attention to the children is more limited than in two-parent families. As a result it is often necessary to make a special effort to set aside regular times to spend with the children. If possible, the child should have a chance to develop a relationship with a loving adult of the

The effects of father absence differ depending on whether the absence is permanent or temporary.

same sex as the missing parent. It might be a grandparent, or an old friend with a stable relationship to the family. Teachers can be important too, and many schools and preschools now make a special attempt to include male staff members.

FROM EGOCENTRISM TO PERSPECTIVISM

role-taking ability Young children tend to be very egocentric. As we have seen, from his observations of children and from his experiments with them, Piaget concluded that young children cannot tell the difference between their own personal experiences and objective reality. In other words, children build their own reality out of their experiences. It does not occur to them that other people may see things differently. Thus, according to the cognitive-developmental point of view, they cannot view a situation from another person's perspective. This in turn limits their ability to take other roles.

challenges to traditional view Supporters of Piaget's point of view argue that children cannot develop taking roles until late childhood or early adolescence (Chandler & Greenspan, 1972). This view has recently been challenged in a number of studies. Using simpler tasks than those used by Piaget, investigators (Borke, 1971, 1972, 1975) have found that children as young as 3 can understand that another person may see things from a vantage point different from their own.

Empathy and Altruism Have you ever become so absorbed in a movie that you could not help crying when one of the characters was hurt? Have you ever shed tears because you heard a sad song about someone who lost a lover? Or has your heart jumped when you learned that someone

Coming to the aid of another is a form of altruism.

close to you received some honor or distinction? If these things have happened to you, you have experienced **empathy.** Empathy is the capacity to feel pleasure when something good happens to someone else, or to feel pain in response to another person's troubles. People must be able to see things from another person's point of view to experience empathy. In turn, empathy is important to the development of **altruism.** An altruistic act is one that is freely given with the aim of contributing to the well-being of someone else.

empathy defined

altruism defined

Recently there has been mounting concern that altruism, which includes sharing, donating, and coming to the aid of another, is on the decline. In one well-known case at least 38 people watched a neighbor being murdered (Milgram & Hollander, 1964). Yet not a soul raised a finger to come to her aid or even phone for help. More recently newspapers reported that a man was hanged from a road sign beside a busy highway, with only the tips of his toes touching the ground. Hundreds of drivers passed by before anyone offered assistance or called for help.

How do people become so cold? Many psychologists who are concerned about the lack of altruism they see around them have been trying to find out what kinds of experiences lead to the development of altruism in children.

Altruism does increase with age. This "natural" change probably reflects the child's increasing ability to take the point of view of others, which also increases as the child grows up (Fry, 1967). This change is probably also due to the fact that as they grow up, children have more chances to learn the values of their culture.

effects of age

But even though altruism increases with age and experience, the advance is not dramatic. And obviously there are substantial individual differences in altruistic behavior. How do these differences develop?

To a large degree differences in children's altruistic behavior are related to differences in their backgrounds. For example, many Mexican-American children in the Southwest come from families that stress sharing, especially among members of the family (Henderson & Bergan, 1976). Descriptive research has shown that children are likely to be concerned about others if they come from families that practice altruism and encourage the expression of feelings (Bryan & London, 1970).

cultural differences

How effective is reinforcement in promoting altruism? For those who think that any behavior can be increased through reinforcement, the findings are likely to be disappointing. The use of social approval, praise, approving pats and hugs, and similar social reinforcements have not been very effective in influencing children to sacrifice *material goods* for the benefit of others (Fischer, 1963; Midlarsky & Bryan, 1967). Social reinforcement seems to be effective only in getting children to make sacrifices that are relatively effortless and that involve no material sacrifice. On the other hand, material incentives (bubble gum) have been effective in getting 3- and 4-year-old children to share things such as marbles (Fischer, 1963). Perhaps these findings simply reflect the values of our highly materialistic society.

reinforcement

Children's moods also influence their altruistic behavior. They are more likely to share when thinking happy thoughts than when thinking sad

emotional states

Modeling by parents influences the development of altruism.

thoughts (Moore, Underwood, & Rosenhan, 1973). We do not have enough information to tell clearly how generalizable these effects are, but it seems reasonable that happy children would be more generous than sad ones.

modeling

A number of laboratory studies have shown that modeling has a very strong effect on altruism (White, 1967; Bryan & London, 1970). This research shows very clearly that parents and others who want to encourage the development of altruism in children had better practice what they preach. Children's generosity is not much influenced by preaching, but it is influenced by the examples set by the people they observe (Bryan, 1970).

This general conclusion was supported by a very important study in a nursery school with children ranging from 3½ to 5½ years old. This study took modeling into consideration just as laboratory studies have, but it also looked at the influence of high and low nurturance. Several different measures of altruism were used.

socialization of altruism

Drawing on the implications of their findings, the authors concluded that "the parent who is an altruist in the world but is cold with his child reaps a small harvest in developing altruism in his child" (Yarrow, Scott, & Waxler, 1973). Their findings also suggested that if adults try to teach altruism by "telling" children how they should behave, and by giving them verbal rules, the children will learn the rules, but nothing else. Knowing the principles will not lead them to follow the rules in practice. Altruism would best be acquired from parents who are altruistic in their own interactions with others and who explain the principles their behavior is based on. Their behavior toward their children should be consistent with the general altruism they advocate.

Middle Childhood

The first day of school brings one of the most dramatic changes in a child's life. The change is usually dramatic even if the child has been in a nursery school or day care or some other institution. The school is a subculture all its own, with its own social dynamics and influences on development. It presents formal demands, frustrations, and chances for failure rarely experienced in preschool.

Even so, parents continue to have an influence, as do the clubs and organizations children join in elementary school. During middle childhood children are subject to many sources of influence, and sometimes these influences are contradictory. For example, their parents may value altruism, while unwittingly allowing their children to watch television programs that suggest that violence is the most effective way to deal with problems. A traditional Mexican-American family may stress the value of cooperation as the way to accomplish goals, while the school stresses competition. These varied sources have an impact upon many forms of behavior. In this section we will look at socialization influences on both negative and positive social behavior. We will use aggressive behavior on the one hand, and pro-social cooperation on the other as examples. And we will look, where appropriate, at how both the family and the school can influence the child.

AGGRESSIVE BEHAVIOR

Americans are becoming increasingly aware and concerned that we live in a violent society. People are afraid to walk through their neighborhoods at night. In some communities they do not feel safe even within their homes. Only the manufacturers of locks and alarm systems benefit from this state of affairs. And the vandals and criminals are not just adults. More and more school children are involved in acts of extreme violence. In some cities the bands of young people who would have spent their time fighting rival gangs in the past are now directing their aggression against adults, and particularly against elderly people. What causes such violent behavior? Is there anything parents and educators can do to curb this destructive tide?

Drive Reduction Viewpoints   Psychologists hold differing ideas about what socialization experiences lead to violence and what means can be taken to control aggression. One of the most popular ideas has been that aggression results from the conflict between inner instincts and the barriers that society uses to block these impulses. This view, of course, is derived from Freud's theories of the psychodynamics of personality. According to this interpretation, aggression is a natural response to frustration (Dollard, Doob, Miller, Mowrer, & Sears, 1939). Freud saw personality as a dynamic energy system. He reasoned that frustration leads to the build up of a supply of aggressive energy. A person might not behave aggressively because of a single frustrating experience, but the effects of that frustration would still be there. As the aggressive impulses to other frustrations build up, they would eventually have to be released.

frustration-
aggression
hypothesis

This set of assumptions has been called the *frustration-aggression hypothesis*. Many people use these assumptions in their daily lives, even though they probably do not know they come from Freud. Many educators assume, for example, that a certain amount of frustration is naturally built into school work. One reason for providing periodic physical activity, through recess and physical education classes, is to allow children to release the energy they have stored up through this frustration. Some non-traditional educational programs try to eliminate the frustration of school work by letting children choose their own activities. Presumably, children will select activities that they enjoy and that are not frustrating.

Theorists who believe that aggression is a natural response to frustration suggest that there are several ways that aggressive impulses may be released. These processes are called **catharsis.** Catharsis can take many forms.

The most obvious form is *direct aggression* against the source of frustration, but it is not always a good idea. An employee may be frustrated by his boss, but to show open aggression against her would not be wise. Similarly, a child may sense that it is not safe to vent her frustration against her parent or teachers. Of course some parents believe in the frustration-aggression hypothesis and therefore encourage their children to express their frustrations directly against them. They feel it is "healthier" to prevent the aggressive impulses from accumulating. Children who know from experience that it is not a good idea to fight back against those who control the resources and the consequences may engage in *displacement*. They redirect their aggression from the source of their frustration to safer targets. For the child, a little kid down the block or a family pet might be a safe target. For a frustrated breadwinner, a spouse or children may be safer targets than the boss. Sometimes a whole group of people become the target for aggressive thoughts and action. Some psychologists believe that this kind of displacement is involved in ethnic prejudice.

Some psychologists recommend that parents and teachers provide objects for children to use in releasing their aggressive energies. For example, sometimes children are encouraged to give a punching pillow a good pounding when they feel frustrated. This procedure is based on the

When children have objects against which to express their feelings of aggression, they seem to learn that aggression is an acceptable way to solve problems.

catharsis

direct aggression

displacement

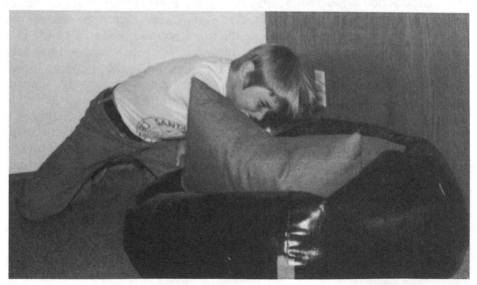

Violence on television may lead to aggressive responses.

frustration-aggression hypothesis. From our point of view, this is not a good idea. Research shows that this approach results in an increase of aggressive behavior rather than a decrease (Bandura, 1969). The unintended outcome of providing things like punching pillows may be to teach children that aggression is an appropriate way to deal with problems. The aggressive behavior is then likely to generalize to other situations and to targets other than the original ones.

Sublimation is another form of catharis. In psychoanalytic theory, this is a way people channel unacceptable impulses and energies into socially approved outlets. According to this interpretation, an activity like sports competition should lead to a reduction in other forms of aggression (Menninger, 1948). Sad to say, this assumption does not seem to hold up either. In fact, aggressive athletic activities are more likely to lead to more aggression than they are to reduce it (Berkowitz, 1973).

Why is it, then, that when people react to frustration by burying themselves in their work or hobbies, they are not likely to be aggressive? One logical explanation is that it has nothing to do with catharsis at all. When a person does something that commands all his attention and concentration, his frustration is forgotten and his anger fades away. Being involved in an interesting task keeps you from brooding about your problems.

Some psychologists think that fantasy can be a form of catharsis. They think that if someone reads about violence or watches it in sports or television dramas, his aggressive impulses will drain off. The research overwhelmingly contradicts this interpretation. Children's fantasy play with aggressive toys increases the chances that they will be openly aggressive (Berkowitz, 1973). Besides, the literature now shows that when children watch violence on television, the likelihood that they will commit similar aggressive acts increases (Comstock, 1977). Television often suggests that aggression is justified, that violence is a socially acceptable way of deal-

sublimation

fantasy

television
influences

ing with problems, and that it pays off. Moreover, television stories with violent action are very exciting and hold the young viewer's attention well. The shows are very realistic because they often depict people and circumstances that are like those in the child's environment. All of these factors increase the likelihood that the child will imitate what he or she sees (Comstock, 1977).

Television does not simply increase the chance that children will be aggressive. It also desensitizes them so that they are less likely to respond to violence in their own environments (Comstock, 1977; Thomas & Drabman, 1975). Increased tolerance for aggression is as disturbing as the violent acts themselves.

Social Learning Interpretations   In general, attempts to control aggression based on the idea of catharsis seem likely to be ineffective. In fact, in some cases, procedures based on this hypothesis may produce more rather than less aggressive behavior. Fortunately, other alternatives are available. Research also provides some very clear insights into what parents and other adults should do to control aggression in children.

When a child hits his little sister and takes a favorite toy away from her, the first reaction of many parents is to punish him. A recent ruling by the United States Supreme Court shows that the justices agree that it is appropriate, and effective, to use physical punishment to control children. Parents might be excused for believing this culturally accepted norm, but the courts should know better. Social learning theorists argue that when parents use physical punishment to control their children, their children learn to use aggression to get what they want. This is certainly not sur-

modeling   prising. When parents use punishment; they are modeling aggression as a
influences   means of solving problems (Bandura & Walters, 1963).

To be accurate, we should say that it is probably not simply because they model aggression that some parents have aggressive children. Parents who use physical punishment a lot also tend to provide very little reinforcement when their children act appropriately. Often they also encourage their children to stand up for their "rights" in their relationships with other children (Becker, 1964). Working together, these practices probably increase the chances that the children will use aggression as a basic means of solving problems.

influences on   But punishment does not always have these negative effects. First, its
outcomes of   effectiveness depends upon a number of factors, including timing and the
punishment   consistency with which it is used. Punishment is more effective when it is used immediately after the misbehavior than when it is delayed until the child has reached her goal (Berkowitz, 1973). Consistency is important because when punishment is inconsistent, the child's world becomes quite unpredictable. When children have difficulty distinguishing between acts that are likely to be punished and those that are not, they often become quite fearful.

Punishment also produces different results in different families. When used by mothers who are warm and affectionate toward their children it may be effective. On the other hand, it is likely to be ineffective when used by mothers who are cold and hostile toward their children (Parke & Walters, 1967; Sears, Maccoby, & Levin, 1957).

In general, parents should avoid the use of physical punishment in favor of more positive control techniques. As we have seen, the effects of punishment are rather unpredictable, and the outcomes seem to be negative more often than not. Punishment can have adverse side effects, such as causing the child to avoid the parent or teacher who punishes her. You will have a difficult time having a positive influence on a child who avoids you. And finally, aggression breeds aggression. If we are concerned about the increasing violence in our society, we should try to find more positive ways of influencing behavior.

positive control procedures

Berkowitz (1973) has suggested several nonpunitive measures that parents and teachers can use to control aggression in children. One technique is simply to not respond to aggressive acts. Some children are aggressive because it is a very effective way to get attention. However, when parents ignore aggressive behavior, the child may interpret it as a lack of concern or even silent approval. Extreme permissiveness can also lead to the development of aggression in children (Becker, 1964). A better approach may be to remove the child from the situation that provoked the aggression as quickly as possible, and to explain why the behavior is wrong. It is important to be consistent. If a child feels guilt, sympathy, or shame, her aggressive behavior may be suppressed, so it is helpful to mention the harm that aggression may cause to innocent people. This approach may also help to reduce the chance that children will be negatively influenced by the violence they see on television. When parents point out that the violence is "bad," "immoral," or "unjustified," the child's aggression may be inhibited (Berkowitz, 1973).

explanation of consequences

Most parents want their children to develop self-control, because as often as not there is no adult around to guide the child's behavior. Children are most likely to become well-socialized and responsible if their parents use logic with them. Reasoning helps children understand and anticipate the consequences of their behavior. These consequences affect both themselves and others. When parents reason with their children and explain the harmful effects of aggression, and when they identify alternative ways to deal with provocative situations, the children are more likely to use reasoning themselves when no adult is around (Berkowitz, 1973).

Probably the most powerful way to teach children how to deal with problems is to show them appropriate ways to respond to frustration. One of the most discouraging things about television is that positive approaches to solving problems or reaching goals are shown much less often than negative means (Stein & Friedrich, 1975). Apparently the television industry considers positive ways to solve problems dull. It is much better to be a good example of the kind of behavior you want to promote in a child than it is to call attention to behavior to be avoided (Bandura & Walters, 1963). In the long run, negative examples that otherwise might not have occurred to the child might be remembered and used later. The danger is the same as with warning a child not to stick peas up his nose when the idea had never entered his head.

modeled responses to frustration

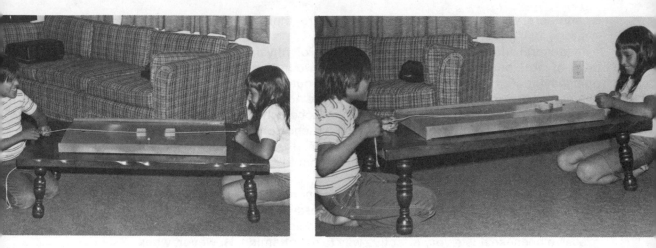

The marble pull game is used to measure cooperation and competition.

cues and
aggressive
behavior

There is one final point to keep in mind. Objects that a child associates with aggression may lead to aggressive behavior under certain conditions. Children who have been given guns to play with often show increased aggression in other play situations (Feshbach, 1956). And while the presence of an object the child associates with aggression may not influence his behavior most of the time, the presence of a weapon may lead to aggression if the child is angry. From his extensive studies of aggression, one noted authority on violence has concluded that:

> An angry person can pull the trigger of his gun if he wants to commit violence, but the trigger (i.e., the sight of the gun) apparently can also pull the finger, or otherwise elicit aggressive reactions from him, if he is ready to aggress and does not have strong inhibitions against it (Berkowitz, 1973, p. 132).

COMPETITION AND COOPERATION

In play situations young children try to get toys for their own use. Anyone who has been around children a while has seen a child suddenly become interested in a toy he had been ignoring as soon as another child begins to use it. We can see that even young children may be very competitive.

It is easy to understand why young children may be competitive since it is easier to compete than to cooperate. To cooperate with their peers, children must be able to communicate well and to set their individual goals aside for the interests of a group. This apparently requires that they understand the benefits of the cooperative effort. They must also be able to take different roles (Wolfle & Wolfle, 1939). Since role taking depends on the child's ability to understand the point of view of others, it seems that children would cooperate more as they grow older and less egocentric. As logical as this seems, it appears to be incorrect. It is certainly not accurate as far as most American children are concerned.

competition and
social values

At a fairly early age, children begin to show the competitive spirit of American society (Gesell & Ilg, 1943), and by middle childhood the pattern is well-established. The specific details of how this happens are not completely understood, but researchers have found a number of important facts of interest.

The major difference between cooperation and competition lies in the goals of the activity. In competition, individuals can achieve their goals only at the expense of the others in the group. There is only one first place available in pole vaulting. In contrast, a cooperative activity is one in which the efforts of every member of a group are directed toward a common goal. The efforts of individuals in a cooperative group are related because each individual's effort increases the chances that the others will benefit (Deutsch, 1962).

goals of competition and cooperation

Laboratory Studies   Most studies of cooperation and competition have been done in laboratories. One device used is the marble-pull game (Madsen, 1971). The accompanying photographs show children playing the marble-pull game. The game consists of a playing board with a rounded top surface. Near each end of the board there is a hole with a container beneath it. Just behind the hole at each end of the board is a small eyelet. The second part of the game is a plexiglass block. In the middle of the block there is a hole large enough to hold a marble. A string is fastened to each end of this plexiglass marble holder and is threaded through the eyelet at each end of the board. Thus, when a marble has been placed in the marble holder, the children can pull on the strings. When the marble holder passes over the hole in front of one of the children, the marble drops into the container. Thus the children can win marbles by pulling the marble

In the country, children have many responsibilities requiring cooperation.

holder to their end of the board. But there's a catch: if the children pull against each other, the marble holder, which is held together by magnets in the plastic, comes apart in the middle and the marble rolls into a gutter at the side of the board. When that happens, neither child gets a marble. Thus, the two players must choose either to compete or to cooperate. If they compete neither one can win, because the marble will always go into the gutter. If they decide to cooperate, by taking turns or some other arrangement, each child can win some marbles. In this game competition is *maladaptive* because neither child can win anything by competing.

maladaptive competition

In a typical experiment one child sits at each end of the board. They are told that they are about to play a game in which they can win marbles. The experimenter places a marble in the holder and pulls on one of the strings. The holder passes over the hole at one end of the board and the marble drops into the container. Then the experimenter repeats the demonstration by pulling the marble holder to the opposite end of the board, and a marble drops into the second child's container. The children are then told that they will have 10 marbles to play for, and that they can keep all the marbles they win. They are not told that the marble holder will break in half if they pull against each other. They will soon learn this on their own. As they play the game, whenever the holder breaks apart and the marble rolls into the gutter, the experimenter picks it up and tells them that neither of them wins it because it did not fall into a cup.

Developmental Changes   This game and several similar ones have been used to study developmental changes in children's cooperative and maladaptive competitive behavior. They have also been used to study cultural differences in these behaviors. Now older children should very quickly see that there is no way to win by competing. They should therefore cooperate more quickly than younger children. Right? Wrong! Madsen (1971) compared the performance of children in the age ranges 4 to 5, 7 to 8, and 10 to 11, and found that American children in the youngest age group won more marbles than American children in either of the two older groups.

Cultural Differences   Madsen also compared American children with Mexican children and found some very striking differences. Mexican children obtained a dramatically larger number of marbles than Anglo-American children. He then tried teaching the Anglo-American children to be cooperative, and even then a majority (62%) of them never won even a single marble. It seems that American children learn to compete so thoroughly that they will give up the chance of winning any marbles themselves to prevent a peer from winning. This tendency is more pronounced in boys than girls (Kagan & Madsen, 1971).

cultural norms

Another interesting pattern has now come out of research comparing cooperation and competition among various age groups of children in different countries, and from both urban and rural communities (Madsen, 1967; Shapira & Madsen, 1969). These studies again show striking differences. Children reared in rural settings tend to be more cooperative and less competitive than urban children. Even among children from urban

rural-urban differences

environments there are ethnic differences, with Mexican-American children showing more cooperation than Anglo-American children. It is quite possible, however, that these differences may be because many urban Mexican-American families have come from rural communities. Whatever the cause, urban-rural differences in cooperation and competition seem to overshadow ethnic differences. Mexican village children are quite cooperative in a cooperation task. Children from Mexico City are more like American urban children than like Mexican village children (Madsen & Shapira, 1970).

FIELD STUDIES OF CULTURAL INFLUENCES

All of this information is merely descriptive. It brings up the question of how these differences come to be, but provides no specific evidence on this point. We can find some additional insights in the writings of anthropologists. Oscar Lewis (1961), for example, studied a village 60 miles south of Mexico City in 1943. He visited the village again in 1956 and found some remarkable changes. During his earlier visit parents had actively discouraged aggression, curiosity, independence, and competition through the use of punishment and fear. At that time the economy was based on agriculture. When Lewis returned 13 years later, the village was no longer   *social change* agricultural. It had become a popular tourist attraction, and the socialization practices used by parents had also changed. Parents had become more permissive and indulgent, and the children were less cooperative and conforming.

More direct evidence of how parents influence children's interpersonal social behaviors is provided in the stories of child-rearing in an Indian **barrio** in Mexico (Romney & Romney, 1966). The barrio was part of a larger Mexican town. Here the parents expected very little of young children, because they were not considered to be old enough to reason. But by the time children were 5 or 6 years old, they were considered old enough to reason. At that point they would be scolded for trying to push other children around or for individualistic achievements. They became very non-aggressive and had difficulty adjusting when they went to the central school. There they had to learn to interact with Mexican children, who were more individualistic and aggressive.

School Influences   Parents undoubtedly influence the development of cooperation and competition in children, but at the age of 5 or 6 children come under the influence of the schools. The schools have a dramatic influence on the development of cooperative and competitive interpersonal behavior.

The point at which competition begins to increase among children in the United States roughly corresponds to the beginning of school. This is no mere coincidence. Teachers can structure learning activities in many different ways. This structure determines how students interact with each other, and many psychologists (for instance, Johnson, Johnson, Johnson, & Anderson, 1976) believe these differences influence both cognitive and affective learning.

A teacher may vary the structure of learning activities in his or her class-room now and then, but most usually stick to one pattern of instruction. The structure of activities depends to a large extent on the kinds of goals the teacher thinks are important. Perhaps the most common goal structure

competition

is competitive. In a competitive activity one child can achieve her goal only at the expense of the others who are involved. One child can win the spelling bee only if the others lose. When grades are distributed "on a curve," only a few students can earn an *A*, even if everyone happened to study very hard.

individualization

Individual goal structures also are used widely in the schools. The stress on individual goals probably results from the admirable belief that instruction should be tailored to meet the needs of each pupil. But often when

cooperation

individualization is carried to extremes, the success of any particular child is not related to the goal attainment of other students (Deutsch, 1962). Moreover, students are not likely to support and reinforce each other for academic efforts (DeVries & Edwards, 1974).

A third goal structure is used much less frequently than competition and individualization. This structure is cooperation. In cooperative activities the efforts of each member of a group are aimed at accomplishing a common goal (Deutsch, 1962). If anyone in the group is successful, everyone else in the group is also. On the other hand, no one reaches the goal unless everyone does.

Given these different possibilities, it is important to understand what effects different structures have on students, beyond success or failure in a particular activity. Johnson and his associates (Johnson & Johnson, 1974; Johnson, et al., 1976) studied this issue. They believed that cooperative goals make it possible for students to share and to help each other. By contrast, they expected individualized activities to lead pupils to ignore each other in order to concentrate on their own tasks. They also had a hunch that children involved in cooperative activities would be more altruistic than those in individualized programs. In addition, Johnson and his associates thought that the goal structure of classrooms would influence student attitudes and achievement. They assigned some fifth grade students to work at individualized activities and others to tasks that required cooperation. The task the students were given was a fairly typical English assignment, but one group of students studied and did the exercise as a group, with everyone contributing to the assignment. Many teachers would consider this approach to an assignment to be cheating, and thus morally wrong, and not likely to help children learn.

outcomes of
different goal
structures

Since this study involved only one classroom and only one academic subject, we must be cautious. Nevertheless, the results are in general agreement with other studies. The findings showed that students who worked on cooperative tasks scored higher on a measure of altruism than students who worked on individualized tasks. The students who had been involved in cooperative activities were also better in recognizing the feelings of others. They also felt that their teachers and peers liked them more than did students in the individualized condition, that their teachers cared more about them, and that their peers liked to help them more.

Students who had cooperated tended to be more intrinsically motivated while students in the individualized condition were more extrinsically motivated. The students who worked on individualized tasks wanted their teachers to set clear goals for them. They also wanted the teacher to keep the other students quiet. Most of the students who were involved in cooperation felt that they had come to like the students they were working with better than they had before.

Teachers and parents sometimes worry that children involved in cooperative group activities will not learn as much as those in individualized instruction. These fears seem to be unfounded. At the end of their study, Johnson and his associates found no differences in achievement between cooperators and the children who received individualized instruction. On the other hand, there seemed to be some academic bonuses from cooperation. Children who cooperated made fewer mistakes on daily assignments and used more complex sentences in their writing than the other children. There was also some indication that cooperators were less self-centered than the other children. Students whose instruction was individualized used the word "I" in their writing more than three times as often as the children in the cooperative group.

From these results it seems clear that cooperative instruction may have a positive influence on interpersonal behavior and attitudes toward learning without hampering the academic achievement of individuals. Researchers using different strategies have had similar results. One strategy has been to set up small groups in which each member learns a portion of the material to be mastered. Each student then teaches his portion of the material to the other members of the group. The process is something like putting a jigsaw puzzle together, because each person has only a portion of the entire puzzle, and the students need each other to put the entire "picture" together. Fifth and sixth grade Anglo, Mexican-American and black students involved in this kind of instruction have been compared with students taught with conventional methods (Lucker, Rosenfield, Sikes, & Aronson, 1976). Both groups studied the same social studies materials. At the end of the experiment, children who used the interdependent cooperative strategies had learned more than children in the traditional classes. The minority students in the interdependent classrooms had the most substantial gains in performance. The academic self-confidence of the minority students also improved (Blaney, Stephan, Rosenfield, Aronson, & Sikes, 1977).

Similar studies show that cooperative instruction is beneficial for the attitudes students hold toward school and toward themselves. With Mexican-American and Anglo junior high and high school students, cooperative learning has led to more students of different groups helping each other. The Anglo students also had more respect and affection for the Mexican-Americans after the experience (Weigel, Wisler, & Cook, 1975). And in classrooms where peer helping is encouraged and rewarded, interracial interaction has increased, and there have been positive effects on school attitudes, self-esteem of students, and social acceptance by peers (Damico & Watson, 1974).

interaction of social and academic outcomes

outcomes of interdependent education

INFLUENCING SOCIAL DEVELOPMENT

The forces that help to shape the development of children's social behaviors are very complex. For example, a parent's attempts to influence a child may have different outcomes, depending on whether the mother or father is interacting with the child and whether the child is a boy or a girl (Harrington, Block, & Block, 1978). Even so, there are a few general guidelines that parents may safely follow in their attempts to help their children to develop social behaviors.

1. Parents who have a warm, nurturant (but not smothering) relationship with their children have a better chance of influencing their children's behavior positively than harsh, cold, critical parents.
2. Provide verbal rules for the child to learn, and explain why the behaviors you want him to develop are important. If you consider cooperation a valuable social behavior, or if you want to promote altruism, explain why. For instance, point to examples of goals that can be accomplished cooperatively but that would be more difficult, or impossible, through individual or competitive effort.
3. Model the kind of behavior you want to promote. Model it in different forms and in different contexts. For example, to model altruism, sometimes you may donate money to a good cause, but other times the sacrifice may involve goods, and sometimes time and effort. The objects of your altruism should also vary. You can preach charity or cooperation all you want; but if preaching's all you do, the child will learn to say the words but not practice the behavior. When you model desired behaviors, take advantage of opportunities to explain your reasons to the child.
4. Give the child the chance to practice the desired behaviors.

Implications for Guiding Development   The evidence we have shows that our society stresses competition and largely overlooks the fact that many of the problems we face are so large that they can only be solved through cooperation. We also know that the school is one place where our current practices lead to competition. Many writers have suggested that cooperation could serve as a constructive alternative to the competition and individualism that now prevails in the schools (Bronfenbrenner, 1970a; Johnson & Johnson, 1974). Teachers who see the value of promoting cooperation should explore these instructional possibilities, and parents may want to see what their children's schools are doing to promote constructive social interaction. The relative advantages and disadvantages of different instructional approaches should be weighed carefully. Open education, for example, is often criticized for not stressing traditional academic skills enough. On the other hand, open education does generally place a high value on cooperation, and there is evidence that children in those programs are much more cooperative than children in traditional classes (Henderson & Hennig, 1978).

Adolescence

INFLUENCES OF PARENTS AND PEERS

We are probably not overstating the case to say that most American adults feel that they do not understand adolescents very well. The phrase "generation gap" has become a cliché, but it is still useful. It suggests the differences between the values of the adult generation and those held by youth. And it also suggests a lack of communication across the generations. Although the idea that there is a generation gap is centuries old, it is still of concern. Traditionally, the period of adolescence has been described by child psychologists as a time of storm and stress (Mohr & Despres, 1958). It is a time of rebellion against parents' standards and control, and a period of uncertainty about individual identity. For a long time, this period of turmoil was attributed to awakening sexual urges. Since these physiological changes are the same in all cultures, it was assumed that the storm and stress of adolescence must be universal. That assumption was disproved when anthropologist Margaret Mead wrote about her observations of Samoa (1928). She reported that, in Samoa, adolescence is not characterized by stormy adjustment problems. Her observations showed that adolescence may be quite a pleasant period, depending on the culture.

generation gap

storm and stress of adolescence

culture-specific phenomenon

Stereotypes of Adolescents Perhaps because it seems beyond our understanding, adolescence has been the focus of strong feelings during the past few years. Not so long ago adolescents were seen somewhat outside the sphere of adult activity. But more recently one emerging stereotype pictures them as *victimizers,* clothed in black leather jackets, being cruel to others, and acting without morals. A contrasting stereotype presents the adolescent as the victim of a corrupt and exploiting society (Adelson, 1968).

As a consequence of these widespread stereotypes, many parents look forward to their children's entry into adolescence with great apprehension. They expect that the child's peers, who may have values different from their own, will have more influence on their child than they will. This expectation is so strong that some parents are surprised if no conflicts materialize.

How accurate are these stereotypes of youth? How realistic is the expectation that the parents' influence that has been built up over more than 10 years can be washed out almost overnight?

Interaction of Parents and Peers Obviously adolescents are influenced by their friends. They adopt the figures of speech, the mannerisms, and the dress styles that are modeled by their peers. The norms of the peer group also influence some less obvious characteristics, including educational and occupational aspirations (Haller & Butterworth, 1960; Lesser & Kandel, 1970). For example, whether or not an adolescent plans to go to college depends on both family background and on the plans of his peer

Adolescents are likely to choose friends who share the values held by their own parents.

group (Bain & Anderson, 1975). While family and peer influences obviously interact, as we have already seen, there is more agreement between the expectations of parents and their adolescents than between these same adolescents and their peers (Lesser & Kandel, 1970).

These findings suggest that perhaps the size of the generation gap between parents and their adolescents has been overestimated. One reason may be that adolescents often choose their friends on the basis of the attitudes and values held by their own parents (Bandura & Walters, 1963). Adolescents are certainly influenced by their friends; but if these friends come from homes that have similar values, there would be some continuity between the influences of parents and friends.

Myths Regarding Adolescents   Albert Bandura (1964) has looked at some of the beliefs that lead parents to expect trouble with adolescents. One common assumption he identified is that conflict is caused by parents' attempts to restrict the activities of their adolescent children. Bandura and Walters (1963) found that this was not the case. By adolescence the boys they studied had internalized their parents' values and standards of behavior. They could take a great deal of responsibility for guiding their own behavior, and their parents trusted in their sons' judgments. Therefore the parents had no need to restrict the boys' activities.

We also tend to overreact to signs of nonconformity that are really quite superficial. Adolescence is often characterized by groups and causes that adolescents join, and by their inclination to follow fads. Bandura suggests that the only reason preadolescents do not do the same thing is that they do not have enough money. He also points out that adults engage in as much faddish behavior as adolescents. How else can you account for

internalized
standards

superficial signs
of nonconformity

the fact that clothing fashions change so rapidly? Commenting on this phenomenon, Bandura recalled a cocktail party at which a lady approached him and

> expressed considerable puzzlement over adolescents' fascination for unusual and bizarre styles. The lady herself was draped with a sack, wearing a preposterous object on her head, and spiked high heel shoes that are more likely to land her in an orthopedic clinic, than to transport one across the room to the olives. (1964, p. 26)

The lady Bandura described would look quite out of place if she showed up at a cocktail party today, but no doubt she would never dream of wearing that outdated outfit now. She would surely be draped in whatever everyone else is wearing to parties these days. People—adults and adolescents alike—imitate the fads and fashions of high-status people.

style-setting and status

There are several other reasons for the somewhat misleading stereotypes of adolescents. A very important source of distorted information is the mass media. The normal, responsible behavior of young people makes pretty unexciting reading, and everyday events would surely kill the ratings of the evening news or a television series. Television in particular is guilty of distorting reality. The unusual is presented as though it were typical. There is no doubt that exciting stereotypes we see in the mass media influence people's perceptions of reality. For example, people who watch a lot of television are more afraid of violence than people who watch less television. Heavy viewers overestimate the violence in society, apparently because it occupies so much broadcast time (Gerbner & Gross, 1976).

mass media and reality distortion

Style-setters must be constantly inventive to keep their superior status.

Durability of Early Parent-Child Relationships A parent's influence on an adolescent is not confined to the interactions that take place during adolescence. Early interactions influence later social adjustment (Becker, 1964). Research suggests that "the heritage of parent-child relationships that the young person carries into adolescence will affect the relative ease with which he adjusts to the changed roles and new demands of this period" (Conger, 1971). The child who has been overprotected may have trouble developing the independence and self-reliance she will need during adolescence outside the home. The child who was overindulged at home may have difficulty when he finds that the wider society is not willing to continue this indulgence (Conger, 1971).

Helping Responses of Peers and Parents There is evidence that adolescents feel a need to discuss problems with their parents. But often parents do not respond to these needs helpfully. One team of investigators (Burke & Weir, 1977) studied the helping responses provided by parents and peers. They were interested in seeing what might influence an adolescent's willingness to disclose his or her problems to peers or parents. They also wanted to know how peers and parents responded to these problems, and how the responses affected the adolescent. Some parents responded with ridicule and attempts at coercion. Others made concrete suggestions for dealing with the problems. Some parents attempted to get the adolescent to think about something else, and others were very detached and simply analyzed the problem.

response to disclosure of problems

The adolescents felt very dissatisfied with the "help" they got from their mothers and fathers when they used coercion and ridicule, detached analysis, or distraction. Their greatest satisfaction came from responses that consisted of concrete suggestions for dealing with the problem.

Adolescents are likely to share their problems with parents who listen sympathetically.

When they went to peers with their problems, their greatest satisfaction came from expressions of interest and concern. Interestingly enough, parents did not respond this way often enough to be included in the study results.

Concrete suggestions from both mothers and fathers were significantly and *positively* related to the adolescent's satisfaction with life, while there was a significant *negative* relationship between the adolescent's satisfaction and parents who responded with coercion and ridicule. Adolescents whose disclosure of problems was likely to be met by coercion and ridicule said that they did not feel free to discuss their problems with their parents, while those whose parents gave concrete suggestions did feel free to discuss these things.

parental response and life satisfaction

The message of these results is if parents want to be in a position to influence their children they should listen sympathetically and actively to their problems. They should not simply analyze the problem. Adolescents want to know that their parents are interested in them, not just in a cool look at their problems. And contrary to what many people believe, adolescents do seem to appreciate concrete, constructive advice, as long as the parent leaves the decision up to the adolescent. Adolescents do not feel comfortable in coming to a parent to discuss a problem if they expect the parent to impose a solution. If adolescents feel more free to go to friends with their problems, *as those studied by Burke and Weir did,* it may be more because of the unsympathetic and coercive reception they expect from their parents than because of anything they get from the peer group.

implications

FATHER ABSENCE AND SEX-ROLE DEVELOPMENT

The effects of different relationships within the family may not be readily apparent. Hetherington (1972) found that young fatherless girls do not differ from girls with fathers in their sex-typed behavior. But by adolescence they tend to differ in their sex-role development, and the daughters of widows respond differently to males than the daughters of divorcees. Fatherless girls were insecure around males, but their insecurity took different forms, depending upon whether their father was lost through death or divorce. Girls whose mothers were widows were rigid and inhibited in their interactions with a male interviewer, but not with a female interviewer. Often they turned their back slightly toward the man, folded their hands in their laps, and sat with their legs held together. In contrast, daughters of divorcees leaned toward the man, made more eye contact with him, and had more open postures. The heterosexual activity of the daughters of divorcees was far greater than that of widows' daughters, and all the differences between the groups were larger for girls who lost their fathers early than those whose loss had occurred later.

daughters of widows and divorcees

Both groups of girls had failed to develop socially appropriate skills for interacting with men, but their efforts to make up for their insecurity and lack of skill took different forms. The differences may be because widows often communicate an idealized image of the father to their daughters, while divorcees are generally quite critical of their former spouses. The

Daughters of widows may feel uncomfortable in the presence of males.

daughters of divorcees saw their mother's life as unsatisfying, and may have felt that marriage is essential to happiness. The widow's daughters, on the other hand, had an unrealistic image of their father, and may have felt that no one else could compare favorably with him.

Another team of researchers (Hainline & Feig, 1978) tried to see if these findings would hold true for older girls. They used some of the same measures with women college students that Hetherington had. They did not find the same differences. There are a number of possible reasons for the differences in the results. For one thing, the older women may have had more chances than Hetherington's adolescents to interact with males in social situations. If there ever had been differences, experience may have eliminated them. And secondly, the college women probably differed from Hetherington's sample in terms of socioeconomic status, educational status and other background characteristics.

Father Absence and Delinquency Psychoanalytic assumptions about the identification process predict that boys who grow up without fathers have trouble developing a conscience. Some studies support this prediction. For example, Hoffman (1971) found that boys without a father showed less guilt, less internal moral judgment, less acceptance of blame, lower moral values, and less conformity to rules than boys with a father. These differences may be due to the lack of a significant male model, but there are other possible explanations. Perhaps the most obvious possibility is that a mother rearing a boy alone may use different control procedures than she would if a father were there to help. If she is frustrated, she may show less affection and use power assertion more often, instead of taking the time to explain and reason with her children. This pattern of discipline is associated with weak moral standards (Hoffman, 1970).

The idea of identification has also been used to explain the fact that there is more juvenile delinquency among children without fathers than in families where a father is present. This reasoning overlooks the obvious pressures and financial hardships that differentiate these two kinds of families. For many reasons, the loss of a father is an economic burden for

development of conscience

economic circumstances and supervision

a family. And when a mother in responsible for earning a living for the family as well as running the household, she is likely to provide less adequate supervision (Herzog & Sudia, 1973). After all, there is only a given amount of time in any day. Poor supervision and economic circumstances seem likely to be responsible for delinquency in fatherless families.

THE SEPARATE WORLDS OF SCHOOL AND WORK

Social Isolation of Youth   The United States today is an age-graded society. Young people are likely to have a close relationship with fewer adults than did adolescents of 20 years back. In part, this is a result of the death of the extended family. Child labor laws and the disappearance of the apprentice system have further separated adolescents from adults. Specialized social activities widen the gap, and consolidated schools cap off the process. These and other social changes have reduced the opportunities for meaningful interaction between adolescents and people who are either older or younger than they are (White House Conference on Children, 1971).

Adolescents have very few chances to see the productive activities of working adults. School is supposed to give them the skills they will need to eventually take their place in this world, but the relationship is often so abstract that many students cannot see the importance of their school work. In fact, the true social function of schools has changed dramatically, although the stated purpose has not. There was a time when children stayed in school just long enough to learn the literacy and special skills they needed to enter the world of work. Today another important but unstated job of the schools is to keep a lot of people out of a labor market

school influences

In today's world there are few chances for adolescents to work alongside adults.

that is not equipped to absorb them (Pearl, 1977). Under these circumstances, school is likely to become very irrelevant.

Many social critics and psychologists argue that we should try to bring the schools and the outside world closer together. Some attempts have been made to give students some experience in a variety of different occupations; but as interesting as these have been, they have generally been abandoned after a short time (Goslin, 1975). To make academic programs prepare students for our economic and political system would require a substantial change in our priorities—a chance we have not been willing to face.

The result is hardly fair. Parents with friends and influence often help their children find a variety of jobs during summers and holidays. These options are not open to children from poor families without economic or political influence. And as long as the bulk of the adolescents do not have any experience with the "real world" of the community, we cannot expect them to understand the problems and concerns faced by adults. In contrast, some nations, such as China (Kessen, 1975) have taken steps to see that children are involved in a variety of productive activities from an early age. Their intent is not just to increase production. They are intended to help people understand and appreciate their contributions to society. In a democratic society, these measures cannot be implemented by law as they are in an authoritarian state. But the current separation between the worlds of school and work poses a problem we should try to deal with.

Suggested Readings

Bryan, J. H. Children's reaction to helpers: Their money isn't where their mouths are. *Journal of Social Issues,* 1972, *28,* 61–73.

Hartup, W. W. Anger in children: Developmental perspectives. *American Psychologist,* 1974, *29,* 336–341.

Hetherington, E. M., Cox, M., & Cox, R. Beyond father absence: Conceptualization of effects of divorce. In E. M. Hetherington & R. D. Parke (Eds.), *Contemporary readings in child psychology.* New York: McGraw-Hill, 1977. Pp. 308–314.

Liebert, R. M., Davidson, E. S., & Neale, J. M. Aggression in childhood: The impact of television. In V. B. Cline (Ed.), *Where do you draw the line?* Provo, Utah: Brigham Young University Press, 1974.

Madsen, M. C. Developmental and cross-cultural cooperative and competitive behavior of young children. *Journal of Cross-Cultural Psychology,* 1971, *2,* 365–371.

McClelland, D. C., Constantian, C. A., & Stone, C. Making it to maturity. *Psychology Today,* June 1978, *12,* 42–53, 114.

Yarrow, M. R., & Waxler, C. Z. The emergence and functions of prosocial behavior in young children. In E. M. Hetherington & R. D. Parke (Eds.), *Contemporary readings in child psychology.* New York: McGraw-Hill, 1977. Pp. 260–263.

14

A Look Ahead

This final chapter takes a look at the science of child development in America today, and how it fits into our society. Most child development books seem to be content to present the scientific "facts," allowing their readers to believe that they have learned some absolute truths. But, as we have seen throughout this book, science—including the science of child development—is intimately related to social values. To act as though science operates in isolation from social reality is self-deceptive and dangerous. Science influences society, whether it intends to or not. And, in turn, science is influenced by the culture in which it is carried out.

In fact, social values even affect the topics that scientists select to study. In the 1960s, for example, there was rising social interest in civil rights and the social and educational inequalities that segregation had caused. This trend sparked many research studies on the design of educational programs to compensate for past inequities and on the influences of a child's early experiences on his or her later development. In the 1970s, growing public concern led to many studies of the causes of child abuse in parents and of programs to deal with it (Nagi, 1975). We could give many other examples; but it is clear that, just as a child's heredity and his environment interact throughout his lifetime, so too do the science of child development and the social values of the society in which research is carried out interact.

Thus, we feel it is necessary to look at our society and some of our common values—social, economic, political, and even scientific—and how they affect the American family and our views on how children grow and how they should be cared for. Pearl (1977) has argued that many of the problems that plague America today are the results of our society's refusal to examine itself. It is for this reason, too, that we are looking at values in this chapter. We feel that today's students of child development cannot be content to merely stop with a grasp of the basic processes and facts of how children develop. Anyone who works with children wants to provide better developmental environments for all our children, and it is up to them—and it will be up to you—to be aware of the differences between our ideals and the reality, between the ways we think children should be nurtured and the ways they actually grow up, and the reasons for some of these differences. Once you are aware of the discrepancies, you are in a position to influence other people to examine the facts and the results of inaction. If our children are our greatest resource, then we should be aware of the long-range economic consequences of our failure to meet their developmental needs. If there is to be any improvement in the quality of life for our children, it will come from the grass roots level— from the people who actually spend their days with kids—from you.

Child Care and the Changing Family

American society is changing rapidly. Changes that were set in motion by the industrial revolution have led to new modes of economic production, new patterns of population, and changes in the structure and function of the family (Toffler, 1970). More and more people live and work on a shrinking portion of the land. City life offers stimulation, excitement, and economic opportunities that people find attractive. But urban life and its attractions also have set the stage for an erosion in the quality of life for our children.

SOCIAL CHANGE AND THE QUALITY OF LIFE FOR CHILDREN

During recent years, the science of child psychology has produced more and more information about the conditions that are likely to help children and adolescents develop. At the same time, it has become clear that some parts of contemporary American life may be harmful to the development of our children. The traditional forms of family life evolved very slowly. Though they stood the test of time, they have not yet adapted to the rapid social changes that we face today.

With urbanization, many families have lost the support of the extended family and networks of close friends. The family is no longer the independent economic unit it once was. Now people must leave the home to find work to help support their families. Conditions are often crowded. Poverty is widespread, and increasingly few families can survive on the income of only one person. Furthermore, more and more mothers are finding work outside the home personally satisfying, even when they do not "have to work."

Because of these and other related social changes, we need to look at the conditions that contribute to the quality of life for children. We must fill a void left by these changes in the family and traditional child care arrangements.

DEFICIENCIES IN CHILD CARE ARRANGEMENTS

Many children today are poorly cared for. Undoubtedly this has always been true, but the problem has been aggravated by the changes in the family that we have been discussing. Some young children are placed in overcrowded, informal day care centers where their caretakers are not trained to work with them. Often even minimum health and safety standards are not met. Other preschool children are cared for by older brothers and sisters who can scarcely take care of themselves. It is not unusual for elementary school children to be kept out of school to babysit for younger brothers and sisters because their families cannot afford anything else.

Compared with many other industrialized nations, the child care arrangements our government provides are grossly inadequate. We could correct the situation, but we don't—because of the prevailing values in this country. Some people feel that providing day care would have a bad effect on the American family, by eliminating one of the reasons families have for sticking together. They overlook the fact that the family has already changed drastically. Many families cannot provide the close personal care for their children that is part of the traditional, romantic image of the American family.

Our economic values also help keep us from providing adequate child care for families who need it. Like apple pie and motherhood, the need for good developmental environments for children of every age is something no one would argue against. But to support national programs and to spend the needed money would take a national commitment. It would mean either taking funds and other resources away from other programs or increasing taxes, and so far we do not seem to think child care is important enough for us to do that.

CHILD CARE IN A PLURALISTIC SOCIETY

It is quite clear that there is an overall need to improve the quality of child care. But beyond these general problems, some authorities (Laosa, 1974) believe that the cultural and linguistic diversity of the American population poses other problems. We tend to make general statements about how children grow and develop. These generalizations may be misleading if they are applied to children from diverse cultural backgrounds. Anyone who wants to work with children must be careful in making judgments based on general statements. For example, there are more educational, economic, and mental health problems among members of ethnic minorities than chance would predict. To some degree, these problems seem to result from the gaps between the culture of the home and of the traditional institutions that provide child care, education, and social services. One psychologist (Laosa, 1974), commenting on this issue, has said that "Neglect on the part of child care personnel to accept, legitimize, and capitalize on the diversity of culture and language characteristics of children may produce alienation, which in turn is manifested in rejection, mistrust, and chronic failure" (p. 214).

Sometimes this neglect is intentional, based on the old idea that minority children should melt into the dominant culture. But there is growing awareness that diversity has value (Galinsky & Hooks, 1977), and the neglect that Laosa mentions is often unintentional. It flows from the fact that few of the people who work with children have the training they need to guide children from varied cultural and linguistic backgrounds.

One way of correcting this problem would be to attract people from varied backgrounds into the helping professions and train them to work with children. By bringing their own cultures into the day-care centers, they would help the children feel more comfortable. If we value diversity, we *must* include a more representative sample of cultural backgrounds among the people who become child care, educational, social service, and mental health professionals.

POLITICAL AND SOCIAL INFLUENCES

Some of the policies that influence families and the environments they provide for their children are structured by political action. Politics, in turn, is affected by social attitudes.

One social attitude that has influenced child care has been called "the myth of independence," the idea that families can and should rear their children without outside help (Galinsky & Hooks, 1977). In the past, this belief was probably reasonable. With the help of members of the extended family, parents could take care of their children without outside agencies. But while the extended family has changed dramatically, this old belief has not been substantially altered. As Galinsky puts it, "Even without this traditional backup system, parents are still supposed to do everything for themselves. They are the sole guardians, the protectors, the providers for their children. To step outside the family for help becomes an admission of failure" (p. 2). Both city apartments and suburban housing developments show us that this independence has "gone askew" (Galinsky, 1977). The support the extended family used to give has vanished, and we have nothing to take its place.

Another striking difference between the ideal version of the American family and reality is the fact that about half the mothers of school-aged children work outside the home. (The percentages vary according to location.) Galinsky and Hooks (1977) tell of a psychologist in New York City who had to abandon his plans to compare infants and toddlers reared by their mothers with those cared for by other people at least part of the time. The psychologist could not find enough children who had been cared for only by their mothers.

Fortunately, there are some outstanding child care arrangements that take our real world into consideration. They have promise for meeting the needs created by changing social circumstances. Galinsky and Hooks were able to find and study a few very good child care arrangements.

They found that these excellent programs differed from each other, depending upon the children and the communities they served. The most significant finding was that the good programs considered the characteristics and values of their local communities. They paid attention to the unique culture and language of their population. It only seems reasonable that there is no single best program for all children. The dilemma is that the programs must be closely tied to local goals, but to provide the number of programs on the massive basis on which we need them would require national political action. Our national policies must therefore be flexible enough to allow local communities to shape their own programs.

Using Science to Our Advantage

The changes we have been talking about place stringent demands on all of us. We find ourselves facing new social conditions, new responsibilities. The future is uncertain; rapid scientific and technological advances demand that we be constantly on our toes, ready to absorb new information. All this change produces stress; it creates a challenge for those who wish to help children make as easy a transition to identity and independence as possible. In this section, we'll look at some of the ways we can *use* developmental science to help us with our children.

RETROSPECT AND PROSPECT

In traditional society, child-rearing practices are handed down from generation to generation, largely through modeling (Bandura, 1977). For example, little girls watch their mothers nursing their babies. Later they may play "house" with friends or their brothers and sisters. Eventually they use the same feeding practices with their infants that they saw their mothers using years before.

The advent of developmental science marked a new force in the socialization process. Now evidence based on scientific studies could be offered as an alternative to traditional, ineffective practices. For example, in the early part of this century, G. Stanley Hall and his colleagues found evidence that growth patterns are, at least in part, controlled by genetics. This information helped foster a welcome movement away from the nineteenth century practices of punishing children to correct their "inherently flawed nature" (Henderson & Bergan, 1976).

Today we are establishing a scientific knowledge base that may one day support a "technology" of socialization, a systematic approach to the raising of children. Many, many scholars are entering the field and doing thousands of research studies on how children grow and develop. It seems certain that our knowledge about children will continue to grow. But although we are accumulating an almost unbelievable amount of information—well over 100,000 research studies relevant to the education of children are published in a single year (Nelson, 1974)—we have not yet come up with an effective network to communicate this information to the adults who are actually in touch with the children. In the past, we have relied upon formal college and university programs to teach adult care-givers about development and socialization. While these programs are and will continue to be important, we must find other, additional approaches if we are to see widespread change. We must find ways to reach all the parents, child care workers, paraprofessionals. Fortunately, there are some new channels of communication developing. Let's look at three of them.

DIRECT INTERVENTION

One way to use developmental science is to directly influence children's behavior through, for example, television. *Sesame Street* is a good illustration. Using pyschologists as consultants, programmers have been able to incorporate scientific knowledge into televised instructional sequences to help preschoolers learn to read (Liebert & Schwartzberg, 1977). Television is also a potentially powerful tool for affecting the ways adults socialize children. Because it is so effective, it seems likely that television will be used more and more to convey scientific innovations to the general public (Bandura, 1977), while being entertaining at the same time.

PRODUCT DEVELOPMENT

Developing educational toys, books, records, films, and curriculum materials that are based on scientific data is another way to get scientific information into the hands of the people. Many educational researchers feel strongly that the products children use should be proven effective first (Short, 1973), and more and more this is being done. This approach does have disadvantages: it is expensive, for instance, to test an arithmetic curriculum for grades K through 6, and it is time consuming. It often takes several years to construct an empirically validated product (Sashkin, Morris, & Horst, 1973). But despite these disadvantages, this approach does hold promise and will probably increase in the future.

CONSULTANTS

Consultants who have special expertise in the areas of development and socialization can work directly with other adults (Bergan, 1977). Consultants are a "knowledge-link" (Short, 1973); they can apply scientific principles to specific child-rearing goals. For instance, a father may employ a consultant to help accelerate his 2-year-old son's language development. The consultant uses available psychological knowledge to formulate a specific plan to increase the boy's vocabulary growth.

At present there are not enough psychological consultants to meet our needs. For example, in the area of children's mental health, the Joint Commission on the Mental Health of Children (1970) estimated that 1,500,000 children under the age of 18 needed immediate professional help. Less than 30% were getting the help they needed. Fortunately, the number of psychology professionals has rapidly expanded in recent years (McKeachie, 1976), and many of these new professionals are becoming consultants. We can expect that the psychological consultant will become a more frequent part of the child-raising "team."

A Final Word

Science is, as we have seen, a source of social change. It provides an objective basis for challenging tradition. For example, as we saw in chapter 2, environmentalists have successfully challenged the idea that intelligence is genetically predetermined by conducting research that demonstrates the influence of home and up-bringing on intelligence-test performance. Science also provides the information needed to develop new products that affect the ways we think about things. For instance, research conducted around the turn of the century provided the basis for the elaborate testing technology we use today to assess children's intellectual capabilities. In fact, more than 250,000,000 standardized ability and achievement tests are given each year (Laosa, 1977).

But although science helps promote social change, it can also retard it—especially in the face of the rapid cultural change we see today. At times, science does not move quickly enough to fill new needs. For instance, the same testing technology we use today was developed at a time when the "melting pot" theory was popular. Thus our intelligence tests are based on the idea that test items should reflect the dominant culture. But as we take a more pluralistic view, traditional testing practices are coming under increasingly heavy attack (Oakland & Laosa, 1977). For example, in one of many recent legal actions, the California State Board of Education was sued for improperly placing nine Mexican American children from predominantly Spanish-speaking homes in classes for the mentally retarded. The suit resulted in several changes in educational practices, including a requirement that children whose first language is not English be tested in both their primary language and in English to determine intellectual ability.

Science also lags behind social change because of the costs involved in changing an elaborate technology (Bandura, 1977). Let's look at testing again. The testing industry brings in millions of dollars each year. To change intelligence testing to be "culture-free," "nonbiased," would be both costly and risky. And furthermore, it takes time—sometimes years— to carry out scientific studies and evaluate them. After the findings are in, comes a long period of debate and more experiments. But this period of testing and retesting, of debate and hesitation, is essential if we are to avoid taking misguided actions based on weak or erroneous results.

Thus science necessarily will be both a leader and a follower in social change. Today, because of the changes we see all around us—particularly the changes in the family that so critically affect our children—we need to make science more responsive to our changing society. As a person who works with children, you can be a part of all this. By keeping informed, by looking at new research and putting it in the context of everything else that is happening around you, by informing others and promoting the new ideas that are bound to develop in the next ten, or even two years, you can help the children you touch. Even better, you can learn to anticipate social needs—to help the science of child development become even more effective.

References

Adelson, J. *The myths of adolescence: A polemic.* Paper presented at the annual meeting of the American Psychological Association, San Francisco, 1968.

Ainsworth, M.D.S. *Infancy in Uganda: Infant care and the growth of attachment.* Baltimore: Johns Hopkins Press, 1967.

Ainsworth, M.D.S. The development of infant-mother attachment. In B.M. Caldwell & H.N. Ricciuti (Eds.), *Review of child development research* (Vol. 3). Chicago: University of Chicago Press, 1973. Pp. 1–94.

Allen, K.E., Hart, B.M., Buell, J.S., Harris, F.R., & Wolf, M.M. Effects of social reinforcement on isolated behavior of a nursery school child. *Child Development,* 1964, *35,* 511–518.

Allison, A.C. *Aspects of polymorphism in man.* Cold Spring Harbor Symposium. *Quantitative Biology,* 1955, *20,* 239–255.

Alpert, J.L. Teacher behavior across ability groups: A consideration of the mediation of Pygmalion effects. *Journal of Educational Psychology,* 1974, *66,* 348–353.

Ames, L.B. The sense of self of nursery school children as manifested by their verbal behavior. *Genetic Psychology,* 1952, *81,* 193–232.

Appleton, T., Clifton, R., & Goldberg, S. The development of behavioral competence in infancy. In F.D. Horowitz (Ed.), *Review of research in child development* (Vol. 4). Chicago: University of Chicago Press, 1975.

Aragona, J., Cassady, J., & Drabman, R.S. Training overweight children through parental training and contingency contracting. *Journal of Applied Behavior Analysis,* 1975, *8,* 269–278.

Aronfreed, J. The nature, variety and social patterning of moral responses to transgression. *Journal of Abnormal and Social Psychology,* 1961, *63,* 223–240.

Ausubel, D.P., & Sullivan, E.V. *Theory and problems of child development* (2nd ed.). New York: Grune & Stratton, 1970.

Ayllon, T., Layman, D., & Kandel, H.J. A behavioral-educational alternative to drug control of hyperactive children. *Journal of Applied Behavior Analysis,* 1975, *8,* 137–146.

Azrin, N.H., & Holz, W.C. Punishment. In W.K. Honig (Ed.), *Operant behavior: Areas of research and applications.* New York: Appleton-Century-Crofts, 1966.

Baer, D.M., Peterson, R.F., & Sherman, J.A. The development of imitation by reinforcing behavioral similarity to a model. *Journal of the Experimental Analysis of Behavior,* 1968, *10,* 405–416.

Bain, R.K., & Anderson, J.G. School context and peer influences on educational plans of adolescence. *Review of Educational Research,* 1975, *44,* 429–445.

Baker, S.L., Fagan, S.A., Fischer, E.G., Janda, E.J., & Cove, L.A. *Impact of father-absence on personality factors of boys: I. An evaluation of the military family's adjustment.* Paper presented at American Orthopsychiatric Association meeting, Washington, D.C., March, 1967.

Ball, S., & Bogatz, G.A. *The first year of Sesame Street: An evaluation.* New York: Teachers College Press, 1970.

Bandura, A. The stormy decade: Fact or fiction? *Psychology in the Schools,* 1964, *1,* 224–231.

Bandura, A. *Principles of behavior modification.* New York: Holt, Rinehart & Winston, 1969.

Bandura, A. *Social learning theory.* Morristown, N.J.: General Learning Corporation, 1971.

Bandura, A. Behavior theory and the models of man. *American Psychologist* 1974, *29,* 859–869.

Bandura, A. *Social learning theory.* Englewood Cliffs, N.J.: Prentice-Hall, 1977.

Bandura, A., & Kupers, C. Transmission of patterns of self-reinforcement through modeling. *Journal of Abnormal and Social Psychology,* 1964, *69,* 1–9.

Bandura, A., & Menlove, F.L. Factors determining vicarious extinction of avoidance behavior through symbolic modeling. *Journal of Personality and Social Psychology,* 1968, *8,* 99–108.

Bandura, A., & Mischel, W. Modification of self-imposed delay of reward through exposure to live and symbolic models. *Journal of Personality and Social Psychology,* 1965, *2,* 698–705.

Bandura, A., & Walters, R.H. *Social learning and personality development.* New York: Holt, Rinehart & Winston, 1963.

Baratz, J. C. Teaching reading in an urban Negro school. In J. C. Baratz & R. W. Shuy (Eds.), *Teaching black children to read.* Washington, D.C. Center for Applied Linguistics, 1969.

Baratz, J.C. Language abilities of black Americans, review of research. In Miller, K., & Dreger, R. (Eds.), *Comparative studies of blacks and whites in the United States.* New York: Seminar Press, 1973.

Barber, T., & Silver, M.J. Fact, fiction, and the experimenter bias effect. *Psychological Bulletin,* 1968, *70,* 6, Pt. 2.

Bardon, J.I., & Bennett, V.C. *School psychology.* Englewood Cliffs, N.J.: Prentice-Hall, 1974.

Barker, R.G. (Ed.) *The stream of behavior: Explorations of its structure and content.* New York: Appleton-Century-Crofts, 1963.

Barnes, K.E. Preschool play norms: A replication. *Developmental Psychology,* 1971, *5,* 99–103.

Baron, J., Lawson, G., & Siegel, L.S. Effects of training and set size on children's judgments of number and length. *Developmental Psychology,* 1975, *11,* 583–588.

Barratt, B.B. Training and transfer in combinatorial problem solving: The development of formal reasoning during early adolescence. *Developmental Psychology,* 1975, *11,* 700–704

Bartel, N.R., & Axelrod, J. Nonstandard English usage and reading ability in black junior high students. *Exceptional Children,* 1973, *39,* 653–655.

Baum, J. Nutritional value of human milk. *Obstetrics and Gynecology,* 1971, *37,* 126–130.

Baumrind, D. Effects of authoritative parental control on child behavior. *Child Development,* 1966, *37,* 887–908.

Baumrind, D. Current patterns of parental authority. *Developmental Pshchology,* 1971, *4,* 1–103.

Baumrind, D. The development of instrumental competence through socialization. In A. Pick (Ed.), *Minnesota Symposium on Child Psychology* (Vol. 7). Minneapolis: University of Minnesota Press, 1973. Pp. 3–46.

Baumrind, D., & Black, A.E. Socialization practices associated with dimensions of competence in preschool boys and girls. *Child Development,* 1967, *38,* 291–321.

Bayley, N. Consistency and variability in the growth from birth to 18 years. *Journal of Genetic Psychology,* 1949, *45,* 1–21.

Bayley, N. Comparisons of mental and motor tests scores for ages 1–15 months by sex, birth order, race, geographical location, and education of parents. *Child Development,* 1965, *36,* 379–411.

Bayley, N. *Bayley scales of infant development: Birth to two years.* New York: Psychological Corporation, 1969.

Becker, W.C. Consequences of different kinds of parental discipline. In M.L. Hoffman & L.W. Hoffman (Eds.), *Review of child development research* (Vol. 1). New York : Russell Sage, 1964.

Beez, W. Influence of biased psychological reports on teacher behavior and pupil performance. *Proceedings of the 76th Annual Convention of the American Psychological Association,* 1968, *3,* 605–606.

Belcher, T.L. Modeling original divergent responses: An initial investigation. *Journal of Educational Psychology,* 1975, *67,* 351–358.

Bell, C.S. Let's get rid of families! *Newsweek,* May 9, 1977, 19.

Bell. R.Q. A reinterpretation of the direction of effects in studies of socialization. *Psychological Review,* 1968, *75,* 81–95.

Bell, S.M., & Ainsworth, M.D.S. Infant crying and maternal responsiveness. *Child Development,* 1972, *43,* 1171–1190.

Beller, E.K. Research on organized programs of early education. In R.M.W. Travers (Ed.), *Second handbook of research on teaching.* Chicago: Rand McNally, 1973.

Bereiter, C., & Engelmann, S. *Teaching disadvantaged children in preschool.* Engelwood Cliffs, N.J.: Prentice-Hall, 1966.

Bergan, J.R. *Behavioral consultation.* Columbus, Ohio: Charles E. Merrill, 1977.

Bergan, J.R., & Parra, E.B. *Variations in IQ testing and instruction and the letter-learning and achievement of Anglo and bilingual Mexican-American children.* Paper presented at the meeting of the American Psychological Association, Toronto, Ontario, Canada, September, 1978.

Bergan, J.R., & Tombari, M.L. Verbal interactions in consultation. *Journal of School Psychology,* 1975, *13,* 209–226.

Bergan, J.R., Zimmerman, B.J., & Ferg, M. Effects of variations in content and stimulus grouping on visual sequential memory. *Journal of Educational Psychology*, 1971, *62*, 400–404.

Berkowitz, L. Control of aggression. In B.M. Caldwell & H.N. Ricciuti (Eds.), *Review of child development research* (Vol. 3). Chicago: University of Chicago Press, 1973. Pp. 95–140.

Bernal, E.M., Jr. A response to "Educational uses of tests with disadvantaged subjects." *American Psychologist*, 1975, *30*, 93–95.

Bernstein, B. *Language, primary socialization and education.* London: Routledge and Kegan Paul, 1968.

Bernstein, B. A socio-linguistic approach to socialization with some references to educability. In J.J. Gumperz & D. Hymes (Eds.), *Directions in sociolinguistics.* New York: Holt, Rinehart & Winston, 1972.

Berzonsky, M.D. Component abilities of children's causal reasoning. *Developmental Psychology*, 1975, *11*, 111.

Bijou, S.W. Development in the preschool years: A functional analysis. *American Psychologist*, 1975, *30*, 829–837.

Bijou, S.W., & Baer, D.M. *Child development I: A systematic and empirical theory.* New York: Appleton-Century-Crofts, 1961.

Bijou, S.W., & Baer, D.M. *Child development II: Universal stage of infancy.* Englewood Cliffs, N.J.: Prentice-Hall, 1965.

Bissell, J.S. *The cognitive effects of preschool programs for disadvantaged children.* Washington, D.C.: National Institute of Child Health and Human Development, 1970.

Blanchard, R.W., & Biller, H.B. Father availability and academic performance among third grade boys. *Developmental Psychology*, 1971, *4*, 301–305.

Blaney, N.T., Stephan, C., Rosenfield, D., Aronson, E., & Sikes, J. Interdependence in the classroom: A field study. *Journal of Educational Psychology*, 1977, *69*, 121–128.

Blank, M., & Solomon, F. A tutorial language program to develop abstract thinking in socially disadvantaged preschool children. *Child Development*, 1968, *39*, 379–389.

Block, J., Block, J.H., & Harrington, D.M. Some misgivings about the Matching Familiar Figures Test as a measure of reflection-impulsivity. *Developmental Psychology*, 1974, *10*, 611–632.

Block, J., Block, J.H., & Harrington, D.M. Comment on the Kagan-Messer reply. *Developmental Psychology*, 1975, *11*, 249–252.

Bloom, B.S. *Stability and change in human characteristics.* New York: Wiley, 1964.

Bloom, L. Language development review. In F.D. Horowitz (Ed.), *Review of child development research* (Vol. 4). Chicago: University of Chicago Press, 1975.

Bogatz, G.A., & Ball, S. *The second year of Sesame Street: A continuing evaluation.* Princeton, N.J.: Educational Testing Service, 1971.

Bogdan, R., & Taylor, S. The judged, not the judges: An insider's view of mental retardation. *American Psychologist*, 1976, *31*, 47–52.

Borke, H. Interpersonal perception of young children. *Developmental Psychology*, 1971, *5*, 263–269.

Borke, H. Chandler and Greenspan's Ersatz egocentrism: A rejoinder. *Developmental Psychology*, 1972, *7*, 107–109.

Borke, H. Piaget's mountains revisited: Changes in the egocentric landscape. *Developmental Psychology*, 1975, *11*, 240–243.

Born dumb? *Newsweek*, 1969, *73* (13), 84.

Bower, T.G.R. The development of object-permanence: Some studies of existence constancy. *Perception and Psychophysics*, 1967, *2*, 411–418.

Bower, T.G.R. The object in the world of the infant. *Scientific American*, 1971, *225*, 30–47.

Bower, T.G.R., Broughton, J.M., & Moore, M.K. The coordination of visual and tactual input in infants. *Perception and Psychophysics*, 1970, *8*, 51–53.

Bowlby, J. *Attachment*. New York: Basic Books, 1969.

Bowlby, J. *Attachment and loss*. Vol 2: *Separation: Anxiety and anger*. New York: Basic Books, 1973.

Bowman, M.J. Learning and earning in the post-school years. In F.N. Kerlinger & J.B. Carroll (Eds.), *Review of research in education* (Vol. 2). Itasca, Ill.: Peacock, 1974.

Boyd, W.C. *Genetics and the races of man*. Boston: Heath, 1950.

Bradley, R.H., & Caldwell, B.M. Early home environment and changes in mental test performance in children from 6 to 36 months. *Developmental Psychology*, 1976, *12*, 93–97.

Brainerd, C.J. Judgments and explanations as criteria for the presence of cognitive structures. *Psychological Bulletin*, 1973, *79*, 172–179.

Brainerd, C.J. Does prior knowledge of the compensation rule increase susceptibility to conservation training? *Developmental Psychology*, 1976, *12*, 1–5.

Brazelton, T.B. Effects of prenatal drugs on the behavior of the neonate. *American Journal of Psychiatry*, 1970, *126*, 95–100.

Bridgeman, B., & Shipman, V.C. Predictive value of measures of self-esteem and achievement motivation in four- to nine-year-old low-income children. Princeton, N.J.: Educational Testing Service, 1975.

Brody, G., & Henderson, R.W. Effects of multiple model variations and rationale provision on the moral judgments and explanations of young children. *Child Development*, 1977, *48*, 1117–1120.

Bronfenbrenner, U. Freudian theories of identification and their derivatives. *Child Development*, 1960, *31*, 15–40.

Bronfenbrenner, U. Reaction to social pressure from adults versus peers among Soviet day school and boarding school pupils in the perspective of an American sample. *Journal of Personality and Social Psychology*, 1970, *15*, 179–189. (a)

Bronfenbrenner, U. *Two worlds of childhood: U.S. and U.S.S.R.* New York: Russell Sage, 1970. (b)

Brown, B. *The assessment of self-concept among four-year-old Negro and white children: A comparative study using the Brown IDS Self-Concept Referents test*. Paper presented at the Eastern Psychological Association Meeting, New York City, April 1966.

Brown, R. *A first language: The early stages*. Cambridge: Harvard University Press, 1973.

Brown, R., & Fraser, C. The acquisition of syntax. In C.N. Cofer & B. Musgrave (Eds.), *Verbal behavior and learning: Problems and processes*. New York: McGraw-Hill, 1963.

Bruner, J.S. *The process of education*. New York: Vintage, 1960.

Bruner, J.S. The growth and structure of skill. In K. Connolly (Ed.), *Mechanisms of motor skill development*. New York: Academic Press, 1970.

Bruner, J.S., Olver, R.R., & Greenfield, P.M., et al. *Studies in cognitive growth.* New York: Wiley, 1966.

Bryan, J.H. Children's reaction to helpers: Their money isn't where their mouths are. In J. Macaulay & L. Berkowitz (Eds.), *Altruism and helping behavior.* New York: Academic Press, 1970. Pp. 61–73.

Bryan, J.H., & London, P. Altruistic behavior by children. *Psychological Bulletin,* 1970, *73,* 200–211.

Burke, R.J., & Weir, T. *Helping responses of parents and peers and adolescent well-being.* Paper presented at the annual meeting of the Western Psychological Association, Seattle, April 1977.

Burt, C. The inheritance of mental ability. *American Psychologist,* 1958, *13,* 1–15.

Buss, A.R. The emerging field of the sociology of psychological knowledge. *American Psychologist,* 1975, *30,* 988–1002.(a)

Buss, A.R. Regression, heritability, and race differences in IQ. *Developmental Psychology,* 1975, *11,* 105.(b)

Caldwell, B.M. Can young children have a quality life in day care? *Young Children,* 1973, *28,* 197–208.

Cardenas, R., & Fillmore, L.W. Toward a multicultural society: Cultural pluralism in the schools. *Today's Education,* 1973, *62,* 83–88.

Casler, L. The effects of extra tactile stimulation on a group of institutionalized infants. *Genetic Psychology Monographs,* 1965, *71,* 137–175.

Cazden, C. Subcultural differences in child language: An inter-disciplinary review. *Merrill-Palmer Quarterly,* 1966, *12,* 185–219.

Chandler, M.H., & Greenspan, S. Ersatz egocentrism: A reply to H. Borke. *Developmental Psychology,* 1972, *7,* 104–106.

Charbonneau, C., Robert, M., Bourassa, G., Gladu-Bissonnette, S. Observational learning of quantity conservation and Piagetian generalization tasks. *Developmental Psychology,* 1976, *12,* 211–217.

Chomsky, C. Language development after six. In C.S. Lavatelli & F. Stendler (Eds.), *Readings in child behavior and development* (3rd ed.). New York: Harcourt Brace, 1972.

Chomsky, N. *Syntactic structures.* The Hague: Mouton, 1957.

Chomsky, N. A review of Verbal Behavior by B.F. Skinner. *Language,* 1959, *35,* 26–58.

Chomsky, N. *Cartesian linguistics: A chapter in the history of rationalist thought.* New York: Harper & Row, 1966.

Chomsky, N. Language and mind: Enlarged edition. New York: Harcourt Brace Jovanovich, 1968.

Claiborne, W.L. Expectancy effects in the classroom: A failure to replicate. *Journal of Educational Psychology,* 1969, *60,* 377–383.

Clark, H.B., Rowbury, T., Baer, A.M., & Baer, D.M. Timeout as a punishing stimulus in continuous and intermittent schedules. *Journal of Applied Behavior Analysis,* 1973, *6,* 443–455.

Cleary, T.A., Humphreys, L.G., Kendrick, S.A., & Wesman, A. Educational uses of tests with disadvantaged students. *American Psychologist,* 1975, *30,* 15–41.

Coghill, G.E. *Anatomy and the problem of behavior.* Cambridge: Cambridge University Press, 1929.

Cohen, S. *Social and personality development in childhood.* New York: Macmillan, 1976.

Cohen, S.A. *Teach them all to read.* New York: Random House, 1969.

Cohen, S.E., & Beckwith, L. Maternal language in infancy. *Developmental Psychology,* 1976, *12,* 371–372.

Coleman, J. D. Equal schools or equal students? *The Public Interest,* 1966, *4* (Summer), 73-74.

Coleman, J.S. The adolescent subculture and academic achievement. *American Journal of Sociology,* 1960, *65,* 337–347.

Coleman, J.S., Campbell, E.Q., Hobson, C.J., McPartland, J., Mood, A.M., Weinfeld, F.D., & York, R.L. *Equality of educational opportunity.* Washington, D.C.: U.S. Department of Health, Education and Welfare, 1966.

Comstock, G. Types of portrayal and aggressive behavior. *Journal of Communication,* 1977, *27,* 189–198.

Conger, J.J. A world they never knew: The family and social change. In J.J. Conger (Ed.), *Contemporary issues in adolescent development.* New York: Harper & Row, 1971.

Conway, E., & Brackbill, Y. Delivery medication and infant outcome: An empirical study in the effects of obstetrical medication on fetus and infant. *Monographs of the Society for Research in Child Development,* 1970, *35,* 24–34.

Cooper, K.H. *Aerobics.* New York: M. Evans, 1968.

Coopersmith, S., & Feldman, R. Fostering a positive self-concept and high self-esteem in the classroom. In R.H. Coop & K. White (Eds.), *Psychological concepts in the classroom.* New York: Harper & Row, 1974. Pp. 192–225.

Corah, N.L. Color and form preferences in children's perceptual behavior. *Perceptual and Motor Skills,* 1964, *18,* 313–316.

Crandall, V.C., Katokovsky, W., & Crandall, V.J. Children's beliefs in their own control of reinforcement in intellectual-academic achievement situations. *Child Development,* 1965, *36,* 91–109.

Crandall, V., Preston, A., & Rabson, A. Maternal reactions and the development of independence and achievement behavior in young children. *Child Development,* 1960, *31,* 243–251.

Cronbach, L.J. Five decades of public controversy over mental testing. *American Psychologist,* 1975, *30,* 1–14.

Damico, S., & Watson, K. *Peer helping relationships: An ecological study of an elementary classroom.* Paper presented at the annual meeting of the American Educational Research Association, Chicago, 1974.

Davé, R.H. *The identification and measurement of environmental process variables that are related to educational achievement.* Unpublished doctoral dissertation, University of Chicago, 1963.

Davis, A. Poor people have brains, too. *Phi Delta Kappan,* 1949, *30,* 294–295.

Dekker, E., & Groen, J. Reproducible psychogenic attacks of asthma: A laboratory study, *Journal of Psychosomatic Research,* 1956, *1,* 58–67.

Dekker, E., Pelser, H.E., & Groen, J. Conditioning as a cause of asthmatic attacks. *Journal of Psychosomatic Research,* 1957, *2,* 97–108.

Dennis, W. *The Hopi child.* New York: Science Editions, 1940.

Dennis, W., & Najarian, P. Infant development under environmental handicap. *Psychological Monographs,* 1957, *71,* No. 7.

Dennis, W., & Sayegh, Y. The effect of supplementary experiences upon the behavioral development of infants in institutions. *Child Development,* 1965, *36,* 81–90.

Deutsch, M. Cooperation and trust: Some theoretical notes. In M.R. Jones (Ed.), *Nebraska Symposium on Motivation.* Lincoln: University of Nebraska Press, 1962. Pp. 275–320.

DeVries, D.L., & Edwards, K.J. Student teams and learning games: Their effects on cross-race and cross-sex interaction. *Journal of Educational Psychology,* 1974, *66,* 741–749.

Dodd, B.J. Effects of social and vocal stimulation on infant babbling. *Developmental Psychology,* 1972, *7,* 80–83.

Dollard, J., Doob, L.W., Miller, N.E., Mowrer, O.H., & Sears, R.R. *Frustration and aggression.* New Haven: Yale University Press, 1939.

Dunn, L.C. *Heredity and evolution in human populations.* Cambridge: Harvard University Press, 1959.

Dunn, L.C., & Dobzhansky, T.H. *Heredity, race and society.* New York: Mentor Books, 1952.

Eckerman, C.O., & Whatley, J.L. Toys and social interaction between infant peers. *Child Development,* 1977, *48,* 1645–1656.

Eckerman, C. O., & Whatley, J. L. Growth of social play with peers during the second year of life. *Developmental Psychology,* 1975, *11,* 42–49.

Eckholm, E., & Record, F. *Worldwatch paper 9: The two faces of malnutrition.* Washington, D.C.: Worldwatch Institute, 1976.

Elardo, R., Bradley, R.H., & Caldwell, B.M. The relation of infants' home environment to mental test performance from 6 to 36 months: A longitudinal analysis. *Child Development,* 1975, *46,* 71–76.

Elkind, D. Erik Erikson's eight ages of man. In S. White (Ed.), *Human development in today's world.* Boston: Little, Brown, 1976. Pp. 224–232.

Engle, P.L. Minority language groups. *Review of Educational Research,* 1975, *45,* 283–326.

Erikson, E.H. *Childhood and society.* New York: Norton, 1963.

Erlenmeyer-Kimling, L., & Jarvik, L.F. Genetics and intelligence: A review. *Science,* 1963, *142,* 1477–1478.

Ervin-Tripp, S.M. Children's sociolinguistic competence and dialect diversity. In I.J.Gordon (Ed.), *Early childhood education: The seventy-fifth yearbook of the National Society for the Study of Education.* Chicago: University of Chicago Press, 1972.

Ervin-Tripp, S. M. Language acquisition and communicative choice. Stanford, Calif.: Stanford University Press, 1973.

Espenschade, A., & Eckert, H. Motor development. In W.R. Johnson & E.R. Buskirk (Eds.), *Science and medicine of exercise and sport* (2nd ed.). New York: Harper & Row, 1974.

Etzel, B.C., & Gewirtz, J.L. Experimental modification of caretaker-maintained high rate operant crying in a 6- and a 20-week-old infant: Extinction of crying with reinforcement of eye contact and smiling. *Journal of Experimental Child Psychology,* 1967, *5,* 303–317.

Evans, P. The Burt affair . . . Sleuthing in science. *APA Monitor,* 1976, *7,* 1, 4.

Faust, M.S. Developmental maturity as a determinant in prestige of adolescent girls. *Child Development,* 1960, *31,* 173–184.

Feeney, S. Child care debate: Key question. *Compact,* 1973, July-August, 25–26.

Ferro, F. Combating child abuse and neglect. *Children Today,* 1975, *4,* i.

Feshbach, S. The catharsis hypothesis and some consequences of interaction with aggressive and neutral play objects. *Journal of Personality,* 1956, *24,* 449–462.

Field, J. Relation of young infants' reaching behavior to stimulus distance and solidity. *Developmental Psychology,* 1976, *12,* 444–448.

Fischer, W.F. Sharing in preschool children as a function of amount and type of reinforcement. *Genetic Psychology Monographs,* 1963, *68,* 215–245.

Flavell, J.H. *The developmental psychology of Jean Piaget.* New York: Van Nostrand, 1963.

Foxx, R.M., & Azrin, N.H. Dry pants: A rapid method of toilet training children. *Behavior Research and Therapy,* 1973, *11,* 435–442.

Fraser, A. *Heredity, genes and chromosomes.* New York: McGraw-Hill, 1966.

Frazer, C., Bellugi, U., & Brown, R. Control of grammar in imitation, comprehension and production. *Journal of Verbal Learning and Verbal Behavior,* 1963, *2,* 121–135.

Freedman, D.G. Hereditary control of early social behavior. In B.M. Foss (Ed.), *Determinants of infant behavior* (Vol. 3). London: Methuen, 1965. Pp. 149–156.

Freud, S. *The basic writings of Sigmund Freud* (A.A. Brill, Ed. and trans.). New York: Random House, 1938.

Fromm, E. *The sane society.* New York: Holt, Rinehart & Winston, 1955.

Fry, C.L. A developmental examination of performance in a tacit coordination game situation. *Journal of Personality and Social Psychology,* 1967, *5,* 277–281.

Gagné, R.M. Contributions of learning to human development. *Psychological Review,* 1968, *75,* 177–191.

Gagné, R.M. *The conditions of learning* (2nd ed.). New York: Holt, Rinehart & Winston, 1970.

Gagné, R.M. *The conditions of learning* (3rd ed.). New York: Holt, Rinehart, & Winston, 1977.

Gahagan, D.M., & Gahagan, G.A. Talk reform: Explorations in language for infant-school children. Primary socialization, language and education (Vol. 3). *Sociological Research Unit Monograph Series.* London: Routledge and Kegan Paul, 1970.

Galinsky, E. *A national study of exemplary child care arrangements.* Paper presented at the annual meeting of the American Educational Research Association, New York, April 1977.

Galinsky, E., & Hooks, W.H. *The new extended family.* New York: Houghton Mifflin, 1977.

Gallimore, R., Boggs, J.W., & Jordan, C. *Culture, behavior and education: A study of Hawaiian-Americans.* Beverly Hills, Calif.: Sage, 1974.

Gallimore, R., & Howard, A. (Eds.). Studies in a Hawaiian community: Namamaka o Nanokuli. *Pacific Anthropological Records* (No. 1). Honolulu: B.P. Bishop Museum, 1968.

Ganby, W. D., & Griffith, B. C. Scientific communication: Its role in the conduct of research and creation of knowledge. *American Psychologist,* 1971, *26,* 349-363.

Gardner, J. W. *Excellence: Can we be equal and excellent too?* New York: Harper & Row, 1961.

Geber, M. The psychomotor development of African children in the first year and the influence of maternal behavior. *Journal of Social Psychology,* 1958, *47,* 185–195.

Gerbner, G., & Gross, L. The scary world of TV's heavy viewer. *Psychology Today,* April 1976, 41–45, 89.

Gesell, A. *The mental growth of the preschool child.* New York: Macmillan, 1925.

Gesell, A. *The first five years of life.* New York: Harper & Row, 1940.

Gesell, A., & Ilg, F.L. *Infant and child in the culture of today.* New York: Harper & Row, 1943.

Gesell, A., & Thompson, H. Learning and growth in identical infant twins: An experimental study by the method of co-twin control. *Genetic Psychology Monographs,* 1929, *6,* 1–124.

Getchell, E.L., & Howard, R.B. *Nutrition in development.* In G.M. Scipien, M.U. Barnard, M.A. Chard, J.Howe, & P.J. Phillips (Eds.), *Comprehensive pediatric nursing.* New York: McGraw-Hill. 1975. Pp. 184–237.

Gleason, J.B. Code switching in children's language. In T.E. Moore (Ed.), *Cognitive development and the acquisition of language.* New York: Academic Press, 1973. Pp. 159–167.

Glick, J. Cognitive development in cross-cultural perspective. In F.D. Horowitz (Ed.) *Review of child development research* (Vol. 4). Chicago: University of Chicago Press, 1975.

Glynn, E.L., & Thomas, J.D. Effect of cueing on self-control of classroom behavior. *Journal of Applied Behavior Analysis,* 1974, *7,* 299–306.

Gold, D., & Andres, D. Developmental comparisons between two-year-old children with employed and nonemployed mothers. *Child Development,* 1978, *49,* 75–84.

Good, T.L. Which pupils do teachers call on? *Elementary School Journal,* 1970, *70,* 190–198.

Gordon, I.J. *Early childhood stimulation through parent education.* Final report to the Children's Bureau, Social and Rehabilitation Service, Department of Health, Education, and Welfare. Gainesville: University of Florida, Institute for Development of Human Resources, 1969. (ERIC Document Reproduction Service No. ED 038 166)

Goslin, D. *Improving the community as a socialization system.* Paper presented at the annual meeting of the American Educational Research Association, Chicago, March 1975.

Gottfried, A.W., & Brody, N. Interrelationships between and correlates of psychometric and Piagetian scales of sensorimotor intelligence. *Developmental Psychology,* 1975, *11,* 379–387.

Gratch, G. A study of the relative dominance of vision and touch in six-month-old infants. *Child Development,* 1972, *43,* 615–623.

Gray, S.W., & Klaus, R.S. The early training project: A seventh year report. *Child Development,* 1970, *41,* 909–924.

Green, P.E., & Cooper, L.M.B. The hemopoietic system. In G.M. Scipien, M.U. Barnard, M.A. Chard, J. Howe, & P.J. Phillips (Eds.), *Comprehensive pediatric nursing.* New York: McGraw-Hill, 1975. Pp. 597–635.

Greenberg, M., Pelliteri, O., & Barton, J. Frequency of defects in infants whose mothers had rubella during pregnancy. *Journal of the American Medical Association,* 1957, *165,* 675–678.

Greenhill, J.P. *The miracle of life.* Chicago: Year Book Medical Publishers, 1971.

Guess, D., Sailor, W., Rutherford, G., & Baer, D.M. An experimental analysis of linguistic development: The productive use of the plural morpheme. *Journal of Applied Behavior Analysis,* 1968, *1,* 297–306.

Guilford, J.P. *The nature of human intelligence.* New York: McGraw-Hill, 1967.

Gunther, M. Infant behavior at the breast. In B.M. Foss (Ed.), *Determinants of infant behaviour.* New York: Wiley, 1961.

Guthrie, E.R. Relationships of teaching method, socioeconomic status, and intelligence in concept formation. *Journal of Educational Psychology,* 1971, *62,* 345–351.

Hainline, L., & Feig, E. The correlates of childhood father absence in college-aged women. *Child Development,* 1978, *49,* 37–42.

Halford, G.S., & Fullerton, T.J. A determination task which induces conservation of number. *Child Development,* 1970, *41,* 205–213.

Hall, C.S., & Lindzey, G. *Theories of personality.* (2nd ed.). New York: Wiley, 1970.

Haller, A.O., & Butterworth, C.E. Peer influence on levels of occupation and educational aspiration. *Social Forces,* 1960, *38,* 289–295.

Harasym, C.R., Boersma, F.J., & McGuire, T.O. Semantic differential analysis of relational terms used in conservation. *Child Development,* 1971, *42,* 767–779.

Harber, J.R., & Bryen, D.N. Black English and the task of reading. *Review of Educational Research,* 1976, *46,* 387–406.

Hardin, G. *Biology: Its human implications* (2nd ed.). San Francisco: Freeman, 1953.

Harlow, H., & Harlow, M.H. Learning to love. *American Scientist,* 1966, *54,* 244–272.

Harlow, H., & Zimmerman, R.R. Affectional responses in the infant monkey. *Science,* 1959, *130,* 421–432.

Harrington, D.M., Block, J.H., & Block, J. Intolerance of ambiguity in preschool children: Psychometric considerations, behavioral manifestations, and parental correlates. *Developmental Psychology,* 1978, *14,* 242–256.

Harris, F.R., Wolf, M.M., & Baer, D.M. Effects of adult social reinforcement on child behavior. In S.W. Bijou & D.M. Baer (Eds.), *Child development. Readings in experimental analysis.* New York: Appleton-Century-Crofts, 1967.

Harris, J.A., Jackson, C.M., Paterson, D.G., & Scammon, R.F. *The measurement of man.* Minneapolis: University of Minnesota Press, 1930.

Hartshorne, H., & May, M.A. *Studies in deceit.* New York: Macmillan, 1928.

Hartup, W.W. Peer interaction and social organization. In P.H. Mussen (Ed.), *Carmichael's manual of child psychology* (Vol. 2). New York: Wiley, 1970. Pp. 361–456.

Haskett, G.J., & Lenfestey, W. Reading-related behavior in an open classroom: Effects of novelty and modeling on preschoolers. *Journal of Applied Behavior Analysis,* 1974, *7,* 233–241.

Havighurst, R.J., & Dreyer, P.H. Youth and cultural pluralism. In R.J. Havighurst & P.H. Dreyer (Eds.), *Youth: The Seventy-Fourth Yearbook of the National Society for the Study of Education.* Chicago: University of Chicago Press, 1975. Pp. 269–284.

Havighurst, R.J., & Neugarten, B. *American Indian and white children.* Chicago: University of Chicago Press, 1955.

Hawkins, P.R. Social class, the nominal group and reference. *Language and Speech,* 1969, *12,* 125–135.

Haynes, C.R., & Kulhavy, R.W. Conservation level and category clustering. *Developmental Psychology,* 1976, *12,* 179–184.

Heald, F.P., & Hollander, R.J. The relationship between obesity in adolescence and early growth. *Journal of Pediatrics,* 1965, *67,* 35.

Heber, R. *Rehabilitation of families at risk for mental retardation.* Regional Rehabilitation Center, University of Wisconsin, 1969.

Heller, M.S., & White, M.A. Rates of teacher verbal approval and disapproval to higher and lower ability classes. *Journal of Educational Psychology,* 1975, *6,* 796–800.

Henderson, R.W. Environmental predictors of academic performance of disadvantaged Mexican-American children. *Journal of Consulting and Clinical Psychology,* 1972, *38,* 297.

Henderson, R.W., & Bergan, J.R. *The cultural context of childhood.* Columbus, Ohio: Charles E. Merrill, 1976.

Henderson, R.W., Bergan, J.R., & Hurt, M. Development and validation of the Henderson Environmental Learning Process Scale. *Journal of Social Psychology,* 1972, *88,* 185–196.

Henderson, R.W., & Garcia, A. The effects of a parent training program on the question-asking behavior of Mexican-American children. *American Educational Research Journal,* 1973, *10,* 193–201.

Henderson, R.W. & Hennig, H. *Relationships among cooperation-competition and locus of control in social and academic situations among children in traditional and open classrooms.* Paper presented at the annual meeting of the American Educational Research Association, Toronto, April 1978.

Henderson, R.W., & Merritt, C.B. Environmental backgrounds of Mexican-American children with different potentials for school success. *Journal of Social Psychology,* 1968, *75,* 101–106.

Henderson, R.W., Swanson, R., & Zimmerman, B.J. Inquiry response induction in preschool children through televised modeling. *Developmental Psychology,* 1975, *11,* 523–524.

Hetherington, E. M. *The aftermath of divorce.* Colloquium presented at the University of Arizona, 1976.

Herson, P.H. Biasing effects of diagnostic labels and sex of pupil on teachers' views of pupils' mental health. *Journal of Educational Psychology,* 1974, *66,* 117–122.

Herzog, E., & Sudia, C.E. Children in fatherless families. In B.M. Caldwell & H.N. Riciutti (Eds.), *Review of child development research* (Vol. 3). Chicago: University of Chicago Press, 1973.

Hess, R.D. Social class and ethnic influences upon socialization. In P.H. Mussen (Ed.), *Carmichael's manual of child psychology* (Vol. 2). New York: Wiley, 1970.

Hess, R.D., Shipman, V.C., Brophy, J.E., & Bear, R.M. *The cognitive environments of urban preschool children follow-up phase.* Chicago: Graduate School of Education, University of Chicago, 1969.

Hetherington, E.M. Effects of father absence on personality development in adolescent daughters. *Developmental Psychology,* 1972, *7,* 313–326.

Hetherington, E.M., & Martin, B. Family interaction and psychopathology in children. In H.C. Quay & J.S. Werry (Eds.), *Psychopathological disorders of childhood.* New York: Wiley, 1972. Pp. 32–82.

Hetherington, E.M., & McIntyre, C.W. Developmental psychology. *Annual Review of Psychology,* 1975, *26,* 97–136.

Hicks, J.D. *The American nation.* Cambridge, Mass.: Riverside Press, 1955.

Hicks, J. D. *The federal union.* Cambridge, Mass.: The Riverside Press, 1952.

Hiernaux, J. Heredity and environment: Their influence on human morphology. A comparison of two independent lines of study. *American Journal of Physical Anthropology,* 1963, *27,* 575–589.

Hiernaux, J. Weight/height relationship during growth in Africans and Europeans. *Human Biology,* 1964, *36,* 273–293.

Hiner, M.R. *Saints and sinners: Images of youth on the eve of the great awakening.* Paper presented at the annual meeting of the American Educational Research Association, Chicago, 1974.

Hoffman, M.L. Moral development. In P.H. Mussen (Ed.), *Carmichael's manual of child psychology* (Vol. 2) (3rd ed.). New York: Wiley, 1970.

Hoffman, M.L. Father absence and conscience development. *Developmental Psychology,* 1971, *4,* 400–406.

Hoffman, M.L. Moral internalization, parental power, and the nature of parent-child interaction. *Developmental Psychology,* 1975, *11,* 228–239.

Hoffman, M.L. Personality and social development. In M.R. Rosenzweig & L.W. Porter (Eds.), *Annual Review of Psychology* (Vol. 28). Palo Alto, Calif.: Annual Reviews, 1977.

Hoffman, M.L., & Saltzstein, H.D. Parent discipline and the child's moral development. *Journal of Personality and Social Psychology,* 1967, *5,* 45–57.

Hofstaetter, P.R. The changing composition of "intelligence": A study in T-technique. *Journal of Genetic Psychology,* 1954, *85,* 159–164.

Honzik, M.P., Macfarlane, J.W., & Allen, L. The stability of mental test performance between two and 18 years. *Journal of Experimental Education,* 1948, *4,* 309–324.

Horn, J.L. Human abilities: A review of research and theory in the early 1970s. *Annual Review of Psychology,* 1976, *27,* 437–486.

Howe, J. & Hunt, H.F. Prenatal development. In G.M. Scipien, M.U. Barnard, M.A. Chard, J. Howe, & P.J. Phillips (Eds.), *Comprehensive pediatric nursing.* New York: McGraw-Hill, 1975. Pp. 87–99.

Hulse, F. *The human species: An introduction to physical anthropology* (2nd ed.). New York: Random House, 1971.

Hunt, J.McV. *Intelligence and experience.* New York: Ronald Press, 1961.

Hutt, S.J., Lenard, H.G., & Prechtl, H.F.R. Psychophysiology of the newborn. In L.P. Lipsitt & H.W. Reese (Eds.), *Advances in child development and behavior.* New York: Academic Press, 1969.

Huxley, J. *Evaluation in action.* New York: Mentor Books, 1953.

Inhelder, B., & Piaget, J. *The growth of logical thinking from childhood to adolescence.* New York: Basic Books, 1958.

Jackson, G.B. The research evidence of the effects of grade retention. *Review of Educational Research,* 1975, *45,* 613–636.

Jackson, G.D. On the report of the ad hoc committee on educational uses of tests with disadvantaged students. *American Psychologist,* 1975, *30,* 88–93.

Jencks, C., Smith, M., Acland, H., Bane, J.J., Cohen, D., Gintis, H., Heyns, B., &

Michelson, S. *Inequality: A reassessment of the effect of family and schooling in America.* New York: Basic Books, 1972.

Jensen, A.R. How much can we boost IQ and scholastic achievement? *Harvard Educational Review,* Reprint Series No. 2, 1969, 1–124.

Jensen, A.R. The heritability of intelligence. *Engineering and Science,* 1970, *33,* 1–4.

Jensen, A.R. The phylogeny and ontogeny of intelligence. *Perspectives in Biology and Medicine,* 1971, *15,* 37–43.

Jensen, A.R., & Figueroa, R.A. Forward and backward digit span interaction with race and IQ: Predictions from Jensen's Theory. *Journal of Educational Psychology,* 1975, *67,* 882–893.

Johnson, D.W. & Johnson, R.T. Instructional goal structure: Cooperative, competitive, or individualistic. *Review of Educational Research,* 1974, *44,* 213–240.

Johnson, D.W., Johnson, R.T., Johnson, J., & Anderson, D. Effects of cooperative versus individualized instruction on student prosocial behavior, attitudes toward learning, and achievement. *Journal of Educational Psychology,* 1976, *68,* 446–452.

Johnson-Laird, P.M. Experimental psycholinguistics. *Annual Review of Psychology,* 1974, *25,* 135–160.

Johnston, M.K., Kelley, C.S., Harris, F.R., & Wolf, M.M. An application of reinforcement principles to development of motor skills of a young child. *Child Development,* 1966, *37,* 379–387.

Joint Commission on Mental Health of Children. *Crisis in child mental health: Challenge for the 1970's.* New York: Harper & Row, 1970.

Jones, H.E. The California adolescent growth study. *Journal of Educational Research,* 1938, *31,* 561–567.

Jones, J.E. The environment and mental development. In L. Carmichael (Ed.), *Manual of child psychology.* New York: Wiley, 1954.

Jones, M.C. A study of socialization patterns at the high school level. *Journal of Genetic Psychology,* 1958, *92,* 87–111.

Jones, M.C., & Bayley, N. Physical maturing among boys as related to behavior. *Journal of Educational Psychology,* 1950, *41,* 129–148.

Kagan, J. Acquisition and significance of sex-typing and sex-role identity. In M. Hoffman & L. Hoffman (Eds.), *Review of child development research* (Vol. 1). New York: Russell Sage, 1964. Pp. 137–167.

Kagan, J. Individual differences in the resolution of response uncertainty. *Journal of Personality and Social Psychology,* 1965, *2,* 154–160. (a)

Kagan, J. Reflection, impulsivity and reading ability in primary grade children. *Child Development,* 1965, *36,* 609–628. (b)

Kagan, J., & Moss, H.A. *Birth to maturity.* New York: Wiley, 1962.

Kagan, S., & Madsen, M.C. Cooperation and competition of Mexican, Mexican-American, and Anglo-American children of two ages under four instructional sets. *Developmental Psychology,* 1971, *5,* 32–39.

Kamin, L.J. *The science and politics of IQ.* New York: Wiley, 1974.

Kandel, D., & Lesser, G.S. Relative influences of parents and peers on the educational plans of adolescents in the United States and Denmark. In M.W. Miles & W.W. Charters, Jr., *Learning in social settings.* Boston: Allyn & Bacon, 1970.

Kantor, J.R. *Interbehavioral Psychology* (2nd ed.). Bloomington, Ind.: Principia Press, 1959.

Keating, D.P. Precocious cognitive development at the level of formal operations. *Child Development*, 1975, *46*, 276–280.

Keating, D.P., & Schaefer, R.A. Ability and sex differences in the acquisition of formal operations. *Developmental Psychology*, 1975, *11*, 531–532.

Keliher, A.V. *Life and growth*. New York: Appleton-Century-Crofts, 1938.

Keller, G. Women and the new physical education. *The Education Digest,* 1976, *41* (5), 42–45.

Kessen, W. *The child*. New York: Wiley, 1965.

Kessen, W. (Ed.). *Childhood in China*. New Haven: Yale University Press, 1975.

Kessen, W., Haith, M.M., & Salapatek, P.H. Infancy. In P.H. Mussen (Ed.), *Carmichael's manual of child psychology* (Vol. 2). (3rd ed.). New York: Wiley, 1970.

Kester, S.W. *The communication of teacher expectations and their effects on the achievement and attitudes of secondary school pupils*. Unpublished doctoral dissertation, University of Oklahoma, 1969.

Klapp, D.E. The fool as a social type. *American Journal of Sociology*, 1949, *55*, 157–162.

Klineberg, D. *Negro intelligence and selective migration*. New York: Columbia University Press, 1935.

Kluckhohn, C., & Leighton, D. *The Navaho*. Cambridge: Harvard University Press, 1946.

Kohlberg, L. The development of children's orientations toward a moral order: 1. Sequence in the development of moral thought. *Vita Humana*, 1963, *6*, 11–33.

Kohlberg, L., & Turiel, E. Moral development and moral education. In G.S. Lesser (Ed.), *Psychology and educational practice*. Glenview, Ill.: Scott Foresman, 1971. Pp. 410–465.

Korner, A.F. Visual alertness in neonates: Individual differences and their correlates. *Perceptual and Motor Skills,* 1970, *31*, 499–509.

Korner, A.F. State as variable, as obstacle and as mediator of stimulation in infant research. *Merrill-Palmer Quarterly,* 1972, *18*, 77–94.

Korner, A.F., & Thoman, E. Visual alertness in neonates as evoked by maternal care. *Journal of Experimental Child Psychology*, 1970, *10*, 67–78.

Kratochwill, T.R. Foundations of time series research. In T.R. Kratochwill (Ed.), *Single subject research strategies for evaluating change*. New York: Academic Press, 1978.

Kratochwill, T.R. Selective mutism: Implications for research and treatment. Hillsdale, N.J.: Lawrence Erlbaum, in press.

Kratochwill, T.R., & Bergan, J.R. Training school psychologists: Some perspectives on a competency based behavioral consultation model. *Professional Psychology,* 1978 9, 71–82.

Kuhn, D. Relation of two Piagetian stage transitions to IQ. *Developmental Psychology,* 1976, *12*, 157–161.

Labov, W. The logic of nonstandard English. In F. Williams (Ed.), *Language and poverty: Perspectives on a theme*. Chicago: Markham, 1970.

Labov, W. *Language in the inner city: Studies in black English vernacular*. Philadelphia: University of Pennsylvania Press, 1972.

Landauer, T.K., & Whiting, J.N.M. Infantile stimulation and adult stature of human males. *American Anthropologist,* 1963, *66,* 1007–1028.

Laosa, L.M. Child care and the culturally different child. *Child Care Quarterly,* 1974, *3,* 214–224.

Laosa, L.M. Socialization, education, and continuity: The importance of the sociocultural context. *Young Children,* 1977.

LaPointe, K., & O'Donnell, J.P. Number conservation in children below age six: Its relationship to age, perceptual dimensions, and language comprehension. *Developmental Psychology,* 1974, *10,* 422–428.

LaRoche, J.L. & Tcheng, F.C.Y. *Le Sourire du Nourrison.* Louvain: Publications Universitaires, 1963.

Leboyer, F. *Birth without violence.* New York: Random House, 1975.

Lee, D. Language and perception of the world. In W. Goldschmidt (Ed.), *Exploring the ways of mankind.* New York: Holt, Rinehart & Winston, 1960.

Lee, E.S. Negro intelligence and selective migration: A Philadelphia test of the Klineberg hypotheses. *American Sociological Review,* 1951, *16,* 227–233.

Leifer, A.D., Gordon, N.J., & Graves, S.B. Children's television more than mere entertainment. *Harvard Educational Review,* 1974, *44,* 213–245.

Lenneberg, E.H. Understanding language without being able to speak: A case report. *Journal of Abnormal and Social Psychology,* 1962, *65,* 419–425.

Lenneberg, E.H. A biological perspective of language. In E.H. Lenneberg (Ed.), *New directions in the study of language.* Cambridge: M.I.T. Press, 1964.

Lenneberg, E.H. *Biological foundations of language.* New York: Wiley, 1967.

Leon, G.R. Current directions in the treatment of obesity. *Psychological Bulletin,* 1976, *83,* 557–578.

Leopold, W.F. *Speech development of a bilingual child: A linguist's record.* Evanston, Ill.: Northwestern University Press, 1939–1949.

Lesser, G.S., Fifer, G., & Clark, D.H. Mental abilities of children in different social class and cultural groups. *Monographs of the Society for Research in Child Development,* 1965, *30* (Serial No. 102).

Lesser, G.S., & Kandel, D.B. Parental and peer influences on educational plans of adolescents. *American Sociological Review,* 1970, *34,* 213–223.

Lester, B.M., Kotelchuck, M., Spelke, E., Sellers, M.J., & Klein, R.E. Separation protest in Guatemalan infants: Cross-cultural and cognitive findings. *Developmental Psychology,* 1974, *10,* 79–85.

LeVine, R.A. Culture, personality, and socialization: An evolutionary view. In D.A. Goslin (Ed.), *Handbook of socialization theory and research.* Chicago: Rand McNally, 1969.

Levy, R.I. Tahiti, sin, and the question of integration between personality and sociocultural systems. In R.A. LeVine (Ed.), *Culture and personality: contemporary readings.* Chicago: Aldine, 1974. Pp. 287–306.

Lewis, O. *Life in a Mexican village: Tepoztlan restudied.* Urbana: University of Illinois Press, 1961.

Liebert, R.M., & Schwartzberg, N.S. Effects of mass media. In M.R. Rosenzweig & L.W. Porter (Eds.), *Annual Review of Psychology,* 1977, *28,* 141–173.

Lipsitt, L.P. A self-concept scale for children and its relationship to the children's form of the manifest anxiety scale. *Child Development,* 1958, *29,* 463–472.

Lipton, E.L., Steinschneider, A., & Richmond, J.B. The autonomic nervous system in early life. *New England Journal of Medicine*, 1965, *273*, 201–208.

Loeb, R.C. Concomitants of boys' locus of control examined in parent-child interactions. *Developmental Psychology*, 1975, *11*, 353–358.

Lorenz, K.Z. *King Solomon's ring.* New York: Crowell, 1952.

Lowrey, G.H. Obesity in adolescence. *American Journal of Public Health*, 1958, *48*, 1954.

Lowrey, G.H. *Growth and development of children.* Chicago: Year Book Medical Publishers, 1973.

Lucker, G.W., Rosenfield, D., Sikes, J., & Aronson, E. Performance in the interdependent classroom: A field study. *American Educational Research Journal*, 1976, *13*, 115–123.

Lyle, J. Television and daily life: Patterns of use (overview). In *Television and Social Behavior* (Vol. 4). Washington, D.C.: U.S. Government Printing Office, 1972.

Maccoby, M., & Modiano, N. On culture and equivalence: I. In J.S. Bruner, R.R. Olver, P.M. Greenfield, et al. (Eds.), *Studies in Cognitive Growth.* New York: Wiley, 1966.

MacFarlane, J.W., Allen, L., & Honzik, M.P. A developmental study of the behavior problems of normal children between twenty-two months and fourteen years. *University of California Publications in Child Development* (Vol. II). Berkeley: University of California Press, 1954.

Macrae, J.W., & Herbert-Jackson, E. Are behavioral effects of infant day care program specific? *Developmental Psychology*, 1976, *12*, 269–270.

Madsen, C.H., Hoffman, M., Thomas, D.R., Koropsak, E., & Madsen, C.K. Comparisons of toilet training techniques. In D.M. Gelfand (Ed.), *Social learning in childhood.* Belmont, Calif.: Brooks/Cole, 1969.

Madsen, M.C. Cooperative and competitive motivation of children in three Mexican-American sub-cultures. *Psychological Reports*, 1967, *20*, 1307–1320.

Madsen, M.C. Cooperative and competitive behavior of young children. *Journal of Cross-Cultural Psychology*, 1971, *2*, 365–371.

Madsen, M.C., & Shapira, A. Cooperative and competitive behavior of urban Afro-American, Mexican-American, and Mexican village children. *Developmental Psychology*, 1970, *3*, 16–20.

Maehr, M.L. Continuing motivation: An analysis of a seldom considered educational outcome. *Review of Educational Research*, 1976, *46*, 443–462.

Mahoney, M.J. Self-reward and self-monitoring techniques for weight control. *Behavior Therapy*, 1974, *5*, 48–57.

Mahoney, M. J., & Mahoney, K. *Permanent weight control.* New York: Norton, 1976.

Mahoney, M.J., & Thoresen, C.E. *Self-control: Power to the person.* Monterey, Calif.: Brooks/Cole, 1974.

Mann, R.A., & Baer, D.M. The effects of receptive language training on articulation. *Journal of Applied Behavior Analysis*, 1971, *4*, 291–298.

Marcus, R.F. The child as elicitor of parental sanctions for independent and dependent behavior: A simulation of parent-child interaction. *Developmental Psychology*, 1975, *11*, 443–452.

Martin, B. Parent-child relations. In F.D. Horowitz (Ed.), *Review of child development research.* Chicago: University of Chicago Press, 1975.

Maslow, A.H. A theory of human motivation. *Psychological Review,* 1943, *50,* 370–396.

Maslow, A.H. Toward a psychology of being (2nd ed.). New York: Van Nostrand, 1968.

Mayer, J. Correlation between metabolism and feeding behavior and multiple etiology of obesity. *Bulletin of the New York Academy of Medicine,* 1957, *33,* 744.

McAskie, M. Carelessness or fraud in Sir Cyril Burt's kinship data. *American Psychologist,* 1978, *33,* 496–498.

McCaffrey, A. *Speech perception in infancy.* Doctoral dissertation, Cornell University, 1972.

McCall, R.B., Appelbaum, M.I., & Hogarty, P.S. Developmental changes in mental performance. *Monographs of the Society for Research in Child Development,* 1973, *38*(3).

McCarthy, D. Language development in children. In L. Carmichael (Ed.), *Manual of child psychology* (2nd ed.). New York: Wiley, 1954.

McClearn, G.E. Genetic influences on behavior and development. In P.H. Mussen (Ed.), *Carmichael's manual of child psychology* (Vol. 1) (2nd ed.). New York: Wiley, 1970. Pp. 39–76.

McClelland, D.C. The importance of early learning in the formation of motives. In J. Atkinson (Ed.), *Motives in fantasy, action and society.* Princeton N.J.: Van Nostrand, 1958.

McClelland, D.C. *The achieving society.* Princeton, N.J.: Van Nostrand, 1961.

McIntyre, C.W., Vaughn, B.E., & Flavell, J.H. Early developmental changes in the ability to infer the visual precepts of others. *Proceedings of the 81st Annual Convention of the American Psychological Association,* 1973, *8,* 99–100.

McKeachie, W.J. Psychology in America's bicentennial year. *American Psychologist,* 1976, *31,* 819–833.

McKusick, V.A. *Mendalian inheritance in man: Catalogues of autosomal dominant, autosomal recessive, and X linked phenotypes* (3rd ed.). Baltimore: Johns Hopkins Press, 1971.

McLaughlin, T.F. Self-control in the classroom. *Review of Educational Research,* 1976, *46,* 631–633.

McNeil, J.D., & Laosa, L. Needs assessment and cultural pluralism. *Educational Technology,* 1975, *15,* 25–28.

McNeill, D. *The acquisition of language: The study of developmental psycholinguistics.* New York: Harper & Row, 1970.

Mead, G.H. In C.W. Morris (Ed.). *Mind, self and society from the standpoint of a social behaviorist.* Chicago: University of Chicago Press, 1934.

Mead, M. *Coming of age in Samoa.* New York: Morrow, 1928.

Mead, M. *Sex and temperament in three primitive societies.* New York: Morrow, 1935.

Mead, M. From the South Seas. New York: Morrow, 1939.

Mead, M. *Culture and commitment.* Garden City, N.Y.: Natural History Press, 1970.

Menninger, W.C. Recreation and mental health. *Recreation*, 1948, *42*, 340–346.

Mercer, J.R. *Labeling the mentally retarded.* Berkeley: University of California Press, 1973.

Mercer, J.R. A policy statement on assessment procedures and the rights of children. In *The rights of children.* Cambridge: Harvard Educational Review, 1974.

Midlarsky, E., & Bryan, J.H. Training charity in children. *Journal of Personality and Social Psychology*, 1967, *5*, 400–415.

Milgram, S., & Hollander, P. Murder they heard. *Nation*, 1964, *198*, 602–604.

Miller, P.H., Heldmeyer, K.H., & Miller, S.A. Facilitation of conservation of number in young children. *Developmental Psychology*, 1975, *11*, 253.

Mischel, W. *Personality and assessment.* New York: Wiley, 1968.

Mischel, W. Sex-typing and socialization. In P.H. Mussen (Ed.), *Carmichael's manual of child psychology* (Vol. 2) (3rd ed.). New York: Wiley, 1970.

Mischel, W. Toward a cognitive social learning reconceptualization of personality. *Psychological Review*, 1973, *80*, 252–283.

Mischel, W. Processes in delay of gratification. In L. Berkowitz (Ed.), *Advances in experimental social psychology.* New York: Academic Press, 1974.

Mischel, W. *Introduction to personality.* (2nd ed.). New York: Holt, Rinehart & Winston, 1976.

Mischel, W., & Baker, N. Cognitive transformations of reward objects through instructions. *Journal of Personality and Social Psychology*, 1975, *31*, 254–261.

Mischel, W., & Ebbsen, E.B. Attention in delay of gratification. *Journal of Personality and Social Psychology*, 1970, *16*, 329–337.

Mischel, W., Ebbsen, E.B., & Zeiss, A.R. Cognitive and attentional mechanisms in delay of gratification. *Journal of Personality and Social Psychology*, 1972, *21*, 204–218.

Mischel, W., Zeiss, R., & Zeiss, A.R. Internal-external control and persistence: Validation and implications of the Stanford Preschool Internal-External Scale. *Journal of Personality and Social Psychology*, 1974, *29*, 265–278.

Modiano, N. Bilingual education for children of linguistic minorities. *America Indigena*, 1968, *38*, 405–414.

Moerk, E.L. Verbal interactions between children and their mothers during the preschool years. *Developmental Psychology*, 1975, *11*, 788–794.

Mohr, G.S., & Despres, M.A. *The stormy decade: Adolescence.* New York: Random House, 1958.

Montagu, M.F.A. Constitutional and prenatal factors in infant and child health. In M.J.E. Senn (Ed.), *Symposium on the healthy personality.* New York: Josiah Macy, Jr. Foundation, 1950. Pp. 148–175.

Montagu, M.F.A. *Prenatal influences.* Springfield, Ill.: Charles C Thomas, 1962.

Moore, B.S., Clyburn, A., & Underwood, B. The role of affect in delay of gratification. *Child Development*, 1976, *47*, 273–276.

Moore, B.S., Underwood, B., & Rosenhan, D.L. Affect and altruism. *Developmental Psychology*, 1973, *8*, 99–104.

Morgan, G.A., & Ricciuti, H.N. Infants' responses to strangers during the first year. In B.H. Foss (Ed.), *Determinants of infant behaviour IV*. London: Methuen, 1969. Pp. 253–272.

Mullener, N., & Laird, J.D. Some developmental changes in the organization of self-evaluations. *Developmental Psychology*, 1971, *5*, 233–236.

Murray, H.A., et al. *Explorations in personality*. New York: Oxford University Press, 1938.

Mussen, P.H., & Jones, M.C. Self-conceptions, motivations, and interpersonal attitudes of late and early maturing boys. *Child Development*, 1957, *28*, 243–256.

Nagi, S. Z. Child abuse and neglect programs: A national overview. *Children Today*, 1975, *4*, 13-17.

Neimark, E.D. Intellectual development during adolescence. In F.D. Horowitz (Ed.), *Review of Child Development Research* (Vol. 4). Chicago: University of Chicago Press, 1975.

Nelson, C.E. Abstract and information retrieval services in educational research: Current status and planned improvement. *Educational Researcher*, 1974, *3*(10), 16–18.

Newton, N. The influence of the let-down reflex in breast feeding on the mother-child relationship. *Marriage and Family Living*, 1958, *20*, 18–20.

Nixon, J.E., & Locke, L.F. Research on teaching physical education. In R.M.W. Travers (Ed.), *Second handbook of research on teaching*. Chicago: Rand McNally, 1973.

Novak, M.A., & Harlow, H.F. Social recovery of monkeys isolated for the first year of life. I. Rehabilitation and therapy. *Developmental Psychology*, 1975, *11*, 453–465.

Nummedal, S.G., & Bass, S.C. Effects of the salience of intention and consequence on children's moral judgments. *Developmental Psychology*, 1976, *12*, 475–476.

Oakland, T., Laosa, L.M. Professional, legislative, and judicial influences on psychoeducational assessment practices in schools. In T.D. Oakland (Ed.), *Psychological and educational assessment of minority children*. New York: Bruner/Mazel, 1977.

O'Connell, E.J., Dusek, J.B., & Wheeler, R.J. A follow-up study of teacher expectancy effects. *Journal of Educational Psychology*, 1974, *66*, 325–328.

Ohwaki, S., & Stayton, S.E. The relation of length of institutionalization to the intellectual functioning of the profoundly retarded. *Child Development*, 1978, *49*, 105–109.

O'Leary, K.D., & O'Leary, S.G. *Classroom management: The successful use of behavior modification*. New York: Pergamon Press, 1972.

Olson, W.C. *Child development* (2nd ed.). Boston: Heath, 1959.

Opler, M.K. Cultural induction of stress. In M.H. Appley & R. Trumbull (Eds.), *Psychological Stress*. New York: Appleton-Century-Crofts, 1967. Pp. 209–241.

Osborn, J. Teaching a teaching language to disadvantaged children. In M.A. Brottman (Ed.), *Language remediation for the disadvantaged preschool child. Monographs of the Society for Research in Child Development*, 1968, *33*, 36–48.

Painter, G. A tutorial language program for disadvantaged infants. In C.S. Lavatelli (Ed.), *Language training in early childhood education.* Urbana: University of Illinois Press, ERIC Clearinghouse on Early Childhood Education, 1971.

Paradise, E., & Curcio, F. Relationship of cognitive and affective behaviors to fear of strangers in male infants. *Developmental Psychology,* 1974, *10,* 476–483.

Parke, R.D. & Walters, R.H. Some factors influencing the efficiency of punishment training for inducing response inhibition. *Monographs of the Society for Research in Child Development,* 1967, *32* (1, Serial No. 109).

Pasamanick, R., & Knobloch, H. Retrospective studies on the epidemiology of reproductive causality: Old and new. *Merrill-Palmer Quarterly,* 1966, *12,* 7–26.

Pearl, A. *The atrocity of education.* St. Louis: New Critics Press, 1972.

Pearl, A. *The drug education program at UCSC.* Paper presented at U.S. Office of Education Preservice Conference, Alexandria, Virginia, April 12, 1977.

Pederson, D.R. The soothing effect of rocking as determined by the direction and frequency of movement. *Canadian Journal of Behavioural Science,* 1975, *7,* 237–243.

Penick, S.B., Filion, R., Fox, S., & Stunkard, A. Behavior modification in the treatment of obesity. *Psychosomatic Medicine,* 1971, *33,* 49–55.

Piaget, J. *The origins of intelligence in children.* New York: International Universities Press, 1952.

Piaget, J. *The construction of reality in the child.* New York: Basic Books, 1954.

Piaget, J. *The child's conception of the world.* Paterson, N.J.: Littlefield, Adams, 1963.

Piaget, J. *Psychology and epistemology: Towards a theory of knowledge.* New York: Viking, 1971.

Piaget, J., & Inhelder, B. *Memory and intelligence.* New York: Basic Books, 1973.

Pinkston, E.M., Reese, N.M., LeBlanc, J.M., & Baer, D.M. Independent control of a preschool child's aggression and peer interaction by contingent teacher attention. *Journal of Applied Behavior Analysis,* 1973, *6,* 115–124.

Potter, M.C., & Levy, E.I. Spatial enumeration without counting. *Child Development,* 1968, *39,* 265–272.

Prader, A., Tanner, J.M., & von Harnack, G.A. Catch-up growth following illness or starvation. *Journal of Pediatrics,* 1963, *62,* 646–659.

Prawat, R.S., & Cancelli, A. Constructive memory in conserving and nonconserving first graders. *Developmental Psychology,* 1976, *12,* 47–50.

Provence, S., & Lipton, R.C. *Infants in institutions.* New York: International Universities Press, 1962.

Pufall, P.B., & Shaw, R.E. Precocious thoughts on number: The long and the short of it. *Developmental Psychology,* 1972, *7,* 62–69.

Ramírez, M. & Castañeda, A. *Cultural democracy, bicognitive development and education.* New York: Academic Press, 1974.

Rappaport, M.M., & Rappaport, H. The other half of the expectancy equation: Pygmalion. *Journal of Educational Psychology,* 1975, *67,* 531–536.

Rau, L. Conscience and identification. In R. R. Sears, L. Rau, & R. Alpert (Eds.), *Identification and child-rearing.* Stanford: Stanford University Press, 1965.

Raven, J.C. *Guide to the standard progressive matrices.* London: H.K. Lewis, 1960.

Reed, E.W. *Genetic anomalies in development*. In F.D. Horowitz (Ed.), *Review of child development research* (Vol. 4). Chicago: University of Chicago Press, 1975. Pp. 59–99.

Reed, S.C. *Counseling in medical genetics*. Philadelphia: Saunders, 1963.

Reichle, J.E., Longhurst, T.M., & Stepanich, L. Verbal interaction in mother-child dyads. *Developmental Psychology*, 1976, *12*, 273–277.

Rheingold, H.L., Gewirtz, J.L., & Ross, H.W. Social conditioning of vocalizations in the infant. *Journal of Comparative and Physiological Psychology*, 1959, *52*, 68–73.

Reisinger, K., Rogers, K.D., & Johnson, O. Nutrition survey of Lower Greasewood, Arizona Navajos. In W.M. Moore, M.M. Silverberg, & O.M.S. Read (Eds.), *Nutrition, growth and development of North American Indian children*. DHEW Publication No. (NIH) 72–26, 1972.

Reisman, D. *Individualism reconsidered*. Glencoe, Ill.: Free Press, 1964.

Reynolds, E.L. Degree of kinship and pattern of ossification. *American Journal of Physiological Anthropology*, 1943, *1*, 405–416.

Rheingold, H.L. Sharing at an early age. In B.C. Etzel, J.N. LeBlanc, & D.M. Baer (Eds.), *New developments in behavioral research: Theory, methods and applications*. Hilsdale, N.J.: Lawrence Erlbaum, 1977. Pp. 489–502.

Rheingold, H.L., & Cook, K.V. The contents of boys' and girls' rooms as an index of parents' behavior. *Child Development*, 1975, *46*, 459–463.

Rice, R.D. Neurophysiological development in premature infants following stimulation. *Developmental Psychology*, 1977, *13*, 69–76.

Richards, J.C. Some social aspects of language learning. *TESOL Quarterly*, 1972, *6*, 243–254.

Richardson, A. Mental practice: A review and discussion. Part I. *Research Quarterly*, 1967, *38*, 95–107. (a)

Richardson, A. Mental practice: A review and discussion. Part II. *Research Quarterly*, 1967, *38*, 263–273. (b)

Ridberg, E.H., Parke, R.D., & Hetherington, E.M. Modification of impulsive and reflective cognitive styles through observation of film-mediated models. *Developmental Psychology*, 1971, *5*, 369–377.

Riegel, K.F. Influence of economic and political ideologies on the development of developmental psychology. *Psychological Bulletin*, 1972, *78*, 129–141.

Riesen, A.H., Chow, K.L., Semmes, J., & Nissen, H.W. Chimpanzee vision under four conditions of light deprivation. *American Psychologist*, 1951, *6*, 282. (abstract)

Rippa, S.A. *Educational ideas in America: A documentary history*. New York: McKay, 1969.

Robertson, J.D. Comparative study of motor achievement of five- and seven-year-old children. *Dissertation Abstracts*, 1973, Order No. 74–9385.

Rodriguez, R. On becoming a Chicano. *Saturday Review Magazine*, Feb. 8, 1975.

Roffwarg, H.P., Muzio, J.N., & Dement, W.C. Ontogenetic development of the human sleep-dream cycle. *Science*, 1966, *152*, 604–919.

Romney, K., & Romney, R. *The Mixtecans of Juxlahuaca, Mexico*. Six Cultures Series (Vol. 4). New York: Wiley, 1966.

Rosen, B.C., & D'Andrade, R. The psychological origins of achievement motivation. *Sociometry*, 1959, *22*, 185–218.

Rosenthal, R., & Jacobson, L. *Pygmalion in the classroom.* New York: Holt, Rinehart & Winston, 1968.

Rosenthal, T.L., & Zimmerman, B.J. Modeling by exemplification and instruction in training conservation. *Developmental Psychology,* 1972, *6,* 392–401.

Ross, D.M. The effect on learning of psychological attachment to a film model. *American Journal of Mental Deficiency,* 1969, *74,* 701–707.

Rotter, J.B. Generalized expectancies for internal versus external control of reinforcement. *Psychological Monographs,* 1966, *80* (Whole No. 609).

St. Petery, J.R. The high-risk infant and family. In G.M. Scipien, M.U. Barnard, M.A. Chard, J. Howe, & P.J. Phillips (Eds.), *Comprehensive pediatric nursing.* New York: McGraw-Hill, 1975. Pp. 294–318.

Sajwaj, T., Libet, J., & Agras, S. Lemon-juice therapy: The control of life-threatening rumination in a six-month-old infant. *Journal of Applied Behavior Analysis,* 1974, *7,* 557–566.

Salili, F., Maehr, M.L., Sorensen, R.L., & Fyans, L.J. Jr. A further consideration of the effects of evaluation on motivation. *American Educational Research Journal,* 1976, *13,* 85–102.

Sashkin, M., Morris, W.C., & Horst, L. A comparison of social and organizational change models: Information flow and data use processes. *Psychological Review,* 1973, *80,* 510–526.

Scammon, R.E. The measurement of the body in childhood. In J.A. Harris, C.M. Jackson, D.G. Paterson, & R.E. Scammon (Eds.), *The measurement of man.* Minneapolis: University of Minnesota Press, 1930.

Scarr, S., & Weinburg, R.A. IQ test performance of black children adopted by white families. *American Psychologist,* 1976, *31,* 726–739.

Scarr-Salapatek, S. Genetics and the development of intelligence. In F.D. Horowitz (Ed.), *Review of Child Development Research* (Vol. 4). Chicago: The University of Chicago Press, 1975.

Schaefer, E.S. A circumplex model for maternal behavior. *Journal of Abnormal and Social Psychology,* 1959, *59,* 226–235.

Scheinfeld, A. *Your heredity and environment.* Philadelphia: Lippincott, 1965.

Schwarz, J.C., Krolick, G., & Strickland, R.G. Effects of early day care experience on adjustment to a new environment. *American Journal of Orthopsychiatry,* 1973, *43,* 340–346.

Schwarz, J.C., Strickland, R.G., & Krolick, G. Infant day care: Behavioral effects at preschool age. *Developmental Psychology,* 1974, *10,* 502–506.

Scipien, G.M. Fetal malformations. In G.M. Scipien, M.U. Barnard, M.A. Chard, J. Howe, & P.J. Phillips (Eds.), *Comprehensive pediatric nursing.* New York: McGraw-Hill, 1975. Pp. 284–293.

Seale, B. How will we raise our children in the year 2000? In S. White (Ed.), *Human development in today's world.* Boston: Little, Brown, 1976. P. 297.

Sears, R.R. Dependency motivation. In M.R. Jones (Ed.), *Nebraska Symposium on Motivation.* Lincoln: University of Nebraska Press, 1963. Pp. 25–64.

Sears, R.R., Maccoby, E., & Levin, H. *Patterns of child rearing.* Evanston, Ill.: Row Peterson, 1957.

Sears, R.R., Rau, L., & Alpert, R. *Identification and child rearing.* Stanford: Stanford University Press, 1965.

Seitz, S., & Stewart, C. Imitations and expansions: Some developmental aspects of mother-child communications. *Developmental Psychology*, 1975, *11*, 763–768.

Shapira, A., & Madsen, M.C. Cooperation and competitive behavior of Kibbutz and urban children in Israel. *Child Development*, 1969, *4*, 609–617.

Shapiro, A.H. Heat, ethnic differences, and creativity in the Negev desert. *Journal of Educational Psychology*, 1975, *67*, 183–187.

Shatz, M., & Gelman, R. The development of communication skills: Modifications in the speech of young children as a function of listening. *Monographs of the Society for Research in Child Development*, 1973, *38* (5, Serial No. 152).

Shavelson, R.J., Hubner, J.J. & Stanton, G.C. Self-concept: Validation of construct interpretations. *Review of Educational Research*, 1976, *46*, 407–441.

Shea, B.M. Schooling and its antecedents: Substantive and methodological issues in the status attainment process. *Review of Educational Research*, 1976, *46*, 463–526.

Sherman, M. The differentiation of emotional responses in infants. I. Judgements of emotional responses from motion picture views and from actual observations. *Journal of Comparative Psychology*, 1927, *7*, 265–284. (a)

Sherman, M. The differentiation of emotional responses in infants. II. The ability of observers to judge the emotional characteristics of the crying of infants and the voice of an adult. *Journal of Comparative Psychology*, 1927, *7*, 335–351. (b)

Sherman, T.M., & Cormier W.H. An investigation of the influence of student behavior on teacher behavior. *Journal of Applied Behavior Analysis*, 1974, *7*, 11–22.

Shipley, C.F., Smith, C.S., & Gleitman, L.R. A study in the acquisition of language: Free responses to commands. *Language*, 1969, *45*, 322–342.

Shirley, M.M. A motor sequence favors the maturation theory. *Psychological Bulletin*, 1931, *28*, 204–205.

Shirley, M.M. *The first two years: A study of twenty-five babies. Vol. II: Intellectual development.* Minneapolis: University of Minnesota Press, 1933.

Short, E.C. Knowledge production and utilization in curriculum: A special case of the general phenomenon. *Review of Educational Research*, 1973, *43*, 237–302.

Siegler, R.S., & Atlas, M. Acquisition of formal scientific reasoning by 10- and 13-year-olds: Detecting interactive patterns in data. *Journal of Educational Psychology*, 1976, *68*, 360–370.

Siegler, R.S., Liebert, D.E., & Liebert, R.M. Inhelder and Piaget's pendulum problem: Teaching preadolescents to act as scientists. *Developmental Psychology*, 1973, *9*, 97–101.

Simmons, K.W., Greenberg, B.J., & Atkin, C.K. The demography of fictional characters in 1975–76. Report No. 2, Project Castle. East Lansing: Dept. of Communication, Michigan State University, Feb. 1977.

Sinclair-de-Zwart, H. Developmental psycholinguistics. In D. Elkind & J. Flavell (Eds.), *Studies in cognitive development.* New York: Oxford University Press, 1969.

Sisson, R., Clatworthy, S., & Zadroga, J. The nervous system. In G.M. Scipien, M.U. Barnard, M.A. Chard, J. Howe, & P.J. Phillips (Eds.), *Comprehensive pediatric nursing.* New York: McGraw-Hill, 1975. Pp. 463–497.

Skinner, B.F. *Science and human behavior.* New York: Macmillan, 1953.

Skinner, B.F. *Verbal behavior*. New York: Appleton-Century-Crofts, 1957.

Skinner, B.F. *Beyond freedom and dignity*. New York: Knopf, 1971.

Skinner, B.F. *About behaviorism*. New York: Knopf, 1974.

Skinner, B.F. The steep and thorny way to a science of behavior. *American Psychologist,* 1975, *30,* 42–49.

Slovin-Ela, S., & Kohen-Raz, R. Developmental differences in primary reaching responses of young infants from varying social backgrounds. *Child Development,* 1978, *49,* 132–140.

Smedslund, J. The acquisition of conservation of substance and weight in children. V. Practice in conflict situations without external reinforcement. *Scandinavian Journal of Psychology,* 1961, *2,* 156–160.

Solnit, A.J. Marriage: Changing structure and functions of the family. In V.C. Vaughn III & T.B. Brazelton (Eds.), *The Family—Can It Be Saved?* Chicago: Yearbook Medical Publishers, 1976.

Spearman, C. General intelligence objectively determined and measured. *The American Journal of Psychology,* 1904, *15,* 201–292.

Spearman, C. *The abilities of man: Their nature and measurement.* New York: Macmillan, 1927.

Spelke, E., Zelazo, P., Kagan, J., & Kotelchuck, M. Father interaction and separation protest. *Developmental Psychology,* 1973, *9,* 83–90.

Spitz, R.A. Hospitalism: An inquiry into the genesis of psychiatric conditions in early childhood. A follow-up report. *The Psychoanalytic Study of the Child,* 1945, *1,* 53–74.

Spitz, R.A. *The first year of life.* New York: International Universities Press, 1965.

Spitz, R.A., & Wolf, K.M. Anaclitic depression. *The Psychoanalytic Study of the Child,* 1947, *2,* 313–343.

Sroufe, L.A. Drug treatment of children with behavior problems. In F.D. Horowitz (Ed.), *Review of child development research.* (Vol. 4). Chicago: University of Chicago Press, 1975.

Staats, A.W., Brewer, B.A., & Gross, M.C. Learning and cognitive development: Representation samples, cumulative-hierarchical learning, and experimental-longitudinal methods. *Monographs of the Society for Research in Child Development,* 1970, *35,* (8), 1–85.

Stayton, D.J., Ainsworth, M.D.S., & Main, M.B. Development of separation behavior in the first year of life: Protest, following, and greeting. *Developmental Psychology,* 1973, *9,* 213–225.

Stein, A.H., & Friedrich, L.K. Impact of television on children and youth. In E.M. Hetherington (Ed.), *Review of child development research* (Vol. 5). Chicago: University of Chicago Press, 1975. Pp. 183–256.

Steinfels, M. *Who's minding the children?* The history and politics of day care in America. New York: Simon & Schuster, 1974.

Stern, C. *Principles of human genetics* (2nd ed.). San Francisco: Freeman, 1960.

Stoch, M.B., & Smythe, P.M. The effect of undernutrition during infancy on subsequent brain growth and intellectual development. *South African Medical Journal,* 1967, *41,* 1027.

Stuart, R.B. A three-dimensional program for the treatment of obesity. *Behavior Research and Therapy,* 1971, *9,* 177–186.

Sunley, R. Early nineteenth-century literature of child rearing. In M. Mead &

M. Wolfenstein (Eds.), *Childhood in contemporary cultures.* Chicago: University of Chicago Press, 1955.

Swanson, R.A., & Henderson, R.W. Achieving home-school continuities in the socialization of an academic motive. *Journal of Experimental Education,* 1976, *44,* 38–44.

Tanner, J.M. Growth at adolescence. Oxford: Basil Blackwell, 1962.

Tanner, J.M. Physical growth. In P.H. Mussen (Ed.), *Carmichael's manual of child psychology* (Vol. 1) (3rd ed.). New York: Wiley, 1970.

Tanner, J.M. Sequence, tempo, and individual variation in growth and development of boys and girls aged twelve to sixteen. In J. Kagan & R. Coles (Eds.), *Twelve to sixteen: Early adolescence.* New York: Norton, 1972.

Terman, L.M. *Stanford-Binet Intelligence Scale.* Boston: Houghton-Mifflin, 1916.

Terman, L.M., & Merrill, M. *Stanford-Binet Intelligence Scale: Manual for the Third Revision, Form L-M.* Boston: Houghton-Mifflin, 1960.

Thomas, M.H., & Drabman, R.S. Toleration of real life aggression as a function of exposure to televised violence and age of subject. *Merrill-Palmer Quarterly,* 1975, *21,* 227–232.

Thompson, W.R., & Grusec, J.E. Studies of early experience. In P.H. Mussen (Ed.), *Carmichael's manual of child psychology* (Vol. 1) (3rd ed.). New York: Wiley, 1970.

Thoresen, C.E., & Mahoney, M.J. *Behavioral self-control.* New York: Holt, Rinehart & Winston, 1974.

Thorndike, R.L. Review of R. Rosenthal and L. Jacobson. Pygmalion in the classroom. *American Educational Research Journal,* 1968, *5,* 708–711.

Thorndike, R.L. But you have to know how to tell time. *American Educational Research Journal,* 1969, *6,* 692.

Toffler, A. *Future shock.* New York: Bantam Books, 1970.

Torrance, E.P. *Guiding creative talent.* Englewood Cliffs, N.J.: Prentice-Hall, 1962.

Trehub, S.E., & Rabinovitch, M.S. Auditory-linguistic sensitivity. *Developmental Psychology,* 1972, *6,* 74–77.

Tuddenham, R.D. The nature and measurement of intelligence. In L. Postman (Ed.), *Psychology in the making.* New York: Knopf, 1962.

Tulkin, S. *Infants' reaction to mother's voice and stranger's voice: Social class differences in the first year of life.* Paper presented at meeting of the Society for Research in Child Development, Minneapolis, 1971.

Turiel, E. Stage transition in moral development. In R.M.W. Travers (Ed.), *Second handbook of research on teaching.* Chicago: Rand McNally, 1973.

Twardosz, S., Cataldo, M.F., & Risley, T.R. Open environment design for infant and toddler day care. *Journal of Applied Behavior Analysis,* 1974, *7,* 529–546.

Veldman, D.J., & Brophy, J.E. Measuring teacher effects on pupil achievement. *Journal of Educational Psychology,* 1974, *66,* 319–324.

Viernstein, M.C., & Hogan, R. Parental personality factors and achievement motivation in talented adolescents. *Journal of Youth and Adolescence,* 1975, *4,* 183–190.

Waber, D.P. Sex differences in mental abilities, hemispheric lateralization, and rate of physical growth at adolescence. *Developmental Psychology*, 1977, *13*, 29–38.

Wagner, I. & Cimiotti, E. Impulsive und reflexive Kinder Prufen Hypothesen: Strategien beim Problem-losen, aufgezeigt an Blickwegungen. *Zeitschrift fur Entwicklungspsychologie und Padagogische Psychologie*, 1975, *7*, 1–15.

Walberg, H.J., & Marjoribanks, K. Differential mental abilities and home environment: A canonical analysis. *Developmental Psychology*, 1973, *9*, 363–368.

Walberg, H.J., & Marjoribanks, K. Family environment and cognitive development: Twelve analytic models. *Review of Educational Research*, 1976, *46*, 527–552.

Warren, N. Malnutrition and mental development. *Psychological Bulletin*, 1973, *80*, 324–328.

Watson, J.B. Psychology as the behaviorist views it. *Psychological Review*, 1913, *20*, 158–177.

Watson, J.B. *Psychology from the standpoint of a behaviorist*. Philadelphia: Lippincott, 1919.

Weatherley, D. Self-perceived rate of physical maturation and personality in late adolescence. *Child Development*, 1964, *35*, 1197–1210.

Wechsler, D. *Manual for the Wechsler Adult Intelligence Scale*. New York: The Psychological Corporation, 1955.

Wechsler, D. *Manual for the Wechsler Intelligence Scale for Children—Revised*. New York: The Psychological Corporation, 1974.

Weigel, R.H., Wisler, P.L., & Cook, S.W. The impact of cooperative learning experiences on cross-ethnic relations and attitudes. *Journal of Social Issues*, 1975, *31*, 219–244.

Weisburg, P. Social and nonsocial conditioning of infant vocalizations. *Child Development*, 1963, *34*, 377–388.

Weiss, B. Clash between culture and biology: Earlier menstruation, longer adolescence. *Psychology Today*, November 1974.

Weiss, B., & Laties, V.G. Enhancement of human performance by caffeine and the amphetamines. *Pharmacological Review*, 1962, *14*, 1–36.

Westinghouse Learning Corporation—Ohio University. *The impact of Head Start*. Springfield, Va.: Clearning House for Federal Scientific and Technical Information, U.S. Department of Commerce, 1969.

Wheeler, L.R. The intelligence of east Tennessee mountain children. *Journal of Educational Psychology*, 1932, *23*, 351–370.

White, B.L. Fundamental early environmental influences on the development of competencies. In M.E. Meyer (Ed.), *Third symposium on learning: Cognitive learning*. Bellingham: Western Washington State College Press, 1972.

White, G.M. The elicitation and durability of altruistic behavior in children. Research Bulletin No. 67–27. Princeton, N.J.: Educational Testing Service, 1967.

White House Conference on Children. *Children and parents: Together in the world*. Report of Forum 15. Washington, D.C.: U.S. Superintendent of Documents, 1971.

White, L.A. *The evolution of culture: The development of civilization to the fall of Rome*. New York: McGraw-Hill, 1959.

White, R. Motivation reconsidered: The concept of competence. *Psychological Review*, 1959, *66*, 297–333.

White, S. (Ed). *Human development in today's world.* Boston: Little, Brown, 1976.

Whiting, B., & Edwards, C.P. A cross-cultural analysis of sex differences in the behavior of children aged three through eleven. In R.A. LeVine (Ed.), *Culture and personality: Contemporary readings.* Chicago: Aldine, 1974. Pp. 188–201.

Whiting, J.W.M., Chasdi, E.H., Antonovsky, H.F., & Ayres, B.C. The learning of values. In R.A. LeVine (Ed.), *Culture and personality: Contemporary readings.* Chicago: Aldine, 1974. Pp. 155–187.

Willems, E.P. Behavioral technology and behavioral ecology. *Journal of Applied Behavior Analysis,* 1974, *7,* 151–166.

Williams, R.L. Stimulus/response: Scientific racism and IQ—The silent mugging of the black community. *Psychology Today,* 1974, *7,* 32–100.

Wilson, R.W. Twins: Mental development in the preschool years. *Developmental Psychology,* 1974, *10,* 580–588.

Winett, R.A., & Winkler, R.C. Current behavior modification in the classroom: Be still, be quiet, be docile. *Journal of Applied Behavior Analysis,* 1972, *5,* 499–504.

Winick, M. *Malnutrition and brain development.* New York: Oxford University Press, 1976.

Winick, M., Rosso, P., & Waterlow, J. Cellular growth of cerebrum, cerebellum, and brain stem in normal and marasmic children. *Experimental Neurology,* 1970, *26,* 393–400.

Winterbottom, M. The relation of need for achievement in learning experiences in independence and mastery. In J. Atkinson (Ed.), *Motives in fantasy, action, and society.* Princeton: Van Nostrand, 1958. Pp. 453–478.

Wispe, L.G., & Thompson, J.N., Jr. The war between the words: Biological versus social evolution and some related issues. *American Psychologist,* 1976, *31,* 341–347.

Wissler, C. The correlation of mental and physical tests. *Psychological Review,* Monograph Supplement, 1901, *3* (16).

Wolf, R.M. *The identification and measurement of environmental process variables related to intelligence.* Unpublished doctoral dissertation, University of Chicago, 1964.

Wolff, P.H. The causes, controls and organization of behavior in the neonate. *Psychological Issues,* 1966, *5* (1, Whole No. 17).

Wolff, P.H. The natural history of crying and other vocalizations in early infancy. In B. Foss (Ed.), *Determinants of infant behavior* (Vol. 4). London: Methuen, 1969.

Wolfle, D.L., & Wolfle, H.M. The development of cooperative behavior in monkeys and young children. *Journal of Genetic Psychology,* 1939, *55,* 137–175.

Wolfram, W.A. Sociolinguistic alternatives in teaching reading to nonstandard speakers. *Reading Research Quarterly,* 1970, *6,* 9–33.

Wulbert, M., Inglis, S., Kriegsmann, E., & Mills, B. Language delay and associated mother-child interactions. *Developmental Psychology,* 1975, *11,* 61–70.

Yarrow, L.J. Separation from parents during early childhood. In M.L. Hoffman & L.W. Hoffman (Eds.), *Review of child development research* (Vol. 1). New York: Russell Sage, 1964. Pp. 89–136.

Yarrow, M.R., Scott, P.M., & Waxler, C.Z. Learning concern for others. *Developmental Psychology,* 1973, *8,* 240–260.

Yarrow, M.R., Waxler, C.Z., & Scott, P.M. Child effects on adult behavior. *Developmental Psychology,* 1971, *5,* 300–311.

Zajonc, R.B. Family configuration and intelligence. *Science,* 1976, *192,* 227–236.

Zajonc, R.B., & Markus, G.B. Birth order and intellectual development. *Psychological Review,* 1975, *82,* 74–88.

Zelazo, N.A., Zelazo, P.R., & Kolb, S. Walking in the newborn. *Science,* 1972, *176,* 314–315.

Ziegel, E., & Van Blarcom, C.C. *Obstetric Nursing* (6th ed). New York: Macmillan, 1972.

Zigler, E.F., & Child, I.L. *Socialization and personality development.* Reading, Mass.: Addison-Wesley, 1973.

Zimmerman, B.J., & Dialessi, F. Modeling influences on children's creative behavior. *Journal of Educational Psychology,* 1973, *65,* 127–134.

Zimmerman, B.J., & Rosenthal, T.L. Conserving and retaining equalities and inequalities through observation and correction. *Developmental Psychology,* 1974, *10,* 260–268.

Glossary

aberrant genes Abnormal genes. Genes carrying biological "errors" which lead to atypical development.

accommodation A Piagetian concept indicating adaptive changes occurring in the manner in which an individual interacts with the environment.

achieved status An earned position in society. Being a farmer is an example.

allele Alternative form of a gene. For example, one form of a gene for color vision may transmit normal color vision. An alternative form may carry the trait for red-green color blindness. In this case the allele for color blindness is recessive.

altruism Behavior reflecting concern for the well being of others, as seen, for example, in generosity and sharing.

amaurotic family idiocy A genetically transmitted disorder resulting in mental retardation. Also known as Tay Sachs disease.

amniocentesis A medical procedure in which fluid is extracted from the amniotic sac of a pregnant woman and analyzed for the purpose of detecting certain genetic characteristics of a fetus. The sex of a child and many genetic abnormalities may be detected.

amniotic fluid A fluid within the amniotic sac which serves to protect the fetus.

amniotic sac A fluid-filled sac, within the uterus, in which the embryo/fetus is suspended.

anaclytic identification In Freudian theory, identification based on the intense dependency relationship of a child on its mother. Considered by Freud to be the main form of identification for girls.

anal stage In Freudian theory, the psychosexual stage in which physical pleasure is associated primarily with the expulsion and retention of feces.

angina pectoris A displase condition involving chest pain induced by an insufficient supply of oxygen to the heart.

antecedent A term used in behavioral psychology to indicate conditions occurring before behavior of interest.

antibody   A protein substance in the blood that reacts to overcome the toxic effects of antigens introduced into the body.

antigens   A substance which stimulates the production of an antibody when produced by or introduced into the body.

ascribed status   A social status assigned independently of behavior. Being a child is an example.

assimilation   A Piagetian concept referring to the acquisition of new information represented by an existing intellectual structure. In anthropological theory, the process by which the members of one cultural group become completely integrated and absorbed into a dominant group.

autosome   All chromosomes except the sex chromosomes.

aversive   A consequence of behavior that reduces the probability that the behavior will occur again.

barrio   In the United States, an area of a community generally inhabited by Hispanic-Americans. Unlike many Anglo-American neighborhoods, barrios are usually named, and residents feel a sense of identification with them.

basic stage   In behaviorist theory, the stage during which interactions with parents are the main sources of influence on a child's behavior; beginning just after infancy and extending through childhood.

behavior-contingency unit   A behavior and the accompanying conditions which control the likelihood of its occurrence.

blastocyst   The stage of prenatal development marked by differentiation of cells of the zygote, and ending when the developing structure is implanted in the wall of the uterus. At this point the organism is considered an embryo.

catharsis   In Freudian theory, the process by which aggressive impulses, accumulated because of frustation, may be released.

centromere   The short region at which two chromatids are joined before separation during mitosis. The spindle fibers are attached at this point.

chaining   The learning of a set of responses in sequence as in learning to tie shoes.

chromosomes   Threadlike structures within biological cells, along which the genes are arranged.

chromatids   The "daughter" chromosomes formed when chromosomes replicate themselves during mitosis.

cirrhosis   Formation of fibers especially in the liver with hardening caused by excessive formation of connective tissue.

clinical method   The method of investigation used by Piaget in his developmental studies. The clinical method is comprised of a set of interviewing procedures to encourage a child to exact or to verbalize his/her thinking processes.

cognitive (behavioral) view   An alternate name for the social learning position.

cognitive structuring   Attempts by socializing agents to describe what they expect of children and to explain why children should behave as expected.

concrete operations   The second major developmental period designated by Piaget. During this period the child learns to represent concrete experiences with symbols and to classify concrete objects in terms of their relationships to other objects.

conditioned stimulus An event which acquires the capability of eliciting a particular response, as the result of being paired with the unconditioned stimulus naturally associated with that response.

consequences A behavioral term indicating events immediately following a behavior of interest.

conservation A Piagetian term referring to intellectual actions displaying recognition that a whole must remain unchanged despite variations in the arrangement of its parts.

contingent A behavioral term indicating that an event such as reinforcement is dependent upon the occurrence of a behavior. For instance, a child might be praised if and only if she picked up her toys.

continuous schedule (of reinforcement) Reinforcement each time the behavior to be reinforced occurs.

correlation A statistical technique which measures the relationship between two variables by quantifying the extent to which they vary in the same way.

cross-sectional method A method of research in which individuals differing in age are studied during the same time period.

cue A signal to emit a response.

cueing The act of emitting a signal for the occurrence of a response.

cultural pluralism The existence of multiple cultural traditions within a single society.

culture The patterns of customary behavior which are characteristic of a particular group of people, transmitted from one generation to another (or from one group to another) through symbolic communication and modeling or demonstration. Culture includes behavior *per se* and the products of behavior.

defense mechanism In Freudian theory, one of a number of ways in which the personality copes with the anxiety created by unacceptable ideas or impulses.

deoxyribonucleic acid (DNA) The amino acid which makes up the genes and contains the genetic code carried by ribonucleic acid (RNA). DNA provides the chemical instructions that determine how the organism will develop.

development Changes in structure, behavioral capability, and process occurring over time.

developmental norm A standard against which to judge level of development with respect to a particular developmental process. Developmental norms specify average, below average, and above average functioning at successive age levels.

dizygotic twins Twins resulting from two separate fertilized eggs; popularly known as fraternal twins.

Down's syndrome A hereditary disorder resulting from an abnormal chromosome condition. Characteristics include severe retardation, flat sunken nose bridge, a fold of skin giving the eyes a slanted appearance, and high susceptibility to infections and disease.

drive reduction Decrease in a biological need, such as hunger, thirst, or sex. Drive reduction theories hold that the effort to satisfy these physiological requirements motivates human actions.

ego   A theoretical construct in Freudian theory. That portion of the personality structure responsible for rational thought and decision making.

egocentric   A term used by Piaget to denote a child's failure to distinguish between his or her own construction of things and the objective reality of the phenomena which he or she experiences.

elaborated code   A term suggested by Basil Bernstein to characterize the language of the middle class. Characteristics of the elaborated code include a tendency to use abstract terms, a tendency to display concern in speech for the intentions and motivations of others, and an emphasis on personal consequences rather than social status as a basis for guiding behavior.

embryonic   Rudimentary, undeveloped, referring to the state of an embryo.

empathy   The capacity to find pleasure in the pleasure expressed by others, or to experience pain, sorrow, or any other affective state in response to the plight of another. In order to experience empathy, an individual must be able to perceive events from the perspective of the other person.

endocrine system   The assemblage of ductless glands which secrete hormones into the blood stream for distribution to body tissues.

epilepsy   A term encompassing a number of nervous disorders involving disturbances of consciousness ranging from brief lapses to convulsive seizures and complete loss of consciousness.

extended family   A family unit consisting of two or more generations, such as parents, children, and grandparents, plus various near relatives such as cousins, uncles, and aunts. Some extended families include fictive kin who are not biologically related.

extinction   A process in which the probability of occurrence of a response is reduced by withholding the reinforcer previously maintaining the response.

fetal stage   The period of prenatal development from about the third month of pregnancy until birth.

fertilization   The penetration of an egg cell by a sperm to form the initial cell of a new organism.

formal operations   The third major developmental period designated by Piaget. During this period, the individual acquires abstract thinking capability making it possible to represent symbolically the full range of hypothetical realities that might exist with respect to a given situation.

functional analysis   Analysis of the contingencies affecting behavior.

gametes   The reproductive cells of either sex; the germ cells.

genes   The basic unit of hereditary transmission. Genes are composed of deoxyribonucleic acid (DNA) and are arranged as segments along the chromosomes.

genetic   Pertaining to genetics, the branch of biology that deals with the hereditary transmission of characteristics of organisms.

genital stage   In Freudian theory, the period during which the individual moves from preoccupation with self-love to the ability to love others for altruistic reasons; corresponding approximately to the periods of pubescence and adolescence.

genotype   The specific genetic endowment of an individual.

germinal stage   The period of prenatal development during which the zygote begins to undergo rapid cell division, to the implantation of the blastocyst in the wall of the uterus; from about a day and a half after conception to the beginning of the embryonic stage at two weeks.

heterozygous   The state in which an individual carries alleles for contrasting characteristics on the two members of a homologous pair of chromosomes.

homologous chromosomes   Chromosomes that normally form pairs during meiosis, each of which becomes incorporated into a separate daughter cell during the reduction division process.

homologues   The members of a pair of homologous chromosomes.

homozygous   The state in which an individual carries two alleles for the identical characteristics on a pair of homologous chromosomes.

hormone   A product of living cells that circulates in body fluids and affects cell activity remote from its point of origin.

hydrocephaly   A genetically determined disorder in which the skull fills with abnormal amounts of cerebrospinal fluid. If untreated, this condition results in enlargement of the skull and in mental deficiency.

hypotheses   A term used in research to denote assumptions such as are tested in a scientific investigation. For example, a researcher might test the assumption or hypothesis that children will learn better when they are praised for learning than when they are not.

id   A theoretical construct in Freudian theory; the aspect of personality structure representing instinctual, pleasure-seeking behavior.

imprinting   A process by which certain organisms become fixated on an object (usually the mother) with respect to a specific behavior, such as following. Imprinting must occur within a critical period of development if it is to occur at all.

intermittent schedule (of reinforcement)   Periodic reinforcement in which some but not all occurrences of a response are reinforced.

IQ (intelligence quotient)   The term IQ originally referred to the ratio of mental age (computed from a test score) to chronological age. Today the term refers to performance on an intelligence test which is described by specifying an individual's relative standing in a norm group established for the test.

Kleinfelters' syndrome   A condition in which male testes are not fully formed and are incapable of producing sperm. Deficiencies in the production of male hormones hinder the normal development of male secondary sex characteristics. This condition is most common in males with an extra X chromosome (XXY).

latency period   In Freudian theory, the period following the phallic stage, during which Freud considered overt sexual activity of all forms to be diminished.

locomotion   A term used in developmental literature to describe movement from one place to another by a child. Creeping and walking are examples.

longitudinal method   A method of research in which the same individuals are studied at different age levels.

maturation   Developmental change controlled by genetic factors.

meiosis   The process of reduction division by which sex cells divide.

menarche   The first menstrual period.

microcephaly   A genetic disorder in which the brain and skull cease to grow at an early age, resulting in severe mental retardation.

miscarriage   The expulsion of a fetus before it is capable of living outside the mother's uterus; a spontaneous abortion.

mitosis   The process of cell division by which body cells divide and replicate themselves.

modeling   The act of emitting behavior to be imitated by an observer. Also, the act of imitating the behavior of a model.

modulator   An action or condition which adjusts, alters, or adapts another characteristic or condition.

monozygotic twins   Twins originating in a single egg fertilized by a single sperm. Early in its development the fertilized egg splits and develops into two organisms; popularly known as identical twins.

multiple discrimination   Distinguishing among individual stimuli in a set which generally includes several stimuli.

mutation   A spontaneous change in genetic structure, resulting in a new variation in inherited characteristics.

negative reinforcement   A behavioral consequence involving the withdrawal of an aversive stimulus to increase response probability.

neonate   A term used to refer to a newborn child during the first month of life.

neutral stimulus   An event that does not elicit a response under natural conditions; a stimulus lacking reinforcing properties.

norms   Behaviors or characteristics of a norm group used as standards against which to judge individual development. For example, information on the average age that children in a norm group learn to walk provides a standard for judging the development of walking skill in children.

nuclear family   A family unit composed of a pair of parents and their own biological offspring.

obesity   The condition of being overweight, generally defined as being 20% or more over a desirable weight determined by health statistics.

ontogenetic skills   Skills which are possessed by some members of a species, but not by others.

operant conditioning   The process whereby a reinforcing consequence acquires control over the probability of occurrence of the behavior that precedes it.

oral stage   In Freudian theory, the stage of development in which the infant is strongly influenced by the ways in which pleasure-seeking impulses centered in the mouth are satisfied.

ovum   An egg, or female germ cell.

phallic stage   In Freudian theory, a psychosexual stage of development in which instincts associated with the genital organs play a predominant role.

phenotype   Observable characteristics of an individual.

phenylketonuria (PKU)   A genetically determined condition which leads to mental deficiency because of damage to the developing nervous system of an infant. It is inherited through a simple recessive gene which leads to a breakdown in the production of the enzyme required for proper metabolism of the amino acid phenylalanine.

phobia   An extreme fear which often seems irrational to observers; resulting in avoidance of situations previously associated with painful or anxiety-provoking experiences.

phylogenetic traits   Characteristics shared by all members of a species.

placenta   A vascular organ within the uterus that serves as the structure through which the fetus receives nourishment from and eliminates waste into the circulatory system of the mother.

positive reinforcement   A consequence that increases or strengthens the probability of a behavior occurring again.

prehension   Seizing or grasping.

preoperational thought   A subperiod of the period of concrete operations characterized by the acquisition of the ability to represent concrete experiences through the use of symbols.

primary reinforcer   A reinforcer directly related to body-tissue needs.

propositional thinking   Thinking involving verbal statements of rules expressing the implications of a set of conditions.

psychometric perspective   A perspective on intellectual development which describes intellectual functioning in terms of test performance.

psychosexual stages   In Freudian theory, stages of development, each of which is associated with pleasure-sensation motives centered in different erogenous zones of the body.

puberty   That period of physical development marked by the rapid enlargement of organs related to reproduction.

punishment   The application of a consequent condition that decreases the probability of occurrence of a response.

readiness   The degree to which the level of development of the individual matches the learning experiences provided for him/her.

reduction division   Another term for the process of meiosis.

reinforcing consequences   Consequences which increase the probability of occurrence of a behavior.

reliability   Consistency in test performance. For instance, if people take a test at two points in time, the test is reliable to the extent scores for the second administration correlate highly with scores for the first administration.

response   A behavior.

restricted code   A term suggested by Basil Bernstein to characterize the language of lower-class speakers. Characteristics of the restricted code include a tendency to use concrete rather than abstract terms, failure to be concerned with the motives and intentions of others, and an emphasis on social status as a standard for guiding behavior.

ribonucleic acid (RNA)   A chemical substance that transmits genetic instructions from a cell nucleus to outer areas of the cell.

rubella   German measles.

schemata   Sets of ideas of things that fit together.

secondary reinforcer   A stimulus which has acquired reinforcing properties through conditioning.

sensorimotor period   The first major period of development designated by Piaget. During this period, the child learns to represent concrete experiences through physical acts.

siblings   Brothers or sisters.

sickle cell anemia   A genetic disorder characterized by the formation of defective red blood cells. The condition is lethal only in the homozygous condition, and occurs in a disproportionately high proportion of people of African ancestry.

signal learning   Learning resulting from classical conditioning.

social learning view   A behavioral theory which holds that behavior results from a process of reciprocal determinism involving interactions among the environment, personal characteristics, and behaviors.

societal stage   That stage of development characterized by extensive contact with individuals outside the home setting.

society   The aggregation of individuals who live together in an organized population.

somatic cells   Body cells. All cells of the organism, other than the germ (sex) cells.

sperm   A male reproductive cell.

stimuli   Plural of stimulus.

stimulus   Something that causes a response or change in activity.

stimulus-response learning   Learning through the presentation of a cue which signals a response that is subsequently reinforced.

sublimation   In Freudian theory, an ego defense mechanism by which an individual transforms unacceptable instinctive impulses into some socially acceptable form, such as athletics. The unacceptable instincts which are sublimated are frequently based on sexual instincts.

superego   In Freudian theory, an element of the personality structure formed from the incorporation of representations of parents' behaviors, attitudes, and values into the mental apparatus. The supergo exerts a guiding influence on behavior.

Tay Sachs disease   See amaurotic family idiocy.

temperament   Constitutional qualities of an individual that may have a generalized influence on behavior.

traumatic experience   An event resulting in great physical or emotional stress and/or injury.

trimester   A period of 3 months. The 9-month period of pregnancy is subdivided into first, second, and third trimesters.

Turner's syndrome   A chromosomal disorder resulting in the incomplete development of female sex characteristics. A female with this disorder has only one X chromosome and may suffer from mental retardation.

umbilical cord   A cord connecting a fetus to the mother's placenta.

unconditioned response   A reflex response naturally elicited by an unconditioned stimulus.

unconditioned stimulus   A stimulus event that normally elicits a particular response without the influence of prior learning.

universal stage   That early stage of development in which child behavior is controlled mainly by biological processes. The universal stage begins at birth and lasts till about the age of 2.

unvoiced consonant   A consonant such as *k* uttered without vocal cord vibration.

validity   The extent to which a test measures what it purports to measure. Validity is usually established by correlating the test with another measure with which it ought to be related. For example, the validity of an intelligence test may be established by correlating the test with a measure of academic achievement.

verbal association   Chaining in which the various links in the chain are verbal behaviors.

voiced consonant   A consonant such as *b* uttered with vocal cord vibration.

zygote   A cell formed by the union of a female ovum and male sperm. The initial cell of a new organism.

Index